LEADING
AT THE EDGE OF
CHAOS

LEADING
AT THE EDGE OF
CHAOS

HOW TO CREATE
THE NIMBLE
ORGANIZATION

DARYL R. CONNER

JOHN WILEY & SONS, INC.

New York • Chichester • Weinheim • Brisbane • Singapore • Toronto

Copyright © 1998 by ODR®, Inc. All rights reserved.

Published by John Wiley & Sons, Inc.
Published simultaneously in Canada.

This publication is designed to provide accurate and authoritative information in regard to the subject matter covered. It is sold with the understanding that the publisher is not engaged in rendering professional services. If professional advice or other expert assistance is required, the services of a competent professional person should be sought.

Library of Congress Cataloging-in-Publication Data:

Conner, Daryl.
    Leading at the edge of chaos : how to create the nimble
organization / Daryl R. Conner.
        p.   cm.
    Includes index.
    ISBN 0-471-29557-4 (cloth : alk. paper)
    1. Organizational change—Management.   2. Corporate
reorganizations—Management.   3. Organizational behavior.
I. Title.
HD58.8.C6518   1998
658.4′06—dc21   98-24357

Printed in the United States of America.

10   9   8   7   6   5   4   3   2   1

PREFACE

This book is a result of the lessons being learned from our continuing research and consulting experience at ODR.[1] My personal interest in the dynamics of change began in the early 1970s when I first became intrigued with the process of human transition (see Appendix A). From a research standpoint, ODR's first comprehensive analysis was published in 1993 in the form of the book *Managing at the Speed of Change*. There, I described the "structure of change": the basic patterns of how people respond to organizational transitions, and the principles that can be applied to manage the change process for particular initiatives. Since then, our pursuit of a more in-depth understanding of the conditions described in that first book has led to an examination of the subject of change from a much wider, more strategic perspective. From this broader viewpoint, the unique challenges about leading an organization during turmoil were discovered. These unique challenges, which we call the struggle to achieve a nimble organization, are presented in *Leading at the Edge of Chaos*. A projected third book will include stories highlighting the day-to-day realities of nimble organizations and show what leaders are doing to operationalize the principles that are described in this book.

I do not dispute that leadership may come in many forms at many levels of an organization. But building nimble organizations, we have learned, requires that change leadership be executed at the most senior corporate levels. The wisdom and skill of these leaders have informed this book. In the past four years, I have listened as many CEOs, COOs, CFOs, and CIOs expressed a key concern of theirs in the following manner:

> Of course we must do an impeccable job of implementing the current reengineering effort [or downsizing, or new technology, or merger]. That goes without saying. What I'm even more concerned about, however, is: What's next? Our market is so chaotic now that the only thing we know for sure is that the way we are doing business today will soon change and then change again. There will be many more major conversions for us to contend with in the future, and what I worry about is how we're to keep up with it all. There

is no longer time to catch our breath. The challenge now is: How do we get ready for the changes we can't even see yet?[2]

This book describes the characteristics and behaviors of leaders who successfully deal with ongoing turbulence in their organizations. These leaders are not only determined to effectively implement the initiatives now holding the attention of their management and employees, but they are equally focused on building corporate capability for addressing the demands of continuously reshaping and redefining their organizations. Within the following chapters, the relationship between market success and what I call Nimbleness and Human Due Diligence™—two central concepts—will be described to show how to properly link these elements to achieve organizational prosperity during unstable times.

The Coming Chaos

Being a leader while an organization pursues important changes used to be fun. It was more enjoyable because there was less change and it was easier to implement. Those days are gone. With new technology, globalization of markets, and increased pressure for shareholder value, the tempo and thrust of change—and the way leaders must lead—have been forever altered.

What formerly excited, stimulated, and inspired us has begun to threaten, terrify, and immobilize. The world is inundated with disruptions: unforeseen dangers, unanticipated opportunities, unmet expectations, alarming new statistics, startling twists of fate, shocking innovations, unheralded improvements, unrealistic requirements, overwhelming demands, contradictory directives, staggering liabilities, astonishing results, sudden strokes of luck, and more. At every turn, there is something that we didn't see coming. Some of life's surprises are good and some are bad, but we seem to be constantly contending with more than we bargained for or less than we think we need.

The act of recovering from these shocks is becoming almost a full-time job. Constant surprises have spawned a new vulnerability for leaders that is unique in history.

As our companies prepare for the next century, we are beginning to confront unprecedented and rising numbers of self-initiated projects and of those imposed by outside forces. Compounding this urgency is the challenge of these projects' increasingly complex implications, which is further exacerbated by the necessity for them to be accomplished faster and completed with fewer resources. These transitions carry greater risks of failure and are more costly should they fail.

Too many of us have already experienced some of this failure and paid the accompanying cost. There is a growing feeling among leaders that they are simply not able to keep up with the shifting nature of their markets and the ever-evolving requirements for remaining competitive. Any system unable to maintain the pace and complexity presented by its surrounding environment cannot survive. Leaders must not only correctly determine what must be done, they must also successfully execute these initiatives. Accomplishing both is becoming more difficult than ever.

Shifting Proportions and Perspectives

To understand the new environment, we will take a closer look at the phenomenon of change in the pages ahead. At the outset, it is important to keep in mind that *change is not an event, it is a process triggered by an event.* Some of these events are voluntary, some are imposed, and many just seem to happen. They may be planned or serendipitous, induced by positive circumstances or traumatic situations. Regardless of the origin of these triggering events, the process that humans rely on to deal with them is what we call "change."

The process of change has many aspects and permutations that will be discussed later; for now, let's think of its basic components as control, balance, disruption, adaptation, expectation, and predictability. These components play out as follows:

- People feel in control when they can get what they want or are prepared for what they are going to get.
- Feeling in control creates a sense of dynamic balance, which is a kind of restless composure that helps people remain poised during uncertainty.
- When this balance is disrupted by unexpected events, people feel uneasy about the ambiguity that is created.
- In response to this discomfort, people engage their adaptation reflex— the process used to adjust to what has happened.
- If adaptation is successful, reliable expectations can be established and the environment, once again, becomes predictable.
- Being in a predictable environment creates the feeling of having control over one's destiny.

This process is summarized in Figure I.1.

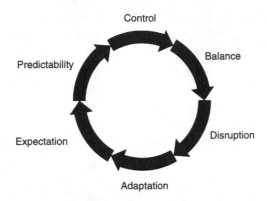

Figure I.1   The change cycle.

The comforting but unsteady equilibrium that is created when people believe they have regained control remains only until it is inevitably disrupted again by the next unexpected event. Each one triggers the change process, which moves a person from a relatively steady state through a period of uncertainty to a new, relatively steady state. Most organizations are beset by too many such change cycles. More often than not, these cycles overlap, greatly amplifying the possible complications. The result is a state of constant disruption that teeters on, and often goes over, the edge of chaos.

The density of the forces of change has begun to compress management and employees alike into a harried and arduous existence that, if not dealt with appropriately, will result in people feeling increasingly intimidated and victimized. The magnitude of disruption is becoming overwhelming, and the consequences for failing to implement important initiatives are quickly reaching prohibitive proportions. The added pressure on people to accommodate new, unfamiliar tasks and circumstances will soon be measured in quantum leaps rather than increments, and the jolts will occur at ever-shrinking intervals. Life within many organizations is already so hectic that the initiatives blur together and there never seems to be a respite.

We are at a point in history where not only is the magnitude of change accelerating and the cost for failed implementation efforts advancing, but the very nature of how to manage change is itself in transition. More and more initiatives with strategic implications are both failing to meet their objectives and overshooting their budgets. The salient question this presents for today's leaders is: If the traditional way we have thought about implementing change is no longer valid, what will take its place? The honest answer is that no one really knows exactly. The framework that will accommodate this kind of turmoil has not yet fully materialized. What we do know is this: The experience of organizational change is no longer what it has been, but neither has it become what it will be.

Caught between two eras in terms of how to orchestrate major transitions in the work environment, we know more about where we've been than we do about where we're going. Like trying to predict the influence the Internet will have on our lives, at best all we can do is grasp the general direction this emerging trend is taking. By definition, if we could comprehend the specifics of its trajectory, we would not be witnessing the birth of a new paradigm.

We are privileged, as well as burdened, to live our lives (more specifically, to attempt to lead organizations) during one of those fundamental breaks in continuity that occur periodically in the course of human evolution. This new era of change will overflow with unforeseen possibilities, many of which will be extremely beneficial. The majority of people are more scared than grateful at the prospect of traveling in uncharted territory. Though it may be uncomfortable, the feeling is typically human. The trough between two different paradigms is always filled with trepidation because it means that the established way of doing things is no longer viable; at the same time, the new ground rules are not yet clear. This in-between state creates uneasiness regardless of how negative the old paradigm was perceived to be or how positive the new one may appear.

Some people can't relate to this new level of change pressure. It seems just too far-fetched to be relevant for their work. Others see it as a likely future scenario for most people, but they cling to the myth that they personally (if not their entire company) will somehow be spared. More than a few people, however, are well past these attempts to avoid the obvious and dodge the inevitable. For them, there is nothing hypothetical about the potential for change to take on a life of its own and overwhelm all those in its path. The only question they would raise is why anyone would speak of this onslaught in the future tense. They see it happening all around them now.

Regardless of how ready people are to face it, more change is moving toward us at greater speeds and with more complicated implications than we have ever seen. Neither ignorance nor denial will serve as a sufficient deterrent. Acknowledgment is the first line of defense in the struggle with constant change and hypercontingency. Only after recognizing that extraordinary levels of change already have invaded or soon will invade their organizations can leaders begin to prepare for the implications. *For those who can see the abyss, for those teetering on its edge, and for those who have already fallen into its depths, there is still hope. This hope comes in the form of a new perspective on leadership for this new age of change.*

Gone are the days of "contiguous progression," when innovations and new ventures were incremental in scope and sequential in nature. In its place is "perpetual unrest"—unending, fundamental changes punctuated by higher or lower levels of urgency. The result is an incessant series of overlapping opportunities for creations, alterations, conversions, and reversals. This kind of leadership challenge calls for a different approach to orchestrating transitions than was feasible during the previous contiguous era. When increases in volume, momentum, and complexity of change constantly reach geometric proportions, we will have entered the new era that represents the ultimate paradox: "uninterrupted discontinuity." The very idea of an unbroken stream of reference-breaking changes is hard to grasp, and yet not to do so means certain obsolescence. Leaders in this new era must be of a certain mind-set to successfully oversee their organizations as they confront an interminable torrent of slight adjustments, significant modifications, and dramatic revolutions.

A Time for Leaders

In a world filled with unending organizational transition, the critical challenge after key decisions are reached is how they can be efficiently and effectively implemented. Assuming leaders possess the intellectual capacity and foresight to properly determine what their organizations' destiny should be, and the resources to provide the necessary infrastructure, the primary task then becomes one of execution. Leaders must not only seek to better understand the factors influencing the outcome of a particular change, but they must also become consciously competent at guiding the generic implementation process itself. They have to ensure that their organizations can consistently apply these lessons to an endless progression of changes. Senior officers must also see to it that the leaders, managers, and employees holding key organizational positions are able to reinforce what they've learned and pass it on to the next generation of corporate citizens. The capacity to do this is a pivotal attribute of what will later be described as the nimble organization.

As an author, I see my readers as people who need no convincing that change has become one of the most important features of our lives. If you doubt the evidence that we are now facing levels of change unprecedented in human history; if you need to be reminded of the disruptions that bombard you daily; or if you seek confirmation that even more change is on the way, this book is not for you. Though I will make passing comments and occasional references to these points, substantiating that we are drowning in a sea of uncertainty and confusion due to an unrelenting advance of change is not the focus of this writing. This is stated as a given, and I ask that you begin reading with this presupposition in mind.

This book has been written for leaders and those closest to them. It is about their new role in implementing critically important changes that are essential to the future survival and/or prosperity of their enterprises. We all tend to feel victimized by things we don't understand. Without grasping the human dynamics of the transition process and how they are specifically manifested, it will be easy for senior officers to become confused and overwhelmed by the actions, consequences, and reactions that unfold during attempts at significant change. Unless leaders understand the process people use in addressing transitions in their lives, it is futile for them to think they can positively influence the outcome of important initiatives.

As in any endeavor where the risks and rewards are high, relying on intuition and luck as the primary bases for your leadership direction is probably not what the shareholders or owners had in mind when you were asked to accept the position of power you now enjoy. In the coming chapters, I will identify the most crucial elements of the change process that you need to be familiar with and the specific actions you can take to instill the nimbleness required for your organizations to succeed in today's volatile markets.

Decision Making and Implementation

I am addressing two primary groups: leaders and those who serve leaders. First, the chapters to follow reflect an ongoing dialogue with leaders in senior positions within an organizational setting: those who have recently been promoted to positions of power within organizations facing major transitions, and incumbent executives who are taking on major new initiatives that surpass the level of change challenge they have previously faced within their organizations. The common denominator linking these groups is the executives who not only face making the right change decisions, but who must also orchestrate the human variables necessary for their directives to be successfully implemented. (I do not exclude those who aspire one day to be in senior leadership positions. They can use the content of this book to assess the actions of current leaders and, in doing so, prepare themselves for the day when orchestrating endless transition will be a critical part of their own duties as senior officers.)

As for the second group of intended readers—those who serve leaders—it is vital that people in key roles like human resources, strategic planning, or information technology be knowledgeable about the various elements and issues related to building nimble organizations. Likewise, external consultants and advisers who may be called on to assist leaders as they pursue the nimble path must be prepared, both conceptually and practically, to fulfill their roles.

For the sake of clarity and brevity, I will maintain a dialogue with the primary audience (leaders). However, those who serve leaders should read from the perspectives of what you must say and do when you are engaged in nimble conversations and planning sessions with your bosses or clients.

Striving to Understand

The stakes are enormously high. Survival, not only as business leaders and organizations but also as a species, depends on successfully accommodating change. Change is a human imperative. The task is both unending and increasingly difficult. Because of the personal, professional, and social implications of the accelerating pressures of change, we must persevere in our efforts to understand human transitions despite the ceaseless nature of this quest.

The response to change can be self-destructive or self-nurturing. As with cancer, we do not completely understand the mechanism that is at work. Sometimes the cures we attempt are as lethal as the disease. It is a humbling experience to write about change. At the end of the day, this author, anyway, must acknowledge how comparatively little he really knows. Even so, despite our primitive knowledge of the transformation phenomenon, we must remain hopeful that it can one day be tamed. It is important that we continue striving toward the goal of being able to diagnose and treat the full array of pathologies that inhibit the successful implementation of important change. Remember, there was a period in U.S. history when polio and literacy were on the list of problems many thought were insurmountable. Unfortunately, neither has been completely eradicated, but significant progress can be declared. One day, the same will be said about our current, rudimentary grasp of the human aspects of organizational change.

DARYL R. CONNER

Atlanta, Georgia
August 1998

ACKNOWLEDGMENTS

I'd like to extend my gratitude to those who allowed me access to their change-related successes and failures, helped me make sense out of the information I gathered, and encouraged me to forge this information into a book.

Thanks to all the senior officers, key executives, managers, supervisors, and frontline workers who granted me permission to observe their actions, share their thought processes, and witness their emotional struggles as they faced the traumas of change within their respective organizations. I also want to extend my appreciation to the many who were willing, through interviews, to share their lessons from past change efforts.

I am eternally grateful to clients and ODR associates who endured the many ramblings, obtuse hypotheses, theories, and convoluted models I inflicted on them as I labored to identify key patterns of executive behavior that contribute to nimble work environments. With their help, I was able to finally determine, from the mass of impressions and information our research generated over the past several years, the most critical components that foster nimble operations. Without these people challenging my thinking, this book would have been significantly less robust and relevant.

During the writing of this manuscript, I was extremely fortunate to be surrounded by people who helped shape my thinking. There were a select few, however, who were more than just contributors to this book's final rendition. These individuals were willing to pour their considerable intellect, experience, and soul into this work so that it could be as comprehensive in its treatment of nimbleness as possible, yet remain practical for the reader. To Dr. Linda Hoopes, Brian Gorman, Dr. Ern Clements, David Miller, and Elaine Fear, I offer my heartfelt thanks for your endless insights, honesty, and patience.

I want to recognize the team that converted the idea of a book about organizational nimbleness into the tangible reality you hold in your hands. The team's first recruit was Margret McBride, whose enthusiasm and talent as a literary agent gave me the confidence that the task was achievable.

Through her efforts, an array of aptitude and ingenuity was added in the form of key players from the John Wiley staff, most notably Renana Meyers and Henning Gutmann. The editorial assistance from Rachael Byrd at ODR transformed my crude renderings into coherent, readable treatments. Ern Clements then added his capacity for reading and rereading the endless stream of drafts, each time improving on his earlier contributions. The editorial genius of Roger Gittines, whose gift for saying more with less words, prevented this book from drowning under its own weight. The team's final contributions were made by the many ODR associates, clients, professional peers, and friends who were willing to read numerous drafts and provide vital feedback.

There is one remaining person who was integral to this book's becoming a reality: Doug Daniel, chief operating officer for ODR. His steadfast friendship and skill at running our company afforded me the luxury of knowing ODR was in good hands as I focused on the process of birthing this baby. His unwavering personal support and talent for navigating our company sets the standard for the term *business partner* and for this, I will be forever thankful.

To all of you, for giving so much of yourselves so that this book might exist, please accept the credit you are due and my personal thanks.

D.R.C.

CONTENTS

PART FIVE
Fine-Tuning the Nimble Organization   209

PART SIX
The Destination Is the Journey   257

APPENDICES

PART ONE

THE NIMBLE CHALLENGE

———

"Chaos" is a frightening word, but you will have to get used to it if you desire or hold leadership positions in today's organizations. Snuggle deeper into the lexicographical security blanket. If you prefer "turbulence" or "unrest," "conflict" or "confusion"—fine. Whatever term you've chosen, my point is that stability is no longer the prevalent condition of our age. All that seems simple and comforting is certain to give way to complex and nerve-wracking substitutes. The very core of success is in the midst of transition.

Change is upon us, and we can neither run nor hide. The only answer is to create new—nimble—businesses capable of adroitly responding to the chaotic conditions produced by constant change. It won't be easy. Decades of deeply ingrained procedures, traditions, attitudes, and cultural biases about managing change must be jettisoned. In their place, new perspectives and frameworks must be embraced.

It won't be easy, but it won't be dull or unrewarding either. Ahead, in Part One, you will gain an overview of where we are and what must be done now to prosper and prevail—and yes, to lead—in a time like no other in our history.

1

Execution, Execution, Execution

T he focal point for this book is leadership's role in building resilient, nimble organizations. I won't be spending much time on decision making. Relatively speaking, that's the easy part of leadership. Execution is hard—very hard. As the world grows more turbulent, organizations unable to execute critical change initiatives will find themselves at a serious competitive disadvantage. In this chapter, I will demonstrate that proper execution is of the utmost strategic importance and that it is imperative to invest in the human side of change if you are to successfully lead at the edge of chaos. To this end, I will bombard you again and again with these special, powerful words:

- Nimbleness.
- Resilience.
- Human due diligence.

And one more:

- Execution.

Yes, there is an echo in this book. Like the joke about the famous maestro who was stopped by a tourist while he walked up Broadway. "How do I get

to Carnegie Hall?" the woman asked, unaware that she was accosting a famous conductor of symphony orchestras. "Practice, practice, practice!" he
bellowed.

How do we build nimble organizations? Execution, execution, execution!

The Foundation of Business Success

Resistance and commitment to change are not merely human relations concerns. Dealing with issues of this nature is a critical strategic part of running any business. Many elements are contributing to your organization's
success: the way it is structured, its use of technology, and the various ongoing processes that influence day-to-day operations. These kinds of success
factors serve as the foundation for achieving corporate goals (e.g., meeting
customer expectations and achieving the desired market penetration). Accomplishing them is, to a great extent, governed by your organization's ability to meet its market's definition for success. When key success factors
central to your organization's goals are correctly identified and skillfully executed, they are said to be "in alignment with" the market's criteria for
prosperity, and your organization is subsequently rewarded.

Alignment between success factors and market is a prized strategic condition. It is every organization's dream to identify its own unique formula
for prosperity and to replicate that success for as long as possible. Once
alignment is created and prosperity is achieved, however, a success formula
only remains viable if these conditions prevail:

- Quality and productivity standards are maintained.
- Customer demands and competitive pressures remain the same.

The more volatile the market, the quicker an organization's success formula
becomes obsolete.

IBM is an example of a company that extended its market alignment far
beyond limits that most companies could only fantasize about. For decades,
IBM was the dominant player in the computer industry. In the 1980s, however, Big Blue shifted to a high-growth strategy focused on the aggressive
selling of hardware that was not always competitively priced. The aim was
to bolster the sales of IBM's traditional product: mainframes. But emphasis
on customer focus lapsed. By the early 1990s, the new strategy had failed;
IBM began to seriously struggle in the market it had once ruled. While customers were moving away from mainframes and looking for better software
solutions and PCs, IBM had held fast to its time-worn preoccupation with

big computers. It wasn't until the company began to listen to clients' needs that it began to recover.[1] As this case demonstrates, continuing to apply the same formula in the same way is dangerous. As with the demise of IBM's predominance in the market, the viability of fixed success formulas tends to diminish over time. The actual length of their shelf life is discernible only in retrospect, but it exists nonetheless.

What this probably means is that your organization's success formulas are losing their durability. To the extent this is true, it demands that you re-craft corporate formulas that you believe in and are committed to, while, at the same time, you remain prepared to significantly alter or completely abandon them if conditions shift. If you lack faith in the formulas, then you won't be able to rally support from your staff and employees to ensure implementation success. At the same time, you must remain emotionally detached or you will miss the cues that indicate when a modification is needed.

If global competition is threatening, or new technology is remolding your market's landscape, or customers are expressing new interests, or your industry is consolidating itself, then your organization must be able to alter its formula to meet those challenges. Some of these adjustments might be no more than minor operational reconciliations; others may represent strategic transformations. The more volatile the environment, the more important the changes become. In highly turbulent markets, your ability to execute changes becomes a key success factor. If your organization falls behind in its capacity to meet the demands for change, it will be unable to accommodate the other success factors necessary to flourish in a churning market.

The mechanics of this realignment process are shown in Figure 1.1.

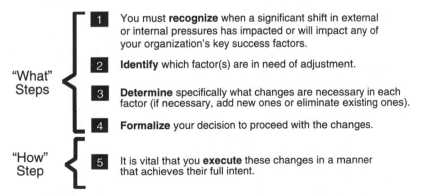

Figure 1.1   The "what" and "how" steps of change.

Nimble businesses and agencies undertake important initiatives by completing all five steps with precision—and they do so faster and more effectively than their competitors. Constrained organizations, restricted in their abilities to carry out critical ventures, falter in one or more of these steps. They are subsequently unable to keep up with the competition.

Many organizations falter because their leaders have not defined, much less updated and/or adequately monitored, the critical factors that contribute to the organizations' success. Even when these factors are known and tracked, some leaders fail to *recognize* (Step 1) the various trends and events, inside and outside their organization, that are likely to influence its future. At other times, leaders realize they are facing new and significant challenges, but either they are unable to *identify* (Step 2) which factor(s) are affected or they can't determine how to alter them in order to maintain alignment with the new requirements for success. For other leaders, their incapacity to act decisively leads to their downfall. Sometimes they make, or appear to make, decisions (*determine*, Step 3) in a way that confuses people or leaves some doubt about priorities. Then there are those leaders who flounder during the *formalization* (Step 4) because either they won't act without a general consensus, or they go to the other extreme and fail to adequately involve others in making sound judgments that can be embraced by enough people within the organization.

Unless Steps 1 through 4 are accomplished, there is no hope for maintaining a competitive position in highly turbulent markets. *Recognition, identification, determination,* and *formalization* are important points in the alignment process. If any one of them is disregarded, it will reduce an organization's ability to correctly determine *what* should be changed in order to succeed in its marketplace. Steps 1 through 4, however, are not the subject of this book. *The focus here is on what happens once a leader realizes a change is necessary and attempts to take what he or she believes to be the correct course of action.* Most leaders accomplish the first four steps relatively well; it's in the fifth step that they fall short. The ability (or lack thereof) to *execute* important change decisions is what ultimately separates winners from losers in volatile and uncertain markets.

It's the People, Stupid

When success factors fall out of alignment, there are plenty of available *whats* to help rectify the problem: reorganization, a new acquisition target, total quality management (TQM), value-based management, enterprise-wide software, a balanced scorecard, or any of the various other business solutions that may emerge. Most of these are expensive; more importantly, they are vulnerable to producing more rhetoric than substance. They must be orchestrated by sound implementation strategies that address the human response to change. Recent confessions by the consultants who sell and the organizations that buy such corporate cures reveal that few ever realize full value. It is the general opinion that the primary culprit in these unsuccessful attempts is poor navigation of the psycho-social-cultural inhibitors that block execution.

Michael Hammer, largely responsible for the spread of the reengineering movement throughout the world, has acknowledged that 70 percent of the efforts to replace corporate hierarchies with "process teams" have been unsuccessful. The main reason, he claimed, is that he and others who promoted this management craze had failed to address the human side of the process. On November 26, 1996, *The Wall Street Journal*[2] reported: "Gurus of the $4.7 billion reengineering industry like Hammer forgot about people. 'I wasn't smart enough about that,' Hammer commented. 'I was reflecting my engineering background and was insufficiently appreciative of the human dimension. I've learned that's critical.'" Ignoring the human dimension is by no means limited to reengineering. It is responsible for most of the mergers, new technology introductions, cost-cutting measures, and productivity improvement programs that fail.

What is missing? For one thing, when most organizations take on new initiatives, leaders often lack the same level of interest and concern about implementation that they show other key metrics like the organization's ROI (return on investment). Leaders are normally very quick to take whatever corrective action is necessary to ensure that their company's ROI remains on target. Yet, most are comparatively passive when it comes to charting the progress or problems associated with what they often declare to be important changes. When leaders take on vital, expensive, and risky initiatives, they should be as vigilant about ROC_{hg} (return on change) as they are about ROI.

Most major change projects are launched to secure, retain, or recover some type of competitive advantage. Because these efforts consume time, energy, and money with no guarantee of results, they should be viewed as risky ventures that are subsidized by shareholders, owners, and other key constituents. In this sense, attempts to implement major change are no different than any other speculative exposure. Those taking the risk expect an adequate ROI to justify the gamble they take with their money. In today's fast-paced and uncertain markets, consistently strong ROC_{hg} has become a prerequisite for attaining expected ROI. It is, therefore, leadership's mandate to be sure investors' assets are used wisely when they pursue critical initiatives involving significant change.

ROC_{hg} does not gauge the activity surrounding a change effort, the energy people put into it, or the passion that might be felt for accomplishing the initiative. Like its financially based counterpart, it is an objective assessment of whether an adequate amount of goal attainment was achieved for the resources invested.

ROC_{hg} is calculated by dividing the yield from an attempted change by the execution cost of that effort (see Figure 1.2). *Yield from Effort* reflects measurable movement[3] toward accomplishing the key objectives of the change. *Execution Cost* comprises four factors: (1) the expense involved in determining *what* to do; (2) the cost associated with *how* the human dynamics of change will be addressed; (3) the lost efficiency (productivity and quality) that typically occurs because attention is shifted from day-to-day duties to the implementation process; and (4) the price of any new infrastructure necessary to support the effort (e.g., corporate structures, technology, people, and training).

What drives the equation into the red is this: When the way people react to change is not dealt with adequately, the combined cost of determining what to do, making up for lost efficiency, and introducing any new infrastructure that is needed pales in comparison to the real expense incurred in addressing human reactions. Most leaders fail to sufficiently prepare employees for transitions that are essential to the future survival and prosperity of their organizations.

Whether due to neglect, lack of awareness, or incompetence, at the heart of the struggle within most organizations is "execution deficiency." Failure to act is so prevalent today that leaders in every organization should be asking:

- How can I better prepare my organization to complete the fifth step in the alignment process (execution) as successfully as we do the first four?
- If we know *what* to change and we have the resources to build the necessary infrastructure, how do we develop an equal proficiency in *how* to orchestrate the human variables related to implementation?

$$ROC_{hg} = \frac{\text{Yield from Effort (Movement)}}{\text{Execution Cost}}$$

Figure 1.2   The formula for return on change (ROC_{hg}).

- How do I create in this organization the knowledge and talent that are required to successfully execute the critically important initiatives needed to secure or maintain alignment with our market?
- How can I improve our ROC_{hg} performance?

If you hope to continue succeeding in fast-paced uncertain markets and achieving a high ROC_{hg}, you must lead your organization through the adaptation process quickly and effectively. To do this, you must orchestrate the human elements affecting the execution of your organization's key initiatives. More specifically, you must implant the characteristics of a nimble operation. Such an organization is skilled at establishing and maintaining its success formula. Of course, this means determining the correct things to change, but, more importantly, the desired agility is most closely associated with the last step in the process: execution. *Nimbleness is the ability for an organization to consistently succeed in unpredictable, contested environments by implementing important changes more efficiently and effectively than its competitors, and thereby maintaining its desired ROC_{hg}.* The task is daunting, but achievable.

2

Confronting the Challenge of Change

N ow that we have established the human side of executing important initiatives as an issue that warrants senior officers' attention, let's explore why this problem has been historically so intimidating to leaders. My research has led me to believe that the key to leadership's poor performance in handling human issues during implementation is the extraordinary challenge orchestrating change poses; for most leaders, it is far beyond what they understand and are prepared to address.

There are eight aspects of change that make it such a formidable experience. This chapter explores each of them in depth:

1. Fear of change—Leaders' fear of major disruption inhibits their learning about it.

2. Demand versus capacity—The current amount of disruption may exceed an organization's capacity for absorbing it.

3. The entangled labyrinth—Transition can create a maze that complicates leaders' efforts to change things.

4. The layered texture of change—The many layers of the change phenomenon increase its challenge.

5. The learning organization and transition management literacy—Because most people have dangerously low levels of transition management literacy, their ability to succeed within ambiguity is reduced.

6. Nimble expectations—Leaders' lack of understanding about the impact of expectations on human behavior lowers their chances of success with new initiatives.

7. Control and disorder—Success rates drop when leaders lack appreciation for how control and disorder affect people's lives.

8. Dynamic balance—Failures increase when the paradox of dynamic balance is not understood.

Fear of Change

A successful change initiative is one that accomplishes its stated objectives within the time and resource parameters deemed acceptable by whoever is sanctioning the effort. To accomplish the intended objectives, there are three interdependent domains that must work in concert:

1. The organization in which the change occurs.
2. The initiative itself.
3. The individuals involved.

As a prerequisite to a desired outcome, the people affected must be able to succeed in the new work environments created by the initiatives introduced. The success of organizational change (1) is, therefore, contingent on the success of critical initiatives (2), which is, in turn, dependent on individuals (3) who can successfully adapt to the new requirements placed on them. Thus, organizational and initiative-level success is ultimately dictated by the ability *individuals* display for absorbing disruption in their lives.

Of the three domains where change is manifested, the human realm is by far the most important. Like former House Speaker Thomas ("Tip") O'Neill's quote from his father, "All politics are local," we have learned that *all change is personal*. For example, when an organizational restructuring has taken place, the psychological evidence usually outweighs the physical traces. To most people, the emotional anguish of a downswing is more real than the reduced headcount on the next quarter's financial report.

Organizations can merge and new technology can be installed, but, like a tree falling in the forest with no one to hear, these events are immaterial until they interface with human consciousness. In this sense, when companies engage in major transitions, they don't "relocate their officers" or "reduce their workforce" as much as they alter the expectations people have about their lives. Disruptive change takes place when people face something significant that they didn't ask for or anticipate. Major organizational change has implications that are deeply personal, but because of its disruptive nature, we are often too scared to allow ourselves the objectivity needed to learn how to manage it.

What do I mean by this? Life has never been easy for our species. We often find ourselves caught between forces that require a negotiated balance to resolve. There is no better example of how this give-and-take is played out than when we address major change. The comfort and solace most of us are so attracted to can only be secured by inhabiting stable environments, but, at the same time, evolution rewards those who can adapt to changing conditions. In the midst of this tension, most people will typically choose to stay in situations that are clearly malfunctioning, improper, or even painful, rather than face their fear of ambiguity. We are so frightened by uncertainty that we often employ mechanisms to deceive ourselves. There are two types of this self-trickery: the *illusion of continuity* and the *illusion of change*.

We use the illusion of continuity when we want to convince ourselves that things will remain basically the same even though much has, in fact, been altered in our lives. Think of this as trying to maintain *superficial stability within fundamental change*. The essential framework of a situation has actually shifted substantially, but we hold one or more components as evidence that nothing has really changed. Here are some examples:

- Over the past few years, an executive has gained 30 pounds, started smoking, increased his alcohol consumption, and no longer exercises, but he still considers himself fit because he eats oat bran and has a low cholesterol count.

- Competition and growing overhead have reduced a company's margins, customers' expectations for support and concessions are increasing, and new technology is emerging that is redefining the market's need for the company's products. The primary sales strategy, however, remains the same: "The buyers know us and trust us. We've been here for them for years. Nothing sells like a good relationship. You can still count on a good meal, fine wine, and a cigar to close the deal."

We use the illusion of change to convince ourselves that small, insignificant modifications have somehow satisfied the requirements for a more fundamental shift. Think of this as seeking *superficial change within uncompromising stability*. The basic framework of a situation remains the same, but a single (or a few) element(s) is modified to give the appearance that dramatic change has occurred. For example:

- A person goes on a series of short-term diets rather than making a significant shift in overall eating habits and lifestyle.
- Training programs that focus on improving quality are conducted, but the basic behavior patterns and reward system within the organization remain the same.

We use these two illusions to try to protect ourselves from the true ramifications of major change. The fear of real transitions is too imbedded in our gene pool to think we can ever totally overcome it. But only by facing our fear of the ambiguity and uncertainty that always accompany significant upheavals in our lives can we hope to learn enough about the process to successfully manage it.

Demand versus Capacity

Most leaders are unprepared for today's turmoil because they lack an appreciation of the struggle between the accelerating transition demands taking place and the diminishing resources available to help organizations adapt to these disruptions.

Three factors can be offered to explain why most executives, managers, and employees report that their professional lives (not to mention their personal ones) have become more inundated with change than ever before. These factors are:[1]

1. Volume—Every year, organizations report dealing with a greater number of significant disruptions in people's lives.
2. Momentum—Organizations demand an accelerated speed when people engage change today, and people are given less time to execute these initiatives.
3. Complexity—The projects taken on today are much more sophisticated and involved than those assigned only a few years ago.

A work environment that has increasing volume, momentum, and complexity of change is defined here as *turbulent*. The basic operating axiom becomes "No time-outs, no substitutions." Under such conditions, ambiguity and uncertainty dramatically rise, thereby reducing predictability and leaving people without the necessary foundation for a sense of control.

Because of this advancing turbulence, we will soon look back on what today appear to be unmanageable levels of instability, and they will look relatively calm. In the past, change meant that, after some initial confusion, a new, steady state was introduced. Now, change breeds only more disruption, not solidity. As the tide of change rises, if the requirements for adaptation exceed our ability to respond successfully, future shock will be the result (see Figure 2.1).

Future shock is where demand begins to exceed capacity—that point where people can no longer absorb major change without displaying dysfunctional behavior (i.e., loss of the ability to maintain quality and productivity standards). Future shock is the boundary that separates the two ends of the predictability/instability continuum.

This aspect of the challenge posed by change is depicted in Figure 2.1 as a contest between adaptation resources (capacity) and adaptation requirements (demand). The diagram helps to show the three main outcomes that are possible from this struggle:

1. The *noncompetitive* realm—The left side of the predictability/instability continuum may initially look attractive because it represents avoidance of *future shock,* but in fact it is filled with its own brand of danger. To keep pace in a fast-moving world, leaders must drive as much change as possible into their organizations without overloading their people with more disruption than they can accommodate. Leaders who opt for this less stressful, more comfortable environment will find it difficult for their company or agency to remain viable among others competing for their customers' business.

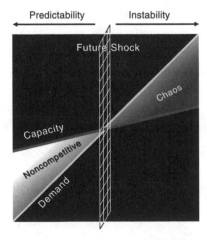

Figure 2.1   Future shock.

2. The *future shock* realm—The middle portion of the continuum reflects the dangers present when the demands of change near or exceed a person's or group's capacity to absorb the implications. Future shock is that point where people can no longer accommodate disruption without beginning to display dysfunctional behavior in the form of lost productivity and inability to maintain quality standards.

3. The *chaos* realm—The right side of the continuum represents the greatest amount of change-related maladjustment a person or group can experience. Chaos is entered into when significant disruptions pile up on people long after they have exceeded their available adaptation resources. When change continues to be poured into a saturated sponge, the consequences are threefold: (a) morale deteriorates, (b) the initiatives that are attempted result in only short-term, superficial application of the intended goals; and (c) people stop listening to the leaders, who continue to announce changes that never fully materialize.

These three realms form a continuum that reflects various degrees of jeopardy. When struggling with change, there is no such thing as invulnerability; there is only greater or lesser risk and liability. The only option is to choose what degree of which hazard will be faced. Given the forced-choice nature of this situation, the optimum move is to stay within the *future shock* realm. Although it is filled with danger, this portion of the predictability/instability continuum provides the greatest hope for survival and prosperity during turbulent times. Why? Because if the adaptation capacity of a person or group can be enlarged without destroying the ability to recover and grow stronger, the end results will be elasticity and agility, not affliction and malfunction.

The Entangled Labyrinth

It would appear that the human form of life has evolved further than other animals, but this status does not come easy for us. We don't pass through the changes necessary to survive and grow by leaving one distinct spot of our development to emerge completely fresh and intact at the next juncture. We progress through our lives, dragging baggage from previous experiences—our unmet aspirations, unrealized potential, and unresolved problems as well as our budding talents and honed skills. As the years of events and learning yield layer after layer of tangled circuitry reflecting our experiences, we become an intricate network of unsolved puzzles rather than a linear, easily understood stimulus-response organism.

All systems operate as subsystems within larger systems. For instance, you are a subsystem of humanity in general. If you are married, your spousal relationship is a system composed of two subsystems—husband and wife. Both are affected by each other and may also be affected by children, extended family, and friends. And don't forget your relationships in the block that you live on, the neighborhood, the city, the state, and on and on. The waves of impingement and influence extend in an almost unlimited fashion. There is no such thing as an isolated relationship. As with a spider's web, touching just one part of the vast network sends ripples through the whole gossamer realm.

Now consider how many of these networked relationships there are in your business, and the enormity of the task called organizational change will begin to come into perspective. Despite these dynamics, leaders must set expectations for people during the change. Those leaders who fail to grasp the depth of challenge that change entails often appear caught off-guard when they introduce initiatives that they hoped would "settle things down." What they usually find is that such efforts, at best, produce only temporary relief. With the onset of perpetual unrest, we have entered an era where change breeds more change, not stability. The individual strands in the corporate web will never again be calm.

With all this occurring in the workplace, it is a wonder that people maintain any image of stability at all. But cling we do to any part of our lives that appears to be undisturbed. Even a hint of the tranquillity we are so desperate for is enhanced and extrapolated into the delusion that our department, company, or industry will once again behave in a completely predictable manner. It is a cruel hoax that we perpetuate on ourselves.

Senior officers within nimble organizations tend to be brutally honest about the escalation of change they foresee for themselves and those they lead. They often take a stand before their direct reports or take the stage in front of thousands of employees in an attempt to prepare them for the continuous advancement of transitions in their organization's future. They use these opportunities not only to announce yet another major initiative, but also to help their people understand that success at the new endeavors will not bring stability, only a more desired version of additional changes.

The Layered Texture of Change

Another reason change is so challenging is because of its multilayered nature. For each aspect of the content or the *what* of change (i.e., what is being changed), there are many more elements hidden in the *how* of change—the human issues associated with implementation. Much like the operating systems embedded in software, the human dynamics concealed within the process of change are infinitely more layered than they appear to be when we look only at the "what-we-are-doing" level. The *how* of change addresses the inherent struggle people encounter when facing transitions, and it lends itself to four tiers of interpretations:

1. The simplistic layer.
2. The mysterious layer.
3. The decoder layer.
4. The tempo layer.

Like the knotty exterior of the geode, the surface of change does not easily betray the complexities within.

THE SIMPLISTIC LAYER

Many people view change only from its first, least sophisticated level of interpretation. From this perspective, getting humans to shift their expectations about things that are important to them appears to be an easy task that requires little more than clarity of thought and communication skills. For the majority of those who see change this way, life's a logical, linear experience, and when a well-thought-out plan of action is carefully explained, they will not only agree with the rationale as presented but will feel compelled to support it and will even be happy to do so. At the risk of stating the obvious, this layer is most frequented by those with little or no real experience with orchestrating major transition efforts involving large groups of people. It is for the uninitiated and untried who can only see change as they wish it were.

THE MYSTERIOUS LAYER

Here, everything looks just the opposite from the simplistic level. This viewpoint makes change appear chaotic, random, and unexplainable. When organizations engage major initiatives, the dynamics encountered often seem so convoluted as to defy comprehension:

- People seem to resist change for no apparent reason.
- Those who were once supporters often become the strongest adversaries.
- Corporate rhetoric praises a new direction while the organizational culture rewards people for maintaining the status quo.
- Staunch resisters suddenly see value in a new initiative.
- Team members start to attack each other.

- Long-standing enemies suddenly form alliances.
- Small, insignificant modifications create vicious battles while announcements with huge implications are ignored by employees.

At the mysterious level, few things turn out as expected and almost nothing is as it appears. This second layer is filled with unbelievable behaviors, indecipherable motives, and incomprehensible emotions. This explains why, for the majority of people, major change is so intimidating.

THE DECODER LAYER

From this exposure, it is possible to see below the intimidating second level to detect distinct patterns of recurring logic, feelings, and actions that people display with fairly predictable regularity. Here can be found numerous identifiable configurations of dynamics that bring shape and form to what previously looked like only baffling puzzles and illusive shadows. This third layer provides a set of lenses, if you will, that brings into focus much of what was vague and distorted at the mysterious layer.

These patterns represent recurring themes that can be identified, isolated, measured, and tracked using either intuition or sophisticated diagnostic tools. Once this kind of monitoring begins, interpretive analysis and prognostic extrapolation are possible. Within this layer is a structure to the change process that lends itself to:

- Thorough investigation (e.g., "How and when will people resist a change?" "Under what circumstances can commitment be developed?" "How will an organization's culture react to change?").
- The development of prescriptive actions (e.g., "This is the resistance you should anticipate after your announcement next week; how do you plan to respond?" "If we follow these implementation guidelines, we can increase the likelihood people will support the project on a sustained basis").

Learning to decode the symptoms, milestones, cycles, and repetitive themes embedded in change allows you to demystify the process and become better able to manage it.

Much of the work presented in my first book, *Managing at the Speed of Change*, is descriptive of the foundation patterns and principles from this third level of change. Understanding these recurring themes reveals the hidden "structure of change" that lies just below the surface. Within this structure are the typical knowledge, behaviors, feelings, and attitudes people demonstrate during periods of major transition.

THE TEMPO LAYER

This last layer of change dynamics is the most inaccessible, yet it has a profound effect on the success or failure of major initiatives. Here, far below the surface, powerful forces affect the fundamental drive and tempo of a change effort. This fourth layer is where the intensity and cadence of change can be exposed. The forces at play here help explain why and when the vigor and energy that drive change sometimes increase and decrease, expand and contract, speed up and slow down.

Because of the depth of these aspects of the change process, we have only a partial picture of what dictates the strides of an initiative. From our observations thus far, what appears to set the tempo of change is the result of at least two forces: (1) the fluctuations of individual factors and (2) the aggregate resonance that is created.

Many individual factors sway, if not determine, the final outcome of an organization's efforts to implement major transitions (e.g., how pressure for change is applied from the marketplace; management's sense of urgency and sustained commitment; employees' ability to articulate their concerns in constructive ways; the extent to which there are cultural barriers toward change). When these factors are examined, they appear neither isolated nor static. A more accurate portrayal is that they are in a perpetual state of interactive agitation; each is displaying its own unique form of oscillation. Envision a room full of tuning forks, with each one vibrating at a different rate and emitting its own particular sound. Some produce a high pitch; others generate a lower tone. Now visualize that all these factors (tuning forks) are pulsating at once and as they begin to influence each other, a collective resonance starts to form. The result is that all the separately vibrating components converge into one vacillating cadence. In any given change project, think of the rhythm of the individual factors as running from high to low and the composite vacillation as running from strong to weak. In a change project, the aggregate cadence formed by the impact each factor has on the others combines to create the overall tempo for an entire change project.

The outcome of all of this generates the swiftness and gait at which a specific change effort unfolds. Whatever pace develops, it does not often look like an evenly distributed flow of activity; it usually appears more like an irregular pulse that reflects the ebb and flow of energy, enthusiasm, interest, and disenchantment so common during the execution of extended change efforts.

The dynamic interaction among and between the factors that affect the outcome of a change effort can produce one of three grades of movement. The cadence of any particular project can be described as filled with: *calm, commotion,* or *chaos.* Sometimes the tempo within a project can be rather sedate (calm). At other times, the resonance that results from the key factors' interacting with each other is modestly energetic (commotion). Then, sometimes without warning, the momentum can reach a pandemonium level (chaos) and just as suddenly return back to calm or commotion.

Part of the discontinuity people experience during major change stems from an unpredictable leap from within any one of these three degrees of movement to another. For example, even though the overall magnitude (volume, momentum, and complexity) of change may be on the rise for an organization, it is quite possible for a particular person or department to go through a period of relative calm just after a particularly chaotic spell. At the same time, in response to the same change, another person or group can make a sudden jump from moderate commotion to frantic chaos.

The Learning Organization and Transition Management Literacy

Whenever people encounter new situations, they draw on whatever prior knowledge they have that might be relevant to the unfamiliar circumstances they are facing. When the existing base of knowledge is inadequate to address the issues at hand, new knowledge must be created.

New knowledge requires the successful application of learning. This, of course, is the antithesis of what most corporate climates foster. Only when data have been assigned meaning do they become useful information. Only when information is successfully applied is knowledge created. This means that the seemingly confusing elements within an unfamiliar situation must be identified, arranged, and indexed in our minds before we can successfully apply them to solving problems or exploiting opportunities.

We can build three kinds of knowledge when adapting to change: specific, systemic, and generic.

PROJECT-SPECIFIC KNOWLEDGE

Specific change knowledge comes from the lessons about an isolated aspect of a particular set of circumstances. These learnings are relevant only to the unique constellation of people, issues, pressures, politics, constraints, and opportunities of a singular situation. The viability of these kinds of learnings is fragile, and their shelf life is often extremely short-lived.

The relevance of specific knowledge is typically tentative and brief because of how systems operate. Change occurs within and across systems.

Systems are made up of interdependent parts that work together to accomplish a common purpose. Within these parts are variables that also operate as systems. This means all systems are made up of smaller subsystems while, at the same time, they are components of larger systems. Because so many variables are interacting during change, what works during one moment in time may not ever be feasible again. Within any system, large or small, a single variable shifting only slightly can, within five minutes, cause a previously impeccable solution to become useless.

When a single action to address change (or a series of maneuvers) is successful, the threat to a personal or group(s) sense of balance is resolved, and the affected person(s) feels once again able to predict and prepare for the future. The lessons learned from these kinds of attempts constitute project-specific knowledge—learnings about a single part or variable in a system. For example:

- "What techniques were used to reduce resistance to the new computer network? Why did they work? Why didn't other techniques work?"
- "How do I convince my boss of the importance of my recommendation?"
- "Why are these people so resistant to the very things they ask for?"
- "Why can't I get these two departments to work together on this project and stop fighting with each other?"
- "What should I do to help the analyst understand that there is a limit to how much change we can take on at any one point in time?"

There is purpose to these kinds of questions and this form of learning if the same kind of situation should arise again with the same people facing the same kind of circumstances. Only if these variables are in place can the lessons already learned be applied again.

SYSTEMIC CHANGE KNOWLEDGE

Systemic change knowledge is extracted from the lessons from the overall impact a particular initiative has had on the various systems in and around which it occurred.

An alteration of any nature and size in one system causes changes in the smaller subsystems it is comprised of, as well as in the larger system in which it participates. For example, in Figure 2.2, when the I.T. department (B) of the Super-Stump Corporation (A) was streamlined, it caused John (C) to lose his job and Mary (D) to be promoted. In addition, line managers with operational responsibilities in the Finance (E), Personnel (F), and Public Relations (G) departments had to reconfigure their monthly status reports.

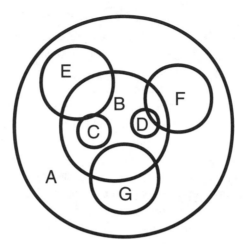

Figure 2.2   Systems and subsystems.

Systemic change knowledge deals with how everything is connected in some way, and it reflects what is sometimes called the *butterfly effect*. This term is a reference to the notion that, theoretically, the flapping of a butterfly's wing in Brazil could stir the air in a way that causes a chain reaction of greater and greater proportions and ultimately results in a raging storm over Europe.

Typical systemic knowledge involves issues like:

- "Why is the eastern region staff so upset about what their West Coast counterparts are doing?"
- "Will this new budgeting process affect the staffing plan in any way?"
- "How can we better prepare our customers for how our reengineering plans might affect their service?"

Systemic knowledge is devoted to the broader-based impact of a particular change effort.

GENERIC CHANGE KNOWLEDGE

Generic change knowledge concerns itself with lessons about the process of change itself. In addition to learning the specific and systemic-level lessons associated with a particular initiative, there are also lessons to learn about the overall transition process as it applies to any set of changing circumstances.

Many aspects of how people respond to a particular change can be generalized to how they would apply to any unanticipated disruption in expectations. These are basic universal mechanisms by which we accept or reject something new; decide why and when we will become committed to it; and determine what can be done to help assimilate it.

These generic mechanisms reflect recurring patterns that form a framework for understanding how people think, feel, and behave during organizational change (described in detail in *Managing at the Speed of Change*). The patterns are manifested differently from company to company and from country to country, yet the fundamental dynamics of how humans operate during transitions remain paradoxically constant. For example, when most people first react to a major positive change in their life, they reflect what is called "uninformed optimism" or enthusiasm based on insufficient information. As they gain more insight about what has happened, they usually shift from the naïveté of uninformed optimism to the doubt of "informed pessimism." This movement from elation to apprehensiveness is a universal pattern; that is, most people exhibit this shift most of the time when they encounter major positive changes in their lives.

Generic knowledge, such as the movement from uniformed optimism to informed pessimism, deals with extrapolating lessons learned from one change effort and applying them to other endeavors. It has to do with capitalizing on lessons from previous change projects that can be used to promote success on future efforts. Once these patterns are identified from one change initiative, they can be applied on completely different initiatives involving different people facing different circumstances. Typical issues raised are:

- "Based on our change history here, how should we anticipate they will react when they hear of the restructuring plan?"
- "Let's set proper expectations for ourselves regarding the amount of difficulty we will encounter in securing the midlevel managers' commitment."
- "Why were we surprised at our own disillusionment? *Of course* this is more difficult than it looked at the beginning."

Specific, systemic, and generic knowledge can be drawn from any change experience. The migration from data to any of these three types of knowledge is a fundamental component of the inner working of the adaptation process. Also, the track record for these three types of knowledge varies significantly. Unfortunately, most organizational change initiatives result in little, if any, change knowledge gain by the people involved. Typically, projects with change implications are carried out, and the subsequent successes or failures are seldom seriously examined for the learnings that could be drawn. Tacit learning of some type may occur to some extent without much effort, but explicit, conscious learning about change requires an investment of intent and energy most organizations fail to sanction.

Those organizations that do encourage learning tend to limit the knowledge they capture to what particular techniques or maneuvers worked or didn't work in a situation (i.e., specific knowledge). It is unusual to find an organization that actually goes to the next level and adheres to the discipline required to thoroughly examine how change in one part of its operation impacts other areas. Although fewer in number, there are still some organizations able to advance past the limits of project-bound knowledge and invest in and secure the value associated with generating systemic knowledge. Even more exceptional are organizations that recognize the inevitable and unending escalation of change demands that is now taking place and methodically acquire new and explicit knowledge about how to better execute any critically important initiatives in unstable circumstances. This is generic knowledge.

Because it is such a rarity, generic knowledge of change represents an important competitive advantage. While most companies are learning very little from their encounters with change (or what they do learn is limited to specific or systemic knowledge), organizations that pursue generic knowledge about the implementation of change build an important distinction that will become more and more valuable as their market grows in speed and complexity. In addition to creating knowledge tied to particular approaches taken during an initiative and how they impact larger and smaller related systems, the leaders of these organizations place a high value on people building mastery of the general change process itself.

Organizations that demonstrate the capacity for all three types of learning go beyond acquiring knowledge about a particular technique used in a specific project, and they propel past learning how the reaction from one part of an organization affects other areas in the same company. In addition to specific and systemic knowledge, these organizations extrapolate generic lessons from one project to the next. Their motivation for doing so is linked to their belief that by taking this action, they will be better able, in the future, to contend with the very changes that will leave their competitors dazed and confused.

By applying all three types of change knowledge, an organization shows that it is ready for a higher understanding of not only the dynamics involved, but also the skills needed to deal with major organizational change. This kind of maturation in the change process, however, requires more than simple exposure to shifting conditions. Most people think that going through a great deal of change automatically increases a person's knowledge of the transition process and strengthens his or her ability to cope with ambiguity. Nothing could be further from the truth. Many people whose lives have been full of changes are no better prepared for the next major surprise than they were before their first encounter with instability.

One of the great myths about humans is that repetition results in expertise. Iteration may lead to heightened proficiency, but only if new learning is associated with each interaction. Recurring episodes of change that lack the benefit of new learning produce little more than redundant experiences; no cumulative value is realized. New learning related to generic knowledge of change is by far the most influential but least observed in organizations today. It therefore represents the strongest competitive advantage.

A person's grasp of generic change knowledge is expanded when new learning is gained that is associated with recognizing common, universal patterns and principles about the human dynamics of change that can be applied to the implementation of virtually any organizational initiative. It is this kind of generic change knowledge that forms the basis for what I call *transition management literacy*.

Transition management literacy reflects the basic knowledge and skill level of a person, group, or entire organization regarding the ability to successfully design and carry out prescriptive plans for the execution of major change initiatives. Low literacy levels are usually associated with either little change-related experience or a weak grasp of the generic patterns that apply to how people respond to disruptions in their lives or of what can be done to facilitate the change journey from one state to another. High literacy levels typically reflect people who have weathered many transitions in their lives and, from this experience, have acquired a general understanding of the universal patterns and principles that can be relied on when planning and engaging change, regardless of the nature or setting of the effort. One of the critical challenges facing leaders today is the dangerously low transition management literacy rate that exists in most organizations.

When a person's surroundings are filled with meaningless data and confusing information, it's impossible to solve problems and exploit opportunities. Unless problems and opportunities can be resolved, success is impossible; and without success, knowledge is unattainable. When facing the unknown, generic change-related knowledge is both the creation of success and its creator.

Nimble Expectations

Change occurs when people face situations they don't expect. But exactly what do they expect? Understanding the process by which expectations are constructed, and later are either corroborated or invalidated, is essential to the prospect of leading the change process. Three key elements interact to form expectations: events, perceptions, and implications.

EVENTS

The experience of organizational change is often first triggered by an unfamiliar event—an occurrence that appears inconsistent with what was anticipated. Think of the triggering event for change as normally coming from objective reality, or the world external to the individual or group that is reacting. Unfamiliar events can be verified by most people who witness them. For example, even though some people at a recent meeting did not want to believe their CEO's announcement regarding an impending plan to merge with a competitor, all who were there confirmed that they personally heard him declare the company's intention to do just that. This is a triggering event—a surprise—that can be regarded as either good news or bad, depending on the perspective of those attending the meeting. Whatever the change entails, it originated from somewhere outside the listeners themselves.

PERCEPTIONS

Incidents, events, data, information—however one characterizes the input—whatever reaches our conscious or even our unconscious threshold does so only after passing through the perception filters we use to explain the world around us.

A printout of raw data, in itself, is nothing but a signal that some type of undefined stimuli has entered an environment. Data alone are without significance or consequence. Until they are ascribed meaning (pertinence and intention), data have no practical value. We gain an understanding of our world by combining bits of related data into information clusters (i.e., formations bound by a logical frame of reference) that are, in turn, grouped into patterns that, when aggregated, form information chains. These chains of information, which are relevant to specific situations, become the basis for what we experience as a spontaneous thought—Car! Danger! Jump out of the way!

When we first encounter events of any kind, our initial reaction is to determine whether the stimuli we are seeing or hearing fit within previously established information chains that are recognizable to us. Whereas information is dependent on data for its existence, knowledge is dependent on the application of information before it can be manifested. Knowledge is the result of successfully administering information chains to solve a problem or exploit an opportunity.

As you can imagine, the path from data to knowledge varies greatly from person to person. Herein lies the basis for the depth of diversity that exists among human opinions. One person interprets the announced merger plan as an example of the inevitable shakeout that must occur because of deregulation; another describes the same event as a reckless action of a power-hungry CEO. These divergent viewpoints of the same event create different valuations of the described incident. One person thinks the merger is an unavoidable dilemma that must be managed and feels it could have positive results. Others see it as a preventable problem that should have been avoided altogether. The meaning an event has for people is a function of what they perceive to have happened and the positive or negative influence they believe this occurrence has had and/or will have on their future.

IMPLICATIONS

This third element of expectation development deals with the assumptions and inferences people make when they project into the future what they think or believe to be true. What's critical regarding how people generate expectations about their future is the relationship that links the *events* that actually take place, how these events are *perceived*, and the *implications* that are subsequently drawn.

When unfamiliar events are filtered through a person's thought processes, the events become meaningful information that is then applied as knowledge when the person characterizes and judges what has taken place. The resulting determinations are usually consistent with what was already believed to be true; that is, we usually make decisions in accordance with our preexisting frames of reference.

Once a person forms an opinion of an event, he or she will immediately anticipate the implications by projecting possible scenarios based on previously established frames of reference. These implications are an essential building block if expectations are to materialize. Once a particular scenario is deemed the most likely to occur, an expectation has been created that this implication will take place. People feel a sense of control in their lives when the expectations they form about the future are verified by what they later experience as actually taking place.

Because all events are interpreted through our perception filters, the important match here is not between expectations and objective reality, but between expectations and our filtered perceptions of reality. When there is general agreement between the two, people feel they can predict and plan for the future, and, in doing so, prepare themselves for what appears to be on the way.

Control and Disorder

Arguably the most demanding reason change is so challenging has to do with why and how people seek control in their lives, and the ways they react to disorder. We are a control-oriented species, and leaders cannot hope to intentionally orchestrate the outcome of an organizational change unless they take this orientation into account when planning and executing the transition process. It is not necessary for leaders to be junior psychologists in order to build nimble systems, but without at least a rudimentary grasp of what influences people as they struggle with control and disorder, it will be impossible for senior officers to move past their existing level of unconscious competence.[2] Becoming consciously competent about leading large-scale change requires a significant investment to understand those aspects of the human mind and spirit that are evoked during transitions.

With that said, let's discuss the human need for control. Regardless of the nature of the circumstances, if people are to enjoy success in any situation, they must be able to solve the problems, and exploit the opportunities presented, in a manner that contributes to accomplishing their goals. It is difficult to succeed in situations that are unstable because they tend to be confusing and ambiguous. This is why we humans are biologically, socially, and psychologically engineered to seek homeostasis whenever possible.

This desire for balance in our lives is expressed in many ways, not the least of which is the kind of settings in which we prefer to operate. Whenever most people have a choice, they will stay within secure environments where there are few fluctuations in the variables that could hinder them from achieving their goals. We do this because ordered surroundings are typically more predictable and thus more amenable to being influenced. Situations that can be anticipated are usually easier to manage and lend themselves to our feeling some degree of influence over destiny. This is true because, except for the impact of luck, people can succeed only in environments they understand. A key test of this understanding is the extent to which a person's expectations match what he or she perceives to be happening. When what appears to be happening validates what was anticipated, people feel they are in a situation that is predictable. The more predictable or stable the environment is judged to be, the more likely it is that success can be achieved.

Reliable predictions allow the time to generate and evaluate alternative response strategies. These strategies may or may not result in favorable outcomes, but, as long as predictability is intact, people feel they have some degree of control over their future.

Though our sense of comfort is highly dependent on the congruity of our expectations and perceptions, a breach between the two is not always a problem. The sensation of being surprised by something can, in fact, be easily absorbed if it occurs in small doses or if we are not very invested in the subject in question.

Sometimes, for example, the break between expectations and perceptions is only a small crack and may go unnoticed, or it may appear to be within acceptable limits—that is, within familiar boundaries. "John is once again late for his own meeting; as long as I've known him, it's been like this. It's hard to tell when his meetings are going to start because of his crazy schedule." The person making this statement might have hoped for the meeting to start on time, but was not too surprised. Delay happens frequently because of John's hectic schedule. These kinds of surprises are encountered all the time and are readily accommodated.

When surprises concern someone or something we are not highly invested in, or if we can view the situation with detached objectivity, the gap between expectations and perceptions is much less threatening and can even be seen as humorous. Jokes are funny because the punch lines depart from what the setup had led us to anticipate. They are not as funny the second or third time we hear them because we know what to anticipate. Usually, the only difference between a hilarious skit and an offensive parody is the sensitivity two different listeners have for the subject. Both people are surprised, but only one finds it funny. The other is alienated.

Small or acceptable shifts from what was predicted are usually not a problem. These kinds of surprises I'll refer to as *minor* changes. *Major change comes about when there are severe disconnections between expectations and perceptions about people or things considered extremely important.* Under these circumstances, the consequences for a breach are often extremely disruptive. When expectations fail to match perceptions, predictability is lost, a feeling of preparedness for what is about to happen is forfeited, control vanishes, and the chance for success is sacrificed.

People need some sort of anchor when struggling through ambiguity and uncertainty in their lives. We humans are arguably the most control-oriented animals on the planet. Securing, maintaining, or regaining a sense of control in our lives is a fundamental need, and it translates into a prevalent, though mostly unconscious, preoccupation for most of us.

Some of our more unpleasant responses when we face unclear conditions are: confusion, anxiety, fear, defensiveness, and withdrawal. Even when our initial reactions to change are more positive, these kinds of situations can still become problematic (i.e., naive enthusiasm and blind devotion can get us into trouble). Regardless of their appearance, most major organizational initiatives generate some level of distress within an organization because people do not like to lose the sense of control that comes from being in a predictable work environment.

THE MANAGEABILITY OF CHANGE

Change is experienced as bewildering chaos when it is faced without the benefit of a sense of control. It is seen as a manageable process only if it can be directed or at least anticipated. The *manageability of change* is therefore explicitly tied to the amount of control available to the people involved and is worthy of further explanation.

First, manageability of change is in the eye of the beholder; it's a matter of one's frame of reference. A new assignment or an upgrade in software may or may not register as a significant change for someone. Even if it does register, the same event may or may not evoke a similar reaction in another person. This is what makes it is so difficult to introduce change into an organization in any kind of systemic fashion. A single effort can produce a broad band of viewpoints based on the number of people affected and how disruptive the impact is to them. The more often people feel disconcerted by change and the more significant the disruptions are to them, the more diverse the interpretations become. A major initiative in a large company can engender thousands of individual interpretations of the same event.

Developing expectations in keeping with what is later experienced does not guarantee a positive outcome, but it allows people to enjoy a sense of control. People feel in control when they can intentionally influence their environment (direct control), or when they can at least prepare to some extent for what is about to happen (indirect control). Confusing and ambiguous situations are frightening to us precisely because they mean we have lost the feeling of having any type of control.

DIRECT VERSUS INDIRECT CONTROL

Contrary to how most people relate to the term *control*, this state of feeling *prepared* for what will happen is not limited to always knowing how to achieve what we want. Being confident that we know what it takes to succeed is only one form of equipping ourselves for the future. A second kind of readiness occurs when we can accurately anticipate the future implications of an event, even though we don't always know what to do to achieve our goal. In either case, we are able to develop and maintain the integrity of our expectations. People experience major change when their circumstances are significantly different from what they expected; that is, when neither direct nor indirect control is possible. When we resist change, we are not so much in conflict with the new conditions as we are acting out our fear of losing access to the direct or indirect control we so desperately seek. Readiness or preparedness is the paramount concern, of which there are two types that produce two very different kinds of control.

Direct control (usually our preference) takes place when we develop accurate expectations about what will happen in the future and about how we should behave when it occurs, in order to achieve what we want. For example: John interpreted the introduction of enterprise-level software into his company as being much more than a means to meet the productivity and efficiency goals declared by management. He, therefore, took it upon himself to start nurturing new relationships in other departments by demonstrating an interest in their work and attending some of their training sessions. Later, he was the only one among his peers who received a lateral transfer when his area was downsized. By taking the actions he did, he felt he had accurately interpreted and responded to the situation. The feeling of being in direct control takes place when people believe they know what is going to happen next, as well as what to do to succeed.

With indirect control, instead of feeling we can directly influence our future, our control lies in anticipating the correct outcome of a situation and preparing ourselves for its effects. In exercising indirect control, just as with its more direct alternative, expectations are developed that later turn out to be correct. In fact, the same sequence unfolds as with direct control: data are converted into meaningful information which, when applied, becomes knowledge that, in turn, creates expectations that prove to be consistent with what later appears to occur. With both direct and indirect control, the congruence between expectations and perceptions makes people feel they can anticipate the future and prepare themselves for what is to come.

The difference between the two types of control is that the readiness created with the indirect version is far less proactive than what is possible with its direct counterpart. If we are primed for what is to happen but are unable to determine how to act in order to succeed in the situation, we usually experience a great deal of frustration and anxiety. This explains why, for most situations, indirect control is far less preferable than direct control.

For most of us, getting what we want (direct control) is the only form of control with which we are familiar. It is a foreign idea that readying ourselves for events we don't like and can't stop is another legitimate form of control. Lacking full appreciation for the readiness value of indirect control increases our already difficult struggle with ambiguity. If we think all we have available to us in the fight against future shock is the luxury of direct control, we are doomed to a life of feeling overwhelmed by the many forces of change that affect our lives. Whenever possible, exercising direct control to achieve what we desire is an important component to success in turbulent markets. As instability grows, however, so does the importance of indirect control, which is far better than having no control whatsoever. Both direct and indirect control are essential elements to the adaptation process, and thus to prosperity in unstable markets.

PREDICTABILITY IS WHAT'S IMPORTANT

Having access to either direct or indirect control means the environment can be viewed as relatively predictable, which, in turn, increases the likelihood of success. Let's take Mary's case, for instance. For the past three years, Mary has worked in an organization she basically understands. Some days seem more difficult than others, but the essentials of her role, goals, responsibilities, rewards, ways to please her boss, and the tools she uses to do her work have maintained a consistency throughout her tenure.

We'll use the color green to represent the continuity Mary has become accustomed to in her workplace. She is familiar with the comfortable green office she goes to each day to conduct her work. There are green tasks with green buttons to push for green results. She can, at times, adjust the various elements in the room to her liking (direct control), and sometimes she endures things she dislikes, but she is at least prepared for them to some extent (indirect control). The surprises that do occur are relatively small and easy for her to absorb. Mary has become confident in her ability to anticipate what will happen in her green situation. In fact, over the years, the color has taken on a soothing quality that gives her a sense of security.

One day, Mary goes to work as usual, walks through the same door, turns on the lights, and is startled by a bright-red glare that almost overwhelms her. The intense red radiates off of everything she sees. No part of her office offers relief. The brilliance is more than distressing: it's confusing. Mary understands green. In the familiarity of her normal work environment, she knows which green buttons to push for her success. In this sea of unconventional red, however, she is disoriented, floundering, and feeling victimized by a work environment she no longer understands. Not only is her energy drained and her spirit dampened, but Mary has no hope of remaining viable in a competitive environment that bewilders her.

Loss of control is a personal experience, but it has some very important organizational ramifications. A green-conditioned Mary will be unable to compete in a red market. She and her company will find it difficult to effectively respond to, much less accurately forecast, customers' red needs and demands as well as they did in the green past.

To say humans try to refrain from these kinds of breakdowns in continuity is a dramatic understatement. Major change is so undesirable, most people would prefer to maintain the continuity of a negative, even self-destructive, but *familiar* situation rather than venture where their predictions are not validated by their perceptions. Even when the consequences for maintaining the status quo are significant, most people avoid dramatically new, unpredictable circumstances whenever possible.

Dynamic Balance

The final reason change is so challenging has to do with the influence of dynamic balance.

Control and equilibrium are what we are drawn to, but we must learn to approach these objectives with an appreciation for the paradox they represent. Because the world we interact with consists of an ever-growing number of variables in various states of agitation, the only stability that is possible is that which occurs as a result of constant movement. Dynamic balance is the closest we will ever come to the tranquil contentment we seek.

Dynamic balance is that quality of well-being attributed to a person's belief that he or she is in a predictable environment where it is possible to exercise some degree of control over his or her destiny. The sense of equilibrium that results from this feeling is a powerful influence in our lives and is fundamental to being able to contend with the various challenges that are inherent to change. This ability to remain poised during unrest is a prerequisite for success in ambiguous and uncertain situations, yet most people have only a faint understanding of what dynamic balance is, much less how it is created, maintained, lost, or reestablished.

Think of dynamic balance as a kind of restless composure. The solidity it generates is not the result of inert passivity; it is the by-product of highly mobile forces interacting with each other in such a way that they create an intensely kinetic steady state. This fosters an equilibrium that is extremely animated, but, relative to the force and intensity of the surrounding environment, it has a quality of calm uniformity.

Dynamic balance occurs when most of our expectations about a situation favorably compare to what we perceive to be happening. The antithesis of this kind of equilibrium is a chaotic environment where ambiguity, confusion, and misunderstandings prevail. When people experience dynamic balance, the various events and processes taking place around them are recognizable, and each has its own meaning and implication. These associations may have positive or negative repercussions, but one thing is certain for the people involved: they experience a sense of indirect, if not direct, control over their destiny. Even if this dynamic balance is operating within an extremely unpleasant situation, the consistency between what was expected and what is perceived creates a relatively predictable environment.

The more familiar our surroundings are, the more chances we have to develop successful ways to deal with the challenges we are presented. Not only are the odds of our success increased, but our functioning in settings we are accustomed to requires fewer resources.

In part, change is so challenging to us because the peaceful presence of mind most of us desire is found within profound disruption. Rather than on the calm waters of a static environment, where logic would suggest the equilibrium we seek would reside, the balance we are looking for is embedded in the very turmoil we are so frightened of.

There are two basic reasons for the constant motion that lies under the stability created by dynamic balance. First, when dynamic balance is achieved, it is the result of a rhythmic, back-and-forth flow that is formed when expectations are in and out of sync with what is being perceived. This kind of uneasy steadiness is like the seesaw symmetry that might occur between two fiercely competitive but evenly matched tennis players. In a game that pits equally skilled and motivated rivals, there are times when the rhythm of their alternating efforts is exactly parallel and they create, for a few moments, a synchronized uniformity to the overall game. During these exchanges, if we were to focus on each player's individual movements, we would recognize only their separate achievements. When the players are viewed as interdependent counterparts, a reciprocating parity is revealed that allows the aggressive competition to take on an almost serene, collaborative quality.

The same is true for most people. When the fluctuations between expectations and perceptions occur close enough to each other, people experience the harmony associated with stability and predictability. It is an uneasy, tentative harmony, but nonetheless, one that lends itself to feeling in control.

The second reason the calm we desire is found only amid intense activity is due to the inherent movement of the world in which we live. Not only is the unsteady equilibrium we seek a result of compensating counterweights, but its vigorous nature is also the result of being constantly bombarded by new environmental elements that pack enough force to throw the fragile congruity between expectations and perceptions out of order. This means that, once achieved, the shelf life for the point of balance is always short-lived. No sooner has it been established than it is shattered by yet more unfamiliar variables that must be accommodated before the sought-after tranquillity can return.

In fact, it is a testament to how powerful intermittent rewards are in our lives that we spend so little time actually experiencing dynamic balance, compared to the time invested in trying to secure this feeling. Attainment of dynamic balance is difficult and infrequent, but there is a powerful incentive to continue trying. Whenever this temporary symmetry is attained, the payoff for the effort is more than worth the trouble. Regardless of whether what was expected was considered an opportunity or a danger, by correctly anticipating what is going to happen a person is able to ready himself or herself in the best way possible.

This sense of preparedness is fundamental to securing dynamic balance. The feeling of being prepared for your destiny is a function of having confidence that the various impending challenges have been accurately anticipated, or having the competence needed to effectively resolve whatever does happen. When these kinds of confidence and competence are combined, they form an alliance that significantly advances your chances of succeeding in a new environment.

ROC$_{hg}$ Revisited

There is a growing likelihood that the demands that result from the eight aspects of change described in this chapter will exceed your organization's capacity to absorb them. If this hasn't already happened, it soon will. As leaders, we are fairly skilled at determining what to do; the issue is that we don't always know how to do it.

Given the scale of change projects we now need to implement and the implications if we fail to do so, this is not a concern that can be left solely at the door of the human resources department. Return on change (ROC$_{hg}$) must become a strategic concern for leaders who wish to create a nimble operation. The task is intimidating in its complexity and resource requirements, but then that's why you have the leadership job and someone else doesn't.

You, as much as the people you lead, fear the uncertainty, ambiguity, and loss of control change brings. You struggle with future shock, you get lost in the tangled web change weaves and the many layers it creates, and you often can't seem to manage your own expectations, much less those that others develop. Like the people you lead, you are able to succeed in unfamiliar situations only to the extent that you can grasp either direct or indirect control of what is happening. Finally, only by achieving the elusive dynamic balance can you stabilize yourself as the world around you becomes more and more chaotic. Despite these challenges, your job is to successfully lead your organization through the turmoil.

It's common to want to avoid that which is both painful and mysterious, but where are you going to go? It is unlikely you will locate a tranquil lake to replace the white-water rapids you are now experiencing. From anyone's particular vantage point, someone else's industry, company, job, marriage, family situation, or professional and personal circumstances may appear more serene and less agitated. After almost two-and-a-half decades of exploring this phenomenon, however, I assure you these appearances are deceiving. If you were inside the situations you see rather than observing from the outside, what appears to be a more restful environment would more than likely prove less placid than it seems.

There is nowhere else to go. Any leadership role in any organization in any industry in any country now requires that you tame the beast.

You didn't do anything wrong, and you're not being punished. The dynamics of change are no more guided toward or away from the righteous of the world than the villains. Like the path of a tornado or the development of cancer, condemnation is not part of the steering mechanism. There is no sin or sinner receiving just deserts. People are simply living out their lives and, in the process of doing so, are encountering surprises that are, at times, greater than they have resources to accommodate.

These chance encounters with overwhelming change are occurring more frequently and with more severe consequences today because our species is maturing. The physical sciences teach us that most living systems increase in complexity and interdependence as they evolve. Quantum theory states that all matter is actually restless and the appearance of stability is only the result of a dynamic balancing act. We must abandon the arrogance that suggests we are immune to these same forces.

We struggle with change because we are alive. This is as true for you as for the people you are attempting to lead. The only difference is: as they struggle, they will look to you for guidance. Anything less than conscious competence on your part will not suffice.

PART TWO

THE CONTAINED SLIDE— CREATING THE NIMBLE ORGANIZATION

Surviving and thriving in the face of constant change has much in common with sports. There are rules, training regimens, mental conditioning, goal setting, and, of course, winners and losers.

Like exceptional athletic performance, organizational Nimbleness doesn't just happen. It is the product of deliberate effort and unremitting hard labor. To me, that is reassuring to know. Change is bad enough; random chance is far worse. The despair that we all feel from time to time when things go awry is a reflection of the human aversion to being caught off guard. When what we expect to happen does not occur, our faith in a rational world starts to wobble. Pervasive change may or may not be rational, but our response to it can be as premeditated as that of an ice skater or skier making a seemingly impossible adjustment to execute a stunning maneuver that will mean the difference between an Olympic gold medal and a footnote indicating participation. There is a split second of sheer, high-risk–high-reward artistry undergirded by years of sweaty toil. Those who are ready and willing to go to the edge get the winning edge.

In Part Two, we will examine how this combination of poetry in execution and the power of extensive preparation comes about.

The Constant Quest

The Nimble Organization Is Always in Flux

C hange is so pervasive these days, many organizations are being danger-ously drained of their time and resources. The pressure is almost over-whelming. Some of us have already surpassed the future shock boundary; the price for doing so is becoming prohibitively expensive. The era of perpetual unrest is upon us, and only the most nimble of systems will survive and prosper.

Nimbleness is the ability for an organization to consistently succeed in unpre-dictable, contested environments by implementing important changes more effi-ciently and effectively than its competitors.

A threefold leadership role is required if you are to help your organiza-tion become truly nimble. First, ensure that the enterprise is an "open sys-tem" (i.e., keeping people and things in an unending growth-and-renewal mode); second, take steps to increase its absorption limits; and finally, con-stantly press the envelope of these boundaries by introducing as many im-portant changes as possible without overextending available adaptation resources.

Before describing the primary features that distinguish a nimble organi-zation, it is important to state that though this quality is much desired, it should never be thought of as a terminal objective. As important as Nim-bleness is, it is no more than the means by which an organization is able to accomplish its true objective, which is to make the adjustments necessary to stay aligned with its market. To be sure this relationship between Nimbleness and market success is firmly grounded, you might review my comments in Chapter 1 about the effect of changing success factors on an organization's market alignment. I will repeat this one important point: The greater the turmoil an organization faces, the more likely that its success factors will require some degree of adjustment to keep them aligned. These adaptations may represent either minor repairs or major conversion.

Nimble organizations have a distinct edge over their more constrained competitors in dealing with constant transition. They:

- Repeatedly succeed in erratic, competitive environments through fast and effective modifications of their operations.
- Demonstrate a superior capacity to deal with unanticipated problems and opportunities.
- Rapidly redefine and redeploy their human, physical, and financial resources following a disruptive change.
- Orchestrate multiple, even simultaneous reconfigurations of their various corporate structures.
- Employ associates who accept frequent reassignment of their duties and perpetual reordering of their priorities as the norm.
- Help their people view a continuous flow of unplanned activities as simply the inevitable price to be paid for competing in volatile markets.

Nimbleness means more than flexibility. It is a term that conveys speed, grace, dexterity, and resourcefulness. As a nimble operation adjusts itself to unfamiliar pressures, people go beyond merely accommodating the new demands. This kind of enterprise is both malleable within its existing boundaries of operation and capable of redefining those boundaries so it can shift its success formula whenever necessary.

Being nimble is not a static position. Organizations must constantly calibrate their agility against not only what it takes to successfully implement the changes they have chosen to pursue, but also the response time of their competitors for achieving similar results. A company or agency that was impressive last year, when it gave a quick and capable response to a situation, can, this year, appear lifeless and cumbersome by comparison, even though its reaction time and capabilities have not lessened. An organization may be no less malleable and resourceful, and may, in fact, be even more responsive and creative than it was in the past; yet it can quickly lose its standing if outdone by an ambitious contender.

Nimbleness is a distinction that is relative to the circumstances in which an organization finds itself. It is a comparative quality, manifested only when an organization contrasts itself to (a) the changing market and (b) the speed and agility of its competitors.

First, let's explore the response to changing market demands. If a company's reaction to pivotal but unfamiliar market conditions is slow or ineffective, it can't secure or defend a nimble standing. Just as Olympic gold medalists meet new and higher qualifying standards for entry to succeeding games, nimble organizations must constantly address tougher standards to maintain their prowess.

Next is the issue of responding to competition. The second way a company can lose its claim to the coveted nimble status is if its reaction to existing market demands is impressive but lags behind that of its competitors. An Olympic runner-up may have broken a world record, but he or she is still noted as the first-place loser. Being nimble in one's market is no different. Winning at change is not a finite challenge; it's a relative one. Winning is contingent on the surroundings. The nimble provider in the market is the purveyor that can successfully solve problems and exploit, faster and more effectively than its competition, the opportunities presented by unfamiliar circumstances.

Nimbleness is not a fixed feature of an organization; it remains very much in flux. It is a virtue that may be powerfully demonstrated or may never exist at all. It may be securely entrenched during one period of time and only a distant memory in the next. After years of work to attain the coveted nimble rank, its advantages can vanish overnight should there be a decrease in ability to meet quality standards, an increase in customer expectations, or an introduction of a new, more spry, less encumbered rival. Unlike the Baldrige award, which, once earned, allows an organization to bask in its glory for an entire year, the status of being the nimble provider in a market can evaporate at any time. Think of Nimbleness as prestigious differentiation that can be won, lost, and reclaimed again in a very brief period of time.

In contrast, operations that are unable to carry out decisions intended to deal with shifting demands for success are referred to as *constrained organizations*. Despite their intention to sometimes do otherwise, constrained organizations rigidly adhere to the status quo. Some of these operations consciously resist change; others see the need for it, but are unable to execute their intent. Even after a concerted effort to conform, most constrained organizations gravitate back to operations that are similar in nature, if not in form, to the way things were before the challenge surfaced.

Being a nimble provider in a market brings with it a number of important competitive advantages above and beyond the obvious ones related to securing and maintaining market alignment. For one thing, a nimble organization is able to attract and maintain more competent employees as well as to design and deliver more creative solutions for its customers.

Another benefit of being nimble—the ability to secure new business and keep existing customers close to home—is due to the organization's capacity to execute that which has not yet even been requested. As more and more companies realize their world is not only changing now but, more importantly, will continue to shift in the future, they will be looking for providers who can be as agile in servicing them as they must be in servicing their customers.

Soon, the competitive advantage will not be in delivering what is needed today, but in being able to have a nimble response to the next generation of needs that are not yet known by the customer. Delighting customers by meeting or exceeding their current expectations will no longer offer differentiation; even second- and third-tier contenders that operate at the rear of an industry's standard of excellence will provide this level of customer satisfaction. Giving customers what they want, when they want it, at a price they will pay will become a commodity that no longer separates those who once dominated from the rest. The defining moment for customer service will not be when established needs are expressed; it will be when the unexpected requirement materializes overnight. The next generation of customer will see it this way:

> I can pick up the phone any day and talk to several providers, all of whom can give me what I already know I need. What is in short supply is a provider that can not only do that on a consistent basis, but can also turn on a dime and reconfigure with me what they deliver and how they serve us in order that we can *together* meet the new, short-fuse requirements given to me by one of my customers. I need relationships with providers that are competitive not only because of who they are today, but, more importantly, because of whom they can become and what they are capable of producing. I need more than current reliability—*I also need future capability.* That's not a "nickel-and-dime" vendor who comes and goes; that's a value-added partner you hang on to.

Nimble companies and agencies believe they must operate within a sphere of incessant novelty, and they treat their ability to manage the unexpected as a strategic asset. They acquire as much of this strength as they can, and they refuse to waste it on frivolous projects that reflect only a casual interest or marginal returns. What results is a stockpile of this versatility that produces some remarkable attributes. For example:

- Nimble organizations are usually distinctive in their deep sense of a shared purpose.
- There is, typically, a strong common belief that, on a frequent basis, the status quo will become prohibitively expensive, driving new changes into the system.
- Employees refuse to be trapped by past success or current pathologies.
- Line and staff personnel operate within flexible interpretations of their existing roles and assume they may face completely new job responsibilities on a periodic basis.
- In addition to individual assignments, people are accustomed to working in synergistic, cross-functional work teams.
- Although opportunities for input are expected from those involved in projects, people also expect fast, insightful decision making.
- Employees and leaders alike demonstrate their ability to focus on the company's ultimate success rather than on the discomforts they may experience in getting there.
- People in these kinds of organizations think it is normal to deal with constantly evolving initiatives and an abundance of diverse ideas.
- It seems only natural to associates in a nimble operation to engage in uninhibited dialogue, straightforward feedback, and open, constructive conflict.
- Management expects to be held accountable for both the quality of decisions regarding "what" to change as well as the implementation architecture necessary to address "how" the human variables will be handled during transitions.
- People at all levels tend to view succeeding in unfamiliar circumstances as one of their top-priority tasks.
- Employees generally feel valued because of their current performance, not their tenure.
- Employees tend to support the organization's cultural values and ostracize those who do not.
- People believe they will earn advancement because of their ability to build knowledge.

This cursory sampling of attributes is not intended to be inclusive; instead, it is meant to portray only a broad profile of the nimble enterprise (other aspects will be discussed in this chapter and other chapters in more detail). What follows is a deeper look at some of the more critical facets that distinguish the nimble organization from its constrained counterpart. These traits include:

- The critical role of staffing.
- How control affects nimble capacities.
- The value of tolerating ambiguity.
- The importance of maintaining a healthy tension throughout the organization.
- The role self-organization plays in an organization's future.
- The shift from an *event* to a *process* mentality.
- The value of orchestrating both trips and journeys.
- How resilience is manifested in a nimble organization.
- Why conscious competence is so essential to a nimble legacy.

Only the Agile Need Apply

In respect to building a nimble operation, your most important leadership task is hiring and retaining the kind of people who can translate the desired vision into tangible reality. Operationalizing the goal of becoming the nimble provider in your market is more dependent on who is on your team than on how they are structured or the responsibilities they are assigned. You must be supported by a cadre of managers, supervisors, and employees who are able and willing to go beyond the guidance you can provide. You need people who can help invent a nimble future.

Achieving the nimble status in your market is an intellectually and emotionally demanding undertaking. It is impossible for you alone to have all the answers, and even when you're right about what to do next, your solution won't be viable for very long or relevant in all parts of the organization. Your contingent must be staffed with men and women who can resonate with your vision of a nimble environment, but who also know much more than you about its fulfillment at a tactical level. Finding these people is not an easy assignment.

It is my strong recommendation that you apply the 80/20 rule to your efforts at staffing your organization for Nimbleness. The overwhelming majority of your company's time and resources should go to matching potential candidates with the requisite skills and predisposition, not trying to mold everyone into being a nimble contributor. Avoid the wanna-bes— those who lack the skill base and/or predisposition that would allow them to advance the effort in a meaningful way. Eighty percent of your resources should be directed toward hiring people who are already prone toward the desired attributes, and then training and coaching them to expand their capabilities even more. No more than 20 percent of your resources should be allocated to assisting those who say they are willing to work against their own instincts and biases and who try to develop completely new propensities that would help them contribute to a nimble environment.

Here, it might be useful to review a few of the skills and predispositions that you should be looking for when staffing. For example, nimble operations tend to attract people who display resilience during change. Resilient people are positive they can succeed in unfamiliar circumstances. They remain focused on objectives during times of confusion, exhibit flexibility about how to address inhibitors, find order within what appears to be chaos, and proactively engage change rather than run from it.[1]

Resilient associates also tend to be resourceful, multiskilled, highly motivated people who have a high tolerance for ambiguity, a desire to experiment, and a willingness to appropriately challenge authority. When an organization creates a critical mass of people with these qualities, its ability to attend to shifting demands dramatically accelerates. These kinds of people converge their energies on making the necessary adjustments so they and the whole operation can succeed rather than fall prey to the dysfunctional behavior associated with people who become overwhelmed with the disruptions in their lives, as is typical of constrained organizations.

The nimble organization tends to attract people who focus on the success of the entire enterprise. They lack the time or inclination to pursue the latest office gossip or engage in provincial battles waged by insecure egos fighting over insignificant issues. These people have no less of a desire to exercise their needs for power than those in a constrained operation, but they feel they have more opportunities to influence the issues and actions that will have a greater bearing on the success of the overall organization, and thus they choose to invest their energy there.

Nimble operations are by no means void of differing opinions, arguments, and heated conflict. The difference is that, in constrained environments, the vehemence and viciousness of the hostility often become counterproductive, if not outright destructive, to the individuals involved as well as to the organization's overall ability to compete. People in a nimble work setting are able to maintain a healthier perspective about their disagreements in two respects: (1) they try to stay centered on what is best for the organization, not what would serve only their parochial interests; and (2) they constantly seek new sources of information, not new ways to protect themselves or subvert the overall system. They don't often forget that their adversary in an organizational disagreement is also their partner in success. They may have different opinions about means, but they share a common goal of market success and they know they are dependent on each other in achieving it.

The result of all this is a bond that allows people who sometimes don't even like each other to work together effectively. Regardless of their personal relationships with each other, an interdependent bond is formed in the environment so there is actually more expression of differing opinions than may be seen in a constrained operation, but seldom does the conflict escalate.

People working in a nimble organization have no less of a need for clout than those trying in vain to control a constrained system. They simply go about meeting this need very differently. Instead of pursuing issues of negligible importance to the organization, they seek to fulfill their power needs by pursuing matters that produce a sense of accomplishment for themselves and contribute to the overall success of the organization. This alignment of personal potency with organizational benefit is much more likely when the organization keeps pace with the escalating and oscillating demands it faces.

When an institution lacks the agility to flex with and adapt to shifting pressures and opportunities, its workers not only dissociate from its success but may even rationalize undermining the organization's efforts to better its position. The grousing sounds like this:

> This place is filled with losers; don't believe a word they say around here about involvement in decisions. Management never has paid attention to our opinion, and they aren't going to start now.

In contrast, when an organization quickly and effectively turns uncertainty and adversity into advantages, the employees usually want to strengthen their identification with the company and attempt to parallel its success with their own. The tone and tenor are a lot different:

> I know it's not easy to trust that management really wants your opinion, but it's true. They will solicit your opinions on all sorts of things. They may not always follow your advice, but if you earn management's respect they will listen to you and value what you have to say. By the way, you should say what you think to everyone here, not just to management. It's how we all relate to each other.

Another important aspect about the people attracted to nimble organizations is their ability to not only engage in and sustain important changes within existing frameworks, but also to create new operating paradigms when necessary. People like this neither hold on too long to the way things worked in the past, nor do they prematurely abandon structures and systems before they have fulfilled their value.

When nimble employees encounter the unanticipated problems and opportunities that proliferate under the stress of change, they don't simply bounce back from the initiatives put in place, they seem to spring forward. That is, after successfully implementing one project, rather than feeling depleted, they are actually renewed in strength to address the next set of initiatives. They may become tired, even exhausted, from the demands of change, but they recover quickly and, more importantly, they gain an expanded capacity to absorb even more change in the future.

To successfully negotiate the turbulence in its market more efficiently and effectively than its constrained competition, a nimble company requires the right people. Staffing the organization with people who are predisposed toward the traits just described will go a long way toward building a nimble system.

Forewarned

As a nimble leader, you need to help those in your organization to appreciate the role control plays in navigating them toward market success.

Constrained organizations have a history of introducing significant, disruptive modifications for which associates have little warning and/or are unsure of how to develop adequate response strategies. In effect, they are asked to perform their assigned duties while facing unmanageable change and without the benefit of direct and/or indirect control. Most importantly, these unmanageable initiatives are usually placed before people with marginal or low levels of resilience to change. The combination of little direct or indirect control and insufficient personal resilience is a formula for transition disaster.

Nimble organizations are characterized by just the opposite kind of circumstances. Their associates are typically caught less off guard by announcements of impending change, and when they are surprised, they are usually more confident in their ability to deal with the situation. Leaders of these companies tend to create environments where most changes are introduced to highly resilient people with as much direct and/or indirect control provided as possible. Whenever leaders are unable to offer direct or indirect control (that is, the circumstances don't allow them to forewarn people about an impending change, or allow them much of an opportunity to influence its impact), high resilience among the people involved can be relied on to help them regain a sense of themselves.

The Two Faces of Ambiguity

Entering the era of perpetual unrest means confusion, mixed feelings, and ambiguity are here to stay. The ability to perform in highly ambiguous situations is, therefore, a core competency for those on a nimble team.

Unfortunately, the notion of tolerating ambiguity has become supercharged with misinformation and misunderstanding. It is not unusual for intriguing words or phrases like this to enter management's lexicon and become popular long before most people have a firm grasp of what the terms really mean. To get a handle on this term, substitute "the unfamiliar" for "ambiguity."

When facing the unfamiliar, fight or flight is the option we usually exercise first. To reduce the malaise we experience in confusing situations, we either try to fight or counter our bewilderment by attempting to make sense out of the quandary we find ourselves in ("Maybe this is how they treat all the companies they acquire") or we try flight—some way to get out of the predicament as fast as we can ("I put my resume on the street as soon as I heard the announcement"). In either case, by bringing meaning to the confusion (even if we don't like what this tells us) or fleeing the circumstances, we can regain a sense of control and reestablish the balance we seek.

When fight or flight appears to be unfeasible, I've observed that a third option, actually a pseudo alternative, sometimes develops. I call it *immunity*. If people find it's impossible to overcome or run from confusion, they will sometimes make an effort to intellectually accept things as they are. In doing so, they unconsciously hope to reduce the distress they feel. Individuals who use this tactic aren't really seeking a higher tolerance for ambiguity; what they want is indemnity from its impact. They hope to use this bogus acceptance as a way to circumvent the real issues and secure an exemption from the emotional stress of uncertainty rather than learn to operate within it.

The immunity approach seldom works because of the faulty logic it presents. Ambiguous situations cause vexations that appear to be relieved only by fight or flight. If neither fight nor flight strategies are available to relieve our stress, the symptoms associated with loss of control don't disappear simply by acknowledging their presence. Accepting that neither the fight nor the flight alternative is feasible doesn't mitigate the remaining vagaries and confusion. There are no pardons from the uneasiness that comes with uncertainty; the discomfort remains intact.

Most people who make reference to "tolerating ambiguity" are hoping consciously or unconsciously that somehow, through the miracle of acceptance, they will be able to rise above the uneasiness that unfortunately always coexists with uncertainty. They usually assume that the acceptance process yields some mystical means for becoming content with their discomfort. This, of course, is not the case. Think about the logic involved in the immunity strategy. By acknowledging the inevitable, it is supposed to somehow transform anxiety, dread, and despair into tranquillity, appeasement, and calmness. Really? I don't think so.

When neither the legitimate fight/flight strategies nor false immunity are considered options for adequately dealing with the burden of ambiguity, a fourth alternative still remains—tolerating the ambiguity while maintaining high performance. This last strategy is the most difficult and, therefore, usually the least preferable of the choices, yet it is the only one that is really viable when circumstances remain muddy and equivocal for long periods of time.

This final strategy also calls for a form of acceptance, but of a very different kind from that associated with immunity. Here, a person fully recognizes that discomfort is the constant companion of significant uncertainty. As such, he or she understands that major change always will be tied to some level of unpleasantness, irritation, and aggravation. More importantly, the person using this approach is able to acknowledge that, regardless of the pain and suffering endured, he or she must still be held accountable for whatever job responsibilities or duties have been assumed.

Tolerance for or acceptance of ambiguity has nothing to do with lowering the fear and anxiety that accompany confusion, nor does it involve reducing performance expectation. Like courage, the true nature of tolerance for ambiguity must be understood. Courage is not *taking action fearlessly*, it is *acting despite feeling fearful*. Tolerance for ambiguity means performing well despite the discomfort one is sure to feel when facing the unknown. It means working with, not somehow sidestepping, the distress caused by loss of direct and indirect control.

Nimble companies consistently operate within this fourth option. They hire and promote people who have a strong tolerance for ambiguity, and then they train, coach, and reward this behavior to fortify it further. What these organizations look for and cultivate is the antithesis of the binary mentality that constrained organizations tend to promote. No gray areas, fuzzy interpretations, or dilemmas exist in the linear, sequential, logical world of a binary thinker. All eligible options are clearly defined or they are assumed to be unsuitable for consideration. Once facts appear and executives make a selection, alternatives cease to exist and the execution of a decision is considered synonymous with its announcement.

Because organizational life has become so fast-paced and complicated, the binary approach is not currently enjoying much popular acclaim, but it is important to remember that it has proven very successful in the past. In earlier times, when there was less speed and complexity, this way of seeing and relating to the world actually contributed to prosperity. The key to its success was to be sure its interpretation of reality was only applied in uniform and uninterrupted settings.

Nimble organizations compete in markets distinguished by their hyperdiscontinuity; binary thinking would be disastrous. Leaders and employees in these organizations, out of necessity, display a highly evolved tolerance for ambiguity. They maintain their quality and productivity standards despite any confusion, setbacks, or affliction they may experience as a result of facing unfamiliar challenges, fragmented information, and unpredictable events. They are not immune to the stress of feeling near the point of losing control; they simply perform regardless of the discomfort that stress generates.

In contrast, constrained organizations tend to hire associates who become dysfunctional when confronted with accelerating ambiguity. Though discomfort is a natural and inevitable outcome of the stress created by uncertainty, for these people it becomes the focus of their attention. They are so distracted by it they are unable to properly perform their responsibilities and/or assigned duties. They are not only unable to relieve the strain created by ambiguous circumstances, but organizational productivity and quality suffer while they attend to their own overextension. They often become immobilized by fear and anxiety and cannot engage in the proper problem-solving activities that are necessary to succeed on the job. Frustrations, conflicts, worries, and grief become the converging points for their energy consumption, leaving precious little for recalibrating expectations. This, of course, renders their adaptation capacity severely weakened.

One final but tremendously important benefit of the ability to tolerate ambiguity has to do with working synergistically with others, and, more specifically, finding creative solutions to presenting problems. By tolerating ambiguity, we delay judging new situations and are more likely to find value in them and to creatively transform them into opportunities.

Using Creative Tension

Nimble organizations do not hide from the challenging reality of change. They assume that a work environment filled with unbroken transition will create a great deal of emotional strain, intellectual intensity, physical tension, and psychological pressure. Nimble companies and agencies seek out resilient people to employ, and they structure their enterprise to conduct its business in such a manner as to exploit the energy created by this atmosphere. It is the intent of such organizations to stay focused on the task at hand and use, rather than try to avoid, the stress that exists. They seek to conduct their business within the tension generated by uncertainty rather than try to maneuver around it.

The space between apparently contradictory alternatives (e.g., increase quality versus reduce expenses; reward innovative thinking versus minimize costly mistakes; or value diverse backgrounds versus form cohesive teams) is fertile ground. For nimble institutions, the continuum formed when two such objectives become critical to success demands that the path between the two is traveled over and over again.

The answer lies in the struggle that is intrinsic to moving from one extreme to the other. We labor to reach one pole because it looks like the answer for a given endeavor or for a period of time, but usually, before we get there, the circumstances shift and the other end of the path becomes more appealing. We toil for access to one end only to find that it is nothing more than a temporary solution and, once attained, we feel the need to move again in the opposite direction.

In a similar fashion, leaders within nimble organizations not only envision many destinations that are paradoxical in nature, but they also know prosperity does not reside solely within any one of these objectives. What is considered important with each of these continua is the struggle to get from wherever they are to wherever they need to be next. Rather than this realization producing disillusionment, disappointment, or emotional trauma, it generates a hardiness among nimble leaders that results in a steady hand at the helm. These senior officers, in turn, tend to hire and retain people who are also able to struggle with, but value the tension that comes from, living between the various paradoxical extremes chosen by organizations.

This composure within distress is accomplished most often by utilizing one of two maneuvers. When faced with the need to pursue multiple options, people from nimble organizations tend to either float among the alternatives (rather than "lock and load" on one) or synthesize a solution from the choices available (rather than compromise between the opportunities).

- Floating—To stay within the tension of uncertainty, the nimble company seldom takes a position that could be seen as permanent. While constrained organizations battle to find a single correct answer among two or more opposing possibilities, nimble organizations pontoon along the continuum formed when apparent contradictions are viewed as paradoxical aspects of the same thing. For example, as shown in Figure 3.1, the binary executive in a constrained company will attempt to choose

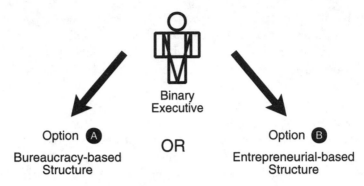

Figure 3.1   Example of constrained decisions.

between an organizational structure that is bureaucracy-based and frugal with expenses (option A), or one that is entrepreneurial-based and revenue-hungry (option B).

To the contrary, the nimble leader may reward one component of his or her organization for being cost-conscious and risk-averse (Dept. A), while forming a different function (Dept. B) around more entrepreneurial values (see Figure 3.2). This allows any point on the continuum between *bureaucracy* and *entrepreneurial* to be used, based on the unique circumstances in each area of the company. It also provides for any one functional area to be guided toward a particular spot on the continuum during one period (Dept. C now). Later, if the situation changes, an alternative point for the same function (Dept. C 18 months from now) can be pursued. In either case, nimble floating entails contextual choices that may be slightly modified or totally abandoned later, depending on the circumstances.

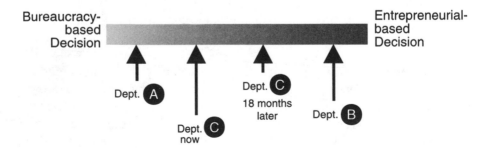

Figure 3.2   Example of nimble decisions.

- Synthesizing—The second way people in nimble organizations remain in the tension of uncertainty originates in their ability to integrate options instead of choosing one over another. A nimble operation may sometimes choose to identify and then merge the best attributes from two or more possible choices and/or reconstitute the contents of these choices to form a completely new alternative with a combined strength greater than any of the separate options.

Although floating and synthesizing can generate optimum solutions for a particular part of an organization at a specific point in time, neither maneuver provides relief from the strain that exists within nimble operations. Nimble operations believe creative tension is necessary to select the proper placement when surfing any continuum of alternatives in search of the correct $1 + 1 > 2$ solution for a given group at a given time. Making the right call is possible only through the pressure and strain generated when diverse views collide in an atmosphere of mutual goals and interdependence. The tension (i.e., energy) brought to life by the clash of different viewpoints is an absolute necessity if truly creative alternatives are to result.

Furthermore, nimble organizations are convinced that, in turbulent environments, an ongoing uneasiness is always present because of the short shelf life that exists for the feasibility of ideas. People can't let their guard down or rest on their laurels in a highly volatile, competitive market because the variables change so often and so profoundly. What last week was a synthesized solution perfectly suited to the circumstances could prove disastrous today. Sleeping with one eye open and being a little paranoid are considered healthy symptoms in an unstable, cutthroat environment.

The key to success when using the floating and/or synthesizing techniques is identifying the proper continua that will allow an organization to stay in alignment with its market. Even though these techniques are powerful tools to help evade the binary pitfalls of single-reality answers, the techniques alone will not produce the desired outcome. The dexterity and agility these methods permit are of little value if they are used to move quickly from one point to another between paradoxical alternatives that don't really help an organization compete in evolving, unstable, complex industries. Leaders must help their organization up and down a wide range of continua. Table 3.1 offers a sample of those commonly pursued.

Tolerance for or even attraction to the grief and irritation generated by the tension of living between these kinds of extremes is an important aspect of the nimble environment. By valuing the gray that separates black and white, people have a greater likelihood of another important nimble feature: self-organization.

Table 3.1   Nimble Continuua

1. Individual effort ... Team work.
2. Improvisation ... Discipline.
3. Defined structure ... Fuzzy boundaries.
4. Diversity of ideas ... Shared perspective.
5. Continuous improvement ... Exploit what works as long as possible.
6. Trust logic ... Rely on intuition.
7. Zero defects ... Learn from mistakes.
8. Near-term results ... Long-term vision.
9. Tactful feedback ... Frank dialogue.
10. Patience ... Urgency.
11. Pride in accomplishments ... Humility for what is left undone.
12. Forgiveness for being human ... Insistence on accomplishing important tasks, no matter what.
13. Leading the whole ... Managing the segments.
14. Attract unorthodox thinking ... Eject destructive conflict.

Self-Organization

Competing in unstable markets means that, at any given point in time, what should have worked but did not, or what did work but no longer does, must be replaced with a new approach that will lead to success in the current circumstances. The ability to reconfigure itself to better meet the needs of external or internal customers is another essential feature of the nimble system.

When an enterprise redefines its own structure to achieve market success, it is demonstrating its ability to self-organize. An organization's structure consists of the arrangement of elements such as employees, technology, and capital; or patterns of activities like procedures, processes, and habits used to operate its basic business. Self-organization is the ability to create new structural options out of existing resources. "Self" in this term means that the search for a new order is not imposed from outside the system's boundaries. Whether minor adjustments correct small deviations, or complete transformations evolve into something never before seen, if the impetus for movement comes from within, the principle of self-organization is at work.

All living systems gravitate toward some type of regularity and harmony. Sometimes this drive for equilibrium is led by something (or someone) from outside a system's boundaries that offers or mandates new arrangements. For example, this can occur after an acquisition, when one company's property and buildings are purchased by another and later sold, or after a bank forecloses on an unpaid loan and claims the collateral as its own. In both cases, the relocation of assets is a result of outside forces at work. When a system self-organizes, however, external influences are less influential in the search for a new order. The reassignment, reallocation, redeployment, or reconstruction of available assets to better meet the challenges at hand is an initiative primarily driven from within the company or agency.

The need to self-organize occurs when whatever has promoted success in the past no longer does. It is the same ability that allows a burned forest to emerge with new growth, a person to find a new focus after the death of a loved one, or a company's assets (e.g., people and materials) to find new uses and value when rearranged to hold off an unfriendly takeover. Think of the capacity to self-organize as nature's way of keeping things going, no matter what happens. For example, a small trickle of water flowing down an embankment will find its way around rocks and into crevices as it descends. In doing so, in a manner of speaking, it is organizing itself to deal with the competing demands of gravity and the physical impediments it confronts. It always remains flowing water, but it keeps shifting its course to accommodate the rocks and branches it encounters. In response to the heat from the sun, that same water will eventually evaporate and rise as steam to collect with other minute water particles in the clouds. Though the cloud formations pose a very different image than the flowing water, it is the same resource transformed into a new structure to better accommodate what it must do to survive. The path the water takes down the embankment and the moisture in the clouds are both the results of self-organization at work.

Nimble organizations rely heavily on their ability to self-organize because they operate in a world that demands that they constantly reinvent themselves in order to remain viable. To achieve and maintain the nimble status in today's market requires that the foremost drive and urgency for change come from within the system.

When applying this concept to a business operation experiencing major change, the value for two of the most important features of self-organization is increased: viability and self-referencing. First, let's explore viability. When conditions endanger the future of any living system, the natural response is self-protection at all costs. This principle of autopreservation may be engaged at any point where danger threatens a system. It can be triggered early on, when abundance and prosperity are at stake, or much later—just before final annihilation. Regardless of the timing or tactics used, the struggle to maintain some form of presence is inherent in all living matter, and self-organization capabilities are central to that struggle.

The second, and possibly less evident, feature of self-organization deals with the paradox of how continuity can thrive inside change. The capacity to remain the same while change takes place is called "self-referencing." This process can be seen in organizational settings when a company or agency is contending with highly turbulent conditions (i.e., nontrivial, rapid, and discontinuous disruptions to the status quo) and undergoes a radical restructuring. Under such circumstances, new strategies and procedures are engaged, yet they reflect self-referencing in that they evolved from the organization's own history, culture, remaining assets, and accumulated learnings. Progress relies not only on the energy derived from innovation, but also on the foundations accumulated from prior experiences.

An automobile manufacturer cannot refine a car, year after year, until one day it becomes a plane; and workers cannot be trained to become machines. Though computers are more proficient at replicating and even exceeding some human capabilities, they will never actually become human. Improvement requires both advancement and continuity. Without internal reference points to guide decision making during major change, it would be impossible for a new order to emerge that could take advantage of past successes and failures. It is precisely this principle that forms the basis for the saying: "The more things change, the more they stay the same."

When self-organization takes place, the resources being restructured or reallocated become different in some way from their previous form, but they also maintain certain properties of the original state. With self-organization, what is being newly formed is a reconstitution of the old self in an unfamiliar form. Even if a former structure failed entirely, causing what appears to be a total collapse of a system, the basic elements live on and become the building blocks for the next generation of order. The fundamental composition of the water trickling down the embankment includes the same particles of moisture that are suspended in the clouds.

In an organizational setting, when many of the incumbents who presided over the last operational paradigm are called on to reengineer their company into a totally different entity, we should not be surprised that some of the previous logic and assumptions have survived the transition. Even what is thought of as a *green-field* start-up operation with all new people is actually a compilation of multiple thoughts, feelings, experiences, and frames of reference from the backgrounds of the various people employed.

It's impossible to create something new that does not in some way reflect and, therefore, replicate history. The new modes of operating created through self-organization are the processes by which systems adapt to unfamiliar environmental demands without losing their identity. Even when the most dramatic shifts take place, some aspects of the original framework remain to serve as a footing for the next cycle of autopoiesis or self-reinvention. The extent of the changes is always limited by the boundaries of the organization's cultural history and the personal identities brought to the situation by the people involved in the adaptation reflex.

In recent years, it has become popular to promote self-organization as a trait companies should aspire to develop in themselves. For example, self-directed work teams have become very popular, prompting many organizations to have at least a few of these efforts around for experimental purposes, if for no other reason. As is usually the case with such fads, along with the well-deserved adulation some of these teams have enjoyed have also come some misconceptions and problems. One of these is the fallacious notion that only the more enlightened companies are capable of this kind of self-organization. If we accept this logic at face value, operations that are not blessed with such teams are apparently doomed to suffer from the antithesis of self-organization by virtue of the limitations imposed when functioning under the disadvantage of only management's direction. This interpretation infers that only when subordinates, either independently or in groups, are allowed to direct themselves does an organization enjoy the benefits of self-organizing.

My observations of the past two decades have not supported this thesis, to say the least. Such logic suggests that leaders are somehow outside the boundaries of their own corporate system, and that true self-organization is demonstrated only when manifested through employees who are unencumbered by management's directives. Somehow, management's input about how to operate is seen as alien ideas that inhibit true self-direction for the organization. This logic implies that when management unnecessarily imposes their views from outside, work teams are hindered from pursuing their own perspectives.

Leaders of nimble operations have learned that the important issue is not what part of their system starts the self-organizing process, but that the process is engaged somewhere within the existing structure. They know that self-organization is contagious. Once any part of a system starts to reconstitute and reconfigure itself from the remains of a previous structure, the rest of the environment will likely follow. When the flora around Mount St. Helens first started to regenerate after the volcano's eruption in 1981, no one complained that certain flowers had begun to grow sooner than others. There was no concern expressed that one type of ground cover was coming back faster than another and that somehow this would result in domination of the slower growing plants. The only thing that mattered was that the forest was once again showing signs of vitality.

Because of the interdependent nature of a forest, one form of plant life, regardless of what it is, helps set the stage for another and then another.

The key to this who-cares-where-it-starts approach is the realization that once true self-direction begins, it usually becomes pervasive within the operation.

From Event to Process Mentality

As I pointed out earlier, during uncertain times, in order to maintain or regain control, we must choose stable reference points to tether ourselves. Many things in our lives can serve as anchors, such as home, family, religion, and work. Within an organizational context, senior officers must choose, among numerous options, which anchors they want people to relate to for their bearings. Regarding change, two options that are particularly important to choose between are events and processes.

Leaders of constrained organizations usually try to maintain their organization's equilibrium by directing and predicting events. In contrast, nimble leaders invest their resources into directly influencing what they can and then rely on responsive processes for meeting the rest of their organization's security needs.

Attempting to establish stable conditions in which to work is not the primary way people in nimble organizations provide security for themselves. They prefer, instead, the safeguard of understanding and knowing how to utilize various forces that can influence a situation as their strategy for securing control. Rather than clinging to a concrete pillar embedded in the ocean floor, they would feel more confident surfing the waves of change. Even though, in the short term, the pillar appears more stable, over time its rigidity works against itself as powerful waves batter it relentlessly. Although the surfboard looks frail compared to the formidable, churning sea, it is designed to ride the energy of the wave, not fight against it. The flexibility and agility it offers become a key asset that, in the long run, proves the more dependable choice.

One of the ways nimble leaders promote surfing behavior instead of entrenching behavior is: they help people learn to trust the processes they use more than their predictions about forthcoming events. Constrained leaders find it difficult to place their faith in fluid processes, in part because many were taught by corporate mentors who owed much of their success to foretelling events. Whether predicting the products and services customers would want in the coming year, or how employees would react to a new operational procedure, leadership competency in earlier, less chaotic times was defined in large part by the ability to foresee what "events" were going to happen next.

In the past, when there was less uncertainty and a longer shelf life for solutions, it was possible to lead this way. Leaders of nimble organizations have learned that in turbulent waters concrete predictions are unreliable. They know from experience that, in an unstable business environment, it is useless to try to maintain one's sense of balance by trying to foresee distinct events.

Trying to outguess a world that has grown too cryptic and abstruse to accurately forecast is a losing battle. Today, the magnitude of change has accelerated beyond our capacity to predict many specific events. Who would have guessed what has happened to desktop computing? In 1981, the newly introduced IBM PC with 64K of RAM, two 160K disk drives, a monochrome monitor, and an 80-character-per-minute printer sold for $4,385. As I write this, the standard is an IBM clone with a Pentium chip that can process 100 million instructions per second and sells for under $1,000.

Only because of our naïveté and an occasional lucky guess do we continue to pursue the illusion of being able to speculate about the future with any precision. Does this mean we should stop guessing about what lies ahead? Absolutely not. For one thing, we never know when the odds will fall in our favor and we'll correctly predict an upcoming event. The problem is not the guessing per se; it's the fact that so many executives make it their primary means to prepare for the future. Market success then becomes a matter of guesswork and long odds.

Instead of trying to predict events, nimble companies focus on developing processes that will allow quick and effective responses to events as they unfold. This process approach to maintaining control requires the nimble leader to pursue a different path than his or her event-based, constrained counterpart. The typical preoccupation with "what" will occur in the future is replaced with a new focus on "how" to address key events as they unfold. For example, nimble companies pay more attention to how they will identify customer needs than they do on guessing exactly what particular needs customers will have. They believe it is more important to develop a plan for making key decisions than to know specifically what decisions they will face in the future.

Focusing on responsive processes to secure a sense of control is by no means a passive act. It calls for early detection systems that alert the proper personnel at the first signs of a new threat or opportunity and for procedures that can determine what the proper response should be. For example, nimble organizations don't manage their customer relations by hoping they have correctly guessed the details of next year's demand and then tooling up to provide only that product or service. Instead, they build a responsive process that can: provide what the customer wants now; react quickly to unanticipated needs; and scan the horizon for early signs of emerging customer requirements so that an early onset of the development cycle for an innovative response can occur. Finally, the nimble operation educates customers about capabilities and possibilities they did not even realize were feasible.

How nimble companies manage their relationships with customers is but one example of their reliance on process development rather than event prediction. In the functional areas vital to a nimble organization's operations (e.g., technology, finances, and personnel), there is usually a dedication to building and constantly updating rapid response processes. In some cases, these courses of action are formalized and documented; at other times, they are more intuitive and are applied with much less structure.

Instead of trying to predict what single implementation strategy would work for all initiatives, nimble organizations tend to rely on a general collection of guidelines, principles, and procedures from which certain elements may be used for a given situation, depending on the nature of the change and the circumstances presented. This approach uses what amounts to a process within a process: There is a process for determining what elements will go into the process that will be used to execute a particular change.

Orchestrating Trips and Journeys

The focus on processes rather than events has many implications for the nimble organization, but none is more important than how this kind of thinking applies to movement from the current to the desired state during critical change efforts. The shift may be slight or dramatic, but all organizational change efforts imply some kind of movement from one state to another. The extent of this kind of displacement comes in one of two proportions: a trip or a journey.

Nimble leaders understand these two dimensions of change and leverage both to their advantage. Constrained leaders usually fail to grasp the distinctions and connections between the two. Because of this, they tend to underperform when attempting trip-level change, and they fail to successfully orchestrate their broader, journey-level transitions.

The American pioneers who crossed the country toward the California goldfields faced the same two scales of movement as do today's enterprise leaders. For example, consider the following scenario. A shopkeeper in Boston sold his store, packed all his belongings into a covered wagon, and started working his way westward. In doing so, he not only began the first of many individual trips that collectively formed a key journey in his life, but he fundamentally altered his destiny.

If the pioneer's movement from one coast to another represented only traversing the physical space between these two points and the time it took to cover the distance, the entire experience could be called a *trip*. A trip reflects minor changes in a person's life. The defining characteristic for this kind of movement is that the traveler is basically the same—only a little older—before and after the excursion. What the former shopkeeper experienced on the trail west, however, was no trip. The decision and subsequent actions associated with the move to California represented no less than a fundamental shift in his life—a shift that would unfold as an uninterrupted progression of experiences, not as a series of disjointed events.

Journeys, as used here, are transforming experiences that defy total predictability. They may start intentionally, like deciding to get married, or they can be thrust on someone, like Lyndon Johnson's 1963 presidency. A journey can begin with an awareness of the significance of its onset, like the first day at college, or it sometimes can be recognized only in retrospect, as when a soldier looks back over his or her tour of duty in a combat zone. There may or may not be a clear point of departure, but once the first steps of a journey are taken, the final outcome can be predicted only in the most general terms.

Trips, on the other hand, take place when people move from a specific starting point toward a distinct, predetermined destination. Trips are discrete episodes that occur within precise time frames. Although not a requirement, they often are planned with precision down to the last detail. When a course of action is formulated, a trip results in no more than the plan has anticipated.

Although trips and journeys are linked, there are important distinctions. Journeys are comprised of many trips, but a trip may or may not lead to a journey. Trips produce changes in the tangible aspects of our lives, but not in the nature of who we are. We take a trip to the store, to the office, or to another country to accomplish a specific purpose, but this kind of movement does not necessarily alter our character or represent a defining moment in our lives. On the other hand, significant experiences like being exposed to profound knowledge, recognizing previously untapped skills, first meeting a lifelong partner, or losing the ability to perform one's profession can occur without traveling very far from home.

Journeys not only contain aspects of their more obvious surface characteristics, but they also possess powerful hidden surprises. Our trailblazer did end up in California exploring for gold as he intended, but what he couldn't have foreseen was the time lapse of three years between start and finish, rather than the few months he had initially planned. Nor could he have predicted the loss of his right leg due to an infection he suffered on the open plain. When he embarked, he was unaware of the courage and tenacity he and the others in his wagon train would summon as they faced starvation and the loss of lives. He had no hint when they departed Boston that he would leave the wagon party at Flagstaff, in the Arizona Territory, to care for a sick friend and, while there, would take a part-time job in the general store, learn the trade, and later open his own dry-goods establishment. He left the East with barely enough money to pay the wagonmaster's fees and buy provisions, yet he eventually found himself in the goldfields of California with enough profit from selling his store to start his own mining operation. His primary objective was achieved, but he ended up with more maturity, knowledge, and skills (not to mention one artificial leg) than when he started.

While pursuing his uncharted journey, this traveler took many trips. These didn't always turn out as he had hoped, but he started each trip from a particular standpoint and had a specific goal as his desired outcome. Journeys often begin with only a broad vision that may or may not ever materialize, but what always does take place is a dramatic shift in the makeup of whoever takes that path.

Leaders of constrained companies who attempt landmark change usually fail to grasp the importance of the similarities and differences between their organization's trips and journeys. This lapse produces some significant problems. For instance, constrained leaders often become so intrigued with the tactical trips they engage that they fail to provide the organization with adequate navigation for the more strategic journeys, or they err the other way around and leave a tactical guidance void. As a result, they are vulnerable to either providing too little specific guidance about the trips that are necessary or imposing too much direction and not enough latitude. Also, they often fail to recognize when an old viewpoint or operating procedure has completed itself and a new one requiring a fresh paradigm (journey) should be started. Additionally, they frequently think a short, inexpensive excursion will accomplish what only a transformational, journey-level passage can achieve.

Another of the more common confusions about movement from one organizational state to another is the tendency for leaders to drive toward journey-proportion outcomes under the mistaken assumption that the destination they seek is a terminal objective. This fallacy comes in many forms and is often accompanied by heightened pressure to perform from various constituencies. Examples include:

- "The board is insisting that we reengineer the company."
- "The market demands that we focus more on our customers."
- "The analysts told our investors that our cost structure is out of line."
- "If we don't secure this merger, we won't be large enough to be considered a key player in the industry."

These examples represent compelling, serious changes, but most of the time they result in no more than organizational trips, not journeys. There is no denying that such treks are sometimes strategic in their intent and may even have a powerful impact on the future of an enterprise, but the transformational nature of a journey is missing. Did management by objectives or quality circles really make much difference within the majority of the organizations where they were used, or were they merely diversions that kept people busy until the normal rhythm of an industry or the whims of Wall Street fundamentally changed conditions for the better or worse? As many have learned who had hoped for a paradigm shift from their reengineering effort, sometimes all that occurs is insignificant movement within existing confines.

In no way do I want to suggest that trips are unnecessary. To the contrary, they are vital to an organization's market viability. It's not that trips are bad and journeys are good, but trips that are pursued without the overall direction provided by more strategic journeys can be an unwise use of resources. Equally dysfunctional is journey leadership without enough trip guidance.

There is no doubt that for an organization to achieve and maintain a competitive position it must demonstrate a facility for taking trips. These event-based expeditions are necessary to address the array of day-to-day dangers and opportunities encountered in the normal course of operating a business. On the other hand, it becomes problematic when trip mentality so predominates an organization that leaders lose their ability to navigate the company's more strategic journeys. The primary symptom of institutions consumed by trip mentality is their persistent belief that they are but one event away from sustained success:

- "We pull off this merger and we're home free."
- "If we can convince the analyst of the power of this technology, nothing can stop the stock from going through the ceiling."

In a constrained system, usually buried beneath such comments is the unconscious wish that life's more complex problems could be resolved with the selection and successful execution of the right singular effort.

When people allot a disproportionate amount of hope to any of the solitary trips they take, they tend to also invest disproportionately in the resources that go toward managing those trips. These mythical "home runs" consume so much time and effort that people often feel depleted after the emotional highs and lows that accompany them.

Think of a journey as reflecting a map with a specific point of departure, but only a general destination identified. Most journeys are comprised of several legs, or segments. These legs represent movement from one location to the next; each segment is one of the separate trips that collectively make up the journey. Leaders should select the map to suit their desired destination. Managers should then set the course for each leg, steer the vessel and keep it maintained, and fix anything that breaks.

If necessary, trips can be coercive in nature and driven by brute force. The change journey, on the other hand, can only be propelled by energy from within people who willingly subscribe to its requirements. Leaders can articulate a vision that attracts attention, but people ultimately decide on their own whether a journey is worth their personal time and other resources. Trips can be directed by linear administrators; journeys are guided by creative, facilitating leaders. Trips are steered by pilots; journeys are kept on course by navigators.

To lead a journey means drawing out the strengths and talents of those who choose to participate. The selection of people who will assist the effort is at least as important as the coaching techniques used to strengthen existing capabilities once someone has been hired. If proper recruitment has been done, navigating a team on its change journey is mostly about preparing mentally, setting expectations, and establishing the proper frame of reference so associates can exploit their natural capacity to absorb change and succeed in turbulent circumstances.

Another differentiation between trips and journeys is the emotional reaction people have to the ambiguity inherent in each. When major change occurs, associates experience fear and anxiety. Trips tend to produce fear of the unknown. Fears have specific objects: a sense of impending threat from a particular person, thing, or circumstance. Trip fear might be reflected as: "How can I acquire enough time to learn the new system before we go on line?" or "I'm not sure I've got the experience to handle my new scope of duties."

Journeys tend to generate anxiety, not fear. Anxiety is more free-floating than fear. It is not attached to anything specific, yet there is a sense of dread. Journey anxieties reflect unidentified and unspecified potential threats: "I don't know where this merger is taking us as a company" or "What will the shareholders demand next if we successfully restructure ourselves as we promised?" Journey anxiety has to do with longer-range issues than trip fears and is dealt with not by providing specific answers, but by establishing a broad context of expectations.

During major transitions, people experience both trip and journey anxiety. Management addresses trip fears by answering precise questions about current and expected events. Leadership responds to journey anxiety by describing possibilities and probabilities.

There are many journeys an organization will pursue over the course of its history. One that is central to this book is the journey of change itself. An organization's change journey reflects its performance when implementing past, current, or future critically important initiatives. The purpose of an organization's change journey is to advance, over time, the company's capacity to absorb major disruption. Additionally, a change journey includes preparing an organization for even more challenging turbulence in the future.

There is no choice about whether change trips will occur. The only question is: In what environment will these initiatives take place? Change trips are inevitable; change journeys are discretionary.

Building a nimble organization involves managing the many trip fears that will surface, while also establishing the proper frame of reference for people to understand and deal with their journey anxieties. A typical expression of these anxieties is: "I'm concerned about what things are going to be like around here, now that we've met our goals. What does our success mean? What should we expect next?" The proper response from a leader might be something like:

> First, let me thank you for your contribution. You helped us accomplish the market share increase we worked so hard for during the past two years. The good news is: we did what we set out to do and now we must prepare ourselves for the implications. You know there is always a price to pay. We didn't want to pay the price for falling behind our competition, so now we will pay the price that comes with success. Capturing the market share was an important task, but now we must maintain it and, frankly, we aren't structured, nor do we know how to operate, in a manner that will let us keep the victory we just achieved.
>
> Because we were so successful in implementing these recent initiatives, we will now face even more changes as our customers raise their expectations about what we can do for them. We have some dramatic modifications we will have to install if we plan to be on top of the competition this time next year.
>
> We cannot afford to seduce ourselves into complacency now that we are winning. The challenges to our position as industry leader can, and will, come from all directions. We must be in a position to make some fast

decisions about critically important issues, and then execute them with a level of mastery.

Each time we do all of this, we have to be quick with our celebrations because every victory brings new rivals and the shelf life of success is roughly 24 hours. Prepare yourself to expect anything, and then anticipate even more than you can expect.

Nimble organizations apply their agility to the execution of specific initiatives (trips) and to equipping themselves for the longer-term voyage of unending change demands—the journey. Both are important (see Table 3.2 for a summary).

Well-executed trips in an environment unprepared for the next, as yet unidentified, change challenge will produce only brief tactical-level success, at best. An operation that has prepared itself for ongoing transition but lacks the ability to fully achieve the intent of its various separate initiatives will never gain the momentum necessary to enact its long-range vision. Both trips and journeys must be achieved in a nimble fashion.

Table 3.2   Trips and Journeys

Nimble Trips . . .	Nimble Journeys . . .
Are brief in duration.	Are extensive in duration.
Implement a specific objective.	Build a paradigm with change at the center.
Execute a precise action.	Succeed in ongoing disequilibrium.
Move from spot to spot.	Move from place to place.
Have final destinations that represent slight modifications to what is seen today.	Have final destinations that represent the means for continued progress.
Expect the short-term future to be some variation of what is seen today.	Expect the long-term future to be whatever it is.
Treat change as a strategic or tactical shift.	Treat change as an evolutionary process.
Rely on the skill to execute.	Rely on learning from the failures that occur.
Apply what you know.	Enhance how you learn and build knowledge.

Resilience in Organizations

Just as the Boston clerk-turned-pioneer drew on many resources, so must would-be nimble organizations. Like individuals, organizations may or may not have the necessary resources of resilience for this task.

Resilience is the ability to absorb large amounts of disruptive change without a significant drop in quality and productivity standards. A highly resilient organization is one that: regains its equilibrium quickly after the disruption of change, accomplishes important tasks during periods of confusion, and makes sure that its people are physically and emotionally healthy and that its systems remain operational despite high levels of stress. After implementing key initiatives, it gains in its assimilation capacity rather than becoming depleted and unable to face the next transition demand.

Nimble operations are highly dependent on their resilient attributes to accommodate the disruption in their marketplace faster and more effectively than their competition. Businesses that are constrained are weak or altogether deficient in this resilient quality and suffer the competitive consequences when instability reigns.

For an organization to respond to change in a resilient fashion, it must initiate actions to reshape the flow and dynamic balance of the system's inputs, outputs, and processes while displaying minimal dysfunction. The success of these actions is highly dependent on the five most critical resilience characteristics:

1. Positive—Security and self-assurance that are based on a view of the marketplace as complex but filled with opportunity.
2. Focused—A clear vision of what must be done to prosper.
3. Flexible—A creative ability when responding to uncertainty.
4. Organized—Structured approaches to managing ambiguity.
5. Proactive—Engaging change rather than defending against it.

These five characteristics come into play at individual, team, and organizational levels. At any given time, an individual has a limited supply of adaptation resources—the cognitive, physical, and emotional assets that enable him or her to absorb change. When this supply depletes, levels of dysfunctional behavior start to rise and the ability to adjust to the new environment is reduced. Resilience characteristics operate by increasing the amount of adaptation resources that are available and by enabling people to use these resources more efficiently. As individuals and groups encounter change, they perform effectively and use their resources efficiently to construct new responses to the challenge they face.

Extending this logic to leadership, context, and culture—three elements that research has identified as important to the transformational process at the organizational level—we can see how resilience characteristics, or their antitheses, are manifested.

LEADERSHIP (EXECUTIVE BEHAVIOR)

Leaders, as individuals and as a group, will guide the organization most effectively in changing circumstances if they are predisposed toward opportunities both inside and outside the organization (positive); remain attentive to the more critical objectives (focused); display pliability in the variety of information they consider when making decisions and considering the possibilities they create (flexible); are able to structure the ways they interpret data and information (organized); and build implementation plans around their new ideas and eagerly try new approaches (proactive). Low-resilience leadership is pessimistic about resolving problems and exploiting opportunities; scatters efforts in unrelated directions; closes itself off from new information and innovative possibilities; fails to see and create patterns that can guide actions; and waits for certainty before acting. Low and even marginally resilient leadership consumes high levels of resources in responding to the challenge of change and usually meets with little success.

CONTEXT (VISION, MISSION, AND STRATEGY)

To succeed in unstable market conditions, the context set by leaders needs to articulate and embody the characteristics of resilience as well. In times of frequent or continuous change, the organization's guiding framework must prepare associates to readily alter processes to meet shifting demands. Thus, it is important that the statements of direction and purpose, which create the common frame of reference, emphasize certain themes. These themes should stress that opportunities exist and can be grasped (positive); that a direction, whatever its content may be, has been set (focused); that the gathering of information and the creation of new approaches are essential (flexible); that high levels of ambiguity can be addressed through judicious application of structure (organized); and that engaging action in the face of uncertainty is critical (proactive).

CULTURE (BELIEFS, BEHAVIORS, AND ASSUMPTIONS)

The shared, underlying patterns of premises, sets of values, and behavioral activities displayed by the organization's associates must reinforce the characteristics of resilience. To help create the desired enterprise-wide agility, leaders should encourage individual and group behavior that facilitates resilience and Nimbleness. Leaders should look for and talk about the opportunities to succeed, even when how to do so is not clear (positive); use a well-defined set of priorities as a means of differentiating and prioritizing activities (focused); seek out novel perspectives and incorporate them into their work (flexible); create structured approaches to deal with the ambiguity they feel (organized); and take measured risks in trying new ways of doing things (proactive). In addition to any predisposition toward these behaviors that a person may display, an organization's culture must overtly state and reward the value it places on these actions.

An organization in which the five resilience and three organizational variables (leadership, context, and culture) are in place and are supportive of each other will have contributed toward creating a powerful, nimble quality. The organization will be positioned to recognize potential disruption early, to target its adaptation efforts in critical areas, and to create and implement effective solutions. This, in turn, will increase the likelihood that it will survive and thrive in the midst of extremely turbulent conditions.

THE IMPORTANCE OF BALANCE

Maximizing any one component of a system has a cost for the system as a whole. For example, attempting to guide an organization by using strong leadership (without attention to the context and the culture) can lead to an overreliance on leaders to provide coordination and guidance in day-to-day activities. A strong emphasis, throughout the organization, on structuring information (reflecting the organized characteristic for resilience) may result in excessively rigid adherence to existing structures, which could interfere with the search for new and better ways to achieve goals (the flexible characteristic). This lack of optimization would impair the system as a whole.

As I noted earlier, this kind of dynamic balance is not the result of a steady state; it is an illusion of stability created by an energetic equilibrium of components. This means that all the components will exist in a balance that fluctuates according to circumstances. At any given time, an effective system may go out of balance to meet the needs of a situation, but it will eventually restore its symmetry. The goal of the system and its components is to establish fervent balance that is effective under whatever circumstances currently exist. Every time the situation changes, it places a new demand on the system, and each part of the system must respond to that new demand. If any individual component of a system is weak, the greater system will not be able to respond effectively to the demands of certain situations.

Because constrained businesses don't attract and can't maintain resilient individuals and subsequently fail to show much resilience at the team level as well, it should come as no surprise that this quality is also missing at the enterprise level. In nimble organizations, the resilience characteristics are not only manifested at the individual and team levels but are also displayed via the transformational variables (leadership, context, and culture). Thus, organization-wide Nimbleness is also further strengthened. Nimbleness requires that each of the five aspects of resilience be represented in a strong and balanced way through each of these transformational factors; that is, *an organization will enhance its nimble quality during change if its leadership, its context, and its culture are positive, focused, flexible, organized, and proactive.*

The balance among these elements is something like that of a wheel (see Figure 3.3), which can only be stabilized while in motion.

The enterprise-level system for maintaining organizational resilience can be viewed as four wheels, each wheel spinning in the opposite direction from the wheel(s) next to it. As the wheels spin in opposite directions to each other, they create a kind of gyroscope effect that generates the energized balance. When seen from this perspective, it becomes clear that leadership, context, and culture must each have the capability to be positive, focused, flexible, organized, and proactive at various times to meet changing situational demands. The optimum alignment of the four wheels at a given time is a function of the circumstances at the time.

To say that system components exist in an animated balance does not mean they must all be expressed equally. Rather, the system fluctuates to meet the needs of each individual situation. Each change is unique and draws on the resilience characteristics and transformational variables in

Figure 3.3   Balance.

different ways. For instance, a merger might initially require a culture that is more flexible than focused. Or, when entering a new market, to express proactivity in leadership may be more important than to focus on proactivity in culture. The nimblest organizations will have a well-rounded set of strengths to draw from, allowing them to succeed in any change endeavor.

Conscious Competence

The final distinction between nimble and constrained business operations has to do with how knowledgeable people are about the strengths they possess. Truly resilient and nimble organizations rarely achieve their enviable status through ignorance and/or luck.

I have observed that most organizations that achieve a nimble status do so even though their leaders, managers, supervisors, and employees do not know explicitly what contributed to their success. They may be tacitly aware that they have an ability to move through change with a level of proficiency not experienced in a constrained system, but they usually are unsure about how this happens. Though Nimbleness in any form is a competitive advantage, this kind of intuitively-based dexterity can limit success and may even present some problems.

The requirements for remaining the nimble player in one's market will escalate over time, because of more change demands and/or because of an increased agility demonstrated by competitors. Regardless of the cause, nimble organizations must rise to the occasion. Meeting each new level of challenge, however, calls for more than mere passion and resolve. It is also essential to know explicitly what to do. If an organization is nimble but lacks the insight into what it is actually doing to produce this powerful quality, it will more than likely lose its agility over time and ultimately become constrained. When the need arises, its leaders won't know how to protect or strengthen the versatility the organization has. Leaders and the various levels of management and employees can't develop skills they don't know how to identify and intentionally replicate. When an organization loses its intuitively based Nimbleness, it can only rely on luck as it vainly attempts to reproduce the magic it never fully understood.

To avoid Nimbleness as being only a mysterious and fleeting experience, companies and agencies need to study the phenomenon they seek to master. I cannot overstress this point. It is imperative that leaders understand not only the individual features that contribute to Nimbleness, but also how these separate aspects form the interdependent relationships that compose the whole. Organizations must have the ability to successfully wage a campaign to become the nimble provider in their market as well as position themselves to determine whether and when that status is in jeopardy. When the danger signal is triggered, leaders should be ready to diagnose what needs to be done to protect or regain the nimble status, and build plans to focus on the precise elements that need attention. This is not a task for people lacking an explicit understanding of their own nimble skill base. Unconscious adeptness is not enough. Leaders must be consciously competent about how to plan and execute their organization's transitions.

Conscious competence is not the exclusive domain of currently nimble operations. This trait is also relevant for those organizations that are only beginning to pursue Nimbleness as part of their strategy for competitive advantage. For example, some companies are forced to build a nimble capacity from the ground up. They are faced with trying to demystify what appears to be the nimble magic their competitors are displaying but they cannot. They hope that by studying nimble providers they will learn enough to replicate their success with change. Through identifying the "best-practice" behavior demonstrated by nimble organizations, leaders of these aspiring organizations can determine what contributes to this powerful quality. For example, they can intentionally hire people with the proper predisposition, and then train, coach, and reward them toward the desired outcomes. In addition, organizational structures, policies, and cultures can be redesigned to establish the infrastructure needed for nimble behavior to flourish.

For companies and agencies inundated with constrained symptoms, it won't be easy. Hard work, perseverance, and a significant investment of time and money are necessary. The reason the investment is so high is that the requirements for attaining a nimble operation go far beyond the mimicry that occurs all too often when one company tries to emulate another's operation. Many organizations benchmark each other, but replicating the behavior, processes, and structures of their nimble rivals does not always pay off. This kind of parroting, even when all the correct actions appear to be in place, is seldom able to produce the desired result. *Nimbleness has a soul that can't be faked.*

Seeking guidance about becoming a nimble organization is no different than wanting to learn how to be a good parent, a high school teacher, or a practicing Buddhist. If your heart isn't already there, techniques won't get you where you think you want to go. Mimicry accomplishes only a shadow of the true goal, and the full intent is never achieved. Sadly, this axiom holds true even for those leaders who honestly want their company to be the nimble provider. If desire alone was sufficient for the ambitious standards we strive for in our lives, there would be many more successful managers than there actually are. The company that is the nimble provider within a market is at the top of its game. Achieving that mark will be possible only by those who can match their heads and hearts with the demands of the task. They must have a sincere, honest, and deep passion for the nimble actions they pursue.

It would be at least politically correct if not entrepreneurial on my part to say at this point that our research has led us to believe that anyone who reads this book can become the kind of leader it takes to make his or her organization the nimble provider. The reality is, however, that most readers will not even try, and most of those who try will not accomplish the objective. Rather than viewing these odds as depressing and unnecessarily restrictive, may I suggest a different perspective.

This book will bore readers who have never failed at implementing an important change due to a lack of support from the people involved. They won't have any idea what all this is about. The book will be at least instructive, if not modestly inspiring, to the many who can relate to the issues I'm raising and who will attempt to move their organizations closer to the nimble designation. Most of these people, however, will never actually gain the coveted status itself. For the majority of the leaders in the latter group, who will at least attempt to pursue the prize, progress in the nimble direction—even slight movement—would be a welcome relief from the high level of constraint their companies now endure. For the relatively few who had already started gravitating toward Nimbleness before reading this book, but who did not know what to call it or how to articulate the key milestones, the guidance within these chapters will resonate like a long forgotten song from their childhood.

What all this means is that the only leaders who will really experience, to its full extent, what this book is trying to convey are those who are already unconsciously competent at the stated objective. Their instinct and intuition have long urged them toward the nimble mind-set and framework, but their lack of an explicit understanding of what to do and how to replicate success has hindered their progress. This writing is intended to offer the techniques and processes whereby reliance on gut feel and educated guesses can give way to an explicit understanding of the structure and discipline necessary for organizations to succeed in highly unstable conditions.

The Nimble Provider

At any single point in time, there can be but one company that is able to recalibrate itself to the shifting needs of its customers faster and more effectively than the competition. We refer to this as being the *nimble provider* within a particular market segment. Just as there is only one business more profitable than its rivals, or one with the highest stock price, only one organization at a time can claim its operations are the nimblest among its opponents.

The singular nature of this distinction makes it both appealing and intimidating. Holding such a unique status is a powerful differentiation, but, at the same time, the odds of actually securing this rank are inherently low. There are many people who would like to be the best tennis player at their club or the most accomplished equestrian on their riding team, but most people view the top position as unattainable and don't even strive for the goal. In a similar vein, some readers may have doubts about the value of pursuing Nimbleness if the ultimate coveted status can never be obtained. In this sense, the issue becomes whether a company should strive to be nimbler than in the past even if it has no hope of actually becoming the nimble provider in its chosen market. The answer is an emphatic "Yes!"

Just as increased profitability and accelerated share price are worthwhile goals in themselves, even if a company never outperforms its competition, increased Nimbleness is a justifiable ambition regardless of the organization's nimble rank. Although being the nimble provider carries with it some powerful implications, all businesses that advance their ability to absorb change will benefit from doing so.

The reality is that many leaders reading this book may find the nimble challenge intellectually stimulating, but beyond the practical reach for themselves and/or their companies. Rarely will these leaders act to implement the perspectives or actions described in this book and intended to increase Nimbleness, although they will gain some consolation in knowing what to do to gain the coveted status. Even when full application is not feasible, people seek out the latest information on a subject just to stay abreast of the most current views. We can sometimes do without actually using the latest models, techniques, or tools, but it would be foolish to be unaware of them.

Among those who actually do attempt to become the nimble provider in their market, most will not prevail. I realize that with today's entitlement mentality and the emphasis on egalitarianism, most readers would prefer not to hear this stated so directly. Facing the statistical reality of uniqueness has fallen out of favor. It is considered more appropriate to at least imply that somehow each person has the ability to achieve individual greatness. For example, if we were to believe the promoters of the various panaceas that become popular, it would be possible for hundreds, thousands, even millions of us to purchase the same formula for success and have each person win at whatever game he or she has chosen to play. We are told anyone can be a leader, we all can be empowered, and everyone can have the whitest teeth. All we have to do is follow the directions for the latest snake oil that reflects our unmet dreams. Brace yourself; it isn't going to happen.

All of us would be better served by facing reality. We can all buy lottery tickets, but only the incredibly lucky will take home any winnings. Everyone can enter the Fourth of July marathon, but only one runner will cross the finish line first. The local health club is full of people, but few will resemble the fit, hard bodies in the ad. We can all read about Wall Street successes, but only a small percentage of us will ever know real wealth.

Knowing what we want usually proves to be somewhat advantageous in getting it. In this respect, it is important for leaders to be realistic about their nimble aspirations. Most organizations should follow the challenge stated in the United States Army's ad campaign: "Be All That You Can Be." The key for success will be to stay focused on the benefits gained from being a formidable nimble contender despite the possibility of falling short of the ultimate objective. Not only is there true competitive value in becoming more agile than most of your market rivals, but also keeping close to the leader means you are within striking distance of the company with the most nimble status when (not if) it falters.

The nimble provider in a market will achieve this standing through the inherent strengths it possesses, a tremendous amount of hard work, and, of course, the ever present possibility of good fortune. The length of time a business will enjoy this prestige is a function of the degree to which its leaders are consciously competent at putting distance between themselves and other organizations that aspire to be the nimble provider but lack the commitment and resources to do so.

Working in the Nimble Zone

P eople often put their trust in concepts and statements that are quite beyond their realm of understanding. For example, the majority of us accept that there are billions and billions of dollars in the economy, but few of us have ever seen that much money. In a similar fashion, most people are familiar with the axiom "Change is now the only constant," yet we still ask ourselves, "How can this be? How can everything—from sub-atomic particles, to the planet we inhabit, to the entire universe—be in constant transition?" We intellectually accept the notion that all forms of matter are in some stage of passage from one state to another; still, this idea of ceaseless movement is difficult to come to terms with.

To understand the true nature of change requires a view that all existence is constantly engaged in a struggle between order and chaos. Each of these forces represents a separate and powerful influence that acts to balance the impact of the other. The nexus, the eye of the storm, is where we want to be.

Getting a Load On

The choreography between order and chaos reveals that they are, at once, counterweights to each other and inextricably bound together. In the midst of this clash/attraction between order and chaos resides the realm where organizational Nimbleness is fostered. *At the point where order and chaos most closely resemble one another, there exists the greatest possibility for broadening the human capacity to adapt to instability and uncertainty.*

To understand this, it is necessary to explore in more detail the attributes that both separate and join order and chaos. Let's first examine how much change can survive within an organization at a given time. The environment within an organization can be characterized by one of six degrees of pressure from transition demands. I will be referring to this kind of pressure as the *load* that change imposes on an organization. The change load carried by an organization in order to compete comprises the *magnitude* (volume, momentum, and complexity) of the initiatives it has chosen to pursue and the *consequences* it will incur if these endeavors are not successfully implemented. An environment saturated with disruption demands is one with high magnitude and consequences. A crowded but less compacted environment may have a moderate level of both. A sparse change environment presents both a low magnitude and low consequences.

The six degrees of change load are as follows:

1. Complacency—There are few major initiatives an organization must contend with, and those are only minor incremental movements within the operational framework. The pace of these changes is slow, their complexity is slight, and the cost of failing to properly implement them is inconsequential.

   A complacent work setting is created when leadership is convinced that there already is a proper alignment between an organization's success factors and its market's demands for success. It requires that most senior officers believe they can maintain the desired alignment by reinforcing the status quo. For this to be true, both magnitude and consequences must be at their lowest point, triggering leadership to display an equally low tolerance for anything that could disrupt the system.

2. Continuous improvement—When the concentration of change demand increases beyond the level that complacency can accommodate, a value for improving the status quo begins to emerge. During such periods, customer expectations and competition are less stable, requiring some adjustments for an organization to maintain alignment.

   The pace of changes is leisurely and the complexity they manifest remains in the low range. The consequences for failing to properly implement changes that are attempted are not burdensome. The ongoing improvement-type modifications that are engaged are usually slight in nature, although they can become fairly consequential in scope. The objective is to keep change projects at a modest level; therefore, smaller and more frequent efforts are encouraged.

3. Intermediate movement—A significant number of initiatives are occurring that represent prominent, but still relatively modest, movement within the operational framework. The pace of these changes is brisk and their complexity is of an intermediate level. The consequences for failing to properly implement them have reached a moderate standing.

4. Dramatic movement—Myriad initiatives have started to unfold. They represent powerful, yet still incremental movement within the operational framework. The pace of these changes may be breathtaking, and the complexity they drive can be overpowering. The cost for failing to properly implement these changes often reaches considerable proportions.

   When magnitude and consequence become this significant for an organization, the demands of change consequence have reached a dramatic standing. Initiatives are sometimes sequential, but at other times they may come in surges of overlapping efforts. These kinds of projects have a major impact on how a company functions, and they generate a serious drain on its adaptation resources. Such endeavors are taxing but typically remain incremental in nature; they stay within the existing paradigm of operations.

5. Paradigm shifts—Each of the first four degrees of change load represents varying levels of change that fall within existing paradigms, but at this level, the number of separate change efforts has become difficult to distinguish. It appears as though there is an endless flood of disruption. Many of the varied initiatives represent formidable shifts. The pace of these changes is relentless, and the complexity they demand can be convoluted, perplexing, and confusing. Additionally, the cost for failing to properly implement these changes has become prohibitively high.

   When demands for changes within existing frameworks intensify beyond the boundaries of incremental movement, the load has reached paradigm shifting proportions. Rather than a change project creating more (or less) of what was already in place, some aspect of the essential fabric of the organization is altered in a fundamental way. This results in not a better version of what existed before, but something completely different.

An organization comprises many paradigms—e.g., how assets are invested, what types of companies are considered viable acquisition candidates, the long view of an industry's stability, how people are trained and promoted, and so on. When an organization is involved in shifting one or more of these kinds of paradigms, it is fundamentally reconstructing the way it views events and functions. The integrity of an organization's overall equilibrium is being protected by completely redefining one or more aspects of its operation. This allows the total organization to survive and prosper in somewhat the same way it did previously, except in the areas modified.

6. Chaos—This level represents an intensity of change demands that is too massive for an organization's digestive system to absorb. Dysfunction, in the form of lost productivity and quality, is created. It first jeopardizes, then hinders, and finally completely blocks a company's ability to compete. The full force of this kind of chaos often contributes to people viewing events and behaviors as purposeless, random, unpredictable occurrences that result in a state of pandemonium. When this takes place, people become confused and disoriented, structures become cluttered and disarrayed, and eventually the overall operation slips into entropy.

Within these six degrees of pressure, the amount of challenge and resources required to adequately accommodate disruption steadily advances from the relative stability of complacency to the ultimate uncertainty and confusion of chaos. In the first four of these gradations, order resides. The last two levels are the habitat for bedlam.

The Unquiet Zone between Order and Chaos

Among the first four levels of change load is a common denominator that makes it possible for organizations to regain their equilibrium within the existing paradigm. The process used to accomplish this is called the adaptation reflex, and it is discussed in detail in Appendix B. Basically, with this process, it is possible to maintain a sense of control by adjusting current frameworks to accommodate accelerating change demands. The four steps in the reflex are:

1. Recognize the presence of unfamiliar data that could jeopardize a previously established balance.

2. Render an interpretation or judgment as to the meaning of the new element.

3. Respond to the situation by determining a strategy for restoring equilibrium.

4. Realign expectations and perceptions by applying the correct strategy.

When the total weight from all the changes occurring in an organization forms an aggregate load at the paradigm shift or chaotic level, the adaptation reflex can no longer accommodate the disruption. The fourth degree of load is where order still exists but at its weakest; the fifth degree is where future shock begins, and the sixth degree is where order is completely lost and dysfunction takes prominence. Although this kind of chaotic change load is dangerous and can be destructive, within this realm also lies the zone where nimble organizations thrive.

The demarcations that separate any of the first four levels of change load (complacency, continuous improvement, intermediate movement, and dramatic movement) are not fine, discrete lines, but more like overlapping margins or perimeters that gradually shift in character until they begin to incorporate the adjacent category. The brink between dramatic movement and the last two levels—paradigm shifts and chaos—is more distinct. A system is either out of control or it isn't. Though, in one respect, order and chaos represent a partnership because they are alternative ends to the same continuum, at a certain point they also become mutually exclusive. That point is referred to as future shock.

The passage from order to chaos is, therefore, a binary distinction. Once the boundary has been crossed, the inevitable dysfunction begins to occur; that dysfunction, however, is contained within the system. This means that though a subsystem may be in the midst of a paradigm shift or even chaotically out of control, the larger, primary system of which it is a part may or may not be in a state of decomposition. As I noted earlier, all systems are made of smaller subsystems and are themselves subsystems of larger systems. So, the eastern region of an operation is only one component of a company that is, in turn, one of several organizations in the holding company.

A primary system's state of health is a function of how many subsystems regain their balance after being disrupted, and how crucial these subsystems are to the system's operation. For instance, a car can still operate quite adequately if only a dashboard light fails. The consequences to the vehicle's viability are more severe, but still recoverable, if the light goes out at the same time that the automatic door-locking mechanism, the muffler, and the radio die.

When larger numbers of subsystems break down, however, it may take only one more relatively modest problem to make the automobile unusable from the owner's standpoint. The final breakdown that crosses the line may be a faulty cigarette lighter or the air conditioner. By themselves, neither of these problems would constitute any real jeopardy to the usefulness of the car as a whole, but combined with the other subsystems' failures, the owner may refuse to drive it again until it is repaired, or may opt for a new one. On the other hand, most of the car's other features can remain completely functional, but if its battery, transmission, or engine-ignition mechanism should fail, the utility of the entire primary system is lost.

This raises a crucial question: How many, and which, subsystems must fail before a primary system slips from order to chaos? Will it be the cigarette lighter or the air conditioner that trips the entire system past its capacity to regain control? Or is it possible that the car only appears to be near the edge because of all the owner's complaints? Perhaps the cigarette lighter and the air conditioner, along with the power windows and the tires, can all break down and the owner will still remain as loyal as ever. The critical issue here is determining just where control leaves off and chaos begins.

Look closer at the curious and vastly important realm that separates order from chaos. Of particular interest is this area's capacity to allow a system to move itself back toward order or over to chaos. If a system should fall back into a strained, but still predictable, orderly state, it can, at any later time, once again tempt the chaotic threshold. If, however, the chaos boundary is penetrated, it cannot return in any form or version to the kind of control it previously employed. Why not? Resources that were present are absorbed into another existing system or they are used to form a new system. Whether the aftermath of chaos proves to be better or worse for those involved is, of course, subjective and immaterial to this dialogue. Once control is truly lost, it cannot be regained. The dynamics of chaos then take over.

From one perspective, the threshold between order and chaos is crisp and unequivocal; yet, from another standpoint, it has emergent qualities. Chaos doesn't explode on the scene, it unfolds. Both exactness and vagueness are present at the same time and the definitive binary nature of this zone is reflected. Once a critical mass of transition magnitude and consequences has formed that exceeds an organization's available resources, the symptoms of chaos suddenly spring forth. On the other hand, the progressive nature of the zone is revealed once chaos has clearly taken hold: The load level produced severe problems gradually, not suddenly. For example, within a corporation that has crossed its chaotic border, dysfunction steadily advances until there is maximum destruction.

It is this progressive aspect of chaos that warrants further explanation. The early phases of chaos, when bedlam is just beginning to form, I call *formative future shock*. This is where the change load is such that people can no longer adapt to disruption without beginning to display some level of dysfunctional behavior (the inability to maintain quality and productivity standards). Within this clearly dangerous area, however, exists the potential for the greatest flexibility. It is at this early stage of future shock that the optimum amount of agility can be attained before the cost of dysfunction becomes too great (see Figure 4.1).

Although future shock is when people begin to display significant levels of dysfunctional behavior, it precedes full-scale chaos, and, in its early phases, it creates a zone where Nimbleness can thrive. The idea of formative future shock may appear contradictory in that it represents a time when the organization is literally poised at the point of dissolution, not formation. Yet, it is the very energy generated at this point that leadership can be leveraged to create the strategic advantage of Nimbleness. Another way to think of this early future shock is as a potentially dangerous medical treatment that, if administered properly, can become a lifesaving remedy. There are several examples of these types of therapies: radioactive material is used to fight cancer; warfarin, used to kill rats, is given in small doses to humans as a blood thinner; and polio and measles vaccinations work by injecting small amounts of the offending substance.

If calibrated appropriately, certain adversities can be used to promote opportunity. The same can be said for future shock. Even in moderate doses, the inability to accommodate change without a significant loss of productivity and quality can cause insurmountable blockage to an organization's

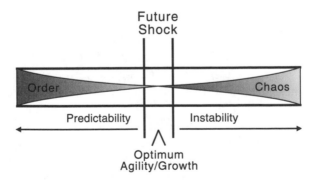

Figure 4.1   Order/chaos continuum.

competitiveness, if not its viability. Yet, a lighter measure of the same future shock symptoms allows an organization to stretch, even strain, its ability to adapt to the unexpected, and the price for doing so does not exceed the gains that are achieved.

Formative future shock is that part of the realm between order and chaos where the factors that contribute to dysfunction are just forming and are only beginning to have an adverse impact on productivity and quality (see Figure 4.2). In recent years, this area has become the subject of intense investigation in such areas as biology and physics. From this kind of study a new science of complexity has unfolded that is attempting

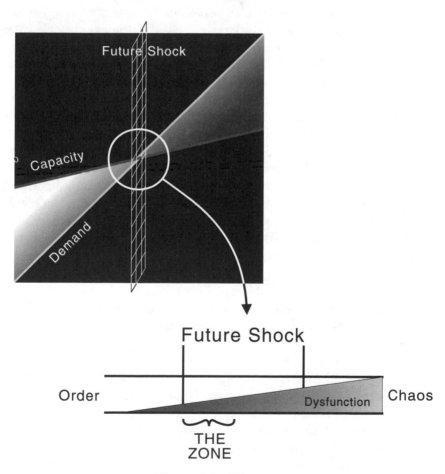

Figure 4.2 The zone.

to better understand what happens just before and just after loss of control. The scientists in this new field call this a bifurcation zone—when something that was whole and consistent splits and goes in two different and unpredictable directions.

What has been learned about bifurcation zones is that the period just before a system goes out of control is perilous, but this is also when a system can squeeze the optimum agility from its resources. For example, ice skaters must contend with pushing the limits of the ratio between their speed going around a corner and the resistance occurring between the blade on their skate and the surface of the ice. There is an optimum point when pressing this boundary, and it produces what can best be described as a *contained slide*. Skaters rely on their ability to read the subtle information gained from their senses and experience to accelerate or slow down so they will only briefly lose their balance (order), but will then quickly be able to regain it. Just as the speed begins to exceed a skater's ability to regulate further action, he or she backs off enough to reestablish control and then presses on faster again.

This sequence does produce some loss of control, but not much and not for very long. In effect, with a contained slide, we have an acceptable amount of dysfunction. Any dysfunction is costly, but this level is generally considered admissible because of the speed being achieved as the corner is taken. To accomplish the maximum speed while maintaining balance, the skater will suffer some reduction in progress. The act of sliding slightly out of control, however briefly, lowers efficiency and effectiveness to some degree. In addition, the risk of a minute miscalculation or momentary loss of concentration can produce a disastrous fall. The only way the skater can invest all his or her strength and endurance without going over the edge and losing control is to find and stay within this elusive, but essential, zone where a contained slide is possible.

All systems, be they mechanical, human, or social/political, have limits to their operations. The zone where a contained slide is possible is equivalent to what pilots refer to as the "edge of the envelope." In an aircraft, pushing the limits of the envelope means taking the flight equipment up to and slightly beyond its known capabilities in terms of such characteristics as speed, turning capacity, and wing stress. In a leadership context, "pushing the envelope" is an often-used phrase meaning pressing the limits of one or more subsystems within a company. Sometimes it refers to pushing the limits of the entire organization.

When pressing the limits to find the edge of any envelope, there are two kinds of systems (or subsystems): Fixed and open. In a fixed system, various components have not been developed or in any way functionally advanced.

A fixed-system organization is one that is not growing its people, resources, or competitive advantages. The boundaries of a fixed system do not fluctuate much, aside from chance occurrences and plus/minus marginal errors. For example, suppose a plane is built for a range of 10,000 miles. Its performance record, however, is held by one pilot who once flew it 12,500 miles and landed with nothing but fumes in the fuel tank. Attempting a 15,000-mile nonstop trip in this aircraft does not make sense unless some significant modifications are made to its engines or structure.

Evaluating the limits of an open system is very different. An open system is permeable to influence. Due to internally and/or externally driven modifications, it is always in some stage of development. Indianapolis Formula One race cars are good examples. Every day, the mechanics, engineers, and drivers try new ideas that may advance the car even a fraction beyond its previous performance. Once something new has been tried, the only way to test its impact is to take the vehicle to—and, if possible, slightly beyond—its previous limits.

Each of the many paradigms within an organization has an envelope. "How far can we press the negotiation without losing the deal?" "How much more capital can we get from the bank without jeopardizing their confidence in us?" "How many weekends can we ask our people to work without risking their emotional and physical health?" The organizational envelope I am most concerned with, and the subject of this book, is the one that reflects the amount of disruption humans can absorb before displaying unacceptable dysfunctional symptoms. It is referred to as the "adaptation envelope."

Many senior officers of fixed-system organizations who are undertaking multiple change initiatives inappropriately push the limits of their organization's adaptation envelope. They don't stretch beyond their company's known transition limits because of some new variable they are testing, nor are they experimenting with an innovative way to better prepare people for change. Rather, these leaders push the envelope simply because they lack the discipline and/or discernment to know when it's best to let the pressure or opportunity for change pass.

This kind of change leadership is no more than a roll of the dice camouflaged with plenty of macho posturing and a solid dose of "I-know-we-can-do-it" motivational hype. The hope is that, through all this, employees will somehow come up with the heroic effort needed to make it all work. These leaders not only surpass their company's adaptation limits without any attempt at expanding the boundaries, but, more importantly, they don't have a clue as to what factors go into determining adaptation limitations. In addition, they lack an understanding of the real ramifications for extending beyond the future shock borders or of the options for what can be done to heighten an organization's absorption level.

The Advantages of a Contained Slide

Leaders of nimble companies perform differently. They are always pushing their organization beyond previous change boundaries, but they do so with the belief that their company is an open system and that something they have done has increased its capacity to absorb disruption. They may or may not be successful in raising the future shock threshold, but they only exceed existing change limits after they have taken some action that was designed to extend these limits: hired more resilient people; better prepared those already employed; eliminated peripheral, less critical initiatives that were draining adaptation resources; or maybe tried being more careful than in the past when preparing for the inevitable resistance that surfaces during major change projects. Regardless of the nature of their actions, before they press the adaptation envelope, these kinds of leaders do something that they believe will further enhance their organization's ability to cope. Such intervention(s) establishes the groundwork for attempting more change than has been absorbed in the past.

Leaders striving for or maintaining a nimble status know that the only way to test the results of their efforts to increase change capacity is to cautiously but decisively thrust the system past its previous benchmark and into uncharted waters. Just as some losses are incurred with any investment strategy and a certain number of failures result from innovative solutions, the price for increasing an organization's ability to accommodate change is always the inclusion of some level of future shock. If the future shock jolt is too great, however, the current project will fail to meet its objectives, and the damage done to the organization's absorption mechanisms will reduce the likelihood of success with future change initiatives. On the other hand, if the boundaries of change are not seriously challenged on an ongoing basis, an organization will be unable to keep pace with the accelerating magnitude of the transition demands being imposed by a competitive market. Leaders must keep their organizations in a never-ending contained slide, always pushing the limits of the adaptation envelope without losing control and falling into full chaos.

In a world defined more by its variations than its redundancies, the Nimbleness required for an organization to remain viable can only be achieved by embracing the very state we humans fear. We must inoculate our companies with just the right amount of future shock to prevent a more lethal case of adaptation deficiency than we can survive.

Tenacity and Detachment Are Required

Ferreting out this elusive perimeter requires leaders to be both tenacious and thick-skinned. First, a word about tenacity. It is easy to become satisfied and even smug when high demands for change have been efficiently and effectively accommodated by your organization in the past. If this should happen, unless there is a strong determination to do otherwise, senior officers will tend to shift their attention to other issues and concerns and lose sight of the ongoing nature of securing and maintaining a nimble status. What is required is an unwavering commitment to the pursuit of extending the limits of transition capability.

But unyielding commitment is not enough; thick skin is also mandatory. The border that delineates the human capacity for change can only be revealed by its penetration. The true parameters that establish how much unanticipated variation a person, group, or entire organization can really accommodate without displaying disabling dysfunction are not made known without imposing far more change than people find comfortable.

Since we are all frightened, to some degree, by the prospect of losing control in our lives, we tend to at first just grumble, then complain, and finally scream when our sense of balance is threatened. If leaders are overly sensitive to these expressions of discomfort, they will mistakenly come to rely too much on the "I'm-frustrated-and-unhappy" scale to determine the limits of change people can successfully undergo. Most of us can adjust far better than our tears, pleas, and threats would suggest.

Senior officers cannot afford to disregard the human anxiety and distress that almost always coincide with discontinuity. These concerns, however, must be responded to with sincere empathy and respect, without leaders' necessarily feeling compelled to withdraw the initiatives. Senior officers may choose to abandon a change project at any point, but that decision should not be based on the inevitable discomfort people will feel. Leaders of nimble organizations are able to relate to the hardship people experience during these periods of uncertainty while often remaining on course.

A chaotic environment, to varying degrees, always manifests the dysfunction of future shock. Mid-range future shock produces a greater loss of productivity and quality than any single change effort is worth, and higher levels of future shock are even more destructive because, in addition, they erode the organization's overall capacity to engage in future change efforts.

At the lower end of the future shock continuum, however, there exists a dangerous, but nonetheless potentially beneficial, amount of dysfunction. Somewhere in the early development of this future shock domain is the portal that separates the discomfort that must be endured in order to amplify adaptation capacity from the level of dysfunction that is too costly to justify. Leaders who seek the elasticity of a nimble operation know that as risky as high levels of change are for an organization, they must flirt with the rim of chaos if they are to keep their organization competitive in today's markets. With tenacity and thick skin, they must push themselves and the people around them to ever-advancing thresholds of adaptation by surfing the zone between order and chaos.

Powering Up for the New Game

M any years ago, Charles Darwin observed that within most species there are more individuals who desire command over their domain than actually achieve it. The implication is that there have always been fewer winners than losers. With respect to the human animal, this means that many more of us try to win at the various games we play than really end up doing so. I'm not using "games" here to refer to the assorted intellectual contests, sports, or other entertaining activities we engage in from time to time. I'm using the term in a broader sense to reflect the more purposeful endeavors we pursue that bear meaningful consequences for us. Our lives are filled with many such games. We try to win (achieve success) as partners, parents, peacemakers, pundits, professionals, parishioners, and patriots, to name but a few examples.

The Games Humans Play

All our games have certain characteristics in common:

- Purpose—They have a point. The intent of some of these games may be frivolous, like participating in office gossip or playing practical jokes on people. Others are designed for more substantive outcomes like treating patients in an emergency-room trauma center or being responsible for maximizing shareholders' return on investment.

- Rules—Some games have explicit directions about how to play, like what it takes to graduate from college, but most are implicit, like the ground rules of a friendship.

- Time boundaries—Some games are brief, like the time it takes to make a first impression with a prospective customer. Others, such as personal development, can last an entire lifetime.

- Spatial parameters—Some games are confined to small physical spaces, like the computer used to produce work. Other games command larger arenas, like the corporate structures where we pursue our careers or the global marketplace within which we help our organization compete.

- Prizes—Being the designated winner, being ranked as a top contender, or sometimes just being able to stay in the game, are all forms of rewards.

- Intensity—Some games are fun, like dating or succeeding at a challenging corporate objective, and some are more serious, like the tenacity displayed when competing for business with a hard-to-penetrate customer or the personal sacrifices that occur in warfare.

- Emotional reactions—Some games bring us pleasure—for example, parenting or achieving financial objectives. Others are more of a burden, like paying taxes or downsizing an organization.

- Prescribed number of players—Some of our games are played with other people, such as a spouse or a management team, but there are also solitary games, like meditation or making tough management decisions.

- Intentionality—Participation in some games is at a conscious, intentional level, like seeking a promotion or getting married. In other games, involvement is more of an intuitive or unconscious activity, like sibling rivalry or unintentionally intimidating coworkers.

- Language—Most games use terms, phrases, and symbols to convey specific meanings that are relevant only within that context, like "sucking up" to a new boss or "going out on a limb" when presenting an innovative idea.

- Roles—Regardless of their nature, most games include generic roles people must play. Examples are: spectators, rookies, seasoned players, and, finally, masterful artists—those who have learned to take a game beyond its normal boundaries.

From this perspective, managing organizational change is but one of the games we play. All the above characteristics apply.

Games with a long history tend to mature over time, which makes their current play much different than in years past. Some games have evolved in speed, complexity, and proficiency to the point that superstars of the past, arguably, would be less able to compete by current standards. For example, how well would Andrew Carnegie be able to keep up with the likes of Bill Gates and Jack Welch?

Managing businesses that are changing is a prime example of how far a game can progress from its inception. Because institutions of all kinds have been altering themselves for as long as humans have been building hierarchical structures, the game of managing organizational change has had many years to develop and refine itself. Although other aspects of the game have advanced considerably, the purpose has always remained the same: to align key success factors with the marketplace's criteria for success. Despite this consistency of intent, the sophistication of the game and the requirements for success have accelerated dramatically and have forced a shift in paradigm that has altered how we look at and manage change.

A New Paradigm Unfolds

To examine the shift, let's first explore some general features of how paradigms operate. First, regardless of their composition, place of origin, or substance, paradigms eventually outlive their viability. Whether it's the mere seconds of existence afforded certain microbes, the few days in the life of a bee, the modest number of years we humans survive, or the millions of centuries during which a star releases light and energy—all paradigms, all systems, have a definitive shelf life. Just as from the microbe's point of view the bee appears to live forever, some frameworks may seem to be indestructible. But, this is only an illusion formed when one standard is viewed from another's frame of reference.

Second, paradigms don't just materialize out of thin air; they are a response to people trying to make sense of their world. When the range of responses suitable for one set of circumstances gives way to a completely different level of options, a new paradigm is born. Figure 5.1 shows the relationship between the questions and challenges posed by an environment and the formation and shelf life of a paradigm that can address those issues. What precedes the forming of a paradigm is a set of questions that cannot be adequately addressed (A = unanswered questions). Often, the time period in which a paradigm remains intact extends beyond the relevance of its original questions and concerns (B = old answers trying unsuccessfully to contend with new questions).

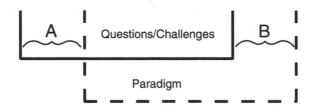

Figure 5.1   Paradigm shelf life.

Figure 5.2 shows the natural extension of this pattern into the set of questions and concerns that replaces the first set. When the old questions and challenges become irrelevant, a new set of demands is created, thus presenting a new set of questions and challenges. These, however, are first dealt with from the standpoint of the old paradigm (A). The new paradigm becomes necessary only when the new questions and challenges would otherwise go unresolved because they are being addressed by the old paradigm. At some point, however, the utility of the answers provided by this paradigm will fall short (B) of the more demanding questions and challenges that will later emerge.

As we apply this paradigm framework to building the Nimble organization, it becomes clear that there have been two distinct periods of organizational change. Each period reflects its own unique paradigm or way of thinking and behaving toward change.

OLD PARADIGM

The first era of change may well hold the paradigm longevity record. Right up there with cockroaches and taxes, this perspective on change has prevailed for an unusually long time. This framework for how to think and act toward organizational transitions has, until recently, served as the commonly accepted context for leaders during periods of major upheaval.

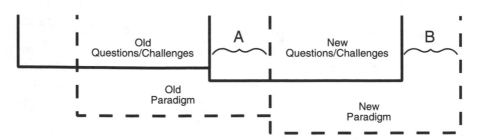

Figure 5.2   Paradigm shift.

Referring back to issues I raised in the Preface, I will refer to this paradigm as having its origin in the contiguous era.

In the change game, the questions and challenges that form the need for a new paradigm are reflected in the pressure from the "load" of change in the environment. The load rating that fostered the first era of change management thinking was of an incremental nature. That is, the magnitude (volume, momentum, and complexity) of the changes and the consequences incurred if they were not successfully implemented represented only first-order, straight-line change, which was merely a modest improvement over existing conditions. The contiguous era of change is characterized by a belief that organizational transitions should unfold in an incremental fashion, where innovation is relatively sequential in nature. That is, alignment between an organization's success factors and the market's criteria for success should be achieved by step progression, not quantum leaps.

NEW PARADIGM

We are now at the point, within many organizations, where the pressure caused by the load of change has outstripped the usefulness of the contiguous approach for managing transitions. We have more and more unanswered questions and unaddressed challenges. This means that many of today's leaders are playing the change game the way their fathers and grandfathers did. Imagine the Wright Brothers bidding against Lockheed-Martin with the same approach and skills that once made them successful. How competitive could Henry Ford be today against the modern assembly lines of Nissan or BMW? When one era passes into another and the paradigm for success shifts radically, intelligence and hard work are not enough.

The purpose of the change game is the same, but a new paradigm of perpetual unrest has emerged. These are its characteristics:

- New rules—The operator's manual for implementing major organizational initiatives is filled with new instructions, actions, and prescriptions that must be followed if success is to be attained.

- New time boundaries—The length of time between change requests and the amount of time allowed for implementation of each request have been dramatically reduced.

- New spatial parameters—The arena for change has now been significantly broadened and, at the same time, has become more confined. The game is played around the globe, and yet often involves subtle nuances within the psyche of those involved (i.e., building commitment and reducing individual resistance).

- New prizes—Physical compliance is not enough; we must secure genuine internalized commitment from all participants or the game is lost.

- New intensity—This is no longer a game for the timid or those seeking lighthearted amusement. What is often at stake is shareholders' equity, people's jobs, billions of dollars in assets, someone's career, or the well-being, if not the sanity, of those who are being affected.

- New emotional reactions—No longer is comfort or pleasure one of the benchmarking criteria for how well people are dealing with change. For many initiatives, high spirits, irrepressible buoyancy, and happy faces are not likely during the uncertainty of implementation.

- New number of players—More participation, across more categories of constituents, is now required than ever before.

- New roles—Gone are the days when there were only those who made the decisions about change and those who read the announcement memos. There are now highly specialized duties and responsibilities for the leaders, sponsors, agents, targets, and advocates of change, and, to make things even more interesting, these roles often overlap within the same group of people.

- New intentionality—Intuitively based gut-instinct is no longer sufficient to successfully lead the change game. Conscious competence is necessary today to ensure not only that victories can be replicated, but also that the cadres of people within an organization can be educated about how to apply structure and discipline to the execution of important initiatives.

- New language—Terms used in the new era of change would be unrecognizable to players of the old paradigm (e.g., ROC_{hg}, and Human Due Diligence).

The shifts required in the way change must be addressed as we move from the contiguous era to the perpetual unrest era are so dramatic that, other than the game's purpose remaining the same, little else will be recognizable in the new paradigm. This kind of movement is not unlike the evolution that has taken place in aviation over the past 50 years. Prior to the introduction of computers, pilots had a manual relationship with their planes. There was a direct mechanical connection from the captain's hands on the stick, through the rods and cables, to the rudder or wing flaps.

This kind of straight-line, uninterrupted hookup produced two important features: (1) The plane was flown by "feel"—the pilot operated the aircraft by using his or her senses of touch and hearing as much as intellect—and, because of this, (2) the plane could respond to events and conditions no faster than the pilot's reactions would allow. Today, flying is very different. For example, sophisticated, high-performance military aircraft must be able to operate in situations where the equipment's speed and response time are many times faster than the old manual system would allow. The new planes are operated on a fly-by-wire basis: most of the planes' functions are performed by a computer, not guided directly by the pilot. The speed and accuracy of the feedback mechanism in a computer allow the plane to increase its velocity and maneuverability by a wide margin compared to manual flight control.

When limitations are simultaneously pushed to extremes in several aspects of an aircraft's operation, the equipment begins to function as a high-performance system that is nearly out of control. In fact, if any one of several critical automated components should malfunction, the plane does lose control. This is why there are backup computers for the backup computers. Aviation engineers refer to this as "contained instability." The overall system achieves its greatest performance when it's on the edge of losing control, with only the various high-speed computers maintaining its stability. Success is dependent on a set of extremely sensitive, accurate, fast-feedback systems that work in concert to create the overall required agility.

The new era of perpetual unrest makes it imperative that leaders shift from the old manual approach of implementing change (i.e., relying on instinct and slow reaction time) to the new fly-by-wire paradigm. Today's leaders must learn to break the habit of depending on luck and unconscious competence and instead rely on the more effective Human Due Diligence approach, described in Chapter 6.

It takes much longer and is more expensive to build today's high-performance aircraft, compared with the planes of the Second World War. Likewise, it requires more time and investment to construct a Nimble organization than it does to run the more constrained operations many of us are used to working in. But, by a wide margin, the competitive advantage is worth the cost. The odds that a constrained company will survive in the fast-paced environment of the perpetual unrest era are no greater than if the old F-16 jets were going up against the newest F-22 fighters.

Nimbleness cannot be attained by leaders who are trapped within the change game as defined by the old, contiguous paradigm. The new game represents a fresh framework with a new array of options that are different in scope and reach from the "change management" approaches used when infrequent, incremental change was predominant.

As it has been practiced since its formulation in the early 1980s, change management's primary feature has been a conceptual and philosophical reliance on psychology and group dynamics to create human-relations-type interventions that were most often applied through the corporate training or organizational effectiveness departments. This way of relating to change has run its course, and taking its place is a more substantial approach I refer to as *Human Due Diligence,* which assumes people have an elastic but, at any point in time, finite reservoir of adaptation resources. Out of necessity, therefore, Human Due Diligence involves a level of structure and discipline far beyond anything seen under the change management banner.

If our problem is that we will soon be experiencing more change than our organizations can absorb, the answer is to develop a greater *Nimbleness.* A nimble workplace is one that consistently succeeds in unpredictable, competitive environments through fast and effective modifications of its operations. Human Due Diligence is the means by which a nimble work environment can be achieved. It consists of gathering information, planning, and engaging in actions related to the impact change is having, or will have, on an organization's human capital. The sole purpose for Human Due Diligence is to help create a nimble work setting in which changes critical to prosperity in the marketplace can be successfully implemented.

In this new era of perpetual unrest, Nimbleness and Human Due Diligence are key leadership tools for achieving and maintaining a competitive advantage. These tools are more than simple extensions of the techniques and philosophy that have characterized the practice of change management in the past. An important evolutionary step has been taken in how we survive and prosper in work environments that continue to grow in speed and complexity.

For most of us, the sponge we use to absorb the unexpected disruption in our lives is already saturated, and yet something or someone is about to pour even more on us. This book, therefore, is not about whether we have a problem keeping up with change, but rather what to do about that problem. The defining feature of the perpetual unrest era will be an unprecedented pace of change, and only leaders who are well versed in the mechanics of the new change game will be able to maintain the hectic pace.

PART THREE

HUMAN DUE DILIGENCE

Change is a process. But if that sounds reassuring to you, Part Three may come as a rude awakening. The process is unfamiliar to most leaders and, in such situations, there is a tendency to fall back on precedent. But the era of perpetual unrest has no real precedent. We are kidding ourselves if we assume otherwise.

The human element alone makes today's change process unique. It won't work to say, "First, kill all the people"—a variation on Shakespeare's famous dictum for revolutions: "First, kill all the lawyers." Nor will it be productive to ignore, torture, or marginalize them. Just as we carefully account for financial resources, we must be vigilant toward the human equivalent.

The process is also singular in that it is imperative. It can't be ducked without paying a heavy price. Increasingly, the option of swallowing hard and taking the hit inflicted by sticking to one's established ways of implementing change is becoming too costly for any organization to bear.

Part Three is about these difficult dilemmas. Change is not just another process that can be treated as business as usual. Now, it requires structure and discipline as never before.

The Human Side of Change

Human Due Diligence

Masters of the new change game pay far more attention to the human aspects of implementing major change than do those who will fall short of their transition objectives. Their dedication to structures and discipline around "people" issues clearly distinguishes these masters from players who operate in a more constrained fashion. This commitment to a serious, rigorous approach to the human side of change forms the basis for Human Due Diligence. To understand this approach, it is helpful to draw further comparisons between it and its predecessor, change management. But first, a definition.

The term "due diligence" refers to the investigation done before taking important actions. Most people are familiar with financial or technological due diligence: critical information is gathered before key decisions are made and carried out. The term implies not a cursory review, but an extensive and comprehensive investigation of the issues and implications surrounding vitally important decisions. Instead of instinct or guesswork, a serious, rigorous effort is made to be sure the findings are as reliable as possible. For example, during the deliberations surrounding a merger or acquisition, each party engages in a due diligence inspection of the other's financial standing, tax returns, bank relations, borrowing record, receivables and payables history, and annual earnings. Thanks to being rooted in finance, due diligence carries images of a thorough inquiry into a matter of the utmost importance. By its nature, this kind of rigorous investigation is time- and resource-consuming, and can only be justified if significant consequences could result from making a wrong decision. In such circumstances, full knowledge of all the relevant information is vital.

Financial due diligence is seldom an afterthought that executives try to remember to engage in before taking action on matters that are pivotal to their organization's future. Such scrutiny is so much a part of the decision-making process when pursuing strategic negotiations that failure to conduct the expected investigation would be considered at least an unprofessional omission, if not an illegal one.

Leaders of nimble organizations don't limit themselves as to when they apply this same kind of due diligence mind-set. They not only use this approach when investigating traditional factors like potential market share gain from a merger, or the cost of capital to be used in a possible restructuring. They also expand the general concept of serious fact finding and potential problem solving to include the investigation of the human features of all-important initiatives involving significant change.

Because most senior officers relate to the due diligence process as a serious matter, Human Due Diligence is the term I use with leaders who are serious about orchestrating the people aspects of implementation architecture. It brings to the people side of change the same demanding meticulousness and painstaking thoroughness normally associated with financial due diligence. To the emotional, social, and cultural aspects of change, it applies the exactitude and attention to detail typically put to use during important acquisitions or vital technical matters that are under consideration.

The Evolution of Human Due Diligence

Now, the history. Just a few years ago, the field of change management emerged as one of the hot new entries on the list of what leaders were expected to be familiar with if they wanted to remain professionally current. It came to represent an array of models and techniques focused on reducing the resistance and increasing the commitment people felt toward organizational changes affecting them. It was and still is a blend of management science, psychology, anthropology, and group dynamics. It deals with the human aspects of implementing major corporate initiatives such as mergers, acquisitions, business process reengineering, and the introduction of new technology. Once written about in business-related articles and books, it quickly became a popular item on the menu of topics executives were seeking answers to and consulting firms were offering advice about.

Despite this initial surge of interest, it is both ironic and symptomatic of our times that change management has so soon become obsolete. Like a satire of itself, change management has been unable to keep up with the dynamics it was created to address. Although still a relatively new tool in the executive's survival kit, it already shows signs of faltering as a reliable mechanism for dealing with what it was suppose to address—the human side of major transitions.

Barely four or five years ago, even talking about change management, much less applying its concepts and techniques to the implementation of major corporate initiatives, was regarded as cutting-edge awareness. Today, it is considered common practice among leaders who hope to succeed with important change projects. More importantly, the magnitude of turbulence now prevalent in the workplace and the cost incurred when initiatives are not implemented correctly have both advanced to previously unheard-of levels. The people problems associated with executing change today are no longer as responsive as they once were to the change management approach. In a relatively brief period of time, this orientation toward organizational transitions rose and is now in the process of being discarded as the darling of those who think of themselves as architects of organizational transitions.

It's not that the answers that were provided in the past were wrong; it's that, given today's level of organizational turbulence, the same questions now encompass additional and more complex elements that influence the success of change efforts. New factors have emerged that evoke reactions and intensities not previously encountered, which suggests that a different set of assumptions and implications is in order.

If the process of implementing important strategic initiatives is to be advanced beyond its current state, the lessons learned from attempts at organizational change must delve far below what has been revealed under the auspices of change management as we have known it. If the true intricacies of the transition process are to be understood and managed, we must break new ground. (See Appendix C for a brief history of how change management evolved and how it compares with Human Due Diligence.)

Our society has plenty of examples of how we thought we understood how to deal with something, only to find out later that our answers were embarrassingly simplistic and sometimes tragically naïve: toxic waste (bury it), drug abuse (just say "no"), national security (defeat communism), or

AIDS (condemn homosexuals). Our current grasp of the dynamics that drive the human side of organizational change is no less superficial. We are vulnerable to suffering from equally dangerous implications if we don't pursue a much more robust command of the variables that influence the outcome of important organizational initiatives.

If we are going to keep pace with the ever growing challenge of transitions, the game must change. Human Due Diligence reflects the kind of paradigm leap we must take if we are to deal with the level of uncertainty and instability inherent in an era of continuous change. It represents a much more in-depth treatment of the issues surrounding how and why people respond as they do when faced with unfamiliar circumstances in the work setting. Only by applying to the process of organizational change the rigor and seriousness this approach offers can we make the headway required to remain viable in progressively unstable world markets.

A Nonnegotiable Factor

Given the level of difficulty associated with Nimbleness, it becomes apparent why so few nimble companies exist. Yet, there is always one nimble provider in each market—one organization that executes, more efficiently and effectively than any of its competition, the necessary adjustments in its key success factors. Let's review what is entailed when this Nimbleness is achieved on an intentional basis.

An organization must remain vigilant in its efforts to maintain market alignment. Because accomplishing this alignment during turbulent times requires constant adjustments to key success factors, a nimble work environment is crucial. This nimble quality can be either obtained through luck and intuition or achieved with structure and discipline. When consistency and transferability are important, Nimbleness must be engaged with the rigor and seriousness achieved only through the consciously competent application of Human Due Diligence.

Once an organization's leadership has decided to pursue a particularly important change initiative, or recognizes that it has entered an extended period of uncertainty and many changes lie ahead, one question becomes critical: "How will people be managed during the transition?" The "how" of change has to do with orchestrating the human variables that influence an organization's success during change (e.g., commitment, resistance, and culture). In this regard, issues that surface relate to how the leadership is to ready the organization for as yet unidentified changes (i.e., enterprise preparation), and how it will execute any particular initiative it chooses to engage (i.e., tactical implementation). The actions taken may be geared toward increasing the adaptation resources employees have available to address future changes, or reducing the unnecessary problems people typically experience when a specific change is introduced. Again, the defining feature of strategies that deal successfully with the "how" of change is the proper application of Human Due Diligence.

Human Due Diligence is applied whenever it is important to generate an adequate Return on Change (ROC_{hg}) from critical initiatives that are pursued. For example, before committing substantial amounts of time and money to a companywide restructuring effort or to the installation of a major new information system, senior management is obligated to conduct a thorough probe of all the critical variables that could impact the success of the venture. They proceed only if they can convince themselves that the potential benefits outweigh the risk and cost involved.

When successful organizations are preparing for turbulent times and the stakes are high if change is not managed appropriately, Nimbleness becomes a nonnegotiable factor in the formula for success, and Human Due Diligence is the vehicle for its intentional delivery. Nimbleness is a critical quality that organizations must demonstrate to survive and prosper in unstable environments, and Human Due Diligence is a disciplined approach to achieve that objective. In combination, these two components both raise and address the one question that becomes most crucial during unstable times: "Do we have or can we attain the human capacity to successfully execute the changes vital to our future?" In this context, "capacity" relates to issues around people's willingness and ability to accommodate a change. "Success" is used here to reflect the achievement of a sufficient number of technical and human objectives to satisfy the time, quality, and budget requirements as defined by the person or group sanctioning the action.

If leaders fail to apply Human Due Diligence, it is unlikely that the Nimbleness they need to execute their critical change initiatives will be available when and to the degree needed. When a ceaseless advance of ambiguity and uncertainty looms, operating with inadequate speed and agility to carry out important decisions is no different than having an insufficient water supply when crossing a desert. Nimbleness and water represent strategically important resources that must be acquired, stored, treasured, and used with discretion. Human Due Diligence is simply a structured and disciplined way to bring about this nimble quality.

Although Human Due Diligence is vital to guiding the transition process, it should never be thought of as a terminal objective. It is an important ingredient for an organization's success with change, but nothing more. Just as, hopefully, no single change project would ever become an end goal for an organization, Human Due Diligence should be thought of as a vehicle for strategy execution, not the ultimate point of the exercise. It is a means within a means within a means, not the desired end state. Figure 6.1 reflects this point: Market success is based on the appropriate deployment of Human Due Diligence, resulting in a Nimbleness that enables an organization to efficiently and effectively execute changes and attain its strategic objectives.

To position Human Due Diligence in the proper context, let's review the requirements for prosperity in turbulent environments. The central focus for an organization must always remain accomplishing its strategic objectives in its chosen market. Achieving this goal is dependent on constantly modifying the key success factors that contribute to the organization's success. The level of ongoing change now occurring in and around most organizations requires a Nimbleness that can best be accomplished by applying structure and discipline to the human side of implementation. I call this Human Due Diligence.

Because of the consequences for failing to properly implement important changes, structure and discipline are crucial to success. For example, to analyze the likelihood of a particular project's achieving its stated objectives, there must be a structural way to judge the variables. Change and its impediments must be viewed as composed of identifiable component parts and processes that function together (or don't) as a unified system. These parts

Figure 6.1   Market success during instability.

and processes may be configured in many different ways, but all efforts to significantly change things reflect a certain uniformity that can be recognized and measured. By observing and measuring the forces that promote and those that block the desired outcome, a prediction can be made regarding the project's chances of success. Like the weather, this kind of forecast is only possible if the phenomenon is comprised of identifiable components that function separately and collectively in an understandable way.

Discipline is applied when the decision to proceed with the initiative is based on the findings rather than someone's ego or impatience. Achieving discipline means applying guidelines, proceedings, and recommendations even when it's not easy or pleasant to do so. Structure without discipline produces results of little value. We must either live with the structures we have built or build structures that we can live with. Structure without discipline produces good intent but inconsistent and sometimes sloppy results. Discipline without structure creates rigidity for its own sake, without meaning or purpose. Both are necessary for the Human Due Diligence framework to deliver the value of which it is capable.

Human Due Diligence is grounded in a specific structure for understanding the dynamics of change and in a high level of discipline to follow its principles and tenets. This kind of rigor is a necessity for achieving market success during unstable times. Human Due Diligence, therefore, demands a specific flow of events:

- Modifying key success factors (executing change) is but a means to the ultimate desired state.
- Demonstrating the Nimbleness to execute these changes is simply a way by which the modifications are accomplished.
- Applying Human Due Diligence in order to help create this Nimbleness is no more than a mechanism in the chain of events necessary for organizations to succeed when surrounded by uncertainty.

The primary purpose for applying Human Due Diligence is to help create and maintain a nimble environment throughout an organization, as well as to assist in the implementation of specific change initiatives. Human Due Diligence encompasses gathering information, planning, and engaging in actions related to the impact change is having or will have on an organization's human capital. When applied properly, Human Due Diligence will help deliver the two prime objectives necessary for the nimble organization: (1) increasing its adaptation capacity and (2) reducing the unnecessary burdens it faces when implementing new initiatives.

Operationalizing Human Due Diligence

Human Due Diligence has three primary components:

1. Collection—Information is gathered about an organization's overall capacity to prosper during prolonged ambiguity (i.e., enterprise preparation) and/or its ability to successfully implement a specific project or series of projects (i.e., tactical implementation).
2. Planning—Once proper due diligence information has been collected, it forms the basis for planning whatever actions are necessary to mitigate the problems or exploit the opportunities that were identified.
3. Action—Based on the plans developed, the activities engaged in are intended to either increase adaptation capacity and/or reduce implementation demands.

Typical issues that arise when exploring an organization's general readiness for change include:

- How much resilience do people have available to help them absorb change, and how do we develop this trait if it is too low?
- How knowledgeable are people about the human dynamics that unfold during change (e.g., why people resist and how they become committed), and how can we encourage more learning about the people side of change?
- How likely is it that important initiatives will be poorly implemented because of insufficient diagnosis, planning, and execution skills, and how do we enhance these skills if they are insufficient?

Issues related more to the execution of specific projects or tactical implementation include items like the following:

- How close to future-shock overload are people before the change is engaged?
- How much additional change-load demand will it generate for them, and how can the demands from other changes be reduced or people's adaptation capacity be increased?
- How strong is management's commitment to this change, and how can it be heightened if it is insufficient?
- How strong is the employee resistance to this change, and how can it be reduced or, at least, managed?

- How much does the current culture support this change, and how can this support be strengthened if it is too low?
- How prepared are the change agents to provide diagnostic, planning, coaching, and advisory support to management, and how can these capabilities be broadened if currently insufficient?

After an organization collects information and plans what to do, Human Due Diligence calls for action. Two types of action can be taken to maximize the Nimbleness of an organization: (1) adaptation capacity can be increased and/or (2) unnecessary implementation demands can be reduced. The strategies for these two courses of action are dealt with in Chapter 8, "Capacity versus Demand."

Andy's Decision and Yours

When Is Human Due Diligence Considered Critical to Success?

Winning the new change game first requires a committed choice to deal with the human side of change. Accomplishing such an effort would most certainly require time, significant attention, and financial investment. The decision to pursue managing the people side of new initiatives with the rigor and seriousness that Human Due Diligence offers is one that leaders must consider carefully.

After observing many leaders who struggled with this decision for their organization, I have found that, in the logic behind the ultimate determination, there is a distinct pattern that is a function of two factors: (1) the magnitude of the changes the organization actually pursues and (2) the consequences incurred if those initiatives are poorly implemented.

Magnitude

Most people assume that the more agitation taking place in the surrounding market, the more changes an organization must engage to remain competitive. This is often the case, but not always, and even when this correlation is relevant, it's true only to a point. The magnitude of change an organization takes on is not necessarily the same as the degree of turbulence that exists in the surrounding market environment.

Many organizations initiate a response to almost every major fluctuation in the arena in which they compete. The ability to react to market fluctuation is, of course, vital to success, but only to a certain extent. Dangerous problems start to arise if an operation tries to respond to too many pressures at once. With extreme volatility, it becomes important for an organization to discriminate between those pressures and challenges it will take notice of and those it will ignore. To make these determinations, it is important to distinguish between two kinds of motives for change that are often inappropriately treated as synonymous: market turbulence and magnitude of changes.

Change-related market turbulence is a measure of the number, nature, and speed of surprises being generated by such entities as an organization's technology, customers, competition, technology, and governmental regulations. The more things change, the greater the impact these surprises produce and the faster they arrive on the scene the more turmoil and agitation is created inside the organization. A highly turbulent market is rich with unrest, clamor, confusion, and unanticipated happenings. In the opposite kind of environment, customer expectations are constant, the competition maintains a steady state in its operations, the obsolescence of technology is not an issue, and governmental interventions do not significantly increase or decrease in number or influence.

In contrast, the magnitude or amount of change taken on by an operation reflects the initiatives it has chosen to engage, not all the ones it has been exposed to. Challenges and opportunities may be bombarding an organization; yet it may choose to respond to only the two or three it considers most crucial.

The term *market turbulence* is used here to describe a set of forces over which leaders have, practically speaking, no influence. Whereas the magnitude of changes an organization accepts represents a decision or series of decisions by management, market turbulence is completely outside any discretionary action management might take to impact its future. Like a personal credit card statement showing prior purchase decisions, magnitude discloses the number and characters of the initiatives that management has determined were important enough to pursue. Market turbulence would be equivalent to the number of purchasable items the customer had access to, not the number actually bought. Market turbulence is similar to a weather report stating the current wind velocity and precipitation for a local community. As in a weather report, the number and nature of the existing and proposed changes in a work environment can be portrayed but not acted on directly.

Discriminating between the two terms is important because the magnitude of changes attempted by leadership may or may not keep pace with the turbulence in the market. Distinguishing market turbulence from an organization's magnitude of change helps explain the two horns of a powerful dilemma. The first of these was best characterized by GE's Jack Welch, when he said, "Change or die." It is imperative that an organization keep pace with the shifting expectations and demands of its customers and competitors. To fail to do so will lead to certain extinction. Equally capable of fatally goring an organization (the second horn), however, is the fact that, at any point in time, it has a finite capacity to adequately absorb the various initiatives it may want to pursue. A company's range of implementation capability is not forever fixed, but, during any specific period of time, there is a boundary the organization cannot cross without suffering lost productivity and quality. People can only assimilate so much change at a time.

On one hand, there is the market pressure: "Keep up or you're out." On the other is the cry from employees: "There is nothing left to give." As if deciding between these two options were not challenging enough, neither of these alternatives will be sufficient by itself. Either one, taken in isolation, will result in dysfunction.

The two sides must be seen as representing a dilemma to be managed, not a problem to be solved and eliminated. The task is paradoxical in nature, not linear. Both must be pursued simultaneously. The limits of change must be stretched beyond the comfort of most employees, while at the same time, leaders must remain protective of employees and their true capacity to accommodate uncertainties. Each option, viewed separately, represents goals to steer toward as well as dangers to avoid. They are the yin and yang of a single struggle, and neither aspect is more crucial to success than the other.

Magnitude is often not that closely tied to the number of internal change recommendations. Today, more than ever, companies and agencies are deluged with recommendations from inside their organizations regarding what to invent or renew. In fact, there are now so many advocates with so many new ideas that many internal attempts to persuade organizations to change have become all but meaningless to those making the final decision.

What all this means is that the path to influencing senior decision makers has become significantly more limited and more hazardous. Despite all the rhetoric about participation, in order to protect themselves from the growing ease with which employees offer their options and ideas, many executives have all but shut down the corridor between themselves and their employees' useful input. These are typically officers who limit their access for new thinking to only that which comes from boards, outside consultants, or what they read in the *Wall Street Journal*. This dangerous practice provides no avenue for incorporating associates' experiences and historical context.

With some exceptions, most organizations are confusing the number of seminars their Human Resources Department conducts on topics like "Openness and Communication in the Workplace" and "Management/ Employee Joint Involvement" with true employee influence. Actually, many of these types of programs have only exacerbated the problem. Employee recommendations are, for the most part, listened to by gatekeepers who have learned how to display the appropriate eye contact and how to skillfully paraphrase what is said so people will feel that they have been heard. Ultimately, most of their perspectives are either ignored or rejected outright.

Magnitude is not synonymous with turbulence, but neither is magnitude the same as the number and character of the initiatives formally approved and engaged by senior officers. Remember, magnitude is discretionary in that management must make a decision to implement a change before it is added to the actual transition burden for an organization. Because this kind of management decision-making power is disseminated throughout all levels, the number of potential discretionary decision points is equally vast. At each of these points, the respective decision maker is in control of two change-related gates that affect his or her part of the organization's overall magnitude rating: (1) cascaded initiatives and (2) locally sponsored initiatives.

CASCADED INITIATIVES

Change efforts that are legitimized or sponsored at any point in the hierarchy above the individual gatekeepers (e.g., executives, managers, or supervisors) where the projects are to have their impact are called *cascaded initiatives*. Their impetus for change comes from above. Most leaders who are experienced with efforts to implement strategic, companywide change will attest that, despite what organizational charts portray or what formal lines of responsibility suggest, the local gatekeepers of cascaded initiatives have the ultimate decision as to which projects will or won't be fully executed in their area.

The reality of organizational politics suggests that successful projects are the ones that are legitimized by each resident gatekeeper in the system. Local gatekeepers of change contend with much more than the edicts that come from above their position in the organization. The total magnitude of change at the local, working-unit level encompasses change pressure from all directions. The ideas each of these gatekeepers themselves put forth plus any changes that were ordered from above or effectively advocated for by peers, subordinates, or outsiders must be combined in order to accurately reflect the locally sponsored weight of change. This aggregate of decisions makes up the local magnitude of change for any single part of the organization.

Far fewer undertakings that start at the top of an organization ever make it intact to the last level of gatekeepers. In fact, the least reliable group to ask about how much change is really taking place in an organization is senior management. They tend to think their organization's magnitude is equivalent to the projects they have approved and announced. Not only do they vastly overestimate the number of their initiatives that survive the fall through layer after layer of gatekeepers to first-line supervisors, they usually are oblivious to the many changes that are engaged locally at each level of the descent.

In addition, any gatekeeper who implements a significant change affects people at that level, but usually creates some type of reverberation below as well. There is always upward and lateral impact, too. The only way the full weight of change pressure for an organization can be accurately determined is to include all the changes at all the levels of the operation.

It is within this context that magnitude must be understood. As first stated in Chapter 2, the magnitude of change faced by an entire organization is a function of three elements: the volume, momentum, and complexity of all the changes it has actually chosen to engage in at all levels of the organization.

VOLUME

To be a change-related gatekeeper is to be the object of advocacy from all quarters. Gatekeepers or local decision makers are in constant receipt of suggestions, proposals, advice, petitions, demands, requirements, directives, and ultimatums about how to make things better. These come from various individuals, numerous constituencies, and cartels of every possible makeup. There is no doubt that many, if not most, of these ideas could translate into enhanced shareholder value; however, no organization can absorb all the change opportunities that are presented. Gatekeepers must decide which ones to actually attempt. Proposals must pass through management's disposition filter. The number of unfamiliar ideas for change that an organization chooses to materially pursue constitutes the real volume of its changes, not how many ideas were floating around the organization.

MOMENTUM

After volume, the second element that contributes to the magnitude of change an organization takes on is momentum. The swiftness with which an organization undertakes its chosen change efforts has a significant bearing on the impact they have on its operations. The time people have to execute each one, and how long they have to recoup between initiatives, reflects an organization's momentum of change. When these two variables (time available to complete the task and time available to recover) decrease, the velocity of change is increasing.

Organizations today contend with two forms of momentum: contrived and genuine. Both contribute to the pressure people experience during transitions, but the first is artificial, unnecessary, and a waste of resources. The second is authentic and critical to success, and should be the focal point for resource allocation decisions. Contrived momentum is driven by emotional or cognitive influences that reside within the local gatekeeper, such as impatience, ego, ignorance, and/or inaccurate information. Gatekeepers who succumb to these spurious motivations apply real consequences to their people if they do not perform within the specified time frames they set.

Contrived momentum is a form of duplicity, though the gatekeepers' deception is usually not malicious in its intent. Mostly, it is self-delusion. They actually believe the window of opportunity for change is narrow and so they feel completely justified to cajole or compel people to comply with their direction in what they believe to be a timely manner. Either because of unconscious influences like boredom and insecurity, or incorrect information about such things as competition or market trends, these gatekeepers impose false deadlines that needlessly consume time, money, adaptation resources, management's credibility, and employee goodwill.

Genuine momentum, the inverse of the concocted compulsion just described, refers to change driven by legitimate pressures. The market is usually the primary source for the urgency that propels this kind of momentum. Here, the motivation comes from issues like advancing competition, technological development, the necessity to shorten product development cycles, deregulation, or the formation of global markets.

Avoiding the pitfalls of contrived momentum requires a high degree of objectivity, which depends on the gatekeepers' psychological maturity and the factual basis of the market information used to make decisions.

The strength of genuine momentum is due in large part to the lack of contamination between a gatekeeper's personal rhythm for change and the tempo he or she imposes on the organization. Just because a person who has a strong capacity to absorb disruption and who can operate in ambiguous situations happens to also be the CEO, this does not necessarily mean the rest of the organization is similarly prepared. It is equally true that just because someone who is easily intimidated by the exploits of other organizations or wants to build an innovative image for its own sake also happens to be the top executive, this does not mean the rest of the organization can pay the price for these indulgences.

Like parents who must learn to avoid living out their own unmet dreams through their children's activities, decision makers must not impose their needs for change on the organization. Forcing children for long periods of time to participate in pursuits they have little interest in, and/or aptitude for, is unhealthy for both the children and the parents. Genuine momentum is driven by executives, managers, and supervisors who can distinguish their own psychological needs from the capabilities and limitations of the people they lead.

There is nothing wrong with a gatekeeper's realizing he or she has a strong personal need to pursue change, and then channeling that desire into a professional role for a company that requires that very trait. When what the gatekeeper personally wants or needs is well matched with the requirements to succeed in his or her organization, a positive dependency is formed. The problem surfaces when a person fails to realistically compare his or her personal development and ego needs with what's best for the organization.

The objective detachment needed for genuine momentum is also dependent on sound, accurate intelligence about the marketplace. Misinformation, erroneous facts, over- or underestimation of the competition, miscalculation of the impact of new technology, distorted impressions of customer needs, and misinterpretation of trends are all symptoms associated with urgency driven by unfounded pressure. Genuine momentum is characterized by correct, timely, and minimally biased information about current and future market dynamics.

Contrived momentum is all too commonly the propellant for organizational change today. Far too many initiatives are being engaged, and the people involved are overwhelmed because of insecurity, arrogance, or ineptitude on the part of decision makers. Gatekeepers can go to the well only so many times before adaptation resources run dry. The time allotted to implement each initiative and the intervals allowed between initiatives should not be dictated by a gatekeeper's psychological makeup or by faulty information. It should be driven by external forces such as the needs of customers, shareholders, and competitors.

There is nothing wrong, however, with a gatekeeper's deciding to pursue a change in the absence of any apparent operational problem or customer dissatisfaction. Genuine momentum can be driven as much by anticipating what the market will do or what it will need as by responding to manifest trends or events. The key is that genuine momentum is driven by a thrust from outside the gatekeeper's personal needs.

COMPLEXITY

The complexity of a change effort is measured by the quantity, variety, and clarity of information needed to describe it. A simple project requires few words to recount a small number of variables that lend themselves to singular or dichotomous explanations. Complex initiatives involve an imposing allotment of written and spoken words to detail a large number of variables, many of which have multiple, possibly conflicting interpretations. When organizations attempt initiatives with major impact, they are typically engaged in complex change. In today's business environment, this kind of complex change is occurring with more frequency than ever.

The growing complexity of change should come as no surprise. An axiom with broad application—whether referencing the subatomic or the galactic scale—is: eventually, all living systems either grow and become more complicated and perplexing, or they die. This characteristic is certainly evident in the evolution of organizational operations. There are two reasons why this is so. The first is that adding stages to a sequence that has proven itself to be effective is easier than starting over or modifying the initial sequence. Therefore, innovations that enhance competitiveness are accretions on the mature mechanism. The second reason concerns the kind of innovation being implemented. Adding a refinement, as opposed to discarding one, is usually more likely to produce a competitive advantage.

It is typical today for organizations to engage in several complex initiatives at a time, each considerably more sophisticated than people have experienced in the past (e.g., reengineering is more complex than reorganization, globalization demands more than international operations, and enterprise-level software is a cut above the normal new computer program). As these separate efforts are stacked and overlapped on top of one another, the overall work environment becomes a tangled web of unfamiliar circumstances, complicated requirements, unclear meanings, and unanticipated demands. The more people feel encumbered in this fashion, the less likely it is that they will be able to successfully implement many of the undertakings. Generally speaking, as the complexity of the changes an organization attempts increases, so does the rate of failure.

Like volume and momentum, complexity is not determined by the sophistication of the many change options available in the surrounding environment. Only the convoluted nature of those initiatives actually accepted by the various levels of gatekeepers as worthy of pursuit counts toward an organization's magnitude of change.

Adding another layer of burden is the fact that complexity and these two other elements of magnitude—volume and momentum—are accelerating in strength in a less-than-orderly fashion. Rather than growing stronger in a smooth progression, each element is a fluctuating variable that promotes inconsistency in itself, but then the combined interaction among them represents yet another variant that promotes widespread instability across all the variables. Organizations contending with a greater magnitude of change than they are accustomed to are dealing with the gyrations within each of the three elements as well as their combined erratic influence. The success of any major effort for change is, to a large extent, dependent on the amount of pressure generated separately and collectively from these forces.

Consequences

The second component that influences the composition of an organization's success formula is the cost associated with an organization's failing to properly execute the initiatives it pursues. Many people are surprised by the choice of *consequences* instead of *commitment* as the second of these key issues. Most think of commitment to a change as synonymous with the importance of the desired outcome. There can be a strong relationship between the two, but there are important differences as well.

Commitment is the glue that bonds people to their change goals. Commitment to major change is evident when people:

- Invest resources (e.g., time, energy, and money) to ensure the desired outcome.
- Pursue their goal consistently, even when under stress and with the passage of time.
- Reject ideas or action plans that offer short-term benefits but are inconsistent with the overall strategy for ultimate goal achievement.
- Stand fast in the face of adversity, remaining determined and persistent in their quest for the desired goal.
- Apply creativity, ingenuity, and resourcefulness to resolving problems or issues that would otherwise block their goal.

The most credible way to test commitment to change is to observe behavior over time, but this makes it difficult to predict its presence before it is demonstrated. In lieu of observable behavior, most people think it is possible to forecast someone's commitment before it has been manifested by listening to the person talk. The problem is that it is much too easy for people to sound highly committed to something when they're not. It's also common for people to believe that their determination is unyielding, yet they falter as soon as they are challenged or when the task becomes more difficult or more expensive than anticipated.

From our observations at ODR, we have found that the most reliable predictor of commitment is *the price people believe they will pay if they fail to achieve their change.* When calculating the true debt left by a collapsed change effort, the focus should not be on the expenditures made during implementation. It should be on the cost of maintaining what already exists, the status quo.

Even though an organization may state a strong desire to modify one of its key success factors, in fact, it may only experience a mild irritation if things remain as they are. In many situations, the more expensive implication is that, after a defeated change effort, the status quo remains in place and may even gain strength as it retrenches itself. In other situations, the penalty imposed for continuing the present status could be prohibitively expensive. The success of any major change effort is directly tied to the severity of the price for the status quo.

Burning Platforms: Andy's Story

In 1988, I started using a real-life incident to explain to people what we had learned about how the cost of maintaining the status quo plays an important role in creating and sustaining the motivation to change. Since then, in speeches, in executive seminars, and in my previous book, I used this burning-platform story to convey our findings about how fundamental change is the result of not just attraction to the desired state, but also fear of the current state. (See Figure 7.1 if you are unfamiliar with the Piper Alpha oil rig explosion and how I have used this story to describe sustainable commitment.)

The popularity of this narrative has grown over the years. It has been passed to thousands of people all over the world, who in turn have passed it on to thousands more. In fact, to my surprise, the story has taken on a life of its own. Various mutations of the story have evolved— I have heard one about a burning bridge, another describing a burning building. My favorite is the rendition I heard that involved a burning bush (I informed the story-teller that I thought his version had possibly been influenced by a different book than mine). Regardless of the many permutations that have been added, I'm pleased to report that, for the most part, the basic intent for my originally using the story has remained intact. Andy Mochan's decision to jump from the oil rig that night remains a metaphor for the tough decisions leaders must make about which change initiatives to pursue as business

The Burning-Platform Story

At nine-thirty on a July evening in 1988, a disastrous explosion and fire occurred on an oil-drilling platform in the North Sea off the coast of Scotland. One hundred and sixty-six crew members and two rescuers lost their lives in the worst catastrophe in the twenty-five-year history of North Sea oil exportation. One of the sixty-three crew members who survived was a superintendent on the rig, Andy Mochan. His interview helped me find a way to describe the resolve that change winners manifest.

From his hospital bed, he told of being awakened by the explosion and alarms. He said that he ran from his quarters to the platform edge and jumped fifteen stories from the platform to the water. Because of the water's temperature, he knew that he could live a maximum of only twenty minutes if he were not rescued. Also, oil had surfaced and ignited. Yet Andy jumped 150 feet in the middle of the night into an ocean of burning oil and debris.

When asked why he took that potentially fatal leap, he did not hesitate. He said, "It was either jump or fry." He chose possible death over certain death. . . .

He jumped because he had no choice—the price of staying on the platform, of maintaining the status quo, was too high. This is the same type of situation in which many business, social, and political leaders find themselves every day. We sometimes *have* to make some changes, no matter how uncertain and frightening they are. We, like Andy Mochan, would face a price too high for not doing so.

An organizational burning platform exists when maintaining the status quo becomes prohibitively expensive. Major change is always costly, but when the present course of action is even more expensive, a burning-platform situation erupts.

The key characteristic that distinguishes a decision made in a burning-platform situation from all other decisions is not the degree of reason or emotion involved, but the *level of resolve*. When an organization is on a burning platform, the decision to make a major change is not just a good idea—it is a business imperative.

From *Managing at the Speed of Change*

Figure 7.1

118

imperatives and which ones to forgo because they are really no more than good ideas.

I'm gratified by the number of leaders who have told me how they related to the story as a reflection of their own struggle with change. The account has apparently helped many of them clarify for themselves and articulate to others the importance of *pain management*—the conscious orchestration of information to help people understand the high price they will pay if the status quo is left in place. That's the good news. The bad news is that many people have misconstrued Andy's drama to mean that an organization can only muster the kind of commitment necessary to successfully change if it is facing immediate, catastrophic consequences such as insolvency, toppling stock value, unwanted takeover, failing merger, and/or collapsing market shares.

I believe this misinterpretation has been fostered for two reasons. First, the picture of the burning oil rig I use to accompany my narrative is a compelling sight, to say the least. The abandoned shell of twisted, burned steel that was once a productive center of activity for 200 oil workers is a powerful testament to the fierce intensity of the devastation that took place. The story and picture are a potent combination, which is why some people only remember this as an account of how a do-or-die situation was the prime motivator for fundamental change. What gets lost is that Andy's predicament represents only one type of the burning-platform conditions organizations can face. There are actually four kinds: current and anticipated problems and/or opportunities.

Of the four circumstances that can generate the kind of resolve necessary to sustain major change, current problems are the most prevalent motivators for major transformation in our lives. Whether in our personal lives, the corporate arena, the social structures we participate in, or events of a global scale, more change—with more fundamental impact, affecting more people—is driven by the desire to address pressing problems than by any other stimulus encountered.

A powerful combination is formed when the forceful imagery of the story and picture converges with the association most people make between impending danger and the need to alter the status quo. Though I'm pleased people remember the story and even go to the trouble to share it with others, I would like to once again try to place this crisis-centered interpretation of the burning-platform story into proper perspective.

I never intended to give the impression that an emergency was always necessary to motivate sustained major change. If one word is associated with the story, I would prefer *resolve* rather than *peril*. People don't have to face a life-threatening situation or organizational insolvency before they will support efforts at fundamental change. What is required is an unusual level of resolve: the determination, fortitude, and steadfastness to no longer pay what has become an inordinate price for the status quo. The result of maintaining things as they are in a burning-platform situation inflicts a grievous cost. Andy's plight that night represents circumstances that epitomize the "current problem" type of emergency that is so common when people determine that leaping into the unknown *is* expensive, but less so than the costs they already face if they continue with things as they are. By no means, however, is this the only reasoning that will support fundamental transformation.

The second predicament that will cause people to leap into a frightening change is an anticipated problem. Here, existing circumstances do not reflect an immediate threat, but a trend or some type of projection into the future strongly suggests that the situation will deteriorate significantly if the current course is maintained. This kind of anticipated change is a less common driver of fundamental transition than crisis, but most people at least can relate to it. It does occur. For example, maybe Andy would have been able to make a more orderly and safer evacuation if he had known, before it occurred, that the explosion was imminent. Engaging major change is relatively easy to understand if we are pursuing it to solve a problem, current or anticipated.

The third burning-platform type quandary is harder for people to relate to: current opportunities. This type of challenge occurs when we leave problem-centered change. It is much more difficult for people to sustain major conversions in their lives if the purpose is to achieve something desired instead of relieving the burden of something feared. Despite this tendency, there are plenty of examples showing that humans are capable of changing for no other reason than the desire to upgrade their status, not because of a problem that needs to be resolved. These examples include getting married, having children, completing an additional level of education, accepting a promotion, expanding market share, and increasing shareholder value. Current opportunities offer a favorable harvest that can be enjoyed immediately. Though we tend not to think of these circumstances as carrying the importance of problem-centered situations, they do drive sustainable change; as long as failure would be costly to endure, these positive situations can be just as galvanizing as the more negative motivators.

Finally, anticipated opportunities are situations where the benefits of leaving the status quo can only be savored later. The key to determining burning-platform commitment is the consequences the person faces if the desired aim is not achieved in the future. Whether they are current or anticipated, opportunities must be extraordinarily attractive in order to spur the sustained effort implied in business-imperative situations. The lure must be so powerful that the person feels the price for *not* attaining the goal is beyond his or her ability and/or willingness to pay.

The burning-platform story is about *resolve,* not peril—about the tenacity to do whatever is necessary to no longer pay for the prohibitively expensive status quo. When change initiatives are driven by interest of a less intense nature, they are considered "good ideas." They are not imperatives for the business.

Good ideas can be very seductive. They appear potentially profitable, in ways that would delight customers and/or please employees. The intended outcome of a change project can be so beneficial that management wholeheartedly promotes its execution; yet the effort can still fail to hold management's interest until full implementation is complete. When all is said and done, people who pursue good ideas often become "psyched up" at the beginning, in anticipation of the results, but still fail to do what is necessary to ensure the project's success. This means the cost to them, should the effort fail, is expensive but obviously affordable. Despite the commitment rhetoric that may have been thrown about, if an endeavor fails to achieve its stated objective and management believes that it can pay what is perceived to be no more than a moderate amount for the collapse, the project is doomed.

Human Due Diligence requires a significant investment of resources. This expense can only be justified if the negative consequences of the status quo are so high that it is less costly to invest in preventing or minimizing the risk of failing to orchestrate the human aspects of change and not achieving the stated objectives of the overall initiative. When true business imperatives are at hand, due to either current or anticipated problems or opportunities, the penalty for not applying Human Due Diligence is significantly higher than the expenditures for doing so. There is a greater likelihood that managing the human risk of change will be included in an organization's success formula if the consequences for the project's failing represent a personal burning-platform situation for the leader.

Is Human Due Diligence Worth It?

If the volume, momentum, and complexity of the changes an organization engages are high, and if the repercussions would be excessive should the changes fail, it becomes critical to add the human aspects of transition to the list of priority issues leaders must pursue. If a business or agency faces more disorder and risk of failure than it is accustomed to, Human Due

Diligence should not only be added to its success formula, but must be treated with the utmost urgency and care. If the magnitude of change an organization is facing has advanced beyond its prior experience and the nature of some of these initiatives constitutes burning-platform criticality, then Human Due Diligence is called for. All other success factors become dependent on the presence and strength of this one component: the ability to execute important changes. If so, the structure and discipline embedded in the Human Due Diligence approach are designed for just such assignments.

8

Capacity versus Demand

A reliable framework is needed to ensure that the desired Nimbleness is in place for an organization to succeed in turbulent times. Winning the new change game requires a framework with two key elements: an overall strategy and specific tasks.

The Strategies

The PROBLEM being addressed in this book is how to efficiently and effectively execute critically important change initiatives. The intensity of this CHALLENGE originates in the struggle with the inherent loss of control that occurs when familiar reference points suddenly become irrelevant, and new questions surface. The SOLUTION necessitates the creation of a dynamic balance within organizations. HOPE for the future lies in the possibility of building nimble operations. The MEANS for achieving the desired nimble state is through the application of the structured, disciplined approach called Human Due Diligence. To accomplish this, dual STRATEGIES must be pursued: An organization must *increase its capacity* for absorbing disruption and *reduce the unnecessary demands* being placed on its existing resources to accommodate change.

To understand the rationale for focusing on these two strategies, it is important to revisit our discussion of future shock in Chapter 2. Figure 8.1 depicts the capacity-versus-demand forces that underlie future shock.

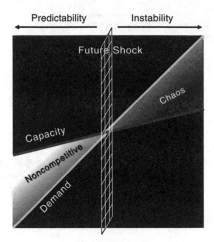

Figure 8.1   Capacity versus demand.

The ultimate intent of the change game, when played within a "perpetual unrest" environment, is to surf the future shock crest, not to try to eliminate it. When the magnitude of change is at levels never before seen and the penalties for implementation failure are prohibitively high, the purpose of the game is to push the adaptation envelope to the contained-slide level. The seriousness and rigor of Human Due Diligence must be applied toward the two strategic objectives that can contribute most to achieving a nimble work setting: increasing capacity and reducing demand on an organization's adaptation resources.

INCREASING CAPACITY

Responsibility for accelerating an entire organization's capacity to absorb major change starts at the top—not near the top, *at* the top. Board members must declare Nimbleness a critical issue worthy of their vigilance, then hire and retain senior executives capable of meeting the challenge. Once in place, these top officers should provide the leadership to ensure that their organization increases its ability to adapt to the advancing pressures of change.

The decision to increase adaptation capacity may be based on (1) a desire to improve on or eliminate a deficient situation (i.e., an organization already experiencing unbearable future shock costs) or (2) a wish to institute preventive measures whereby avoidable future shock is blocked from occurring. Although the first of these approaches is more common and easier to implement, it is actually the weaker of the two options, in terms of the amount of adaptation capacity it ultimately promotes. If the nimble status is to be secured, it usually requires stretching the boundaries of the adaptation envelope to create additional absorption resources before the pressures of change become insurmountable.

Strengthening any capability beyond what is needed to meet existing demands is almost always contentious. Theoretically, it makes all the sense in the world to keep a reserve of key resources in order to respond to peak demands as they occur. The problem is not in the concept of building excess capacity, but in the day-to-day pressures that we've come to think of as practical realities.

Who would argue with the idea of building up more critical assets than are currently needed to achieve our goals? Yet, when the insistence mounts for maintaining pace with the advancing minimum standard of success, leaders usually feel they must draw on every available resource just to keep their heads above water. Organizations can occasionally address these demands with new, untapped reserves that are miraculously discovered in the nick of time, but, for the most part, unanticipated surges in demand are met by borrowing from assets previously designated for other purposes. We tend to "rob Peter to pay Paul" by rerouting what was originally allocated elsewhere. Whether we zero in on the capital that was to fund the new computer system, the energy from the company's brain trust that was to unravel the cause of the recent loss in market share, or the few hours of sleep over the weekend that we hoped would ward off the early symptoms of the flu, when we move assets from one category to another, overall capacity is not enhanced; it is actually diffused.

Reprioritization of existing resources is a vital component to any operation trying to survive, much less prosper, in uncertain times, but this tactic should not be confused with an increase in overall capability. In all likelihood, the borrowed resources will be imported without adequate planning for their best use—a lapse that usually results in the face value of these resources being discounted considerably. More importantly, shifting a key asset from one vital part of the organization to another only perpetuates the illusion of adequacy. The borrowed asset sets up yet another deficit that must be eventually filled from other sources.

This quickly becomes the equivalent of writing bank checks on an account with insufficient funds and using them to cover previous checks written against insufficient funds. Such schemes can only last for so long. The capacity increase in the area receiving the resources is merely short-term, and the energy used to operate this way is itself a resource drain. This combination results in a currency devaluation at each site where transactions like this occur. Eventually, the value of the resource being transferred is seriously weakened.

To some extent, resource shuffling is a necessity for any operation trying to compete in a dynamic environment. But, it's a dangerous sign when this activity becomes a constant stream of emergency drills. There is a major problem if a "run, dive, and catch" mentality becomes the daily routine rather than the exception. When the majority of an organization's legends are based on stories about extraordinary heroic efforts instead of competence and courage, this usually means it has become culturally acceptable to participate in deficit spending of key resources.

"Run, dive, and catch" is the prevailing mentality toward the resources needed to properly address the human side of change within most organizations. The idea of dedicating energy to dealing with the people aspects of corporate disruption is foreign to many companies. There is even more reluctance to accept the notion of building a stronger reserve adaptation capacity. If the human issues are engaged at all, they are typically addressed by borrowing resources from elsewhere. For example, a company I'll call Alstar initiated a process to eliminate several layers of management. The nature and scope of the remaining jobs were also to change dramatically. The senior team at Alstar reallocated money from its new product development coffers to train and coach survivors of the delayering process. As a result, the new product cycle was dangerously delayed. Borrowing money from future product development to address current transition problems only delays the inevitable. In settings where transition demands are already high and evidence suggests that more, not less, ambiguity and uncertainty are in the making, accelerating adaptation capacity beyond what is required to negotiate current levels of change is the only way to stay ahead of the demand curve.

The intellectual, emotional, and physical energy needed to recalibrate expectations is not a resource that is quickly replenished, once it is exhausted. The frames of reference that leaders must possess and the cultural infrastructure that must be in place to create an atmosphere where Nimbleness can be intentionally fostered are not a set of circumstances that is achieved overnight. It can take years for you to create an environment conducive to becoming the nimble provider among your competitors.

A decision to intentionally raise the organization's adaptation capacity must be made far in advance of the rising tide of change. If you wait until lost productivity and poor quality are recognized by customers, recovery may still be possible, but unnecessary costs will be incurred. As you know, the ideal time to ask your bank for an extension of your company's line of credit is when no funds will be drawn on the account. This is also true for raising adaptation capacity. The optimum time to invest in building a stronger capacity to digest the human reaction to transition is before you reach the critical threshold for chaos.

REDUCING DEMAND

As tempting as it may be to think Nimbleness can be obtained by capacity-building alone, this coveted status presents an even more demanding set of requirements. Winning the new change game will be the result of both investments and sacrifices. The investments involved in increasing capacity are significant, but without a corresponding surrender, Nimbleness will still be elusive. In the new change game, what must be sacrificed is the gluttonous appetite most leaders have for innovation on demand.

Despite the persistent myth that bureaucracies tend to shun change, my experience has been just the opposite. Most organizations today pride themselves on how many groundbreaking, rhetoric-laden, paradigm-busting projects they can initiate. The number of cutting-edge concepts and techniques that are floating along the corporate hallways should not be confused with how much fundamental change is really taking place. In fact, typically, there is an inverse relationship between the volume of avant-garde hyperbole and the degree of real transformation. When the true fabric and texture of an organization shift in a meaningful way, the effect is seldom lost amid a barrage of other equally important initiatives. Concrete, sustained change is typically the result of focused attention and dedicated resource allocation.

As will be detailed in Chapter 17, the successful implementation of a particular initiative requires some very specific actions by those sponsoring the effort. Unless sponsors perform properly and ensure that other key players (i.e., targets, agents, and advocates) do the same, new projects will, at a minimum, create an unnecessary drain on existing adaptation resources and could jeopardize a project's success altogether. For this reason, successfully implemented change initiatives typically represent a concentration of energy and attention that can only come at the expense of other existing or prospective projects.

Choosing to narrow our focus during change may or may not be a conscious act. Sometimes, despite ourselves, we become thoroughly engrossed in the compelling nature of a given set of circumstances. Whether we experience the death of someone close, a baby's birth, a business merger, the loss of a job, a devastating hurricane, or a declaration of war, at certain times our focus and energy seem to be held captive by the magnetic force of a solitary issue or event. At other times, we deliberately block outside stimuli to lend full attention to a particular endeavor. Through sheer discipline, we become totally absorbed in a chosen course. In some circumstances, unless we can block out competing problems, opportunities, and the background noise that could otherwise diffuse our attention, our top priorities may never be addressed.

The decision to dedicate resources is more about saying "no" than saying "yes." It's about sacrifice more than contribution. The corporate assets leaders are called on to invest, in order to maintain a company's operation, vary widely. They include: money, time, attention, allegiance, problem-solving skills, ingenuity, emotional support, access, political power, intellectual properties, and reputation. Even during relatively stable times, the number of opportunities and demands for investing these assets can be overwhelming. When there is external and/or internal flux, there is added pressure to dilute the bargaining power of these assets by thinly spreading them over too many ventures. Under such conditions, successfully negotiating the surrounding uncertainty and ambiguity requires not only sound decisions about what the resources will be allocated to, but, more importantly, what they will not be diverted to.

Saying "no" to resource-draining investments that don't promise much of a return anyway requires little more than common sense. More effort is required as the feasibility for a value-added return begins to rise. When viable and compelling alternatives are presented, the struggle elevates to the tough-choices level. Next come those agonizing decisions where mutually exclusive choices are such that the price for not being able to pursue all the options reaches moderate to significant proportions. Finally, there are those "damned-if-you-do, damned-if-you-don't" situations when the cost for declining one or more pursuits to protect the resources for another more important endeavor becomes true sacrifice. The choice becomes extremely expensive, but not to choose is even more problematic.

Competing offers may occur at the time the original decision is made to dedicate resources, or they may come during the course of pursuing the top choice. Sacrificing other critically important options to safeguard what's needed to support an even higher priority is costly. The price for making and sustaining such a decision includes significant amounts of currency in such forms as money, power, and emotional strain.

When senior officers are faced with the need to introduce more change than their organization can adequately absorb, it becomes critical that they place all the various current and prospective initiatives into one of three categories:

1. Unacceptable ideas—Are by definition more expensive to implement than the value they would create.

2. Good ideas—Are likely to generate positive results such as making a profit, delighting customers, pleasing shareholders, satisfying board members, complying with governmental regulations, being attractive to industry analysts, and so on.

3. Business imperatives—Are likely to generate such value that the cost for failing to implement them would be prohibitively high.

These initiatives are beyond good ideas; they are burning-platform-type decisions. The consequences of maintaining the status quo would be inordinately expensive.

Today, executives have to be extremely protective of their organization's capacity to adapt change. Not only must they prevent unacceptable ideas from draining resources, they must also stand guard against many of the good ideas that well-meaning advocates bring forth. Good ideas are attractive, but their appeal is based on the assumption that they can be fully implemented. Without adequate adaptation resources to actually absorb the implications generated from these options, their practical value diminishes greatly. Vigilance must be unrelenting, to be sure that, first and foremost, the organization can successfully execute its business imperatives. Only if this can be accomplished with the remaining adaptation capacity can top-priority good ideas be considered.

The ability and willingness to make this kind of sacrifice are central to your organization's becoming its market's nimble provider. Indeed, major investments are needed to increase the corporate capacity for absorbing more change than is currently required, but, without discipline, the typical appetite for innovation will quickly overrun any surplus that is generated. Doubling the capacity for adaptation serves no purpose if four times the demand is created. Nimbleness comes when one company has more change resources and is more protective of these assets than its competition. Investment and sacrifice are, therefore, key companion strategies. When both are achieved, a powerful advantage is gained.

THE PAYOFF

The investments and sacrifices necessary to increase adaptation capacity are considerable, and herein lies the benefit. The expense in time, money, effort, and lost opportunity is such that most leaders will be reluctant to engage in the process. Those few who proceed will pay dearly for their organization's accelerated ability to adapt to change, but they will also gain a powerful and unique value—they will have access to *preemptive competitive advantage*.

Organizations around the globe seek the elusive mix of value-based products, services, and internal operations to set the standards for their industry or industry segment. If this mix can be achieved, they not only define the boundaries of what customers learn to expect, they also cause competitors to exercise caution when entering their domain of expertise or attempting to lure customers away. Companies that enjoy a preemptive advantage don't eliminate competitors; they intimidate and embarrass them.

The nimble provider in a market lays claim to a potent advantage that makes competitors feel they must operate with a distinct handicap. The nimble organization is able to adjust itself to such high levels of turbulence that:

- Customers see its capacity for agile responses to changing conditions as part of the service they pay for.
- Competitors will either be blocked from implementing needed initiatives because they lack the necessary adaptation resources, or they will unwisely and unsuccessfully attempt such projects and further deplete their resource base.

Let the competition beware!

The Tasks

A key element in creating a nimble framework involves the tasks people in critical roles must perform if an organization is to increase its ability to operate in a nimble fashion.

To start with, an important part of leadership today is fashioning a work setting that is specifically structured to encourage the absorption of change. This is best done by applying the structure and discipline of Human Due Diligence for the purpose of increasing adaptation capacity and lowering implementation demands. (See Table 8.1.)

Regarding the raising of adaptation capacity, there are three main points of application:

1. Strategic oversight—Board members should formally establish a *nimble charter*. The charter may be written or verbal, but it should reflect their resolve to pursue a nimble status for the organization. They must next hire and retain senior officers who are prepared to provide the proper frame of reference about how change should be approached.

2. Change leadership—Once the proper senior-level executives are in place, they must, in turn, prepare employees for ongoing change. This is accomplished by leaders who can:

   a. Understand and convey to others in the organization, in a meaningful way, the critical change priorities.

   b. Exhibit and propagate the proper mind-set about how change should be addressed.

   c. Demonstrate enough of their own personal resilience to engage and sustain the various initiatives necessary to succeed in the marketplace.

Table 8.1   Human Due Diligence

Purpose	To help create a nimble environment where the changes necessary for market success can be accomplished faster and more effectively than the competition.		
Focus	Raising Capacity (Enterprise Preparation)		Reducing Demand (Tactical Implementation)
Who	Board Members	Leaders	Sponsors
Intent	Make Nimbleness a key strategic objective and ensure that appropriate senior officers "sign on" to accomplish this task.	Prepare the organization for ongoing change by increasing reserves of adaptation resources.	Address issues asssociated with implementing specific initiatives by lowering unnecessary implementation demand on assimilation resources.
How	Include the capacity to build a nimble organization as part of senior officer hiring and retention criteria, and match the organization's change load to candidates' leadership orientation.	Demonstrate the personal skill set necessary to lead toward Nimbleness (e.g., exhibit proper leadership style and display adequate resilience). Set the proper conditions for change success (e.g., employ resilient people who are expecting ongoing turbulence, be sure there is a network of prepared sponsors, and ensure people know how change unfolds and can be managed).	Prepare themselves and others to perform their respective roles and to manage the project's implementation risk.

d. Optimize the life span of the primary operating paradigms the business relies on to conduct its work.

e. Create an enterprise-wide envelope that surrounds associates with a work environment that promotes fast, effective adaptation to disruptions.

3. Enterprise-wide envelope—A work environment must be established that will help people adjust to change by:

    a. Hiring naturally resilient people and then providing the training, coaching, and rewards to strengthen this quality to its fullest potential.

    b. Conditioning people, at all levels of the organization, for ongoing upheaval and constantly changing conditions.

    c. Teaching people about the dynamics of change so they feel less victimized by it and more able to manage the challenges it presents.

    d. Extending proper delegation as far down the organizational hierarchy as is feasible, and insisting on empowered relationships around each individual in the decision-making chain.

    e. Establishing procedures and processes that provide structure to ongoing operations while, at the same time, providing the flexibility needed to accommodate ongoing, continuous change.

    f. Creating a powerful network of sponsors to properly sanction needed change in their respective areas.

Regarding the ability to reduce demands, there is one key point of application:

1. Change sponsorship—After local decision makers are prepared for their role as sponsors, they then provide the direction and commitment necessary for specific change projects to succeed. This is accomplished by sponsors who:

    a. Adhere to the limitations of their part of the organization's existing adaptation capacity.

    b. Require themselves to live up to the tough standards set for the kind of sponsor behavior necessary to fulfill critically important initiatives.

    c. Insist that those who hold key positions in the change process in their area (sustaining sponsors, agents, targets, and advocates) are trained and expected to perform in a manner that promotes transition success.

    d. Petition each person or team with implementation responsibilities for key initiatives to include in their plan of action an assessment of the human barriers that could impede success and a description of how they plan to address these vulnerabilities.

PART FOUR

Nimble Leadership Capabilities

———

General Charles DeGaulle said, "Men are of no importance. What counts is who commands."[1] The great French soldier and statesman was only half correct, however. Both are crucial to success.

The nimble organization is as dependent on capable leaders as it is on resilient people below them. In fact, without the right kind of leadership, even men and women with otherwise impeccable qualifications will be swamped by change. Leading near the edge of chaos demands the utmost skill and dedication from those who are at the helm. Even more, they must have the bravery to operate in uncharted waters, and the wisdom to know there are no alternatives.

In Part Four, we will explore why leadership has never been quite so demanding and what it now takes to build a nimble operation capable of navigating today's turbulence.

9

Strategic Oversight

Building and maintaining a nimble organization requires that all of those in the chain of implementation responsibility perform efficiently and effectively. Key players fall into two categories: (1) those outside the organization's formal boundaries who can influence the amount of attention paid to the human side of change (i.e., shareholders and analysts), and (2) those inside the boundaries who can influence enterprise-level preparation for change (i.e., the board).

Influential Outsiders

Shareholders are the nine-hundred-pound gorillas of corporate life. It's not smart to take them for granted. Yet, they are there but not there. On a day-to-day basis, shareholders are highly influential and largely invisible, but most of their clout is wielded by surrogates—Wall Street analysts. These are the people who function as paid detectives and advisers for current and prospective shareholders regarding the near- and long-term viability of a particular company's stock. In this capacity, they are expected to pursue every morsel of information they believe to be relevant to the potential growth or decline in a company's future. For example, industry analysts have always been noted for their tough questioning, and the nature of their intense inquiries was established long ago. Senior executives might not like being asked certain questions and may be reluctant to give completely candid answers, but they generally know what questions are coming and when.

Analysts hunt down anything they consider germane to the long- or short-term profitability of an organization. Though this will remain the analysts' focus, because of the growing impact change has on a company's viability they will soon inquire not only about margins and new-product release dates, but also about the agility of the organization in question. They will be interested in not only what company an organization is going to buy next, but how prepared it is to truly assimilate the two cultures and achieve the synergy being promised shareholders. It will continue to be noteworthy if a company is about to replace its antiquated information system platform with new software, but analysts will pursue further ramifications of this kind of change, like whether employees are ready to absorb yet another major shift so soon after the reengineering, downsizing, or recently announced joint venture with a former key competitor.

Don't think these questions can be brushed aside with a casual assurance that "Everything will be all right; we've got good people in charge of that." That was an acceptable answer when executives and analysts alike thought issues related to the human aspects of a business warranted only collateral senior-level attention. For analysts who go head-to-head with corporate senior officers and understand the interdependent relationships among market success, Nimbleness, and Human Due Diligence, the typical cat-and-mouse game of information exchange that has taken place historically between senior officers and analysts is about to be raised to its next logical level.

As analysts come to recognize how important orchestrating human capital during transitions is to the success of new initiatives, they will demand more than flippant responses from CEOs, CFOs, and COOs to their questions: "What is the specific rollout strategy that will prevent the resistance problems encountered during last year's reengineering failure?" "Have you hired people in the past year who are better prepared to design and guide this implementation effort than those in place during last year's costly misfire?" "The eastern region was three months behind the rest of the organization in adjusting itself to the new requirements from customers. Other than replacing the regional vice president, how is that problem being addressed?"

When characterizing analysts as a group, as is true with any stereotyping, caution should be exercised because there are always noted exceptions. For the most part, however, industry analysts tend to be extremely information hungry, logical, and pragmatic. Although they have, so far, been slow to pick up on perspectives like Human Due Diligence and Nimbleness and the value they could provide them when judging an organization's capacity to implement strategies, this will change shortly. As the magnitude of change and the consequence for poor implementation continue to escalate, analysts will face fewer and fewer situations where they can afford not to take the human element into account. When they do recognize the extent to which this kind of probing can demystify the tangled web of human influence on an organization's success and failure, they will pursue it with the same demand for specificity that they apply to any other factor they deem important to track:

- "Mr. Chairman, you say you are confident your people have learned from their mistakes during last year's implementation fiasco. Can you document for us what the lessons were and how they have been corrected?"

- "In a recent publication, you stated, as head of strategic planning, how confident you were that the employees could absorb all the implications of the recent mergers. Could you share with us the metrics you used to conclude that your employees have remaining capacity to assimilate even more change than they already have during the last eight months of restructuring?"

- "When you say that, from your perspective as the COO, you believe your workforce is better prepared for change than other organizations, are you stating something you hope to be true or can you show us some benchmarking measures to back up your contention?"

Beware, senior officer; in the perpetual unrest era, Wall Street analysts' investigations will require that you:

- Have more than a passing knowledge of how the human element impacts implementation prognosis.

- Be articulate about what you have put in place to prepare your enterprise for ongoing transition, as well as the specific tactics you will use to execute any recently announced changes.

- Provide supporting evidence to claims you make regarding the organization's ability to successfully manage key transitions.

- Document why you believe your organization is the nimble provider in your market, meaning that it is ready to make whatever modifications are necessary to serve its customers' emerging needs more quickly and effectively than your competitors.

Influential Insiders

If Nimbleness is, in fact, vital to an organization's success in volatile and uncertain times, the ultimate responsibility for its presence and strength lies with those serving as members of the board of directors. Only when their resolve for achieving such an agile, flexible system becomes a non-negotiable part of their charter will an organization develop and sustain this quality despite the difficulties that might be encountered in doing so. If Nimbleness is not included in what board members consider the essential components in their mandate to the senior officers they hire, the existence of a truly nimble culture is left either to mere chance or to the personal preferences and personalities of the senior officers. In times of turbulence and upheaval, tenuous and unreliable approaches to Nimbleness should be considered unacceptable.

Board members must establish that a nimble milieu is essential to strategic intentions' being carried out. It is imperative that they operationalize this by emphasizing that the security of a senior officer's position is dependent on the level of agility he or she is able to establish and maintain within the work environment. Not only must the board clearly articulate its desire for a nimble structure and culture in which employees can function, but it must also exercise great care in ensuring that the senior officers they hire are appropriately skilled and predisposed to building such a work environment.

Many responsibilities come with membership on a board of directors, but none is more important than the selection of the people to serve in key senior-level positions for the organization. Filling these positions is a demanding task under any circumstances, but with the uncertainty in today's market environment, the challenge is particularly arduous. Members of a board must hire leaders who, in addition to their other duties, can compel the organization to address the human side of navigating future shock. If shareholders are increasing the pressure for bottom-line results, board members can expect to take the heat at the annual shareholder meetings. When analysts raise the ante by launching probing questions regarding a new CEO's stand on executing key initiatives, or whether there is sufficient resilience in the senior team, it's the board members who are left vulnerable if these elements for change success should prove to be weak.

Even without pressure from the analysts, boards will, on their own, eventually recognize the need for an organization to respond in a nimble fashion when they begin to encounter more uncertainty and turmoil than they can absorb. As the cost of poor implementation starts to increase at a rate that corresponds to the advancing demands for change, it will become more and more difficult to ignore the critical importance of addressing the human side of change in a disciplined manner. Confronted with these circumstances, board members will find themselves with two strategic responsibilities:

1. Incorporating the development and maintenance of a nimble organization into their mandate to senior officers.

2. Determining the organization's transition demands and matching this pressure against the orientations toward change held by both incumbents within and candidates outside the organization who are seeking senior executive positions.

The Nimble Charter

Whether clearly articulated or subtly assumed, whether formally documented or only broadly discussed, there is always some form of charter or mandate, from the board to the senior officers it hires, delineating what is to be accomplished during their tenure. These covenants between boards and members of the senior teams they employ vary tremendously, but most of the time they include some type of strategic initiative (e.g., guidance about the necessity for slight modifications to existing marketing strategies, or directives concerning radical changes needed in the information system infrastructure, prescriptions about raising profitability and stock value, or instructions concerning how much and how quickly to grow through acquisitions).

It is interesting that though most of these charters dictate or assume some degree of change, seldom do they include any stipulations about increasing the organization's ability to absorb the escalating demands on its adaptation resources. Historically, boards have not included such specifications as part of their mandates to senior teams because, in the contiguous change era, the demands of change were nowhere near what they are today or will be in the future. As the magnitude of change advances and the losses from poor implementation accelerate, Nimbleness will become a key strategic asset for organizations. Such a determination should not be taken as a given, however, because building and maintaining a nimble infrastructure is not an inexpensive or easy endeavor. The last thing shareholders need today is another illusory silver bullet for organizations to become enamored with and waste time and resources pursuing. Most of these efforts generate no more than a flavor-of-the-month kind of commitment and produce little shareholder value in the end.

Matching Change Demands and Leaders' Orientation

DIAGNOSING DEMANDS

A decision that a nimble capacity is essential to an organization's long-term viability, and is therefore worth the investment necessary to achieve it, must be tied to an objective appraisal of the demands of change the organization is presently facing and will encounter in the future. A detailed analysis of the present and future change demands on an organization's adaptation resources should be conducted to determine whether Nimbleness is truly a nonnegotiable component to long-term competitiveness or just another whimsical fad that will create its own share of unfounded excitement before it too disappears into the archives of management remedies that proved to be more promise than substance.

Such an analysis should focus on the combined impact from the two key forces that define the burden, or load, that disruptions impose on an organization: magnitude and consequences. If the magnitude of change (volume, momentum, and complexity) has (or will) accelerated well past what has been experienced in the past, and the implications for failure to properly implement these change initiatives are (or will be) prohibitively expensive, a board must declare that the change load has (or will) reached a critical level and requires the same level of serious attention and scrutiny as any other strategic issue the organization may face.

The impetus for Nimbleness should, therefore, start with the board. They should include, in the corporate goals to be accomplished and the criteria for senior executives' success, the securing of a nimble quality to the organization's operations. They must not only charge senior officers with successfully executing the current and pending individual change projects, but, more importantly, they must also require them to prepare the organization to accommodate any vital transitions that may arise in the coming years.

MATCHING DEMANDS
WITH PERSPECTIVES

After careful analysis, if the change load requires strategic-level concern and vigilance, a key responsibility of board members is to align their organization's transition demands with the orientation toward change displayed by senior executives. As obvious as this sounds, most boards fail to recognize the role they have in casting key players so that Nimbleness is at least possible to achieve. Specifically, board members need to understand the critical nature of their hiring and retention decisions as they relate to change readiness and the CEO and his or her direct reports.

It is a fundamental trait of human nature that new, positive relationships are energized by the power of untested enthusiasm. This is true for any relationship in the beginning stages—a euphoric young couple during their first few dates, or the budding relationship between the head of a search subcommittee and the lead candidate. The mutual zeal that can be generated between people when they are first getting to know each other can be quite seductive. The fantasy of the perfect partner invades all kinds of human endeavors, yet it usually ends in disillusionment because, typically, the first stage in an attractive relationship can only sustain itself as long as the facade of perfection can be maintained. Few relationships can make the transition from being dependent on naïve hopes and selective perceptions to being based on full disclosure and balanced assessment.

It is amazing to watch these dynamics apply to the selection of a new member of a company's senior team by its board. For example, boards, as well as the CEOs they hire, are at first inspired by the prospects of what they can accomplish together. Soon, however, the mutual charm and thrill tend to give way to dismay, miscommunication, and tension. Why does this happen? And, perhaps the even greater question: Why does it occur so frequently?

Some degree of these kinds of misgivings is inevitable because the initial eagerness to work together is usually based on a superficial understanding of (1) the strengths and weaknesses of the parties involved and (2) the potential dangers and opportunities the business situation itself might present. The greater the gap between early expectations and subsequently perceived reality, the more unhappy people are about their choice, and the more pessimistic they become about their prospects for achieving their desired outcome. When this pessimism exceeds one or more of the parties' tolerance for disappointment, "checking out" behavior appears. Checking out occurs when either party openly terminates the relationship (i.e., quits or is fired), or covertly withdraws his or her energy and investment in the other person(s) but continues to present a public display of cooperation until a more opportune time for overt action presents itself.

The frequency of this phenomenon in personal, social, and work-related situations suggests that it is a natural component of human interaction. The question is not "if," but "when" will tangible pessimism emerge from what was once considered incontestable positive potential? Will the alliance be terminated or will the issues be resolved and the relationship grow stronger as a result?

A point toward the end of the search process, when final candidates are being identified, marks the beginning of an important rejection or bonding ritual between candidates and the search committee. This ritual helps to cull those who would otherwise be suitable, and further strengthens the relationship with the final choice. A key element in this process is the sharing of information by all parties (e.g., past experiences, future aspirations, needs, desires, and fears). Despite the amount of dialogue that occurs, much is always left unsaid. During this part of the courting period, the board and the candidates operate under many unstated assumptions. It becomes clear only later, after final selection, that these same assumptions turn out to be the bases for both the early, unfounded fervor in the relationship and its subsequent unraveling.

You may recognize this scenario:

Leon was at the helm of a large organization for over 20 years. Most agreed that he had led it ably and it was time to step down. The board was convinced that the successful candidate to replace Leon needed to bring skills and leadership approaches that were vastly different from those he had brought to the table. The organization was facing new realities and was likely to face more in the future. Leon was an affable guy who sought consensus on most major decisions. By contrast, the CEO selected to succeed him was formal, decisive, autocratic, and an "all business" kind of executive.

Not surprisingly, the new CEO's staff, and eventually people below them, had a difficult time getting used to the new leader. His "by-the-book" ways of going about things and his tendency to make decisions without significant discussion among his staff were not insignificant changes. Still, the board remained convinced that the new CEO's tendency for making "snap" decisions was what was required in their turbulent market.

About a year after the new CEO took office, it became evident that the organization was suffering from more than morale problems and resistance to complying with the new CEO's leadership style. Due at least in part to the CEO's making major decisions without input from his staff, some of those decisions turned out to be wrong. The company began to lose market share, quality problems emerged, and new products were not ready for production as had been announced. These downturns worsened to the point that the board could no longer ignore them. Further, the board could no longer deny the possibility that they had become excessively enamored with the new CEO during the courting stage. This undoubtedly contributed to the blind spots they had about his style of operation. Those blind spots came home to roost after the new CEO was in place. By then, it was too late.

Two of these unstated suppositions are related to Nimbleness and the use of Human Due Diligence to achieve it. One is the result of a key omission and the other comes about from an important commission.

The first and biggest contributor to a relationship's inevitable fall from grace is the result of an omission. Seldom is there any direct dialogue between board members and the short list of candidates about the "how" of change. They may discuss in minute detail the candidate's history with other companies, what must be accomplished if the job is accepted, and even the strategies for achieving key goals. Little time or energy is usually invested, however, in examining the candidate's general views about how fundamental change occurs, much less the specific tactics he or she might use to implement particular change initiatives that are currently pending. Some questions that could be asked, but typically are not, include:

- Tell us about the most successful change initiative you personally helped orchestrate. What were the main contributors to that success?

- What about the biggest change disaster you oversaw? What happened and what did you learn? How have these lessons been incorporated into the way you would lead a major initiative today?

- From your experience, what are the key reasons why change efforts fail to meet their full potential?

- As CEO (or COO, CFO, CIO, etc.), what are the important messages you would convey to this organization about change in general, regarding issues like: How much transition can be expected? When will it slow down? What level of involvement will people have? How should they prepare themselves?

- Have you ever decided not to proceed with a major change you were interested in or were under pressure to execute, because you believed the people who would be affected were already overloaded with other change demands? Please explain.

- How do you let people know when you are really committed to a change initiative?

- How do you determine whether others are truly committed to projects you feel strongly about?

- When engaging important changes, do you require those responsible for execution to use structural approaches to implementation, such as diagnostic tools and proven guidelines to deal with the people issues, or is it okay for them to depend mostly on their instinct and intuition?

- What do you rely on to indicate when an organization can no longer absorb more change? What do you do if this point has been reached, yet it's imperative that new initiatives be successfully executed?

If these sorts of questions were pursued while the bonding ritual was still in progress, many of the surprising revelations that later occur between a new senior officer and his or her board could be averted.

The second inhibitor to realistic expectations is the superficial nature of the conversations that do occur about the human factors that impact implementation success. If discussions should take place about the people issues surrounding change, the discourse is usually filled with good intent and platitudes, but not much more. Neither aspirants for the senior positions nor board members typically offer much tangible evidence that they possess a "consciously competent" understanding of the change phenomenon or what practically can be done to increase the chances for a successful outcome. The parties involved may intuitively believe that the human side of change is important enough to discuss, but usually the board can't formulate penetrating questions about how the candidate would approach preparing the organization for change. (It's just as well: most candidates would only respond in vague generalities anyway.)

To summarize, two unstated assumptions play an important part in the uninformed optimism that plagues the selection of senior-level officers. The omission-based assumption is that the "how" of change is a tactical issue, if relevant at all, and need not be discussed as part of the selection process for a senior officer who will have strategic responsibilities. The commission-based assumption is that even if it is considered important enough to raise the issue of the people side of change, it is usually acceptable to keep the discussion lofty and shallow.

What all this means is that search committees can no longer behave as if their job is completed just because they locate one (or more) candidate who:

- Is capable of performing the basic job duties, and,
- Has a compatible chemistry with board members and other key senior officers.

Besides these two classic factors, six more should be added to the hiring criteria:

1. A keen understanding must encompass the reasons the board identified certain changes as imperative to the organization's future, as well as the precise consequences, for the organization and the candidate, if these efforts should fail.

2. A proper match must be made between the candidate's leadership orientation toward the execution of organizational change and the magnitude of change the organization is currently experiencing, as well as the change-related pressure the organization will confront in the next few years.

3. An ability for mastery-level competence in the dynamics of change must be demonstrated.

4. A sufficient demonstration of personal resilience must be present to suggest the candidate can sustain the change-related challenges that will arise while in office.

5. An ability must exist to understand and operationalize the knowledge and skills necessary to optimize the shelf life of the various organizational paradigms in place when the candidate is hired, as well as those that will be developed in the future.

6. A capacity must exist to create the proper working environment (i.e., the enterprise-wide envelope) that will allow people to be hired and managed in such a way as to maximize Nimbleness.

To fully assess a candidate's ability to address the responsibilities of a senior officer's role, all eight of the foregoing criteria should be examined.

The power of Human Due Diligence lies not only in its content (what it examines) but also in its discipline (the degree to which decision makers heed the findings). Boards gain little if all they do is interject into the selection process the concepts and rhetoric related to orchestrating the human side of change. They must then take the next step and closely assess each candidate as to his or her ability to substantially contribute to the organization's becoming a more nimble operation. To realize the full benefits, however, the board must have the strength, when making their final decision, to adhere to the implications of the information collected. If there is too large a gap between the candidate's change skills and the organization's transition demands, no employment offer should be made.

The real test, for any discipline, comes when application is not easy, quick, or politically popular. For example, the day of reckoning for board-level Human Due Diligence comes when there are tremendous pressures to fill a senior executive's position as soon as possible. Let's say one of the existing candidates might have proven to be a star performer if he were measured against only the first two of the board's eight selection criteria (basic job capabilities and compatible chemistry). The problem is: he lacks strength in several of the remaining six criteria.

Here, we have a well-seasoned veteran who is up-to-date on the industry, is familiar with the strengths and weaknesses of the company's existing products, has worked for the competition in previous years, and has some definite ideas about what could be done to improve market share and profitability. In addition, let's say the candidate has the kind of outgoing, charismatic personality that the board thinks could impress industry analysts, motivate the workforce, and scare competitors. Three of the remaining measures, however, come up grossly short. Somehow, this front runner has managed to participate in, and even help implement, many changes in other settings, but still lacks a basic understanding of how organizational change actually unfolds. There is no doubt that the candidate possesses some unconscious competence in this realm, but it is also apparent that the ability to build sophisticated architecture when introducing change strategies is not something this individual was schooled in or is even sensitive to. The candidate lacks the desired orientation to set the right organizational context for change, and therefore his capacity to establish the proper enterprise-wide envelope is in question as well. To make matters worse, the candidate seems to display a relatively low level of personal resilience. Specifically, his history shows signs of inflexibility when dealing with shifting demands, and there were situations in the past when he appeared to be overwhelmed rather than invigorated by ambiguity.

In less turbulent times, these issues might never be raised. Any candidate with credentials that support basic job competence and board chemistry would have been immediately retained. More than likely, issues related to the human aspects of implementation would not even have been incorporated into the regular interview agenda for managers, much less be part of the senior officer's formal selection process. More to the point, if such issues were covered in any of the discussions between the board and candidates, they would have had little bearing on the final outcome. But, in periods of escalating uncertainty, possessing basic job competence or even projecting an exciting personality is not enough.

Today, an organization is in jeopardy if the senior team does not relate to the board's change priorities and does not have the experience, instinct, knowledge, and techniques necessary to set the proper context for change. Moreover, the team must display mastery of the change process and of how to achieve the desired outcomes. Its members must demonstrate sufficient personal resilience and must possess the knowhow to optimize the shelf life of operational paradigms. If these attributes are lacking in the team, it is impossible to create a work environment throughout the rest of the organization that fosters a nimble culture and structure.

Change Leadership Styles

Leaders' Views about Change

One of the six additional factors that boards should use when evaluating candidates and positions deals with the leaders' views of change. It is essential to understand a senior officer's change leadership style because, to a great extent, it influences the decisions he or she will make regarding the effort and resources applied to the human aspects of important change. When major organizational transitions are attempted, it is ultimately the prerogative of the top executive or senior team to determine what approach, if any, will be applied in addressing the people side of implementation. Key questions are: How important are the attitudes and feelings people have toward a specific initiative? Under what circumstances would you require a thorough diagnosis of how employees will react to a particular project before any news of it is announced? These kinds of questions, when properly answered and interpreted, help us gain insights into leaders' perspective on the nature and significance of the human aspects of organizational change.

Because of the critical role senior officers play in the transition process, it is vital that their style for orchestrating the psycho-social-cultural facets of change be classified for easy identification. The need for this categorization goes far beyond any academic use it may have. Today's executives need to be aware of the various leadership styles available in order to decide which one (or combination) would be best to apply to their organization.

What is needed is a menu of styles that includes not only the approaches that have proven effective in the past, but new ones just now surfacing that can be viable in today's unstable market environments. In addition, board members involved in hiring or retention decisions regarding CEOs or other key senior positions need a means of articulating the leadership style that will best guide their organizations to prosperity. Finally, market analysts need a framework and nomenclature to be able to ask senior officers and their board the tough questions about how their organization will address the major transitions required to build financial growth.

During many years of interviewing, consulting with, and working alongside executives in senior positions, we noticed certain recurring themes related to transition management. It was eventually possible to isolate six distinct leadership styles related to change. These styles are referred to as:

1. Anti-change.
2. Rational.
3. Panacea.
4. Bolt-on.
5. Integrated.
6. Continuous.

Each represents a unique set of perceptions, attitudes, and behaviors regarding how organizational disruption should be addressed.

These distinctly different approaches have resulted from the advancing change demands that were placed on organizations in different periods of time. Each style gained acceptance because of the particular transition dynamics present at the time of its greatest popularity and effectiveness. Evaluating the appropriateness of when to use any of these six leadership styles should therefore be viewed as a contextual exercise; that is, each style should be critiqued against the intensity and nature of the interruptions an organization faces, not against each other or some hypothetical, philosophical preference.

It is unimportant which of these orientations comes closest to the latest academic theory. Only two factors really matter when determining which style is best for an organization. The success rate of the various approaches is most influenced by the *magnitude* of these changes and the *consequences* if the initiatives are poorly implemented.

The alternative styles presented in this chapter should be viewed in relation to the two basic types of change that leaders address within organizational settings:

1. First-order change is incremental in nature and reflects movement that is more or less already taking place.
2. Second-order change is nonlinear in nature and reflects movement that is fundamentally different from anything seen before within the existing framework.

The reference to first-order change being incremental in nature implies implementing an initiative that results in going faster or slower, or doing more or less within a relatively stable context. Second-order change requires shifting context; it represents a substantial variation in substance and form that discontinues whatever stability existed before.

First-order change is common to the first four leadership styles, which pursue change (if at all) by extrapolating from past experience. They represent perspectives where future success or failure can be fairly accurately predicted on the basis of historical successes and failures. Although there are gradations of intensity within first-order change, all such efforts are incremental in nature. They run from the lower end of a continuum, where minute adjustments are made, to the upper end, where enormous step increments occur. These extrapolative environments are very different from those that are discontinuous in nature.

At a certain level of turbulence, a work setting shifts from one where new challenges can be predicted and managed based on established trends, to one where it is impossible to infer the future by extending assumptions from the past. In discontinuous settings, second-order modifications of a more profound nature occur. This is where strategies that have been relied on in the past are likely to turn into failures. Here, an organization's historical strengths are likely to become its primary weaknesses (see Table 10.1).

Table 10.1   The Two Eras of Change Leadership

Eras	Types of Change	Leadership Styles
Contiguous Progression	First-order, incremental, extrapolative	Anti-change Rational Panacea Bolt-on
Perpetual Unrest	Second-order, discontinuous, paradigm-breaking (i.e., new game)	Integrated Continuous

As you will see, the Anti-change, Rational, Panacea, and Bolt-on leadership styles reflect history; the Integrated style speaks to today, and the Continuous style is a peek into our future. When the first four styles are aggregated, they form a continuum of what leaders have encountered in the past during the Contiguous Progression era of change. These styles exemplify the various approaches to change as it grew from a minor influence on organizational operations to one of the most significant factors in overall success.

The perpetual unrest era of change, just now emerging, is characterized not by step increments of advancements, but by geometric explosions in both the magnitude of disruptions being encountered and the price being paid for failing to execute key corporate initiatives. This second era represents a paradigm of unending transitions where quantum-leap changes occur frequently and are designed to completely break from the previous integrated order and structure of how things operated. It is from this state of flux that the Integrated and Continuous styles emerge. To stay parallel with the evolution of change, however, we will start with the archetypal Contiguous Progression era styles.

The Anti-change Leader

The premise of this first change leadership style is that senior executives have an obligation to provide their employees with the most composed, stress-free work environments possible. Such environments reflect lower first-order changes where disruptions are relatively inconsequential. These are the kinds of work settings where only minor incremental shifts occur. The Anti-change leader considers the ideal workplace one that has an undisturbed dynamic balance (i.e., stable, secure, and predictable). He or she doesn't believe all change is inherently bad; only those initiatives that really disrupt operations are thought to be unproductive and unnecessary.

Anti-change leaders operate from an underlying assumption that organizational life should be mostly a calm experience, and, therefore, significant modifications of any kind are undesirable. Dramatic deviations are to be evaded at all costs. When they are unavoidable, the implications are to be contained early so as to minimize their impact (see Figure 10.1). In these leaders' opinion, if people are doing their jobs, the few significant revisions required to keep a business going can be handled in small, incremental doses. They interpret their role as basically a protector of the status quo. Believing bureaucratic steadfastness will provide the safest harbor, they consistently give the same messages whenever their organization

Leader's Basic View

We need to fortify ourselves against organizational change. When it is unavoidable, it should be narrow in scope, with as little impact as possible.

Figure 10.1 The anti-change leader.

confronts the unexpected: "Stay the course." "Keep the adjustments small." "No need to change things in any major way."

Anti-change executives try to accomplish tranquillity by applying the thermostat method. Once an organization has frozen itself into a fixed way of operating, it becomes easily threatened by the friction or heat generated if any significant modifications are introduced. These leaders set the organization's fluctuation thermostats at the lowest level possible. This makes the entire operation extremely sensitive to even the slightest signs of increases in temperature (i.e., change). The bureaucratic sensors detect any variation above the narrow band of transition tolerance that has been established. Anti-change leaders make sure that with a rise of more than a few degrees comes a blast of bitter-cold air that people will not soon forget. When the heat alarm triggers, action is swift. Freon starts flowing, fans begin to blow, and the organization's air ducts are filled with a frigid signal: "Cool it." Like a heat-seeking missile filled with liquid oxygen rather than explosives, the source of the temperature irregularity is located, locked on, and engaged in order that it can be refrozen back to the status quo as soon as possible.

These leaders usually act quickly in order to protect "the way things are," and when this occurs, malice is seldom involved. For Anti-change leaders, it's just a matter of survival. They can't conceive of operating in any way other than following the established routine. They fear any significant change could lead to a fundamental shift from what people are accustomed to, a loss of predictability and control, and/or a general meltdown.

To protect the organization from an unwanted thaw, they use the thermostat approach as an effective defense mechanism to keep things in a fixed, frozen state. In doing so, they successfully protect the dynamic balance of the status quo. Because these leaders consider even modest change efforts to be sources of potentially threatening warmth, they react to any initiative that might produce a departure from established procedures as if someone had turned on a blowtorch.

Anti-change leaders have no interest in promoting agility or building a nimble capability; therefore, there is no need to pursue Human Due Diligence. Their resources are devoted to minimizing significant modifications, not facilitating their execution. They would not seek out or be responsive to suggestions about how people and the organization could be better prepared to absorb change.

As shown in Table 10.2, the principal strengths of their approach are: it establishes a mechanism to protect against unwanted vacillation, and it

Table 10.2   The Anti-change Leader's Basic View

Distinguishing Characteristics
Type of change encountered: Lower first-order, minor incremental.
Magnitude of change encountered: Inconsequential.
Cost for implementation failure: Slight.
Interest in a nimble work environment: None.
Application of Human Due Diligence: N/A.
Underlying assumption: Life should be mostly calm. Therefore, significant fluctuations are unnecessary and undesirable.
Goal: Protect status quo.
Comfort is found in: Believing bureaucratic steadfastness will provide a safe harbor in a turbulent world.
Primary message to organization: "Don't change."
Idealized organization: Stable, secure, predictable, and controlled.
Response to change-related people problems: Slow, rigid, and considered uncalled-for.
Management style metaphor: Thermostat.
Principal strength: Provides people with stability and predictability about tasks and roles, and helps organizations reap benefits from previous sound decisions.
Principal weakness: Not suited for highly competitive, volatile markets.

helps reap the benefits from previous strategic decisions that need more time in order to generate their maximum return. It also provides employees with a sense of continuity and equilibrium about their task and roles, even when outside forces may be exerting extreme pressure to change. Remember, a leader who utilizes the Anti-change approach may be precisely what an organization needs if it is encountering only a modest magnitude of change and the cost of implementation failure is slight.

The principal weakness of this style is that it does not position the organization and its people to function in highly competitive and volatile markets. Environments where ambiguity, uncertainty, and unplanned demands are common tend to generate a greater need for Nimbleness than an Anti-change leader can promote.

The Rational Leader

Operations confronting a step-up in change demands, compared to those faced by Anti-change leaders, are best served if their senior officers demonstrate a bias for a rational approach to change. Rational leaders operate in environments where first-order change is prevalent and the incremental movement that does occur is moderate. They seldom initiate major modifications within their organization, but they do occasionally see the need to modestly react to shifting market conditions. These leaders understand that major transitions are, at times, unavoidable; they believe that some upheaval can even be healthy for an organization. They can see the need for some change, but they believe it should always be executed in a logical and linear manner. They show little patience for what they view as the melodrama that people often fall prey to during the execution of important transitions.

These rationally oriented executives tend to see life as mostly a binary experience: things are either good or bad, right or wrong, on track or off. Attached to this general view of life is their general approach to organizational change—something to be implemented in the most sequential and unemotional fashion that is possible. They are confident that the strength of logic will always prevail over frail emotions. They, therefore, believe it is unnecessary and unprofessional to permit sound business decisions to be hindered by feelings or by what people think about the implications. "We can't allow the whiners and complainers of the world to impede necessary progress." (See Figure 10.2.)

The inanimate computer is a useful metaphor for the way Rational leaders engage change. Level-headed logic and sober, no-nonsense thinking

Leader's Basic View

Figure 10.2 The rational leader.

dominate their view of transition management. They are focused purely on the tangible aspects of the task, and they do not allow sentimentality or passion to cloud the issues. Because the human side of change is viewed as unimportant, these leaders would disapprove of Nimbleness as a desirable organizational quality and would see Human Due Diligence as an unnecessary expenditure of time and money.

For Rational leaders, when the inevitable intermittent changes do occur, implementation should be synonymous with announcement. As far as they are concerned, the task of executing a change is all but completed once a decision is made and a well-crafted announcement has been developed and distributed. If any other implementation planning is attempted, it tends to be focused on one or more of the three levers they tend to use to engage the bureaucratic machinery: (1) reason, (2) communication, and (3) project management.

Reason is often considered by Rational leaders to be the most potent of the levers. From this kind of leadership perspective, logic dictates that intelligent, reasonable employees will support any modifications, even those that might be unpleasant, once the rationale for the decision has been explained. Rational leaders, therefore, put great stock in their ability to proclaim to the workforce a powerful, carefully researched, thoroughly analyzed, and well-documented case for realignment.

Rational leaders often believe the only event that could hinder the compelling logic of their change decision would be if the logic had not been properly conveyed. These executives operate on the basis that, most of the time, a well-conceived communication strategy, including detailed memos and meticulous speeches, is all that is needed to ensure that associates will comprehend and support an impending change.

For these leaders, the only possible remaining barrier to full employee commitment toward a new initiative could be the lack of a set procedure for them to follow during implementation. The result is a carefully constructed project management process. Their reliance on project management is a natural fit because it is an engineering-based approach comprised of PERT charts, time lines, and status reports. It provides precisely the kind of logical reference points needed for someone with a bias toward seeing life as a reason-centered flow of sequential events.

As shown in Table 10.3, the principal strength of this view is that it introduces objectivity into the often emotion-laden change process. Without some degree of emotional distance from the pain and anxiety felt by

Table 10.3   The Rational Leader's Basic View

Distinguishing Characteristics
Type of change encountered: Mid first-order, moderate incremental.
Magnitude of change encountered: Modest.
Cost for implementation failure: Noteworthy.
Interest in a nimble work environment: Low.
Application of Human Due Diligence: Believe it is unnecessary.
Underlying assumption: Life is a binary experience. When change is required, it can be accomplished in a rational, linear manner.
Goals: React to external shifts in the market while minimizing melodrama and avoiding mistakes.
Comfort is found in: Believing the strength of logic will prevail over the frailty of emotions.
Primary message to organization: "We can't allow the whiners and complainers of the world to impede necessary progress."
Idealized organization: Mostly stable, but when a change is called for, it is implemented in an unemotional and sequential fashion.
Response to change-related people problems: Cerebral and judicious; problems considered nonessential.
Management style metaphor: Computer.
Principal strength: Introduces logic and objectivity into the often emotionally laden change process.
Principal weakness: Not suited for complex environments where participation and commitment are necessary for change to succeed.

the people struggling through the transition, leaders can lose sight of the bottom-line responsibility they have to shareholders and other key constituencies. Tough decisions have to be made, and it won't serve anyone's purpose if a leader is so sensitive to the discomfort people are experiencing that he or she can't sustain the actions necessary for success.

The major weakness of this style is exposed when an organization faces a higher magnitude of change than usual—one that calls for more sophisticated responses than are traditionally necessary. Rational leaders are not well-suited for complex environments where participation and commitment are necessary for change to succeed. Though they acknowledge that periodic major transitions are a natural part of organizational life, they lack an appreciation for the psycho-social-cultural intricacies. For example, they are usually unprepared for the levels of emotional responses people display when facing increasing unpredictability. They don't know how to deal with people who express strong feelings of ambivalence, skepticism, and hesitancy.

One of the main problems these leaders face is they tend to operate as though logical thought and subjective emotions were separate and mutually exclusive components of the human organism. When confronted with rapidly shifting circumstances, Rational leaders find themselves doing battle against market turbulence, but armed only with concepts and tactics formulated over 300 years ago. Forged by the work of Galileo, René Descartes, and Isaac Newton, the rationalist template—mind and matter are separate and machinelike in operation—abides to this day.

The potency of that template is formidable, as is evidenced by the logic-bound, linear view held by Rational leaders. The weakness of this perspective emerges when Rational leaders are easily overwhelmed by the realization that they find themselves in a world too complex for black-and-white logic alone. Their dilemma is that the logical, empirical, predictable world described by Galileo, Descartes, and Newton has become inconsistent with the irrational, subjective, and seemingly random emotional reactions employees tend to display when their organizations face dramatic change. It has become common for nonquantifiable employee feelings to block the execution of technologically sound, badly needed initiatives. Here, Rational leaders find individuals not behaving in the lock-step, mechanistic fashion called for in their carefully laid plans. Entire organizations fail to respond to the laws that once governed executive use of power.

The Rational perspective is a viable option if the magnitude of change is moderate and the consequences of failing to implement key initiatives is no more than noteworthy. If, however, transition demands and risks become great, the Rational outlook can jeopardize an organization's future.

The Panacea Leader

Panacea leaders face a degree of upheaval that is well beyond anything their Anti-change or Rational counterparts have ever seen. Like the Rational leaders, they are hesitant to initiate any more change than is required by market pressure, yet they believe this pressure has increased significantly in recent years. They view the market they compete in as making more demands for major change more often than ever. When the pace of change becomes this conspicuous, it's difficult to maintain a view of the process as being purely logical. There are simply too many emotionally based issues to ignore the nonlinear aspects of implementation.

Because of the amplified intensity of change bombarding their organizations, Panacea leaders reconcile themselves to the fact that unforeseen, disconcerting transitions have become an inevitable part of their organization's life (see Figure 10.3). They also acknowledge that the cost of failing to properly implement certain of these initiatives can be forbiddingly high. In addition, Panacea leaders have learned that the human aspects of implementing key projects can be tricky, and if not handled appropriately, can endanger the desired outcomes.

As a result, these senior officers face more pressure to change than ever before; yet, employees seem to grow bolder and more skilled at blocking initiatives they don't understand or don't feel comfortable pursuing. It has become readily apparent to this kind of leader that the existence of commitment to or resistance against new mandates is a key factor in the success of his or her business.

For these leaders, the convergence of more pressure to change and greater vulnerability during implementation has created a compelling case for a different approach to managing transitions. Panacea leaders do not want to follow in the Anti-change or Rational leaders' footsteps. Rather

Leader's Basic View

Change is inevitable and so are the related people problems, but they can be dealt with easily.

CHANGE

Figure 10.3   The panacea leader.

than avoiding transitions or looking for the next two decimal points of accuracy to deal with employee resistance, leaders adhering to the Panacea approach choose to fight fire with fire; emotionally based problems should be dealt with by applying emotionally based approaches and techniques.

For example, it is their contention that negative emotions about change can and should be either prevented or converted into positive feelings. They place a high premium on a happy workforce. They expect dramatic change to be implemented with little, if any, of the forlorn, despondent, or recalcitrant behavior they know can derail a project. In addition, their self-image is that of a benevolent, caring leader who is more attentive to people's feelings than their Anti-change or Rational counterparts. Panacea leaders are often pejorative about these other styles of change leadership, believing them too insensitive to the emotional aspects of work. In a similar fashion, Panacea leaders tend to judge themselves harshly if people start to display any signs of low spirits during change. They often take on a protective, if not parental, attitude toward employees, believing it their job to ensure that their workers experience no discomfort.

Panacea leaders believe major changes are inevitable, as are the related people problems that accompany the inherent confusion and anxiety that seem to always occur. They also think, however, that these kinds of problems can be anticipated and circumvented by doing whatever is necessary to put smiles on everyone's faces. If employees should become disheartened, these leaders believe there is always something that can be done to restore an upbeat, cheerful work setting.

They see the people side of change as challenging, but fairly easy to address as long as anything related to temperament and feelings can be passed along to someone who has specialized training in that area. These leaders are usually not sure what to do themselves, but they are confident that by delegating such problems to someone in the Human Resources department or to an outside consultant, the issues can be resolved quickly and effectively.

On the plus side, Panacea leaders are the first of the leadership styles to show some concern about the human side of change and to seek any kind of assistance to address these issues. On the negative side, they tend to avoid direct involvement with the human aspects of implementations, and the experts they gravitate to aren't always adequately prepared for the task. For example, today's Panacea leaders are the main source of employment for consultants and trainers who still utilize the kind of touchy-feely techniques that were popular in the late 1960s and early 1970s. Actual encounter groups and sensitivity training sessions are not used very often anymore, but the same theme—"Let employees vent their feelings and they will feel better"—provides much of what these practitioners continue to promote even today. Panacea leaders tend to believe that their resistance problem will disappear if they administer a few employee attitude surveys, conduct some "How to Be Happy while We Disrupt Your Life" seminars, and provide one-on-one handholding sessions for those who need special attention.

Like dropping soiled garments off at a dry cleaner shop, Panacea leaders expect others to clean up the people problems their change projects generate. Their own involvement consists mainly of paying the bill. They find comfort in believing that complex human reactions to organizational change can be addressed with simple, quick, and inexpensive solutions.

A Panacea leader is looking for a human relations specialist with a sign over his or her office door: "One-Hour Change Martinizing—People predicaments in by 7:00 are resolved, on hangers, and ready to go by 5:00." The underlying assumption is that most people-related change difficulties can be addressed if they are delegated to the right specialist, who, in turn, selects the right video to show and who gives people the correct laminated card to display on their desk.

As shown in Table 10.4, the Panacea approach marks a significant departure from the Anti-change and/or Rational stance. The principal strength of the Panacea approach to change is the value demonstrated for the human aspects of implementing key initiatives. As I said earlier, this style of engaging transition is the first of the six to reflect a significant concern for the impact of important undertakings on people.

The central weakness of this change leadership style, however, is the superficiality of its understanding of the human issues and, consequently, the naïve solutions it employs. It's a plus that Panacea executives have the interest they do in the people side of change and that they make an honest effort to attend to this concern by taking action. The problem is that because they do not grasp the depth of what they are dealing with and the complexity of the dynamics involved, these leaders stay much too disengaged from the process. For example, because of the distance they keep, they will often unknowingly authorize shallow activities that have no meaningful impact. Thinking their role is limited to selecting the right expert, they tend to engage the services of internal or external professionals who either lack an appreciation for the real scope of the task at hand, or who understand what is called for but are unwilling to confront the leader with the true actions necessary to address the issues properly. In either case, management and employees are ultimately left unprepared to deal adequately with the challenge of absorbing badly needed change.

Table 10.4   The Panacea Leader's Basic View

Distinguishing Characteristics
Type of change encountered: Mid first-order, prominent incremental.
Magnitude of change encountered: Strong.
Cost for implementation failure: Significant.
Interest in a nimble work environment: Limited.
Application of Human Due Diligence: Believes employee attitude surveys are sufficient.
Underlying assumption: Any change-related problem can be handled if you show the right video, give people laminated cards to put on their desks as reminders, and give them cool T-shirts to signify they were properly dipped in the correct training "solution."
Goal: React to external shifts in the market while keeping people happy.
Comfort is found in: Believing complex human reactions to organizational change can be addressed with simple, quick, inexpensive solutions.
Primary message to organization: "Human Resources will handle any people concerns that arise."
Idealized organization: Regularly faces disruptive change, but resistance and ambiguity problems are handled without much difficulty.
Response to change-related people problems: Superficial, cursory, emotional, and driven by the Human Resources Department.
Management style metaphor: Dry cleaner shop.
Principal strength: Demonstrates value for attending to the human dynamics of change.
Principal weakness: Employees left unprepared for the human side of major change; management and Human Resources erode their own credibility.

The Bolt-on Leader

The Bolt-on leader works in an environment that reflects the upper end of first-order change. Movement there can be enormous but is still incremental. This leader orchestrates many complex changes in an extremely unstable atmosphere, yet most initiatives remain extrapolations from past experience. As markets turn more complex and begin to shift more often, leaders are forced to not only react to new pressures, but anticipate these demands and engage change more proactively than ever before. When the number of new requirements facing an organization and the depth of the uncertainty faced on a daily basis reach disconcerting proportions, employees start to feel overwhelmed by the adjustment demands being placed on them. Critically important changes begin to produce less-than-expected results, and far too many initiatives are stopped dead in their tracks. When these developments occur, leaders are usually forced to broaden their view of what it means to implement something new.

As the scope of change grows more dramatic, it becomes apparent that success calls for more than good intentions and money spent on training and T-shirts. Simple answers are no longer enough to guide employees through their struggle with the lost predictability and control. The dynamic balance they desire becomes less and less accessible, and with this loss comes the debilitating effects of deep future shock.

As the price for failed change projects reaches critical mass, leaders begin to acknowledge that orchestrating the people side of transitions may require more than their benevolence and peripheral attention. They come to realize that the time and resources necessary to address the human aspects of implementation are significant, and necessary, if they are to achieve their desired outcomes. They start openly declaring (1) an increased value for building a nimble work setting and (2) the importance they place on taking a more professional approach to the psychological issues that arise when change is introduced. Senior officers who come to these conclusions but are uneducated as to what they should do, or who know what to do but refuse to pay the full price for resolution of these issues, are called "Bolt-on" leaders.

"I'M A BELIEVER"

Bolt-on leaders typically think of themselves as sensitive to human issues, and they often boast of their considerable interest in creating the Nimbleness to absorb major change. They honestly believe in and talk openly about the value they place on the people side of change. To act on this, it is common for them to search out experts who can offer advice and conduct training programs for their people. They take pride in engaging these change-management specialists to examine the people problems as they arise, and to provide the necessary educational programs that will help their employees be more knowledgeable about and feel better during the transition process.

As a result of these kinds of activities, rank-and-file employees are usually taught how to recognize and deal with the natural reactions they will experience when significant shifts in their work routine occur. Mid-level managers and first-line supervisors attend sessions to learn about the human dynamics aroused when key change projects are introduced, to recognize what kind of problems typically occur during implementation, and to determine what actions can be taken to increase the chances of success. Senior officers may even attend briefings to gain a broader view of the challenge of managing the human aspects of change. Sometimes thousands of people at all levels of an organization are exposed to various change management briefings or training programs intended to generate an environment more conducive to successful implementation than would otherwise have been possible.

Many of these kinds of activities have proven to be truly helpful and have resulted in an increased appreciation for the more emotional features of the change process. The impact of this kind of work has been so positive that if it weren't for the fact that the magnitude of change and the consequences of poor implementation have continued to advance at unprecedented rates, victory could have been declared long ago in the battle against the dysfunctional aspects of deep future shock. The trouble is: the pace of change has accelerated. Its current rate exceeds that of educational efforts to increase people's capacity to absorb what is happening to them. Given the advancing complexity in the marketplace, the moderate increases in knowledge and skills that are produced by seminars and workshops alone just aren't enough by themselves.

Without question, the Bolt-on mentality represents an important leap forward from the Anti-change, Rational, and Panacea approaches. The Bolt-on leader offers more genuine interest and concern about how people will be affected by important initiatives and how they can be helped to better absorb the changes they must face. The problem is these leaders think change readiness can be secured by simply exposing people at a conceptual level to transition management information and techniques when, in fact, a much more in-depth, practical level of understanding and intervention is required.

FLAWED THINKING

The Bolt-on approach is based on a belief that an organization's inability to execute important initiatives is primarily due to knowledge deficits. The Bolt-on leader thinks it is his or her responsibility to provide employees with education that addresses what they don't understand about managing and absorbing change. Given this task, it seems obvious to them that change management specialists would conduct the seminars. What better information to disseminate than lessons learned from years of experience with the triumphant, as well as the unsuccessful efforts at introducing important new organizational endeavors? And who better to conduct these training programs than change-management practitioners themselves?

There are two flaws to this line of thinking, and ultimately they hinder Bolt-on leaders from accomplishing what they intend. First, although they're right to invest in educating their employees about change, training alone is a necessary but insufficient requirement for new initiatives to achieve their stated results. The hoped-for return on their educational investment cannot be measured by attendance reports or scores reflecting retention rates of the lessons taught. Direct, on-the-job application of the information, tools, and techniques people have been exposed to is the only meaningful gauge of the value received once education has been provided.

This may appear to be so unquestionably obvious that it need not be mentioned, but my experience has been just the opposite. Each year, within many large organizations, millions of dollars and thousands of hours are spent exposing people to the latest change management seminars. No self-respecting training director would fail to have at least one such offering in this year's educational catalog, and any up-and-coming fast-tracking executive-to-be who wants to demonstrate proper respect for the softer side of management will attend. The irony is that the resources are invested to expose people to the knowledge and skills they need to be successful during change, but then there are typically no requirements for people to practice what they learn.

In these seminars, change management concepts and techniques are displayed, exhibited, discussed, and role-played in the classroom, but often, following the session, little else is done to promote application. It is expected and hoped that the training will be so clearly relevant to the participants' experience with change, that the elapsed time between classroom exposure and on-the-job utilization will be minimal. This, of course, assumes that all attendees learn what was intended and are motivated to apply what they studied.

The typical Bolt-on leader cares enough about the impact employees could have on the success of important initiatives to train them, but not enough to track the utilization of what they learn. Without adequate tracking measures, most leaders are reluctant to establish positive or negative consequences that could be used to encourage application of what was taught. Being interested enough in something to invest in the training programs, without the metrics and incentive mechanisms to drive day-to-day practice of the subject's content, produces little more than short-term intrigue on the part of those being trained.

This then raises the second flaw in Bolt-on logic. These leaders' lack of attention to application may appear to contradict earlier statements about their attentiveness to the human side of change. My previous reference to this kind of leader's concern and interest in the human components of implementation can now be refined to reflect a more accurate portrait. Bolt-on leaders can best be described as curious, but usually not serious about, the human side of change. They are willing to give credence to and, at times, even become engrossed in how employees affect the execution of crucial initiatives. Most are eager to give consideration to these issues but are far from committed to their resolution. For example, their unwillingness or inability to establish monitoring systems to track the application of change management concepts and techniques, after exposing employees to them in seminars, is but one example of a much bigger problem. The real issue here is that the interest and concern the Bolt-on senior officer has for the people issues during change are limited by convenience. This is a leader prepared to do "whatever is necessary" to address the human issues of change as long as it can be done without too much trouble and expense.

THE BOLT-ON BIASES

A typical statement reflecting Bolt-on mentality is:

> I believe in *attaching* change management concepts and techniques to our key projects whenever it is a feasible *option,* particularly *after* resistance starts to build. I really do think it is a *good idea.*

This person is revealing a bias that the human side of change is an option that may or may not be attached to a project. If it is included, it will be only after some pesky people problems have surfaced, and only if it is not too time-consuming and doesn't tax the rollout budget too much. The italicized words in the statement are clues to the Bolt-on leader's true level of enthusiasm for application.

Attaching   To affix something to the transition process implies that there is something missing, or a separation is in need of a bridge. Although the emotional and cultural dynamics of organizational change are intricately embedded into the basic fiber of the transition process, the Bolt-on leader thinks he or she has a choice about whether to concede the presence and importance of both. It is an artificial separation this leader is contemplating closing. It's no different from deciding whether to address the psychological impact divorce has on children. The fact that children are affected is indisputable. The only questions are: In what ways and to what extent?

Acknowledging or avoiding reality is immaterial to its existence and effect on people. Recognizing or ignoring the critically important role played by the human factors of change in no way diminishes their existence or impact. What is assured is that if these issues are identified and dealt with appropriately, the prognosis for success is increased. If they are shunned, the forecast usually worsens.

Option   At the heart of Bolt-on leadership is the view that, as critical as the human side of change is to the success of key initiatives, it may or may not be adequately addressed based on the time, energy, and other resources available at the time. Think about the logic being used here. It is no different from declaring we don't have time to fix a car's worn-out electrical system, so we'll focus on the transmission instead; or, we don't have enough capital to buy the technology needed to compete in the marketplace, but we can reorganize so that the customer complaints that are pouring in can be better managed. Triple bypass surgery is an impressive medical miracle in its own right, but it serves little purpose if the physician lacks the time, skill, or inclination to also treat the lungs' filling up with fluid.

The emotionally messy, hard-to-deal-with human side of change is no less vital than the more clearly defined, tangible elements that comprise the logical side of important transitions. They are both interdependent parts of a whole; one part cannot be rehabilitated or saved without a corresponding effort for the other. Yet, the Bolt-on leader sees the people-management issues as discretionary options that may be applied, if convenience allows.

This attitude is reflected in many different ways. One symptom of the problem is that administering change management techniques is often the result of chance, not discipline. Here is a common Bolt-on voicemail message:

> Mary, it's Joe. I'm so glad I saw you today in the hall. We are facing some re-luctance from a few mid-level managers. They don't seem to want to support the new cost-control procedures. Seeing you today made me remember the briefing you gave a few months ago on the importance of building a cascad-ing network of sustaining sponsors for a project like this. We must be doing something wrong because our mid-level ranks are full of those "black holes" you talked about. Please give me a call. I think we need some change man-agement help.

In such situations, bringing skill and experience to the process of or-chestrating the human side of change is at the mercy of a chance meeting in the hallway. Change management might be applied to this project, *if* Joe and Mary should see each other as they pass in a busy hallway, *if* they are not at odds with each other over some turf battle and won't talk, *if* Joe can remember what Mary presented several months ago at the briefing, *if* he can see that her expertise might apply to his circumstance, *if* she is allowed to provide assistance in his part of the organization. With Bolt-on leadership, the key determinants for using change management concepts and techniques are often serendipity, friendliness, and politics—not the most comforting foundation, if what is at stake is the execution of a critically important change project.

When the stakes are high, the critical elements that influence the outcome of change success should not be left to chance. See how ridiculous the following version of the same scenario sounds when we replace change management with something that is more commonly recognized as essential to success:

> Mary, it's Joe. I'm so glad I saw you today in the hall. We are facing some reluctance from a few picky Wall Street analysts I'm dealing with. They are not responding well to the new acquisition we announced. Seeing you today made me remember the briefing you gave a few months ago on the importance of doing sound financial due diligence in order to build a strong case for action that analysts would understand. We must be doing something wrong because they seemed unimpressed when I met with them last week and told them how confident we were that this deal was good for the shareholders. One of them told me after the meeting that having a "good vibe" about the other company and a "gut feeling" it would all work out was not enough for them. Please give me a call. I think we need some guidance about how to develop the financial part of this deal for the analyst.

The only difference that makes the first vignette plausible and the second one inconceivable is the universal acceptance of the importance of financial due diligence when pursuing an acquisition. Those who subscribe to the Bolt-on style fail to see the necessity of thoroughly investigating the human issues associated with pursuing major organizational change. Like a sunroof that could be added to a new car but does not really affect the vehicle's performance, it is viewed as an option that may or may not be applied to important projects.

After   For Bolt-on leaders, implementing the human side of change is seen as no different from any of the other "by-the-way" afterthoughts passed on from management to be carried out by someone down the line. Dialogue between Bolt-on leaders and change management specialists, for example, often sounds like this:

> By the way, as you know, we recently announced some new methods for improving our operations. For some reason, however, the rollout is not going as well as we expected. It's hard to understand since these changes will generate additional profit, delight our customers, and entice the analyst. Regardless of why people are resisting, these are important changes and they must

succeed. Could you drop by one afternoon to meet with the troublemakers and do some of that change management stuff to get things back on track?

This all-too-common view reflects a mentality that considers managing change only after key decisions have been made and problems have surfaced. Bolt-on mentality means that the human issues are usually not thought of or acted on until well into the implementation process.

In the world of the Bolt-on leader, applying change management techniques to a project becomes feasible only after the reaction people are having has generated such a complicated mess that the project is clearly at risk. Change management techniques are occasionally applied in a preventive manner, but more often than not they are engaged when such problems have already surfaced and the only option left is damage control—or worse, an autopsy.

A classic Bolt-on leader's comment:

> Monday is the official rollout for phase three of the reengineering project. This is where we actually start putting into place all the work these design teams have been doing. Since we have already heard a lot of grumbling, maybe we should give the change management group an hour at the next executive staff meeting to present any ideas they have about making this go smoothly. There may even be a couple of areas where we want them to go in and hold some hands.

For leaders who embrace this kind of approach to critical transitions, change management is a reactive tool that can be pulled out and used whenever trouble surfaces. It is not considered a preventive measure. It's seen as an expense, not an investment. Even after psycho-social-cultural difficulties have surfaced and are considered threatening to a project's success, change management is usually bolted on only if it can be done in a manner that is not too draining on people's time and not too expensive.

Good Ideas   These are ideas we are interested in and often initiate but seldom complete. Diets and New Year's resolutions exemplify how we relate to good ideas. They are worth attending to as long as they are easy, fast, and cheap. Good ideas are appealing until they incur more than a modicum of expense; then they are usually abandoned in favor of the next inexpensive illusion. Because they are "easy come, easy go," their inclusion is always on a tentative basis. To the Bolt-on leader, change management is a good-idea option that may or may not be affixed to an initiative, based on whether people problems have already reached critical mass.

When the Bolt-on leader does use change management techniques, it is usually only after people problems have already surfaced, implementation success is threatened, and the time and money involved in dealing with the difficulties are determined not to be too burdensome. It is an afterthought that is not considered necessary until well into the change process. Only when addressing the human side of change becomes a business imperative does an organization have any chance of developing a nimble organization.

WHAT'S CONSIDERED IMPORTANT

Leaders, regardless of their style, tend to raise certain issues whenever informal suggestions or formal proposals involving change are submitted for their consideration. These issues revolve around what I refer to as the "what, why, and whether" questions:

- What is to change—do we have a clear picture of the final outcome?
- Why should it be pursued—do the benefits or profits that will be created by this change outweigh the risks and costs?
- Whether the tangibles necessary are available—do we have or can we attain the resources (e.g., capital, technology, and people) necessary to carry out the initiative?

Each leadership style has its respective position regarding these questions. The Anti-change leader would see no purpose in pursuing any of these questions. The Rational leader, on the other hand, finds "what, why, and whether" questions extremely relevant. They are the kind of logical concerns one would expect in a binary world. The Panacea leader also focuses on these three questions, but would pose an additional, tactical question to any human resources specialist at hand: "Will you please make sure everyone remains comfortable and happy as they transition to the new way of operating?"

It was not until Bolt-on thinking became prevalent that leaders began to take on any real responsibility for a fourth query—the "how" question,

Leader's Basic View

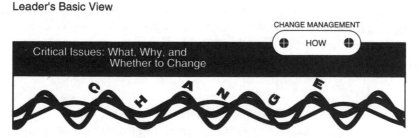

Figure 10.4   The bolt-on leader.

which addresses the manner in which the human side of change is to be guided. Even so, Bolt-on leadership treats the "how" of change as an optional luxury that only sometimes gets addressed if the constraints for doing so are not too great (see Figure 10.4).

A Bolt-on mentality is characterized by leaders' believing that the "what, why, and whether" aspects of change are the only truly critical issues senior officers need address. They believe the question of "how" people and their

Table 10.5   The Bolt-on Leader's Basic View

Distinguishing Characteristics
Type of change encountered: High first-order, formidable incremental.
Magnitude of change encountered: Shocking.
Cost for implementation failure: Considerable.
Interest in a nimble work environment: Significant.
Application of Human Due Diligence: Belief that only a cursory review of people issues is necessary.
Underlying assumption: Change management is an option that may be attached to a project, if after getting into trouble you remember it, and the time and money involved are not too burdensome.
Goal: Engage in reactive and proactive change while taking care of as many people issues as feasible, given the constraints.
Comfort is found in: Believing change-management "S.W.A.T. teams" can be effectively deployed after resistance becomes a problem.
Primary message to organization: "Try to take care of the human side of change whenever you have the time and resources to do so."
Idealized organization: Can recover from any implementation problems by calling on change-management professionals.
Response to change-related people problems: Tentative, discretionary, piece-meal, and delegated to change-management specialists.
Management style metaphor: Optional feature that may be added to a new car.
Principal strength: Brings together reasoning from the Rational change approach and attention to the human dynamics from the Panacea approach to form a more effective change-management framework.
Principal weakness: Usually produces too little value too late to have significant impact on change projects.

emotions are going to be managed during the transition is worthy of attention, but they see it as more of a tactical issue. They feel it isn't necessary for them to be overly concerned with the "how" part of implementation, other than to be sure some specialist is handling it. Their prevailing attitude is that once they assign implementation planning to the Human Resources department or a change management specialist, they have completed their portion of the task.

As shown in Table 10.5, the principal strength of Bolt-on leadership is the desire to recognize and address the human side of implementation as a legitimate component of the architecture of change. Bolt-on leaders attempt to combine the reasoning from the Rational approach and the attention paid to the people dynamics from the Panacea approach to form a parallel change-management framework. To achieve this parity, they place an emphasis on educating and sensitizing the workforce to the emotional aspects of transitions. The basic shortfalls for this style, however, are its discretionary, cursory treatment of a very complex set of issues and the piecemeal, reactionary way it is applied. Generally speaking, what results is a genuine effort to address the "how" of change, but it is done in such a way that it produces too little value, too late to have a significant, positive impact on the outcome of most projects.

The Integrated Leader

As is true for each of the leadership styles, the Integrated leader was forged out of necessity. Orchestrating change poses a new and formidable challenge when the extent of turmoil and uncertainty confronting an organization reaches breathtaking proportions and the cost for poorly executing its initiatives attains dramatic dimensions.

When the magnitude of change increases significantly beyond that faced by the Bolt-on leader, second-order, discontinuous movement starts to occur. This, of course, makes managing the human side of change more difficult and more important than ever. To address this added pressure, the logical/technical aspects of project management must be combined with the emotional aspects of people management. Only when this union is properly formed can an organization be capable of generating the Nimbleness needed to successfully implement its initiatives and keep pace with expanding market demands.

Under such pressurized conditions, Nimbleness not only becomes a business necessity, it must be driven by senior officers, not Human Resources professionals. Leaders who have reached this conclusion know the importance of embedding Human Due Diligence into the day-to-day operation of their organization. This view reflects the more prominent value they place on the "how" of change as compared to their Anti-change, Rational, Panacea, or Bolt-on counterparts. For Integrated leaders, how change is executed takes center stage, putting it on an equal plane with the "what, why, and whether" aspects (see Figure 10.5). The responsibility for the people issues during change shifts from the Human Resources department to the executive suite.

Leaders who place the people aspects of implementation on the same level as these other components are usually veterans from hard-fought battles where important lessons were learned or reinforced about the role of emotions and attitudes. Experience taught them that the what, why, and whether ingredients of change are necessary but insufficient elements for achieving results in a fast-moving world. For the Integrated leader, the "how" of change is equally important and must be inlaid into all elements of the change process.

The cornerstone of the Integrated style of change leadership is the respect and prominence placed on the psycho-social-cultural issues associated with accomplishing important initiatives. Integrated leaders move beyond operating as if the intellectual power of their ideas alone can compensate for a lack of careful diagnosis and skillful navigation. Instead, they blend into their decision-making process: implementation strategies, execution tactics, and the kind of questions, requirements, and resources needed to reflect a balanced concern for both the human and technical aspects of orchestrating change.

Integrated leaders value the people side of transitions not only because of their own experience with innovations that failed due to poor execution, but also because of increased scrutiny from those they must please. Senior officers pay close attention to the issues raised by the constituencies that keep them in power: boards, owners, and analysts. In recent years, these constituencies have begun to ask questions that go far beyond whether an

Leader's Basic View

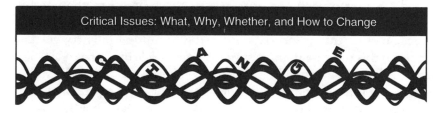

Critical Issues: What, Why, Whether, and How to Change

Figure 10.5 The integrated leader.

impending strategic initiative represents the right thing to do. They have begun to ask how senior officers are going to ensure that employees successfully implement the decision.

Another indicator that demonstrates the priority Integrated leaders place on the importance of the human factor is the number of change management specialists now on staff within the major professional consulting firms. In the late 1980s and early 1990s, Bolt-on thinking grew popular among corporate leaders. In response, the major consulting companies started reassigning people and adding staff to fill the gap. In a very brief period, these service firms dramatically increased the number of professionals who either had this expertise or at least could appear so to a naïve client.

During this period, though the number of consultants from these firms that were presented to the public as change management specialists rose greatly, most played only token roles in client engagements. Many senior partners in these firms reflected the Rational leader's mind-set: they were quite leery about pursuing the soft human side of change. As a result, change management specialists were typically more visible during the business-development phase than in any other part of a client's relationship. They were involved during proposal writing and when making capability presentations to clients, but rarely seen otherwise. If senior partners allowed them more involvement on projects, they were usually kept in peripheral assignments—conducting training programs, developing communication plans, or helping write announcement memos.

By the mid 1990s, the marketplace had grown more volatile and the cost for failed initiatives had become prohibitive, so the demand for change management consulting expanded significantly. The question that started coming to the forefront was: "What are you going to do to make sure our return on this investment in change (ROC_{hg}) is not hindered by poor execution?" Board members began raising these kinds of issues with CEOs before approving millions of dollars for new technology, mergers, or reengineering projects. Industry analysts started to probe top executives about issues beyond "Is there a strategic plan for recovering from your recent problems?" They also wanted to know: "How will it be successfully implemented?" Senior officers, in turn, passed the heat on to the consulting firms competing for their business.

Because of its entrepreneurial nature, the consulting industry quickly responded to this increase in interest in the human side of change. Consultants are in the business of providing clients a conduit to their specialized skill or knowledge, a pair of hands to help complete a task, or the perceived value of being linked with experts in a particular field who enjoy a distinguished reputation. These assets are embodied in the professionals who work with clients and are attractively packaged and sold in units of time (i.e., by the hour, day, or month, or the life of a project).

For the best indicator of what is hot in the consulting industry, look at what expertise, staffing, and reputation asset packages are being sold and how fast these specialty areas are growing. It would be difficult today to find a major consulting company that does not have (or claim to have) change management specialists on staff. More important, this expertise is among the fastest growing specialties in the consulting industry. During the past few years, Andersen Consulting alone added an army of newly hired or laterally transferred people to its change management operation. Coopers and Lybrand has enlarged its ranks of change consultants to approximately 700, and Ernst & Young has amassed around 650 change management professionals. All the projections from these firms suggest the growth in these numbers will continue for the foreseeable future.

The strongest evidence that the people side of organizational transition has become important to Integrated leaders is the actions executives themselves take to ensure that the concerns, threats, anxieties, and misconceptions people have about important initiatives are appropriately addressed. If something is really vital to the bottom line of a business, senior officers in nimble operations tend not to rely on luck or a hope that someone will remember to do it well. Whatever a leader considers critical to running his or her business becomes a nonnegotiable part of how the organization functions. Leaders systematize what they really want to see happen; they embed these things into the fabric of their business.

For example, executives of retail companies cannot afford to hope that their sales clerks collect the appropriate tax from customers. To ensure that this is done properly, they integrate the step of calculating sales tax into their representatives' training and reward systems. More importantly, they embed the sales tax calculation itself into the cash register system used at all counters. In a similar fashion, most organizations cannot afford to leave the annual budgeting process to chance. At a precise time each year, people know to expect the multiple rounds of budget meetings, justification reports, and final negotiation sessions. The sequence is embedded in routine procedures and expectations.

It is no different for leaders who determine that planning how to reduce resistance and increase commitment is essential to the success of major change. Integrated leaders consider these issues just as important as the financial or logistic components of their project's rollout strategy. They believe that careful crafting of the human side of change is essential to the success of new initiatives; therefore, embedding it into the process for introducing all important transitions becomes the norm.

Leaders who subscribe to this approach are not satisfied with anything less than fully integrating both the human aspects and the technical factors of their organization into one comprehensive implementation plan. Just as the diagnostic services a doctor performs before prescribing medication are a separate but inherent part of proper medical treatment, exploring how people will respond to change is an essential part of professional implementation planning.

Leaders who engage Integrated thinking fold people management planning into their operation, not only because of its impact on the success of their organization's initiatives, but because doing so also influences their personal careers. They know they can only maintain their positions of power if people are willing to follow their directives. If employees can't or won't execute the guidance provided by those in leadership positions, then, by definition, new leadership will be forthcoming.

LANGUAGE

Whenever leaders determine that something is integral to an organization's success as well to their careers, it takes on a different priority and visibility than the many other items competing for their attention. A good indicator of the importance something has for senior officers is the language used to refer to it. For example, "strategic planning" will hold most executives' attention, not "action steps." They will make a priority of "critical success factors," but not "things to do." They are interested in "executive compensation," but not "pay." The role language plays in conveying importance can be seen in how executives relate to change as well.

Among the various change leadership styles being described here, concern for orchestrating the human reactions to disruption varies greatly. The language used by the respective styles reflects the priority each places on the people side of change. For example, the Anti-change executive does not need any wording to describe the human side of transitions. As far as this leader is concerned, fluctuations in the status quo are to be avoided as much as possible. The Rational leader does invoke to terms that relate to people problems during change, but they are mostly pejorative in nature (e.g., whiners, complainers, troublemakers, and melodrama). Rational leaders have no need for terminology to describe what to do about the symptoms of human disorientation during change, because they believe these symptoms should be ignored or eradicated anyway.

Panacea leaders also develop distinct nomenclature to reflect their concern for the people side of change. The vocabulary they use, however, usually offers evidence of the ambivalence they often experience toward the subject. Some of the language conveys a value for the people issues (e.g., sensitivity to people's feelings, helping people adjust to the new environment, and keeping morale up). Other descriptions are more derogatory (e.g., touchy-feely, esoteric, and hand-holding).

It was Bolt-on mentality that created the term "change management." It is important to note that as this term gained recognition, the word "management," used in the noun position, has taken on more significance. By referring to it this way, acknowledgment was given that it was possible to actually influence the outcome of the psycho-socio-cultural facets of organizational life. Traditionally, these elements had been considered too ethereal to deal with directly. The term is not "change hope," "change prayer," or "change luck." The choice of "change management" implied that the skills, predispositions, and emotional reactions people experience during transitions were finally being viewed as things that could be at least influenced, if not guided.

The onset of the Integrated style of leadership ushered in a completely new set of nomenclature that reflected a much more comprehensive understanding of the complexity associated with the human side of change. Here is where terms like "change-related dysfunction," "Human Due Diligence," and "ROC_{hg}" began to take on important significance.

NEW THINKING

Two key characteristics set apart the thinking of the Integrated leader from the other leadership orientations:

1. The extent of the executive's *commitment* to seriously address the human side of change.
2. The degree to which he or she *institutionalizes* the thorough investigation of people issues during implementation, instead of leaving it as a discretionary option.

Commitment   Integrated leaders clearly try to avoid the pitfalls to which their Bolt-on counterparts fall prey. For example, the hallmark of Bolt-on leaders is their strong interest in—not necessarily their commitment to—dealing with the people side of transition. They are curious about the human issues, but only to a point. The limits of their interest are evidenced by their attachment to superficial change management techniques rather than the more substantial methods used when applying Human Due Diligence. As a result of this limited interest, the Bolt-on approach usually results in sequential or parallel efforts to address the people side of change.

Sequential use of change management occurs when it is applied after all the other aspects of a new project are in place. An example is:

> Everyone listen up, this is the plan. After we complete our analysis, we present the case for action to the board. I'll lead that effort. Once we get the green light, Bill, you will need to start informing the region heads about what is going to happen. After they are on line, Mary should begin the logistics and project-management work that will have to be done. When she finishes, Joe needs to coordinate with Corporate Communications to get something in our next newsletter and maybe get some local press. Bryan, give the change management team a heads-up that by the time the news hits the street we are going to have some people bouncing off the walls, so let's have them prepared to come in at that point and give us some guidance.

Parallel application of change management takes place when it is viewed as an important task but separate from the other planning necessary for change:

> Beverly, would you and Charlie work together on coordinating your efforts? Beverly, while you're driving the reengineering design teams, I want to make sure you are aware of any concerns being raised by Charlie's change management teams. They will be conducting some training to help people maximize their resilience during the next couple of years until we get through this. I'm sure there will be information they surface that could influence how we design the new structure and roll it out.

Executives who demonstrate more advanced Integrated thinking are not willing to accept this kind of cursory treatment of the human issues that so typically characterizes change management techniques. They refuse to bear the problems associated with sequential or parallel efforts. Their commitment to the people aspect of change translates into the more comprehensive approach of Human Due Diligence being fully embedded into the entire sequence of events for implementation.

Institutionalization   After commitment, institutionalization is the second characteristic way of thinking that distinguishes Integrated leaders. They take their namesake quite literally in terms of what it means for their role in the implementation process. Although they acknowledge the importance of having access to change experts who can provide assistance when needed, they don't view executing important change as something that should be separated from their own direct involvement. Instead, these leaders view Human Due Diligence as one of the core competencies senior officers must personally possess and demonstrate in order for them to provide the kind of strategic guidance their role requires. A typical instruction from an Integrated leader to staff members would be as follows:

> It sounds like we are all in agreement about the part we must play as the senior team. Sandra and Tom will contact the consultants to let them know they got the contract, but only on one condition. They will be told that they had the best technical approach and the chemistry was good with the team they sent in. The one area they were weak in, however, must be addressed or we can't proceed. We must be direct with them about this. They said all the right words about helping us orchestrate the human side of this project, but they were not convincing that they really knew what to do. Sandra, just be honest and say that we noticed there was no real methodology to what they proposed on the people side—just lofty ideals and hand holding. Let them know that we've been burned by that in the past and we can't afford for this project to fail.
>
> Tom, you can explain that we want to work with our own change specialist to break down all twelve phases of their project management process and integrate the diagnostic tools, principles, and training we normally use to make sure we have the commitment necessary for projects like this to be successful. We don't want to waste our people's time teaching them how to go online with this new technology and then separately show them how to deal with the resistance and confusion that are inevitable. One seamless implementation strategy taking care of both is what we need.

VULNERABILITIES

Integrated leadership represents some of the most advanced thinking about how to orchestrate organizational change, but the weakness in this style is also very apparent (see Table 10.6). Its main flaw is that it features a one-at-a-time mentality. Its focus is on the individual project rather than a portfolio of change initiatives. The Integrated leader calls for a tough diagnosis of each project to determine its independent draw on an organization's assimilation resources. But this approach can fall short of adequately preparing the organization for the next volley of change that will inevitably follow whatever current endeavors exist. Without proper care, it is easy for an organization to find itself winning short-term individual change battles (i.e., execution trips), but losing the war (i.e., the change journeys). A particular change project can be well designed, but if its execution leaves the organization physically, emotionally, and intellectually depleted, where do the resources come from for the next round of change demands? The Integrated style is extremely powerful and effective, but it does not represent an adequate response to the challenge of perpetual unrest.

Table 10.6   The Integrated Leader's Basic View

Distinguishing Characteristics

Type of change encountered: Lower second-order, one or more paradigms redefined.

Magnitude of change encountered: Breathtaking.

Cost for implementation failure: Extreme.

Interest in a nimble work environment: Substantial.

Application of Human Due Diligence: Believes it should be fully utilized with focus on specific current initiatives.

Underlying assumptions: Carefully architecting the human side of change is essential to the success of new initiatives, so Human Due Diligence must be embedded in the process of introducing important modifications to an organization.

Goal: Orchestrating massive, complex change while treating people issues as integral to the success of each major project.

Comfort is found in: Integrating the human and technical factors of change and relating to both as inseparable aspects of the same process.

Primary message to organization: "Human Due Diligence must be completed before key change decisions can be made and carried out."

Idealized organization: Has a seamless process that deals with the human aspects throughout the decision-making planning, and execution phases of introducing change. Attempts are made to prevent problems by diagnosing potential concerns, taking early corrective action, and carefully framing the initiative to generate as much support as possible. Also, executives prepare to manage the remaining, inevitable resistance that occurs with major disruption.

Response to change-related people problems: High interest, in-depth concern, balanced perspective, project-specific focus, driven by line management.

Management style metaphor: The diagnosis a doctor performs before prescribing medication is a distinct yet inherent part of proper medical treatment.

Principal strength: Uses the structure and discipline of Human Due Diligence to address individual change projects. Positions change management as a necessity for the success of important initiatives.

Principal weakness: Emphasis is on the success of separate projects, not on the organization's overall capacity to be prepared for ongoing transition.

The Continuous Leader in the Era of Perpetual Unrest

A new leadership style is beginning to surface, with the onset of the perpetual unrest era. The precise dimensions and feelings of the emerging era itself are still in development, so it should come as no surprise that the style of leadership it will require is in its early formalization. Only a few of the more "cutting-edge" leaders are displaying aspects of this new style, and even they are not always consistent with its application. Yet, because enough of those new views and behaviors toward organizational change are now being displayed, the trend in this direction is clear. The type of leader who will be required to drive success must deal with ongoing disruption, so I refer to him or her as the Continuous leader of change.

When the magnitude and consequences of change move beyond incremental implications, a new framework is necessary to understand the dynamics involved and the leadership style implications. When the transition load reaches such proportions that second-order transformations are commonplace, the paradigm has shifted from the first era, contiguous change, to the second era, perpetual unrest. In such environments, senior officers must shift their perspective in order to oversee their organizations' efforts to deal with an unending torrent of modification and resolutions.

There is much to be learned before we can claim any thorough understanding of the true parameters for this new perpetual unrest period in which multiple quantum-leap changes will be common. In fact, the Continuous leader style is only the first of several distinct leadership styles that will surely emerge within this era. Fortunately, our observations have begun to reveal specific characteristics that offer distinctions about this newest leadership approach to change.

The era we are entering will be noted principally by a never-before-seen magnitude of change and by unforgiving implications for poor implementation. This means a fundamental shift is necessary in the way executives view the "what, why, whether, and how" configuration of change questions. The Bolt-on leader delegates the "how" of change to transition specialists and deals with the human aspects only on a discretionary basis. For the Integrated leader, the "how" of implementation has equal status with its counterparts, but he or she keeps its focus on particular projects. The Continuous leader will engage the challenge from a fresh perspective. He or she will view all three issues—*what* should be changed, *why* it should be done, and *whether* the necessary resources are available—as secondary to a more important question: Can the organization maintain its ability to absorb all the major disruptions (known and unknown) necessary to remain competitive?

Because the marketplace is becoming less linear, more complex, and even more uncertain than in the past, leaders in this new era will realize that the orchestration of the human side of change has many far-reaching implications that go beyond the success or failure of any one project. For the Continuous leader, what is paramount is not whether the organization can execute any current, singular change efforts, but whether it can sustain in the future an unending avalanche of dramatic, overlapping alterations in its key success factors (see Figure 10.6). This new era of change will bring endless adjustments to what is sold, how it is marketed, who the customers are, what it takes to satisfy their needs, how to respond more quickly to their requests, and how to deliver higher value-based products and services in cost-effective ways. Consequently, Continuous change leaders will expect that the various initiatives necessary to drive success will be executed with the discipline and structure of Human Due Diligence fully integrated into their implementation plans. They will hold those who report directly to them accountable for doing so, thus freeing themselves to focus on the larger issue of adaptation capacity—*the organization's long-range ability to be as nimble as possible.*

Senior executives with a Continuous perspective will no longer consider their only strategic focus to be making the right change decisions or even being sure they are executed well. It's not that Continuous leaders will totally abdicate the responsibility, but this duty is not their primary concern. They will delegate much of this work to those with day-to-day operational responsibility.

Leaders with a Continuous perspective realize that tactical solutions come and go over the years, and there is never a lack of internal advocates or external vendors from which to choose. Remember, not long ago, everyone thought MBO was the answer to competitive pressure. Then it was zero-based budgeting, quality circles, TQM, and, more recently, mergers

Leader's Basic View

Figure 10.6   The continuous leader.

and acquisitions, process reengineering, client servers, and enterprise-wide software. After watching far too many of these intellectually sound solutions fail to generate their full promised value, these leaders perceive that what people know about executing change, and about the skills needed to manage the process, represents a critically important strength that must be managed like any other strategic asset. They will acknowledge that they will not achieve the ROI promised the shareholders unless they first deliver the proper ROC_{hg}, which will allow their companies to make the necessary adjustments in key success factors.

In no way does this delegation to the senior team of the tactical execution of initiatives imply that important new projects aren't still carefully planned and orchestrated. Continuous leaders, in fact, will require that their top management teams conduct the same rigorous application of Human Due Diligence to projects deemed vital to their organization's success as do Integrated leaders. The key difference between the two, however, is that the Continuous executives maintain oversight responsibility to ensure the attention paid to any one project never supersedes maintaining the organization's overall ability to maneuver and respond to the next set of change demands, lurking just around the corner.

As was true for the other styles, the emergence of this Continuous mentality is, in part, a response to failure. Leaders who develop this viewpoint will have come to realize that one of the main reasons they were hired or promoted into their current position was that their predecessors were unable to prepare the organization for unending change. The previous incumbent may have been a brilliant decision maker when it came to what modifications would keep the business competitive, and may even have been skilled at integrating change management concepts and techniques into the implementation process. What will be clear for the Continuous leader, however, is that none of these accomplishments provide adequate job security if the organization can't absorb the total number of changes needed to survive and compete. It is no longer career-enhancing to blow all the available adaptation capacity on current changes when even more grueling initiatives must be accommodated in the future.

Continuous leaders will see their organizations' adaptation resources in the same light as other strategic assets that must be developed, nurtured, and protected. They will be just as concerned about their organizations' readiness to bring about future, unidentified changes as they are about their managers' ability to carry out any one particular initiative currently being implemented.

In the more challenging era of perpetual unrest, finding meaning and direction while operating at the rim of chaos will be the hallmark of the

Table 10.7   The Continuous Leader's Basic View

Distinguishing Characteristics
Type of change encountered: Second-order, numerous paradigm reconfigurations, nonconforming movement.
Magnitude of change encountered: Relentless.
Cost for implementation failure: Prohibitive.
Interest in a nimble work environment: Extensive.
Application of Human Due Diligence: Believe it should be fully utilized, with focus on both general preparation for the organization and the execution of specific projects.
Underlying assumption: It is no longer career-enhancing to consume all the available adaptation resources for the changes presently at hand, when even more demanding initiatives must be accommodated in the future.
Goal: Succeed with current projects while ensuring that the organization maintains adequate assimilation resources for the changes it will face in the future.
Comfort is found in: Realizing that assimilation capacity can be managed like other strategic assets. It can be measured, developed, harvested, and used with caution after careful consideration and planning.
Primary message to organization: "We must prepare ourselves to survive and prosper during constant turbulence. This is possible if we build a nimble organization capable of addressing, with speed, agility, and skill, the ceaseless advance of uncertainty and ambiguity that will be coming our way."
Idealized organization: The attention paid to any one project is never allowed to supersede the overriding priority the organization has set on maintaining the assimilation resources needed to respond when the next set of change demands inevitably surfaces.
Response to change-related people problems: Among top priorities; constant vigilance, future-oriented, and driven by executive leadership.
Management style metaphor: Tao—the Chinese word for continual flow of energy, the endless motion that occurs in all living systems.
Principal strength: Provides people with a feeling of control when in turbulent work environments. Helps them gain confidence in the organization's Nimbleness to respond to any significant disruption.
Principal weakness: Unknown.

successful, nimble organizations. Realizing that ongoing disruption is the new norm will be a strong motivator for leaders to learn that people cannot properly respond to the demands of unfamiliar market situations unless they feel in control. Remember, being in control means being able to make sense out of what you perceive to be happening. When employees can alter objective reality, shift their expectations, and/or match the new demands and restrictions coming out of the marketplace, they are able to grasp the kind of control that makes success possible. The Continuous leader commits to building a work environment that is conducive to fast, efficient recalibration of business-related expectations and perceptions. In such a setting, the adaptation reflex (described in Appendix B) is completed, and new ways of operating are engaged faster and more effectively than the competition (see Table 10.7).

Continuous leaders know the importance of the rigor and seriousness of Human Due Diligence when addressing the people side of any specific change. More to the point, they have gained an understanding of and respect for the full chain of support necessary to succeed during unending instability. The Continuous leader respects the underlying relationship Human Due Diligence has with organizational Nimbleness which is the next higher link in the chain necessary for prosperity in turbulent environments (see Figure 10.7).

Figure 10.7   Market success during instability.

Success and the Six Leadership Styles

Each of the leadership styles has a set of assumptions and goals that, when properly applied in the correct environment, can result in success (see Table 10.8). The key is to match the load of change being faced by the organization (magnitude and consequences) with the corresponding leadership mind-set toward change. When this pairing is appropriately accomplished, the organization can be guided toward the optimum amount of change and a high degree of attention to the human aspects needed for successful implementation.

Students of Change

Over the years, as the complexities associated with organizational innovation have multiplied, so have the creative adaptations people have come up with to accommodate the heightened challenges they have faced. Leaders are no exception. They have always evolved new skills and priorities that reflected a growth in their understanding of the human side of change. They have been students, if you will, enrolled in the university of change. The tutelage they received came from the real-life classrooms of their day-to-day operations as their organizations tried to keep pace with all the turmoil they confronted. The lessons learned were a natural result of their struggle with the increasing magnitude and failure costs associated with the real changes taking place. Leaders have always been students of change, and it's time to go back to school.

We are in the process of moving from the Contiguous era to one of perpetual unrest, and new approaches to transitioning are in order. Here, the volume, momentum, and complexity of change increase exponentially, and the cost of the status quo accelerates to prohibitive levels. When uncertainty and ambiguity are the norm, school is in session and the subject is how to provide leadership during unpredictable and precarious times. The instructor is the hard reality of a fast-paced, competitive market. Although all the students who attend study the same leadership curriculum, some are at a freshman level, learning the rudiments of change dynamics, while others are pursuing postgraduate challenges in an attempt to master the craft of piloting an organization at the edge of chaos.

Corporate leaders are students of the change process and must approach their assignments in a manner consistent with the knowledge and skills they seek. For example, the key lesson for the Anti-change leader is how to

Table 10.8   Styles and Environment Match

Style	Underlying Assumption	Goal	Optimum Environment
Anti-change	Organizational life should be mostly calm; therefore, significant fluctuations are unnecessary and undesirable.	Protect the status quo.	Magnitude: Inconsequential Cost of failure: Slight
Rational	Organizational life is a binary experience. When change is required, it can be accomplished in a rational manner.	Minimize the melodrama and avoid mistakes.	Magnitude: Modest Cost of failure: Noteworthy
Panacea	Any change-related problem can be handled if you show the right video, give people laminated cards to put on their desks as reminders, and give them cool T-shirts to signify they were properly dipped in the correct training solution.	Keep people happy.	Magnitude: Strong Cost of failure: Significant
Bolt-on	Change management is an option that may be attached to a project, if after getting into trouble you remember it, and if the time and money involved are not too burdensome.	Take care of as many people issues as feasible, given the constraints.	Magnitude: Shocking Cost of failure: Considerable
Integrated	Careful architecting of the human side of change is essential to the success of new initiatives, so Human Due Diligence must be embedded into the process of introducing important modifications to the organization.	Treating people issues as integral to the success of each major project.	Magnitude: Breathtaking Cost of failure: Dramatic
Continuous	It is no longer acceptable to consume all the organization's assimilation resources to satisfy the changes presently at hand, when even more demanding initiatives must be accommodated in the future.	Succeed with current projects while ensuring that the organization maintains adequate assimilation resources for the changes it will face in the future.	Magnitude: Relentless Cost of failure: Prohibitive

avoid as many fluctuations as possible. The Rational leader is focused on how to contain change with logic and linear execution. For the Panacea leader, the solution to disruption problems is found within such things as communication and motivational training. The Bolt-on leader is trying to learn how to regain a sense of control by attaching change management techniques to projects on a discretionary basis. The Integrated leader is searching for ways to use the structure and discipline of Human Due Diligence as individual change projects are addressed. The Continuous leader is trying to leverage Nimbleness into a strategic asset by the comprehensive application of the Human Due Diligence methodology to increase adaptation capacity and reduce unnecessary implementation demands.

Any of the six approaches can, of course, be either poorly executed or applied under the wrong circumstances. When this occurs, the organization's ability to make the necessary adjustment in its key success factors is usually greatly restricted. In today's markets, this makes it difficult, if not impossible, to remain competitive. When there is a complementary pairing, however, between leadership's disposition toward change and the load of change demands in the environment, the probability for leadership students to learn and for their organizations to succeed is significantly enhanced.

Who's Right?

Examples are plentiful regarding how each of the six styles has been successfully applied. These examples come not only from the records of how leaders have dealt with ambiguity and uncertainty in the past; they can also be found in the way senior officers today are addressing the challenge of change. As you read this page, somewhere there are executives trying to hold back the tide of transition while others are hoping their logical presentations to promote change will prevail. Somewhere, right now, someone is calling on a human relations expert to take care of his or her company's people problems while another leader is calculating whether the time and money needed are available to apply change management techniques and tools to an important initiative. Still others are desperately trying to fully embed Human Due Diligence into the project management process being used for separate projects. Even though they are few in number, there are even leaders today who are trying to express as much concern about their organizations' long-range adaptation capacity as about the execution of near-term change initiatives.

Not only are all six leadership styles being played out separately in various settings; somewhere right now there are executives who, within the same organization, are using two or more of these approaches at the same time. While one division of a company may be enjoying the luxury of a brief respite between avalanches of chance, another may be facing unprecedented pressure to completely abandon its operating paradigm for a new one that is more suited to its fickle market. The same leader may apply Anti-change thinking in one area while simultaneously using the Continuous perspective in another.

Although the choice of which leadership approach to apply in various situations is often driven by unconscious habit and personality preferences, it should be based on a conscious effort to match the appropriate style with the environment's change load. Regardless of the motives for selecting one style over another or even the suitability of the choices made, these six leadership approaches to change are all well established on the landscape of contemporary management practice. What all this means is that none of the approaches to disruption are inherently good or bad, right or wrong, helpful or destructive. Each predisposition has produced its share of success and failure. If one appears to offer little redeeming value to you, it's probably because of the change load your organization is presently encountering, not some congenital flaw in that style's composition.

Given the right situation, any of the leadership approaches may be fitting for all or part of an organization, but each can also be inappropriately applied. Because each approach reflects a distinct perspective toward change, rather than a segment of time, it is not uncommon to find executives exhibiting holdover thinking—that is, inappropriately using a style that was popular during a previous period when it was more suitable. For instance, many organizations are finding it difficult to remain viable in today's fast-moving markets because they are burdened with leaders who never developed beyond the Rational or Panacea style. This can pose some very real problems because the speed and efficiency with which an organization absorbs change have become key strategic assets, and leaders who adhere to less sophisticated, holdover viewpoints are putting their companies at a distinct competitive disadvantage.

In a world characterized primarily by escalating uncertainty, an organization cannot maintain its viability unless its executives keep current with the latest thinking about how change can be managed. Just as the product life cycles for new technology continue to decrease dramatically, the half-life of "cutting-edge" thinking about how to manage change has also grown shorter. Not long ago, it was possible to secure 24 to 36 months of competitive advantage for a company by purchasing the newest software with the latest innovations and speed enhancements. Today, that advantage can be maintained no more than 3 to 6 months. The same is true for organizations that wish to enjoy the benefits of absorbing and exploiting change faster and more effectively than their competitors. The competitive advantages of change victories are often just as short-lived as their software equivalent.

Being one or two generations behind the competition in the ability to implement needed changes is no less dangerous than being one or two generations behind in computing capability. Just to compete, leaders must stay up-to-date with at least the rate of change most of their marketplace rivals are able to absorb. To set the pace within an industry, however, an organization must remain on a constant search for the most current advancements in approaches and methodologies that will facilitate absorbing the unfamiliar.

It's not even as simple as deciding which leadership style is a good match for the change load a particular organization is experiencing. Today, leaders are usually not afforded the luxury of determining which style best fits their entire organization's circumstances and narrowly applying that singular view. Instead, they face the much more formidable challenge of keeping a constant watch on the magnitude and the failure costs of change throughout their organizations. Sometimes, certain parts of an organization may require leadership that promotes an Integrated or Continuous environment while other elements of the business may be in need of more stabilization. The Rational, or even the Anti-change, style could be just what is needed.

None of these six perspectives should, therefore, be treated as either the preferred leadership approach to be used under any circumstances, or the scourge of change guidance to be avoided at all costs. Each must be considered a legitimate point of reference on a continuum of ways organizations can respond to disruption.

Leadership's Personal Resilience

S ustaining organizational performance in the controlled slide zone is not just professionally challenging, but also personally demanding. As you balance conflicting demands and priorities, move through days that are full to overflowing, make decisions that affect the lives of countless others, respond to challenges, and shape new organizational directions, your personal adaptation capacity is taxed to the limit. In order to hold the enterprise on the brink of chaos, your own capacity to thrive in the midst of disruption cannot be compromised.

Each individual has a personal speed of change. Your speed of change is the rate at which you can move through the adaptation process with a minimum of dysfunctional behavior—the pace at which you can bounce back from the confusion caused by uncertainty and grasp the opportunities that the new environment presents. The single most important factor for enhancing this speed of change is *resilience*. Resilient individuals—those who operate at a high speed of change—have an advantage over their less resilient counterparts. They are able to take on more change without becoming so intellectually, physically, and emotionally drained.

Keeping a steady hand on the helm requires you to practice and consistently display certain resilient habits of mind—characteristic approaches to unfamiliar and uncomfortable situations that maximize your ability to perform during chaos. Our research, combined with a great deal of work done by other students of human adaptability, has identified five personal characteristics that define resilient behavior:

1. Positive—Resilient individuals effectively identify opportunities in turbulent environments and have the personal confidence to believe they can succeed.
2. Focused—Resilient individuals have a clear vision of what they want to achieve, and they use this as a lodestar to guide them when they become disoriented.
3. Flexible—Resilient individuals draw effectively on a wide range of internal and external resources to develop creative, pliable strategies for responding to change.
4. Organized—Resilient individuals use structured approaches to managing ambiguity, planning, and coordinating effectively in implementing their strategies.
5. Proactive—Resilient individuals engage action in the face of uncertainty, taking calibrated risks rather than seeking comfort.

The combination of these attributes is powerful. Each characteristic plays a role in protecting assimilation resources during change; when they are balanced wisely and used faithfully, they create a strong force for effective transformation. Let's explore each characteristic in greater depth. I will then assemble them into a portrait of the resilient leader.

Positive

Turbulent environments, and the ambiguity they create, present the business-world equivalent of a Rorschach inkblot test. Each person who views such an environment sees something different, and what a person sees says more about him or her than about the situation. In the midst of change, both dangers and opportunities are present. To ignore either of them is to run the risk of missing important information. At the same time, a perspective that overemphasizes the potential dangers may lead to inaction. Worse, it could cause a heavy drain on adaptation resources expended in worry and rumination.

Resilient individuals do not overlook dangers; rather, they focus their attention on opportunities. Two specific aspects of their approach to disruption are important. First, they believe that the environment presents to them a stream of opportunities (albeit sometimes disguised as dangers).

They characteristically choose (or create) one that offers new possibilities rather than one that reinforces frustrations or difficulties. Unexpected events become stimuli for positive action. Second, they have a high level of confidence in their own capabilities. Rather than a vague, fuzzy sense of self-esteem, they have a reality-based understanding that they can succeed in difficult situations, along with a willingness to tolerate occasional failure as the cost of learning. This enables them to move decisively into action and to persist in the face of setbacks.

Focused

Resilient individuals bring clarity of purpose to their actions. Disruption, by nature, throws people and organizations off course, introduces uncertainty into objectives and plans, and presents a wealth of challenges. Without a means of determining how to select and prioritize activities, assimilation resources can easily be wasted.

Resilient individuals usually have a well-thought-out set of values and priorities. They use these to make effective choices. Whether this focus comes from strong identification with the organization's vision and mission, or from a deep spiritual center, a political or moral philosophy, or some other source, it enables the resilient individual to conserve his or her assimilation resources for those tasks that are most critical.

Flexible

Unfamiliar situations, by their nature, can rarely be conquered with familiar means. As obstacles are encountered, it is often necessary to modify strategies repeatedly. Without the capacity to create new solutions, many resources can be wasted in using worn-out and/or ineffective methods. A third critical element of resilience, therefore, is the ability to construct diverse solutions and to alter them if necessary. This capability draws, in fact, on two sets of personal strengths. First, resilient people are conceptually flexible. That is, they can generate a range of thoughts and possibilities relative to a particular problem without feeling the need to decide on one immediately. High levels of creativity, tolerance for ambiguity, and fluency of ideas are all components of this skill. The resulting wealth of options provides the means for attacking a problem from many angles.

Second, resilient people tend to draw effectively on the resources of others. They are able to supplement their own knowledge and skills with the talents of others, and are not only willing to do so but recognize that others often have critical pieces of the answer to an unfamiliar problem. Without depending exclusively on others for solutions, they are actively open to input and they build effective networks to ensure that information and other resources are freely exchanged.

Organized

An overwhelming amount of data must be managed when the demands of disruptive situations are combined with the range of possible action plans. A key to success, therefore, is the ability to swiftly convert data to information and then structure this information into effective plans for moving forward (knowledge). Without appropriate structures in place to set boundaries, resources can be lost in disorder, confusion, miscommunication, and lack of coordination. A fourth crucial element of resilience, therefore, is the ability to impose structure both internally and externally. Resilient individuals are able to categorize information, sequence elements in a plan, attend to necessary details, and discipline themselves to utilize the structures they have created.

Proactive

Effective approaches to change are only useful if they are applied when the time is ripe. As circumstances change, windows of possibility open and close swiftly, and the person who awaits complete certainty before deploying a strategy loses the chance to take advantage of them. The failure to capitalize on an opportunity through inaction based in risk aversion can be extremely costly, in terms of both lost opportunity and the resources spent to build plans that become obsolete before they can be tried. The fifth and final element of resilience, therefore, is the willingness to pursue action experimentally. Resilient individuals will move forward into unfamiliar, uncertain settings, taking action even when the risk of failure is substantial. Rather than ensuring that every "I" is dotted and every "T" is crossed, they will test their ideas, learn from the experience, revise their plans, and test again.

The Balancing Act

Each of the five elements of resilience is important. Although they are interrelated to some extent, they represent separate facets of a fully formed approach to change. They are not equally critical in every situation: one situation may call for decisive action without a great deal of attention to the balance of perceived danger and opportunity; another may call for a high degree of adherence to structure; yet another may require a heavy use of resources from colleagues. Because each situation calls on a different configuration of resilience characteristics, it is impossible to say that there is a single "trait" called resilience. Rather, we have come to view resilience as the ability to draw effectively on whichever characteristic, or combination of characteristics, is called for in a particular situation.

Physical Well-Being

High levels of change demand place a heavy strain on adaptation resources. Although we may think of these demands primarily in terms of their emotional and intellectual impact, they also affect physical well-being. The physiological impact of stress is substantial, contributing to both acute and chronic illness and injuries. Although the majority of our research on resilience has focused on demonstrating the ways in which the resilience characteristics protect and augment cognitive and emotional resources, there are also direct links to physical well-being. It is clear that individuals who are physically robust are more likely to demonstrate psychological health, and that physical toughening has benefits in the psychological realm as well. This has been shown in several studies, including one that demonstrated a link between the frequency of exercise and levels of the five resilience characteristics.[1] Interestingly, the link may run in both directions—increased physical fitness may enhance one's ability to operate in a positive, focused, flexible, organized, and proactive way; at the same time, displaying these attributes may increase the likelihood that individuals will be motivated not only to engage in regular exercise, but also to overcome the inevitable challenges involved in doing so in the midst of an extremely busy life.

The Good News/The Bad News

We have argued that personal resilience is an important characteristic of a leader who undertakes the challenge of guiding a nimble organization. Indeed, data from several thousand individuals indicate that resilience and leadership go hand-in-hand.[2] There is a positive relationship between an individual's strength in the resilience characteristics and his or her level in the organization. That is, people who have risen to leadership positions in organizations and who describe themselves as going through high levels of change tend to be more resilient than individuals at lower organizational levels, even after taking into account such elements as age and education.

The good news is fairly obvious: if you are currently in a leadership position with an organization in turbulence, you have probably gotten to your present position at least partially because of your ability to demonstrate resilience during change. The bad news is this: Because of your resilience, you are likely to set a pace that others cannot match. Situations that look like exciting challenges to you are actively uncomfortable for many others. It is probably difficult for you to view things from a less resilient perspective and see how disruptive certain changes are—they simply don't look that hard to you. As a result, you may become very frustrated with the amount of resistance to change that is expressed by those around you, and with the level of disruption created by seemingly minor disruptions. One of our clients offered the following example:

> One of the senior executives had scores above the 90th percentile in every resilience[3] characteristic. This individual was personable, energetic, and willing to join in on work teams whenever his schedule allowed. One of the greatest dilemmas that he faced was the fact that none of the many projects underway in his division seemed to be running on time. Throughout his division, overtime was far over budget and he admitted that many of his staff seemed somewhat burned out. As we explored this situation, we identified the problem. Because of his high level of resilience, many of the changes in which his division was involved seemed minor to him. As a result, he continually initiated new challenges for his division. One level down, however, these same changes were having a significant impact. He had no idea of the effect that his strong ability to absorb one change and move on to the next had on those around him. Once he understood and took steps to be more sensitive to the resilience of his staff, there was a noticeable turnaround in many of his projects.

Is the answer, then, simply to live with low resilience in others and reduce the amount of change you undertake? Absolutely not. In order to build a sustainable competitive advantage, your challenge is to maximize the resilience of those around you while continuing to refine your own skills. Two aspects of your own role that can support these efforts: (1) modeling resilience and (2) shaping a resilient system.

MODELING RESILIENCE

You need to pay special attention to how you display resilience in your actions and reactions during disruptive change. First, become consciously competent about your own resilience. This requires you to understand each of the resilience characteristics clearly, know when you are displaying it, and be able to explain to people what you are doing. Second, seek to operate resiliently at times when you are experiencing high levels of disruption, and to do so in a way that does not seek to conceal the extent to which you are disrupted. Employees will benefit more from knowing that you are challenged although you look calm; you are choosing to respond in a way that is positive, focused, flexible, organized, and proactive. Third, let people see the efforts you are making to improve your own resilience. One way to do this is to identify a characteristic you would like to enhance, let others know that you have challenged yourself to do so, and actively seek feedback about your own performance. If you can serve as an effective role model to others, you will lay the groundwork for efforts to help them increase their resilience to the point where their speed of change matches the level you need for success.

SHAPING A RESILIENT SYSTEM

Your actions in building organizational resilience can foster resilience in those around you. One especially important challenge is to guide the operations of senior-level teams so that resilient behavior is expected and reinforced in team settings. Few individuals on a team have strength in all of the resilience characteristics. When the profiles of team members are combined, however, most teams possess a strong mix of characteristics. Effective teams draw on resilience strengths while minimizing weaknesses and supporting and coaching one another in their efforts. This allows them to devote resources to finding solutions rather than to arguing, posturing, and devaluing one another's contributions.

Second, shape the context that guides individual behavior by articulating the organization's context (i.e., vision, mission, and strategy) in a way that promotes and reinforces resilience. Statements of context can be developed to reflect high resilience or to embody a much more reactive, defensive point of view. In looking at context statements for a variety of organizations, we have found that some contain language that emphasizes opportunity (Positive), a sense of clear purpose (Focused), a combination of flexibility and structure (Flexible, Organized), and a bias toward action (Proactive). Others reflect the opposites of these traits. Most commonly, I see statements that embody one or two of the resilience characteristics, but do not include each of them as an explicit part of the organization's direction. To the extent that you can weave resilience into the organization's formal statements of context, you will create guides to action that lead people toward resilient behavior.

Third, define and shape the organization's culture by creating systems that influence individual beliefs, behaviors, assumptions, and actions. These systems include hiring, orientation and training programs, performance appraisal and compensation systems, decision-making processes, work settings, and a wide range of other elements. These systems can value and reinforce individuals who challenge the status quo, or they can punish them. They can place a positive weight on actions that involve experimentation and risk, or they can ensure that individuals adhere rigidly to a highly structured set of rules. To the extent that you can shape a system that reinforces people who display the resilience characteristics, you will reap the benefits by finding yourself surrounded by people who can match your speed of change.

Optimizing Paradigm Life Spans

A s you recall, we discussed the idea of games and paradigms in Chapter 5. Now I would like to use the idea of paradigms in a slightly different context, that of the operational paradigms of your organization.[1] For the purpose of discussing how leaders can develop nimble systems, the basic definition I will use for an organizational paradigm is: "a generally accepted view of an important operational framework that supports how an organization is perceived to function and how it represents its true rules for success." This interpretation of paradigm has several components that include assumptions, beliefs, behaviors, systems, and methods. The combination of these components forms the basis for people feeling in direct or indirect control of themselves and their organization. Examples of organizational paradigms include: the way people are hired, how new customers are secured and current customers are served, how technology is used, and the way a company is perceived when compared to its competition.

Many aspects of these kinds of operational frameworks are worthy of pursuit, but the *life span* of a paradigm is of particular importance to managing change. As stated earlier, all paradigms, regardless of their composition, place of origin, or substance, will eventually outlive their viability. Once built and functioning, paradigms will continue to operate in a useful manner until the inescapable entropy that eventually consumes all systems overtakes the momentum toward sustainability. Whether it's the mere seconds of existence afforded certain microbes, the few days in the life of a bee, the modest number of years we humans survive, or the millions of centuries that a star releases its light and energy—all paradigms have a definitive shelf-life.

Organizational paradigms are no different; they all have a period of viability that is governed by the relevant variables at play. Just as from the microbe's point of view the bee appears to live forever, some organizational frameworks seem to be indestructible. But, this is only an illusion formed when one standard is viewed from another's frame of reference. All frameworks eventually fall prey to dysfunction and decay. Given today's turbulent environment, the basic operating paradigm of an organization may remain productive for weeks, months, years, or possibly decades, but it is inevitable that at some point it will no longer perform as desired. In this respect, all operational paradigms have two alternative trajectories: one reflects the natural course of events (unaided by leadership's intervention), and the other reflects leadership's intentional efforts to influence a paradigm's shelf life. Which of these two alternatives is selected dictates the length of time a paradigm can remain sustainable.

Organizational success in turbulent times, however, requires definitive leaders who are both willing and able to be the architects of their vision of a nimble future and to build it into the day-to-day operations of the institutions they were hired to run. This kind of architectural approach to dealing with uncertainty and transition requires an understanding of how organizational paradigms are formed and sustained, as well as how they become dysfunctional and/or are reconfigured for greater strength.

Paradigm management deals with intentionally orchestrating an organization's trajectory; that is, building and harvesting for the appropriate amount of time, intentionally dismantling, and, when necessary, forming completely new operational frameworks that are critical to a company's success. The model shown in Figure 12.1 offers a means of understanding how paradigms function in organizational settings, and suggests how they can be managed for optimum results.

This model is used to describe the five phases in the life of organizational paradigms: (1) building, (2) harvest, (3) uncertainty, (4) decay, and (5) renewal. It depicts how, over time, the performance of an organization is affected by its relationship to the prevailing assumptions, beliefs, behaviors, systems, and methods used by employees to guide and interpret their actions. These elements and their interrelationships form what is described as an organization's paradigm.

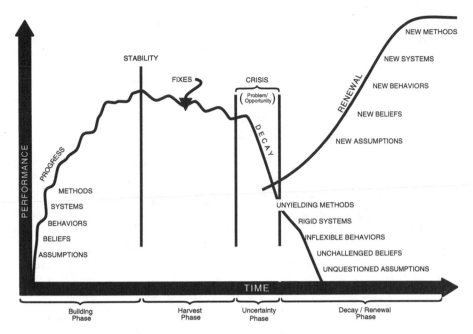

Figure 12.1 Organizational paradigms.[2]

The Art and Axioms of Paradigms

There is much to be learned from this model.

PARADIGMS MUST BE MANAGED

Once a successful paradigm configuration is formed in the building phase, its useful life span is directly related to the stability of the market environment for which it was constructed and the skill displayed by leaders for applying fixes to extend its shelf life.[3] Sometimes, paradigms become obsolete or misaligned because customers are demanding more—better and faster—than the old framework can deliver. At other times, a paradigm loses its vitality because leaders have not staffed the organization with talented people capable of identifying and carrying out the correct fixes that could extend the viability of existing frameworks. In both cases, the robust state of Nimbleness is absent.

One of the key responsibilities of leadership is to ensure that the organization is prepared to manage its critical paradigms in an optimum fashion. Optimal paradigm management involves:

- Forming paradigms throughout the organization that provide the necessary common understanding and structures to support a successful operation.

- Prolonging the life of each of these frameworks as long as possible by deploying efficient, effective, and creative fixes.[4]

- Maintaining the necessary objectivity to permit a speedy dismantling of these mechanisms when the time comes.

When paradigms are abandoned too early, regardless of the reason, it produces a change-for-its-own-sake situation, and the full value of the frameworks in question is never realized. On the other hand, when a crisis signals the final phase of usefulness for a way of viewing things or conducting operations, but the people involved can't or won't let go of the past, what Joel Barker calls *paradigm paralysis* has set in. Both these options represent a potential for significant penalties in terms of the time, money, and opportunity loss incurred when a paradigm's existence outlives its usefulness. To avoid this, leadership must ensure that people in all key areas of the operation are trained and given incentives to properly manage the paradigms under their care (i.e., build good ones, "milk" them for as much as is practical, and then move on to new ones when necessary).

RENEWAL MEANS REBUILDING FROM THE GROUND UP

At or near the beginning of the harvest phase, performance (as measured by achievement of productivity and quality goals) is often at its highest point.[5] Over time, the configuration gradually (often imperceptibly) begins to weaken. As more and more fixes are required to maintain performance goals, the fabric of the initial framework is slowly replaced by a patchwork of bandages, baling wire, and exceptions to the rules—all designed to keep the original paradigm operational.

Paradoxically, it is during this harvest phase that the organization sows the seed of its paradigm's demise. At the very time performance measures are being met or exceeded, the dynamics that will eventually undermine this success are beginning to unfold. During this period when the harvest phase generates goal attainment, the sequence of paradigm development that spawned the original success (assumptions > beliefs > behaviors > systems > methods) begins to reverse.[6] Because they are often the most tangible, performance gaps during the harvest phase are primarily addressed with method-type fixes. The new methods that are constructed then begin to demand system modifications designed to foster the use of the methods themselves rather than to increase productivity and quality. These new system fixes, in turn, start to require certain behaviors that will ensure their own integrity. Over time, these behavior fixes generate a new set of conscious beliefs about what is true or false, good or bad, important or irrelevant, manageable or unmanageable, and so forth. These beliefs gradually become incorporated into unconscious assumptions and eventually alter the core foundation of people's thoughts.

As the shelf life of a paradigm's utility is extended by more and more fixes, the ultimate (though usually undeclared) purpose of the organization becomes the success of internal mechanisms (methods, systems, and behaviors) rather than success in the external marketplace. If this happens, an organization is operating within a different paradigm from the one actually developed during the building phase. Not only is this new paradigm's purpose divergent from the initial one, but its methods, systems, and behaviors are now driving the fundamental beliefs and assumptions, instead of the reverse. When this kind of environment exists, the lessons people gain from their experiences are being applied for the purpose of preserving the status quo, not for promoting success in the market.

True organizational renewal is achieved by thoroughly investigating and, when necessary, dramatically altering each key component in the existing paradigm. The renewal process begins with the difficult task of bringing to the surface previously unquestioned assumptions that have served as the foundation for prior decisions and actions. This enables you to make a more objective analysis of incoming information. From modified or altogether new assumptions, fresh implications are generated concerning what is believed to be true, relevant, and so forth. From these beliefs, priorities emerge and specific behaviors are identified that can best manifest the intent of the new beliefs. As all this unfolds, certain clusters of assumptions, beliefs, and behaviors are modified, or altogether new systems are designed to accomplish specific outcomes (e.g., hiring people, using information technology). Finally, these systems demand fresh methods (e.g., rules and tools) to support the new framework and a renewed dynamic balance.

Renewal is the result of drawing on the dynamics used when original paradigms are built from the ground up. It represents a replication of the sequence that generated success for the old paradigm in the first place: assumptions > beliefs > behaviors > systems > methods. The difference is that the new paradigm is built with conscious competence instead of relying on trial and error, intuition, and luck (as is often true during the evolution of the initial paradigm). Constructing a new paradigm means intentionally challenging what has worked in the past and deliberately constructing a fundamentally different alternative.

PARADIGMS ARE NOT BROKEN
BY CONSENSUS

The nature and purpose of consensus is to protect the status quo. Usually, by the time the majority of any population becomes truly convinced of the need for an organizational paradigm shift, two things have happened: (1) the time and resources needed for fundamental transformation are diminished, and (2) the opportunity for securing a competitive advantage has been jeopardized. In such circumstances, the only reward for all the expensive reframing work that has been done is that the organization can settle for minimal survival or an "also-ran" status.

When new paradigms are constructed, usually a single determined individual with the appropriate power or a small group with the ability to sanction dramatic change has come to the conclusion that short-term fixes are no longer sufficient. These kinds of leaders perceive that something in the market environment has shifted, and they realize it is time for the organization's core assumptions and beliefs to be reexamined. Recognizing the opportunity that is embedded within this crisis being faced, they decide that the timing is right to seize the moment.

Although paradigm shifts require very strong and decisive executives who are often willing to pursue unpopular paths in order to accomplish corporate objectives, leaders are only as powerful as their constituencies allow them to be. The paradox is that, although paradigms are not dismantled as the result of a democratic vote, people at all levels of an organization's hierarchy must be responsive to the guidance being offered by senior executives, or leaders can't accomplish the move to a new framework.

Most leaders who motivate others to follow their direction do so by either instilling fear or fostering faith and credibility. Both strategies can result in a paradigm shift, but, in the majority of cases, trust and respect are required if the new framework is to remain viable in turbulent times. The stress and strain can be massive when new operational mechanisms are designed to conduct business in churning, uncharted water. For the mechanisms to become and remain functional, the necessary level of commitment to such processes, procedures, and structures is extremely high. It is unlikely this depth of commitment will be generated by a leader whose only tool is sanctions.

Usually, trust and respect must also be at the heart of subordinates' loyalty to a leader if a new and more capable paradigm is to emerge. These attributes, however, should not be seen as synonymous with other leadership qualities, like personableness and warmth. It is possible for followers to have an infinite trust and respect for someone whom they find personally uncomfortable to be around or even intimidating. The point here isn't whether the follower would feel comfortable enough to invite the leader to his or her house for dinner. The question is whether there is enough trust in the leader's judgment, and enough respect for the leader's unique skill or perspective, for the follower to leap from a familiar (though maybe unproductive) framework into the untested environment of a new way to operate.

Leading organizations through the ambiguity, confusion, anxiety, and fear that separate one operational paradigm from its successors demands that strong, definitive guidance be balanced with an appreciation for the complexity and ever-shifting nature of the task. In a nimble organization, focused energy, decisiveness, and tenacity from senior executives are evident, but these characteristics are manifested in a manner that promotes and utilizes employee empowerment and participation. (This point is further developed in Chapter 15.)

INCUMBENCY IS AN INHIBITOR TO TRUE PARADIGM RENEWAL

It is possible, but extremely difficult, for incumbent leaders to see the need to dismantle the paradigms they helped to build. It's not unusual for senior officers to espouse the rhetoric of fundamental change, intellectually embrace significant shifts in the operation, and even become emotionally attached to the success of these initiatives. The logic and passion that are sometimes associated with change are relatively easy to come by, even in turbulent environments. When the world around you is falling apart, it's not hard to make a case that change is necessary. What sometimes is really in short supply is existing leadership's willingness and ability to carry out the full intent of these respective initiatives. When the expensive invoices for paradigmatic change start to come in, it is difficult to find many leaders motivated and skilled enough to sustain the effort. The task becomes dramatically more challenging and costly when an incumbent tries to not only break his or her own frame of reference about how things should be done, but must also contend with others who may be disappointed and dismayed that the leader would abandon the tradition they still believe represents success.

The combination of these kinds of pressures on incumbent leaders to maintain the status quo prompts many organizations to look elsewhere for their guidance. These organizations fill vacancies at the senior level with capable, experienced people from the outside who are less familiar with the rationale behind the company's status quo. In order to have access to both strong, decisive leadership and a willingness to explore what has been previously unquestioned, companies like this often opt for importing the leadership talent they are seeking. They determine that acquiring someone with a preset disposition for exploring new alternatives can be a better use of corporate resources than attempting to develop the existing players. It's not that leaders who have served their organization for some time are completely incapable of dismantling the frameworks they helped construct, but, in order to do so, the price for the status quo will generally need to be much higher for incumbents than it will be for leaders brought in from the outside.

CRISIS IS A PREREQUISITE TO RENEWAL

A common wish for most of us is that if we can understand how certain things work, we can circumvent some of the more unpleasant parts. Unfortunately, life doesn't seem to work this way. Learning about the phases of child development won't allow you to skip those awkward teenage years with your son or daughter, and marriage counseling doesn't permit you to bypass the arguments with your spouse and go straight to the fun of reconciliation. The value in gaining access to the inner workings of the forces that affect our lives is not only to maneuver around the ones with negative implications (although many can be avoided), but also to set realistic expectations and prepare ourselves as best we can for what is to come. Remember, we gain some element of control by either getting what we want or preparing for whatever we are going to get.

Once leaders understand the dynamics of paradigm development and the forces at play during decay/renewal, many immediately want to find out how they can accomplish a needed paradigm shift without the pain of a crisis.[7] The answer is as unpleasant as it is simple: It can't be done.

Shifting paradigms is a long, hard, expensive journey. It may be intriguing at the beginning, but this is only due to the enthusiasm that always accompanies new, positively perceived endeavors. This excitement will quickly dissipate once the tough realities of what such a challenge entails begin to set in. One of the many expensive aspects of this kind of effort is that you can't even begin until the pain of the status quo exceeds the cost of the transition process. The crisis may be embedded in problem avoidance or opportunity exploitation, or it may be an impending crisis or one projected based on current trends. Regardless of the circumstances, some combination of current or anticipated problems or opportunities must reach crisis status before enough tenacity develops to sustain a person or group through this difficult process.

PARADIGM RENEWAL IS EITHER FACILITATED OR LIMITED BY THE ORGANIZATION'S ABILITY TO LEARN FROM ITS EXPERIENCES

Because of the growing magnitude of change companies face today, renewal, like Human Due Diligence, is not a point in time; it is a state of mind. It is not a project; it is a way of leading. The ability to respond quickly and effectively to a paradigm crisis depends greatly on the organization's capacity to learn. This kind of learning is characterized by the willingness to question what has worked and what may still be working; the skill to develop new alternatives within the context of the market being served; and the capacity to turn those ideas into action. An organization that fosters this kind of environment values learning for the future as much as learning from the past.

During the harvest phase, organizational success results, in part, from lessons applied to either existing or anticipated short-term performance problems (fixes) within the existing paradigm. Three levels of these kinds of corrective actions are available for an organization to choose from:

1. Methods fix—Alter existing tools, techniques, forms, and so forth; or purchase or develop new ones.

2. Systems fix—Alter existing procedures, routines, structures, and so forth, or purchase or develop new ones.

3. Behavior fix—Alter existing skills, demeanors, actions, and so forth, or purchase or develop new ones.

These three levels of learning and corrective action are generally associated with first order incremental modifications and continuous, improvement-type efforts.

To address second order, current or forecasted performance deficiencies with longer-term and broader implications, the transformation-type learning that is applied must result in two additional levels of corrective action:

1. Existing beliefs must be revamped, altering or developing new values, convictions, or judgments.

2. New assumptions must be formulated, altering or developing new categories of unconscious thought, unquestioned biases, unstated expectations, tacit fields of meaning, or unchallenged frameworks of understanding that relate to how people and things operate.

Paradigms enter the renewal phase of the cycle only when the organization's fundamental assumptions and beliefs are examined and significantly altered. From these remodeled foundations, new behaviors, systems, and methods are then designed and implemented to complete the paradigm's transformation.

NEW PARADIGMS CANNOT BE SUPPORTED BY OLD CULTURES

Many initiatives that carried the label and expectations associated with paradigmatic shifts turned out to be nothing more than elaborate, expensive fixes that really only modified or rearranged certain features within an existing framework. When this happens, it is another example of the illusion of change discussed in Chapter 2. In these cases, the paradigm stays intact even though a great deal of money and energy may be displaced in an effort to cause a shift of greater magnitude. Typically, when the pomp and ceremony of quantum-leap change efforts result in nothing more than a modest actual shift, it is due to leadership's inability or unwillingness to address the lower-level elements (assumptions, beliefs, and behaviors) of a paradigm's framework that constitute an organization's culture.

Organizational culture reflects the interrelationship of shared beliefs, behaviors, and assumptions that are acquired over time by members of an organization. An organization's collective beliefs, behaviors, and assumptions affect daily business operations on two levels: (1) the overt level, representing observable, intentional, or direct influences on operations (goals, policy-and-procedure manuals, and corporate philosophy statements); and (2) the covert level, characterized by more obscure, unintentional, or indirect influences on operations (informal ground rules, unofficial guidelines, or "the way things are done around here"). These latter influences are particularly difficult to change because they often lie below the surface of our awareness and/or we may be reluctant to discuss them openly.

Whether the influence is unstated or directive in nature, a corporation's cultural beliefs, behaviors, and assumptions serve as a powerful means for defining, justifying, and reinforcing business operations. Culture provides ways for employees to understand important decisions. Based on this understanding, expectations develop that limit possible responses. Because of these responses, employees make certain decisions and behave in accordance with those expectations, confirming and reinforcing the culture's original patterns. This self-fulfilling process reinforces a strong corporate identity but can also restrict the introduction of new beliefs, behavior, and assumptions that may contribute to success in a changing environment.

If an organization's current culture and the objectives of a desired paradigm change have little in common, the chances of successfully achieving that change are slim. The odds of implementing the change increase as the similarity grows between the existing culture and the beliefs, behaviors, and assumptions required by the new initiative. Whenever a discrepancy exists between the current culture and the objectives of the change, the culture always wins.

This is why most efforts at applying innovative approaches to organizational crises are not ultimately successful. These initiatives typically fail because they lack the cultural support necessary for people to see their relevance or sustainability. Organizational renewal demands a reexamination and, if necessary, a significant modification to the basic assumptions, beliefs, and behaviors serving as the cultural infrastructure for the enterprise. Without this type of cultural context to reinforce the innovations emerging from a learning environment, important changes tend to be initiated but not sustained.

You have two choices in how to approach the management of your organization's operational paradigms. One is more laissez faire and noninterventional. The risk of this approach is your vulnerability to both internal and external fluctuations in the environment that may result in your being unable to meet, let alone beat, your competition. The cost of this approach is a tremendous waste of adaptation resources. You and your organization are reduced to reactivity and the threat of dwindling profitability. On the other hand, you may take a proactive approach to paradigm management, which, as stated in this chapter, is yet another key feature of a nimble organization.

PART FIVE

FINE-TUNING THE NIMBLE ORGANIZATION

Up, down, left, right. It's everywhere. Surrounding each person and work team is a habitat, if you will, that reflects the various pronouncements, instructions, guidelines, and behaviors regarding what the company considers the optimum way to relate to change initiatives.

This milieu—which I call the enterprise-wide envelope—*is created by the structures as well as the verbal, written, and symbolic messages conveyed that collectively establish a set of skills and cultural expectations for how people within an organization should interpret and respond to disruptions. Although it may be manifested in several different ways, depending on what part and level of the organization it is focused on, the key elements for a frame of reference predisposed toward a nimble response to change must be consistent throughout the company or agency.*

Aside from its imagery as an all-encompassing entity, I use the term envelope *because, as a leader, you must learn to expand the envelope, much as jet fighter pilots do when they take themselves and their aircraft up to and beyond the known range of capability. The envelope is the boundary between the known and the unknown; between the amount of change load you and your organization have endured in the past and what is yet to come.*

What follows are the critical components to focus on when stretching and strengthening the enterprise-wide envelope.

209

13

Conditioning for Constant Turbulence

The Readiness Game

T he first element to address in the enterprise-wide envelope involves creating the proper predisposition in people's minds about the ongoing nature of change.

In any serious game, it is not the motivation to succeed that poses a problem, it's the conditioning necessary so that winning is possible. Bear Bryant, the legendary football coach for the University of Alabama in the 1960s and 1970s, was often asked how he was able to motivate his players on game-day to give their all. His response was typically something like the following:

> The challenge isn't on game-day. With thousands of people watching and the adrenaline flowing on the day of the game, the players' drive to win is the last thing I have to worry about. The problem is motivating them throughout the week to practice, practice, and practice some more when they are hurt, exhausted, wet, and cold.

Serious athletes are not people with a natural gift for their sport who simply show up on game-day, don their uniforms, then go out and perform at levels of proficiency that far exceed what the casual player ever could.

211

Yes, they are inherently talented at their game, but they also make a huge investment in conditioning themselves so that on game-day their innate abilities have been strengthened to the point of maximum efficiency and effectiveness. Long hours of training are devoted to practicing the basic skills and rehearsing the proper mind-set so that when the actual contest takes place, they are at their peak of readiness.

Change leaders are like the coaching staff of an organization preparing for the big game with its arch rival, perpetual unrest. Managers, supervisors, and salaried employees are like the players themselves, who must combine their natural talent with intense preparation to condition themselves for the contest. This analogy can be carried only so far, however, because of one key distinction. In the sports world, the bouts last only a brief period of time (a few minutes or hours) and are separated by several days (for example, with football) and sometimes several months (with boxing) of recuperation and further conditioning before the next match. Organizations seeking to be the nimble provider in their market are in a game of quite different dimensions.

Companies seeking to be more nimble have entered a competitive match that never ends. There are no three-minute rounds separated by rests in a corner of the ring, and no marching bands perform at halftime. There may be lulls in the game from time to time, when the pace of disruption settles down to a less frenzied level, but, for the most part, the action is fast and furious throughout the game. There are no practice fields where the team can try out strategies and run through moves in a safe environment without fear of consequences if their timing is off or someone fails to execute his or her assignment. There is only the game itself.

Rookies may be placed in less demanding aspects of the game where they will face fewer consequences, but, for the most part, after a brief orientation about the rules, everyone is thrust into the fray. People either perform well under these kinds of on-the-job training (OJT) conditions or they don't. With so much at stake for both the players and the organization, leaders must be as vigilant as possible about recruiting only talented people who demonstrate a predisposition for the game (e.g., innate resilience), and who can resonate well with the mental and emotional conditioning necessary to succeed.

To do this, people need a clear sense of what it will take to succeed and a practical view of how that translates into day-to-day behavior for themselves and those they work with. There are many elements to the kind of conditioning required to be a contributing player on a nimble team. They all, however, relate in one way or another to demonstrating a strong tolerance for ambiguity, that is, being able to deliver high performance despite the discomfort and confusion that typically exist when facing uncertainties. In addition to any natural tolerance for ambiguity demonstrated by players, leaders can coach their team members toward even greater displays of this quality by helping them establish appropriate expectations about life within a nimble organization.

Nimble companies continually reinforce for employees that the organization is competing in volatile, extremely inconsistent, risky markets. People at all levels must learn that the shelf life for assignments, responsibilities, solutions, tools, and techniques will be measured in days, weeks, or maybe months, but probably not often in years. People are taught that change is about dealing with the unfamiliar and, given the number of unforeseen events taking place in their markets, they should not waste much energy being caught off guard by the unexpected.

Nimble organizations are less focused on anticipating what surprises they will encounter; what is more important to them is to be prepared for the surprises that will occur. They help their people understand that the broad range of emotional reactions to change includes fear, anger, elation, anxiety, relief, discouragement, happiness, grief, and satisfaction. Some reactions are more pleasant than others, but as long as they are appropriately expressed and don't become destructive, any of these responses is considered understandable and acceptable. In a nimble operation, employees and management alike know that only one response to change is considered unsuitable—*being surprised at surprises.*

In a constantly changing environment, people cannot afford to be stunned or amazed at unexpected events. Nimble organizations inform their associates that there is little patience for staff members who register major surprise about changes. Such a reaction is considered a waste of time and resources. Because disruption is inevitable, agile operations want their associates' energy invested in problem solving and opportunity exploitation. They don't want people diverting their attention and spirit to the unproductive, self-indulgent exercise of being aghast when life does not unfold as expected. A nimble operation expects its people to accept the unstable nature of today's work environment as a normal phenomenon.

Nimble companies believe that while strategic planning and scenario development are helpful to building confidence during uncertain times, it is also important to temper this self-assurance with a healthy dose of humility. A humbling factor is needed here because when facing major change, impeccable preparation can never fully eliminate the inevitable surprises that will still occur. Nimble operations teach their people to analyze, study, plan, and train as much as they possibly can before facing the unknown. This preparation allows them to learn this important lesson: *You can't sidestep the inevitable surprises coming your way, but you can avoid being surprised that you are surprised.*

When their copious preparations turn out to be insufficient for the actual task at hand, many people are caught off guard and waste more resources than they can afford. When (not *if*) the major changes you engage are more demanding than you thought possible, don't waste your time and energy wondering why this is so. The watchwords for a nimble organization are: "Anticipate all you can, and then expect more."

Leaders can help set the proper expectations for this kind of constant upheaval not only by what they espouse, but also by how they behave when faced with unfamiliar circumstances themselves (e.g., what they show concern about and what they reward). Below is a list of the kinds of messages leaders need to send loud and clear—in words and deeds—concerning what people should start doing, or do more of, to condition themselves for constant upheaval.

THE "DO'S" OF ONGOING TURBULENCE

- Start being honest with yourself and your employees: more, not less, turmoil lies ahead.
- Start interpreting extended periods of calm as a distress signal—it means your sensors aren't working properly.
- Start thinking of things that appear stable as really being composed of rhythms or fluctuating waves of movement that form predictable patterns.
- Start paying more attention to how you learn than to what you know.
- Start concerning yourself with whether people you are responsible for can successfully assimilate additional changes when new initiatives are being considered.
- Start reminding yourself and your employees that everyone's job now is to succeed in unfamiliar environments.
- Start increasing your tolerance for ambiguity during periods of uncertainty.
- Start viewing some of today's disruptions as the bases for tomorrow's new possibilities.
- Start operating as if anything that looks like "the answer" to a major problem or opportunity is more expensive and less durable than is apparent.
- Start thinking about many contradictions as paradoxes.
- Start recognizing when to slow down (and do things right the first time) in order to move faster through change.

- Start translating "either/or" choices into "both/and" thinking.
- Start experimenting with everything you can, but remember to maintain the core values of who you are so you will have an internal reference point for making key decisions.
- Start taking some of the mystery out of change by learning to understand its patterns and dynamics.
- Start learning from your previous attempts at implementing change, and incorporate these lessons into new behaviors when facing major transitions.
- Start taking responsibility for architecting the future.

Listed below are messages that leaders should convey and model to people throughout the organization to let them know what they should stop doing, or do less of, in order to help achieve the nimble status in the market.

THE "DON'TS" OF ONGOING TURBULENCE

- Stop waiting for things to slow down.
- Stop promising yourself and your employees that your organization is just one change project away from tranquillity.
- Stop feeling sorry for yourself because life has become so challenging.
- Stop feeling like a victim when you don't get what you want.
- Stop assuming stress is always bad; a certain amount is necessary for learning.
- Stop thinking that you and your employees are entitled to always feel comfortable during change, or that your organization has failed if this doesn't happen.
- Stop being distrusting or resentful when your boss doesn't have all the answers about the future.
- Stop depending more on rhetoric and hype than on action to achieve your change goals.
- Stop being enamored with your own achievements—complacency and arrogance inhibit your ability to develop new expectations.
- Stop being drawn to the excitement of initiating change but bored or distracted with what it takes to sustain it.
- Stop relying on your own knowledge, assumptions, and perceptions as the only valid bases for determining what to do next.

- Stop thinking that any one person or any single group can resolve the really important issues in isolation.
- Stop running from the unexpected—instead, move closer to identify what new dangers are to be avoided and what new opportunities can be expected.
- Stop thinking only in terms of your own survival during change—it will invariably destroy the people and things around you and ultimately lead to your own self-destruction.
- Stop being afraid of abandoning things that have worked for you in the past.
- Stop being surprised at life's surprises.

These are the dos and don'ts of perpetual unrest. The conditioning necessary for players to really contribute to their organization's quest for Nimbleness is heavily dependent on these kinds of expectations being firmly embedded within individuals as well as within the collective corporate culture. Leaders can help entrench these expectations by constantly reiterating their importance and practical relevance to the everyday actions and circumstances people encounter. This can be done by:

1. Modeling for employees what it looks like to operate within the guidelines of these kinds of expectations.
2. Being available to serve as an interpreter, adviser, mentor, or coach as individuals and teams struggle to understand and apply these guidelines.
3. Hiring, promoting, and retaining people who are predisposed to operating in a manner consistent with these general guidelines.
4. Bringing significant positive (or negative) consequences to bear for those who do (or do not) operate consistently with these expectations.

William Shakespeare wrote: "Sweet are the uses of adversity" (*As You Like It*). But adversity is only positively useful, productive, and *sweet* if one undergoes constant conditioning.

CHAPTER

14

Expanding Change Knowledge

T he next element to the enterprise-wide envelope deals with the proper knowledge base. A basic and shared knowledge about the mechanics of organizational change can serve as the foundation for a strong transition management literacy, mentioned in Chapter 2. By being armed with a shared understanding of how change unfolds, people can conserve their adaptation resources significantly. For example, we know that it is perfectly normal and predictable that employees will resist, at some point and to some degree, even change projects they initially perceive as positive. When associates understand this dynamic, they can better manage their own and others' reactions to unfamiliar circumstances.

Also, whenever an individual's change knowledge is strengthened, it supports personal resilience by providing additional concepts and techniques that can be used to more easily manage transitions. The categories of this kind of change knowledge are referred to as the seven *support patterns* that compose the structure of change (see Figure 14.1). Each pattern can serve as a source for strengthening the primary resilience pattern of an individual by the application of the related skills and techniques of that support pattern. Here, I will give you a very brief overview of the conceptual content, some of which we've discussed earlier. All the patterns are

Figure 14.1   The support patterns.

more thoroughly covered in my previous book, *Managing at the Speed of Change*.

The Nature of Change

The importance of control in our lives must be recognized, as well as the fact that there are three levels of change pressure on people today: (1) micro change is when *I* must change; (2) organizational change is when *we* must change; and (3) macro change is when *everyone* must change. If we expect to manage major shifts in our lives effectively, the total adaptation demand from these three levels must be within our absorption limits.

The Process of Change

People and organizations develop the resolve to change when they recognize that the change is truly a business imperative (i.e., burning platform-type situations). In these situations, the issue is not *will* the necessary commitment to act be generated, but *when* (i.e., the timing of the resolve).

Pain and remedy are two prerequisites for successful organizational change (see Figure 14.2). The pain referred to here is the critical mass of

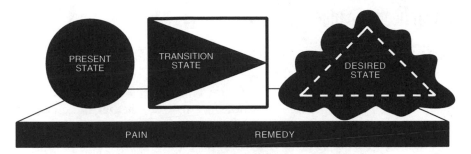

Figure 14.2   Change is a process.

discomfort associated with staying in the status quo; it justifies suffering through the transition state while moving toward the desired state. Remedies are actual behaviors in which people need to be engaged to achieve the desired state on time and within budget. To sustain change, pain and remedies must work together to create the desired outcome.

The Roles of Change

Another support pattern that helps explain change is the various roles that must be played in the organization if a particular initiative is to gain full acceptance. In addition to the leader role described, there are four additional roles in the transition process:

1. Sponsors—The individuals or groups who have the power to sanction or legitimize change. They ensure that changes are accomplished on time and within budget.

2. Agents—The individuals or groups who are responsible for actually carrying out the change. Agents' success depends on their ability to diagnose potential problems, develop a plan to deal with the issues, and help execute the change effectively.

3. Targets—The individuals or groups affected by the change. They must be educated to understand the changes they are expected to accommodate, and they must be involved appropriately in the implementation process.

4. Advocates—The individuals or groups who want to achieve a change, but lack the power to sanction it. Change ideas can die an early death if those who generate the ideas do not have the skills to gain support from those who can approve them.

Resistance to Change

Although resistance during a major change is inevitable, its expression can vary greatly. It can take the form of overt resistance, such as memos, meetings, or other public exchanges, or covert resistance, such as loss of trust, loss of morale, or even sabotage. It does not matter whether the change is originally seen as good or bad; when people's expectations are disrupted, the end result is always some form of resistance.

It comes as no surprise that we resist change we don't like. As depicted in Figure 14.3, people pass through seven main stages whenever they perceive a change as negative from the beginning (they don't want it and can't stop it):

1. *Immobilization* is the initial reaction to a negatively perceived change (shock).

2. *Denial* is characterized by an inability to absorb new information into the current frame of reference.

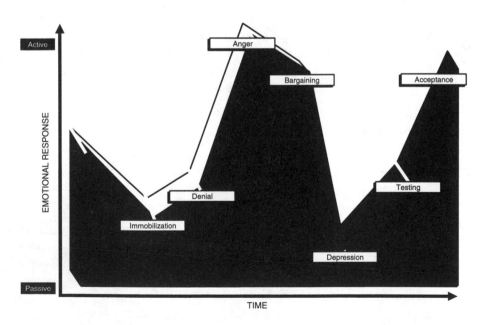

This model is an adaptation of Elizabeth Kubler-Ross's clinical work with terminally ill patients (*On Death and Dying,* New York: Macmillan, 1969).

Figure 14.3   Response to negatively perceived change.

3. *Anger* involves frustration with the change and often includes irrational and indiscriminate lashing out.

4. Afterward, people resort to *bargaining* to avoid the negative impact of change.

5. *Depression* is a normal response to major, negatively perceived change. The full extent of clinical depression, helplessness, and hopelessness is not usually found in organizational settings, but resignation to failure, a feeling of being victimized, a lack of emotional and physical energy, and disengagement from one's work are likely symptoms.

6. *Testing* helps people to regain a sense of control and to free themselves from feelings of victimization and depression.

7. *Acceptance* involves realistically facing the change, but this is not necessarily synonymous with liking what has happened.

People also resist change that first appears to have beneficial implications. A response to positively perceived change includes the following stages: uninformed optimism, informed pessimism, hopeful realism, informed optimism, and completion (see Figure 14.4):

1. *Uninformed optimism* is characterized by naïve enthusiasm based on insufficient data.

2. As major change unfolds, much of what we were promised does not come to pass, and much of what begins to take place we are unprepared

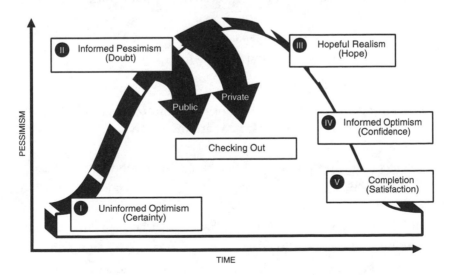

Figure 14.4 Response to positively perceived change.

for. This is called *informed pessimism*. If this pessimism should surpass a person's tolerance for doubt, the withdrawal from a change that occurs is called *checking out* (either privately or publicly).

3. When the concerns of the *informed pessimism* begin to lessen, people move into *hopeful realism* (i.e., having a realistic understanding of the change and a sense of hope of moving through the transition successfully).

4. As more and more issues are resolved, people become increasingly confident. They then move into *informed optimism*.

5. They then can either *complete* the change or begin the cycle again via another change.

Commitment to Change

This support pattern is about the resolve to sustain change. Most change failures can be traced back to some lack of commitment, either by obvious signs (the sponsor cancels the project) or more subtle means (target apathy). Your commitment to a specific outcome is evident when you:

- Invest the necessary resources.
- Consistently pursue the goal.
- Reject ideas or action plans that are inconsistent with ultimate goal achievement.
- Stand fast in the face of adversity.
- Apply creativity, ingenuity, and resourcefulness.

To help increase commitment to change:

- Refuse to take commitment to change for granted. Approach the development of commitment to change as an understandable and manageable process.
- Remember that people respond to change at different intellectual and emotional rates.
- Realize that commitment is expensive.
- Don't assume commitment will be generated without a plan of action.
- Keep in mind that building commitment is a developmental process.
- Either build commitment or prepare for the consequences.
- Slow down to increase the speed of progress.

Culture and Change

Culture is the frame of reference that helps distinguish one group of people from another and establishes a unique set of formal and informal ground rules for opinions and actions. The following characteristics are crucial for understanding the impact culture has on people:

- Culture is composed of three components—(1) The prevailing beliefs, (2) behaviors, and (3) assumptions of an organization. They serve as a guide to what are considered appropriate or inappropriate actions to engage in for individuals and groups.
- Culture is shared—It provides cohesiveness among people throughout an organization.
- Culture is developed over time—An organization's culture is the product of beliefs, behaviors, and assumptions that have, in the past, contributed to success.
- Culture is nurtured in a self-fulfilling cycle—Culture provides a means of understanding strategic decisions, which allows expectations to be developed, which generates thoughts and emotions, which leads to decisions about implementation, which guides and justifies activities that are supportive of the culture.

Culture usually develops in one of two ways: it is either evolutionary (reactive) or architectural (proactive). A key element to enhancing resilience and minimizing the chance of dysfunctional behavior is to actively manage your organization's culture. Whenever a discrepancy exists between the current culture and the objectives of your change, the culture always wins. The odds of implementing a change increase as the similarity grows between the existing culture and the beliefs, behaviors, and assumptions required by the new initiative. Either introduce changes that are consistent with the existing culture, or alter the culture to support any new initiative you want to introduce.

Synergy and Change

Before you attempt to make a change, you must examine the relationships among the project's key sponsors, targets, agents, and advocates (see previous discussion of the roles of change). These relationships can be viewed as self-destructive, static, or synergistic. Self-destructive relationships require more energy to sustain than they produce, and they usually are full of miscommunication, defensiveness, and blaming. Static relationships have an even mix of negative, backstabbing behavior and productive, team-oriented behavior. People in this situation are as effective working together as they are working alone. The synergistic relationship, however, creates a sum that is greater than its parts.

Applying Change Knowledge

A key aspect of the enterprise-wide envelope is your employees' mastery of the transition process. This calls for developing personal resilience and enhancing it by using a disciplined approach to change found in the Human Due Diligence process. A basic knowledge of the "structure of change" is a requisite to the achievement of this goal. It calls for recognizing the characteristics of resilience and its support patterns and respecting them as vitally important to absorbing change. It also requires using knowledge of these patterns to conserve existing adaptation assets and liberate previously untapped resources. Expanding resilience by using principles from the seven support patterns results in a powerful personal and organizational advantage in building a nimble organization.

Genuine Delegation and Empowerment

T he next contribution to the enterprise-wide envelope is the proper mix of delegation and empowerment. Both of these features in a work environment are essential for survival and prosperity in uncertain markets. Between the two, however, empowerment is the term more in need of clarification. Delegation is fairly straightforward. It is the act of granting someone in the lower levels of the organization responsibility and accountability for decision making. The key to its success is for management to stand firm on its decision to pass authority and accountability down to someone lower in the chain of command. Once such responsibility has been delegated, management should support the delegate's decisions unless the company can no longer afford the mistakes being made, at which time that person should be released from his or her responsibilities.

Empowerment is quite a different concept, yet, more often than not, the two are treated as synonymous. This is my definition: *Empowered employees are those whose input is considered valuable enough to influence the outcome of key decisions, but who are not in a position to make the final decisions themselves.* Empowerment represents an inclusive aspect of the decision-making process where employees have influence based on their knowledge or expertise, rather than their organizational position or tenure. It involves decision makers' allowing others to influence their deliberations rather than relinquishing the decision-making authority itself. With empowerment, a decision maker values the person's or group's input enough to consider it, but the responsibility for the decision still remains with the decision maker.

When someone has been assigned the right to make his or her own decisions, it is more appropriate to call this *delegation*. The term *empowerment* should be reserved for those situations where employees are *not* granted permission to take action on their own, but instead are asked to provide input to management as decisions are being made. They are empowered when they are seen as valuable enough to leadership and management to influence decisions—not when they are allowed to make their own.

As a senior decision maker, you maintain a strong position, but an empowered environment reflects a balance of power. As a leader, if you want valuable input from employees, you must deal with them from their true power base. Their power lies in the value their perspective has when you make a sound decision.

A nimble organization is one that displays strong, decisive decision making at all levels of the organization while, at the same time, it exploits the vast array of talent and ideas that exists throughout the entire workforce. In constrained organizations, delegation and empowerment usually have become so confused with one another that their important distinctions have been all but lost. When this happens, delegation becomes the overwhelming term of choice, and the concept of empowerment loses much of the distinction it originally possessed. The history of this convergence is fascinating and instructive.

The Delegation of Responsibility

The concept of delegating responsibility and authority has been around in a formal, institutionalized manner at least since the Catholic Church first organized its hierarchical structure. Why then would a new term need to suddenly emerge to take its place? It's my contention that two things have influenced the rise in popularity of the notion of empowering people instead of delegating to them the power to make decisions and then live with the consequences:

1. Misuse and abuse took place under the auspices of delegation.
2. A dramatic shift occurred in the number and nature of changes affecting the workplace, which caused managers to be unsure about what tasks or duties they were supposed to pass on to others.

The experience many employees have had with delegation is that they received the responsibilities associated with a task or job, minus the authority to carry them out. This, of course, created much frustration and wasted effort. Another more common situation was when responsibility and authority were granted but only on a provisional basis. It goes without saying that if a delegate consistently makes decisions that are not supported by management, then that person will be relieved of his or her delegated responsibilities. This action is wholly consistent with the consequences inherent in the delegation process. What often happens, however, is that a subordinate will be delegated duties only to have his or her decisions or actions second-guessed by management as soon as or even before they have been made or carried out. When this happens, management intervenes to correct a situation before it gets out of hand, thereby undermining any authority the subordinate was supposedly granted.

This kind of subversion of the true intent of delegation is even more destructive than micromanaging subordinates. Micromanaging may or may not be appropriate for a given set of circumstances, but when it occurs, management is maintaining direct control over that aspect of the operation and makes no pretense to the contrary. At least, when this happens, there are no mixed signals.

When responsibility and accountability are properly delegated, it is not under the condition that the person always performs as expected. Delegation is based on the hope that the employee will make sound decisions and engage the correct actions, not on a guarantee that this will always take place. To delegate a task or duty to someone means either you are confident that person will perform well but you can live with the consequences even if they don't, or you know the subordinate is not quite ready for the challenge but feel the lessons he or she will acquire from the inevitable mistakes that will be made are valuable enough that you will support the endeavor. In either case, once delegation has occurred, it is inappropriate for a higher level of management to step in and take action unless there is a declaration that the task or duty is no longer the responsibility of that person.

Delegation does not operate like a toggle switch that is turned on and off to accommodate the anxiety level of the next tier of management. It is a binary decision about a defined assignment at a specific time and with a particular person. Another assignment or time frame, and certainly another person, might preclude or advance the decision to delegate. But once delegation occurs, it is an all-or-nothing decision. Autonomy is central to delegation. Failure to adequately grant this kind of autonomy has undermined the credibility of the process within many organizations.

I believe this kind of corruption of intent became so pervasive by the mid-1980s that few people thought it was possible to resuscitate the process and reestablish delegation's original integrity. Which brings us to the second reason empowerment has become synonymous with and, for the most part, has replaced delegation. By the mid-1980s, not only was delegation broken and in need of repair or replacement, but management was quickly losing faith in its ability to determine what should be done to address the mounting chaos of change. Corporate management came under so much change-related pressure that companies not only turned to consultants (who didn't always have the answers), but also started soliciting the opinions of employees.

At about the same time, the human resource community conceived a new bit of jargon, empowerment, that was sufficiently vague so as to allow for a broad range of interpretation. As indeterminate as the concept was, it led to many people believing that they should be more assertive in expressing their ideas related to how their organization could better contend with the unprecedented change pressure that was building. Beset by these changes, leaders and managers decided to open the gates and get more employees involved in finding solutions. The combination of management's realizing that the way delegation was being deployed wasn't working—but not knowing what to do about it—and the human resources concept of empowering everyone, suddenly presented a very appealing package. What emerged was a vein of hope that perhaps by labeling delegation differently, past sins would be forgotten: "Let's call it empowerment and maybe it will work."

Here is a representative statement from management to the workforce:

> Okay, listen up. You're empowered now. Don't wait until someone tells you what to do. Take action as you see fit. You're bright and often closer to the customer than we are, so you take charge. We will support you. Instead of just doing what you're told, carry some of the responsibility for decisions we managers have made in the past. By the way, it wouldn't be fair to give you responsibility without authority as well, so congratulations, you now have that, too.

At the time, most leaders and managers knew that seeking input from employees was not going to be as easy as it sounded. They were aware that the workforce had long been overexposed to training programs and leadership rhetoric about the importance of participative management without much tangible evidence that anything ever came of it. It occurred to many of them that a well-crafted memo and an expensive video with the president saying, "Okay, we really mean it this time," probably wasn't going to work. Collective managerial wisdom concocted a new image and promise:

Not only would they seek employee input, but also transfer the responsibility and accountability to do such things as stop the production line when they deem it necessary, approve more loans without appealing to higher authority, and do whatever they think is necessary to satisfy the customer. With all this, the phenomenon called *empowering the workforce* was born.

Let's sidestep the lack of logic when what for hundreds of years has been known as delegation suddenly became labeled empowerment. This makes about as much sense as "the artist formerly known as Prince." We can chalk this up as one of those illogical quirks of human behavior that is best to smile at and move on.

What are worthy of examination are the implications that can be drawn from a combination of delegation's loss of integrity and the ambiguity created when mounting change caused leaders and managers to solicit employee participation to help steer their corporate ships. These forces, plus the confusion surrounding the terms *delegation* and *empowerment*, have not only generated untold anguish and consternation within organizational settings, but, more seriously, have hampered employees' much needed involvement in critical change decisions.

Empowerment has also been confused with democracy, consensus management, and self-management. Inviting participation in the decision-making process does not mean the decision maker has given up responsibility for the final determination. The decision maker is instead exercising his or her responsibility by choosing to involve others in reaching decisions. Empowerment is not an abdication of management control; it is another form of management control.

Empowerment is not the same thing as courage. At times, people must act on their convictions even though they know they will not be very influential with others. Yet, employees' submitting their perspectives on something does not constitute empowerment unless those offerings are considered valuable enough by you to influence your thinking. Therefore, empowerment represents both employees' willingness to provide input to a decision maker and an environment in which that input is valued. When someone chooses to express an opinion despite the fact that you do not seek or value that person's input, the act should be referred to as possibly courageous (or, stupid, given the circumstances), but not empowered. The students at Tiananmen Square were courageous but, from their government's perspective, they lacked the value to be influential. Therefore, they were not empowered.

We have observed thousands of people, in hundreds of organizations, enduring the pressures and responding to the challenges brought on by continuous change, and it is abundantly clear that more nimble operations utilize a decision making process that encompasses both definitive guidance by those in authority and influential involvement by the people who are impacted once these decisions are enacted. The nimble system is characterized by strong decision makers who have been properly delegated to and who take definitive action after receiving the broadest base of empowered input possible.

The Empowered Relationship

To be empowered is not a personal characteristic someone possesses; it is a description of a relationship between people involved in a common situation that requires a decision one person makes after listening to and valuing the viewpoints of the other(s). Empowerment describes a process where those who have useful contributions can influence decisions, and those responsible for making decisions are open to qualified input.

Given this perspective on empowerment, its application is not limited to employees' influencing those whom they report to. Empowerment can originate at any level and go in any direction in a hierarchy. Depending on the situation, people in any organizational position can be decision makers or participants in decisions at various times. Empowerment can apply down, up, or sideways in an organization. Managers may involve employees who have valuable contributions to certain decisions, or an employee may empower his or her peers, or even a manager, to influence a decision he or she has been delegated to make.

Teams and work groups can also reap the benefits of empowerment. In empowered groups, each person can influence decisions according to his or her ability to contribute. One person is usually responsible for a decision, even if the decision-making task rotates from member to member due to the subject matter. Although empowered input is always listened to, respected, and considered, the actual decision-making influence that team members contribute to the final decision is variable. For instance, an executive director may solicit ideas from his senior team on how to cut spending in his division. The final decision, however, is his to make, and he is usually influenced to varying degrees by the different viewpoints he hears.

In a team or work-group context, people often fail to distinguish empowerment from consensus-based or democratic forms of decision making. Each of these has value in certain situations, but empowerment is unique. The ultimate goal of consensus is common agreement. The downside of this approach is that it can produce decisions based on the lowest common denominator. In a democracy, all decisions must be supported by a majority. This makes it difficult for the group to take unpopular positions on issues.

With empowerment, the decision need *not* be supported by the entire group or even by a majority. The group's direct control over the decision is limited to its influence with the decision maker.

The demands of the situation also help determine whether empowerment will develop among people. Individuals themselves are not universally empowered—this would imply that it is an immutable trait that exists in any situation. People are empowered only in the context of certain relationships at certain times. One example is when a decision maker develops an empowered relationship with some—but not all—participants in a task. This will happen when some individuals are considered to have more relevant input than others. For instance, a department store manager looking for ways to boost customer service might seek input from the sales associates with the most experience or the most insightful points of view.

Another situation often occurs: someone is empowered by a decision maker only with regard to certain decisions. For example, a sales associate who can influence management's decisions about customer service may have no leverage whatsoever when it comes to marketing strategies. An individual's empowerment is usually specific to a decision, or even several categories of decisions, but it does not usually extend to all decisions.

It is also not unusual for an individual to be empowered with some decision makers in the work environment, but not others. Someone from the production department may be influential with his or her manager, but not with the director of information systems.

For an empowered relationship to thrive, it must be reciprocal; participants and decision makers must each have important roles to play. It is not possible to empower someone without seeking his or her opinions; likewise, an individual cannot declare himself or herself empowered with a decision maker who is not open to the input offered. Empowerment doesn't exist until a decision maker recognizes value in the individual's input. When the person's input is paired with genuine recognition of value for the ideas offered, empowerment grows. By the way, valuing others' ideas should not be confused with agreeing that their views are viable and should be implemented. I can appreciate your particular viewpoint and still disagree with what you suggest.

The term empowerment has often been interpreted as applying primarily to how employees feel about their worth to the organization and their capacity to influence management. The assumption here is that managers are automatically empowered by virtue of their status. For many managers, however, this is not the case. In fact, it only adds insult to injury when managers who do not feel empowered enough to influence their own bosses are told to foster empowerment with employees in their respective work areas. Empowerment must exist on all levels of an organization, otherwise a dangerous situation develops regardless of who possesses this sense of power. Feeling valuable and influential is therefore an essential component to both employees' and management's being empowered.

To be empowered is to believe that you can significantly influence your own destiny. Some people consider themselves lucky to have had, during their entire lifetime, one or two relationships in which they felt empowered to influence the decisions being made. Others feel they spend a great deal of their time either making decisions or influencing those who do. Yet, even the people who enjoy this status do not think they can directly control all elements of their lives. They generally don't think they are going to get everything they want, but they do believe they are responsible for much of what they get.

I'm using the notion of responsibility here to suggest neither blame nor acclaim, but rather the belief that the majority of the circumstances in which we find ourselves are the result of how we define (1) the situations we face, (2) the decisions we make, and (3) the prices we are willing to pay for what we say we want. The hallmarks of an empowered person are: taking responsibility for creatively framing situations so that success is possible; having the capacity to make tough decisions about what to do; and being willing to pay the price for achieving what is desired.

Victimization

The antithesis of empowerment is victimization. Within the context presented here, victims are people faced with negative situations who believe they have no alternatives available to them. In actuality, most victims do have options, but they can't define the troublesome situation in a way to succeed, they won't make a tough decision about what to do, or they refuse to act because they view the options before them as too expensive.

Anyone can fall prey to this trap. Victims convince themselves they have no choice, but, in fact, choices are available. They are simply difficult to define, hard to select, and expensive to execute. For example, an individual could confront another person he or she is having problems with, but may then face anger or punishment. People could risk offending or irritating someone at work, or take the chance of losing a key position or possibly even their job. They may not like these alternatives; nonetheless, they exist. Victims, however, take the easy way out.

People who see themselves as victims usually resent feeling that they are being used and abused, and are, therefore, eager to retaliate against the system. For example, they tend to demonstrate little interest in contributing beyond what is necessary to protect their employment during unsettled times. An organization profits little, if at all, from its investment in such people. In contrast, empowered employees appreciate being fully utilized during change and feel enriched by their experience. They are, therefore, motivated to look for new ways to help the organization maintain its competitiveness. The organization, consequently, enjoys a high return on its human resource investment.

Although the amount is never known at the beginning of employment, everyone operates with a certain measure of resources (i.e., time and energy) that they will ultimately utilize while working for a particular organization. Victimized employees and managers spend a great deal of their time and energy complaining about who or what outside themselves dominates their life. Empowered people spend their time and energy deciding what they want to achieve and what price they will pay for that success. What both of these groups have in common is the inevitability that the people in each group will run out of their allotted resources by the end of their employment. The difference between the two has to do with what is achieved with a person's resources while he or she is employed.

When Does Empowerment Happen?

Two factors encourage a decision maker to surround himself or herself with empowered people who can influence the decision(s) that must be made: (1) the latitude allowed by the situation and (2) the other person's ability to add value to that decision. The first factor deals with the degrees of freedom to involve others in a decision. Latitude becomes a constraint when logistics, budgets, or other parameters mandate that the decision maker must act without much meaningful input. There is no purpose in soliciting ideas and opinions from people when the decision has already been made or must be made within such tight parameters that any input would prove useless.

The second issue that impacts when empowerment takes place relates to an individual's unique contribution of knowledge, experience, and skills to a decision. A decision maker's openness to a certain individual's ideas grows as that person establishes a track record of adding value to decisions. Decision makers soon realize that they cannot afford to ignore someone who consistently offers sound advice. Empowerment is not something that an organization grants to its people or can transfer to them through training. It is a special status that is merited by building credibility through previous interactions.

Work environments can be established that attract people capable of becoming empowered, and empowerment can be fostered by acknowledging its importance, teaching what comprises the empowered relationship, and rewarding it when it occurs. Empowerment, however, is not a quality that can be given to people simply because an organization has decided that it would be beneficial to all concerned.

Three primary aspects of a situation influence whether employees are willing to offer suggestions to their boss. First, they must perceive the decision maker as open to input (this depends heavily on how that person has responded to ideas in the past). Second, they must have faith in the decision maker's ability to make sound decisions. Third, they must perceive the decision as important; it must have enough ramifications for them to warrant the investment of time and energy needed to become involved.

Empowered relationships tend to foster trust between people. Trust, in turn, strengthens the relationships. Trust grows over time as each party earns the right to influence the other by genuinely considering the other's perspective, and feeds back the outcome of that influence. Decision makers gain respect by genuinely listening, even to unpopular ideas, and by making sound decisions that in some way reflect the value of the input. For example, even when they don't adopt a recommendation, effective decision makers explain their rationale and demonstrate that the input was not disregarded. In turn, participants earn the trust of decision makers when they consistently support the final decision, even when it differs from their suggestions.

Building Blocks of Empowerment

The responsibility for building and maintaining empowered relationships lies with both the decision makers and the participants who offer their ideas and options (subordinates, superiors, and peers). Empowerment can only occur when fueled by certain supporting beliefs, motivations, and actions from both parties.

Beliefs are the foundation of empowered relationships. Decision makers in empowered relationships believe they:

- Must earn the right to lead.
- Don't have enough information to make the best decisions; others often have better access to information.
- Can improve the quality of their decisions by obtaining the input of those who have valuable perspectives.

- Can benefit from respected participants' feedback, even when it is difficult or painful to receive.

For their part, participants in empowered relationships believe they:

- Can contribute to the quality of decisions for which they have specialized knowledge, unique perspectives, or considerable experience.
- Must earn the right to influence the decision maker's thinking by providing valuable perspectives.
- Are responsible for helping decision makers make the best, most informed decisions possible.
- Have no direct control over the final action but can influence decisions by offering their input.
- Are working with a decision maker who is willing and able to be influenced when the advocacy comes from a source he or she deems credible.

Motivations are the driving force behind empowerment. Decision makers in empowered relationships want to:

- Make decisions that achieve the best immediate and long-term results.
- Ensure their decisions are thorough and technically accurate.
- Increase others' commitment to their decisions.
- Engage in breakthrough thinking and creative problem solving.
- Foster an environment where people are involved and feel valued.

Participants' motivation tends to come from the desire to:

- Shape decisions that produce immediate and long-term results.
- Work where they have an opportunity to influence their own destiny and that of the company.
- Increase the likelihood that decisions are well thought out.
- Work for a company in which they feel valued.
- Help produce breakthrough solutions.
- Share in the organization's vision.

Actions are the behavioral evidence of empowerment. Decision makers encourage empowerment when they:

- Select and develop people who will offer ideas and support their decisions.
- Determine when and how much to solicit the input of others.
- Send clear messages that participation is expected and will be rewarded.

- Appropriately involve specific people in the decision-making process (according to their qualifications and the amount of flexibility the situation allows).
- Employ techniques that facilitate participation (such as an open-door policy, focus groups, or hotlines).
- Carefully listen to and consider the ideas of others.
- Demonstrate the permeability of their frame of reference by using the input of others.
- Explain the rationale behind their decisions to those who offered input.
- Use consequence management to reward those who support the decision and impose sanctions on those who do not.

Participants enhance empowerment when they:

- Recognize situations where they have input to contribute, and then offer it.
- Identify problems early and prepare adequately before offering suggestions to decision makers.
- Share their honest perspective, even when this challenges the decision makers' views or desires.
- Show support for the decision maker and/or the decision, even when it was not what they advocated.
- Follow up with the decision maker to determine the impact of their contribution.
- Share with others examples of successful participation with decision makers.

Sequence of Building an Empowered Relationship

The decision-making sequence in an empowered relationship is shown in Figure 15.1, which represents the sequence of steps that satisfies the requirements leading to a participative and empowered outcome. Steps 1 and 2 reflect an atmosphere of mutual respect between an employee and decision maker, at least in the context of the issue at hand. The employee's input is valued by the decision maker, and the decision maker acknowledges that the presenting problem will be best resolved if they work together (Step 3). As a result of this declaration, the employee decides (Step 4) whether he or she is willing and able to assist the decision maker. If the conclusion is yes, the employee proceeds to prepare a case (Step 5) and

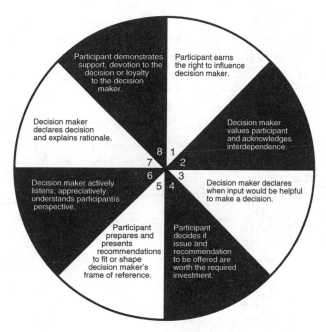

Figure 15.1   The decision-making sequence.

presents it to a receptive decision maker (Step 6). This is a critical point in the process. At Step 7, the employee must appreciate that the decision maker does, in fact, make the final call. On the other hand, the decision maker must explain his or her reasoning to the employee as fully and respectfully as possible. If the decision is explained in terms that the employee can understand—even though he or she may not agree with it—the stage is set for empowered interactions in the future. At Step 8, the employee in a mutually respectful and truly empowered relationship with a decision maker will either be devoted to the decision (agree with it) or, lacking full agreement, will be loyal to the decision maker or organization and will properly comply with the decision. Finally, by successfully completing Step 8, both participants in the process are typically eager to reiterate the empowerment sequence when the need next arises.

Benefits of Empowerment

When faced with the challenges of a volatile market, decision makers must fully tap all their resources in order to meet increasing change demands. People represent one of an organization's greatest natural resources, yet their skills, experiences, and viewpoints are often underutilized. Miscommunication, high turnover rates, turf wars, sabotage, and apathy are symptoms of unempowered employees in a workplace where their input is neither solicited nor valued. These kinds of unproductive actions serve to undermine leaders' efforts to keep up with massive changes, and ultimately create a drain on the organization as a whole. Successful organizations are learning to optimize their resources by channeling energies away from dysfunctional behaviors and toward change-related goals.

Building empowerment between decision makers and employees can be expensive. It often requires education, coaching, training, and consequence management. The payoffs, however, are substantial:

- During periods of high volatility, empowerment often results in more viable solutions.
- Empowerment increases commitment to decisions by involving employees across levels and functions in decision making.
- Empowerment sets the stage for synergistic teamwork.
- Empowerment fosters mutual trust and credibility among people across levels and functions.
- Empowerment increases vertical and horizontal communications in the organization.
- Empowerment creates a climate where conflict can be dealt with openly.

Delegation and Empowerment

Decision makers who wish to support a nimble work environment can no longer afford to confront the throes of change armed with limited input from a select few and burdened by petty internal warfare from impassive employees. To reach breakthrough solutions in an unstable market, leaders must incorporate diverse perspectives and solicit multilevel feedback. This is only effective when people, across the board, who have critical information and insight are involved in the decision-making process. In order to do this, it is necessary to delegate to decision makers the responsibility to:

- Build an environment where employees can help shape the organization's course in those areas in which they possess special expertise and/or insight.
- Be thoughtful and open to input during deliberation, definitive in decision making, and tenacious and tough, but fair, in executing key initiatives.

Involvement at all levels of an organization is key to the successful execution of a major change. In fact, in complex and turbulent environments, it is often the only way to reach sound decisions that can be widely supported. Employees can be integrated into this decision-making process and represent a valuable resource, or they can be overlooked and underutilized and may eventually become a potential drain. Delegation *and* empowerment are key to channeling employees' diverse energies into areas and activities that will help an organization achieve its long-term goals. It will then not only survive, but will thrive in the midst of future shock.

CHAPTER
16

The Value of
Structured Flexibility

O ur lives are comprised of many continuua. Each consists of two extremes that, under the right circumstances, can respectively satisfy our
needs. We maneuver between these continuua, seeking to obtain
whatever is the opposite to our current circumstances. When we're busy, we
long for a rest, but once granted one, we eventually get bored. We can't wait
for the kids to go to camp, then we miss the noise and confusion when
they're gone. We encourage employees to be frank about their views, but
then feel miffed when we are the object of their complaints.

The length of time needed to be at or near either end of a continuum in
order to satisfy a particular desire varies from person to person. You may
need days of solitude before you are ready to interact with people again, or
the one-hour commute to and from work may suffice. Sometimes, the mere
idea of losing what you have is enough to hold onto it even tighter; then
there are those things you don't really value until they are gone for good.

This facet of our existence can be a source of frustration for those who
are either unaware or unaccepting of how fundamental this dynamic is to
the rhythm and direction of our lives. Each of us has our own unique way
of moving from one end of the continuua in our life to the other. Regardless of a person's particular pattern, this oscillation in our lives opens up

opportunities for growth and progress. Without unmet needs and desires to motivate us, we would tend to remain fixed and stagnant at some point on the various continuua we encounter. To say this is not optimum is an understatement. Lack of movement up and down these continuua is synonymous with intellectual and emotional death.

Navigating between these opposing destinations is not a choice we are afforded; it is intrinsic to being alive. What does vary, however, is our perspective on this travel. When some people move back and forth between poles, they do so with anger and resentment because they can never find that perfect place to be. Most of the energy that they could apply to learning and growing is expended instead on self-pity and feeling victimized by life. Other people become stationary at one end or the other of their various continuua, and though they periodically gravitate back in the other direction, this movement is so slight and infrequent that, for all intended purposes, they have taken permanent residence at a particular pole. Included in this category are the compulsive, fanatical types who opt for extremism rather than growth. Constrained organizations are typically populated with both types: people who are resentful about the movement between poles and fail to grow much as a result, and people who move very little on their continuua and, likewise, fail to grow much as a result.

Nimble organizations tend to attract and retain people who have an unconscious, if not overt, appreciation for the movement they experience between the ends of their personal continuua. That is not to say that this movement is always pleasant or comforting. The greater the distance being traveled, the more uneasy they become because each time they migrate they leave the familiar for the unknown. Nonetheless, developing an enterprise-wide envelope that can support a nimble environment requires attracting and keeping people who value the unending passage from one end of life's continuua to the other.

Rather than feeling they waste resources when they retrace the same path every time they move toward the opposite pole, people in nimble operations tend to stay motivated for constant movement. From a nimble perspective, each venture brings new insights and learnings, which are then used to reinterpret what can be gained by accessing the alternatives at the other end of one's continuua. Even though the limits of a particular continuum's extremes may be reached over and over again, there is usually some new aspect to the endeavor that is revealed, and, in this way, progress results instead of redundancy. This progress is manifested in the process of learning something valuable about the respective ends of a continuum each time it is engaged, and then incorporating those lessons into one's perspective and mode of operation.

My own experience in this process may provide a useful example. A major portion of my professional life has involved moving back and forth on a variety of learning continuua. The poles of one continuum are my work on the road with clients and my work in the office. The first pole is focused on experiential learning while its opposite involves learning from a more theoretical perspective. The work on the road with clients is application-oriented: identifying change behavior patterns, testing new ideas and techniques, and observing results. All this occurs while I'm actively involved in consulting and educating around a client's specific need. When I return to my office, my attention turns to the conceptual end of the continuum. Here I review the feedback I've received and the observations I've made during application, in order to identify any generic change knowledge that may in turn be taken back to that situation or to another client's circumstances.

I find that both poles are attractive and alluring in their own way, making it easy for me to be seduced into overextending my stay at either end. What's needed is a mechanism to help me avoid the pitfalls that await me should I succumb. What I use is my understanding of the payoffs and costs associated with moving back and forth on the continuum.

It plays out this way. The gratification I receive from the direct experience of seeing clients gain value from my work is most enticing. If I pause too long at the application extreme, however, I will be constantly reinventing the wheel. Each new engagement would have to be approached without the benefit of my documenting previous observations and learning. On the other hand, I also find it captivating to reflect back on specific client situations and see whether there are any patterns to what was or what was not occurring that are similar to other client situations I've seen in the past. As attractive as this is for me, if I enjoy my research role too long, I end up being trapped in an ivory tower. The price I'll pay is: the muddled, confusing, contradictory, messy, and often unpleasant reality organizations actually operate within would gradually be replaced with sterile theory, hypothetical problems, abstract politics, ideal solutions, and speculative outcomes.

Mine is the world of the entrepreneurial researcher; to afford the luxury of investigating how humans change, I must present my findings in a manner that reflects true practical value to clients. This means my time is spent running from the field to the laboratory with observations and learnings, and then making them available to clients in order to fund my next excursion back into the field. To be successful in this endeavor requires two points of focus: I must have the freedom to creatively experiment in the field, and the discipline to translate the experiences into worthwhile information and knowledge. Both ends of this learning continuum are important to my professional pursuit.

The Structure/Flexibility Continuum

This ability to find practical value in what appears to be contradictory positions is in itself extremely critical to a nimble work setting, but of particular importance is the application of ability to the continuum formed by structure and flexibility. Order and chaos are the two extremes you must contend with when trying to find a balance point that will allow your organization to operate within its contained-slide zone. If order and chaos are seen as mutually exclusive, it is unlikely that an optimum course of action that addresses both conditions will ever be formulated. If, however, they are viewed as two extremes on an interdependent continuum that can be traversed as often as necessary to harvest the important lessons from each end, then a powerful integration of the two can occur.

STRUCTURE AND FLEXIBILITY

Should the goal be *flexible structure*, meaning an organization that places the priority on order while leaving room for creativity and spontaneity, or should a company pursue *structured flexibility*, implying that the hoped-for agility can best be attained in a state of true organized flux? Either interpretation is a healthy alternative compared to the working environment in a rigid, constrained organization. Nimble operations generally opt for the riskier version, where structure is used to support the primary value being placed on flexibility. Instead of being versatile in their conservatism, people in this kind of system are careful not to lose total control as they go about the limber, pliable manner in which they operate.

Though it is difficult to achieve, structured flexibility is not an oxymoron when it occurs as a paradoxical result of many years of an organization's bouncing back and forth between order and chaos. Over time, leaders come to realize that not only are both extremes equally dysfunctional, but so is the wasteful practice of each management regime's overcompensating in the opposite direction for the structures and practices put in place by the last group of leaders. Structured flexibility is an effort to practically apply the value both ends represent. Its goal is for people to take advantage of the collective experience and intellect of those who came before by staying within the guidelines provided, unless new circumstances arise that were not considered when these original guidelines were developed.

In constrained organizations, either people are taught to rigidly adhere to the directions they are given, regardless of what occurs, or they have too few procedures to follow and are left to reinvent the wheel each time they pursue a task. Unyielding rules won't allow for the constant shifting of variables. On the other hand, free-form, creative response to whatever is happening not only neglects to take advantage of history's lessons from failures, but it generates no viable format for passing on what works to others when success does occur.

Although an organization may be constrained, the people within it must still find ways to survive and remain sane even when the environment around them seems less and less able to control its destiny. One of the classic techniques for trying to accomplish one's job when bureaucracy inhibits success is to covertly circumvent the barriers causing the blockage. The ability to evade and outwit the officially sanctioned restrictions that prevent us from accomplishing our assigned duties, without drawing attention to ourselves, is an absolute must in a constrained bureaucracy. The energy that goes into the creative ways people elude the rules, plus the time they devote to bragging about such accomplishments to their peers, usually adds up to a huge, unintended investment on the part of the organization.

A nimble operation will choose to invest its resources very differently. Instead of an environment that requires people to either get their job done or follow procedures, it provides a mechanism for adhering to, as well as officially breaking from, sanctioned procedures. Rather than driving dissenters underground, an agile operation becomes an ally to those who want to fight the system and introduce modifications to established structures. They do this by operating within the boundaries of structured flexibility.

This kind of approach is an attempt to capitalize on the positive attributes of both ends of the order/chaos continuum by teaching people along these lines:

> Do what we've asked you to do in the manner you were taught, unless you face an exception that the guidelines didn't take into account. If this occurs, and there is not the time to get any advice from your boss, then use your best judgment, prepare to explain your position, and help us all learn from the experience.

The bottom line on Figure 16.1 makes a crucial point: Regardless of whether permission was granted or the employee acted independently, it is critical that whatever happens is translated into learnings that result in either a formal modification of the procedure or clear reasons why the standard approach should prevail.

Without the benefit of procedures that have drawn on past learnings received from people who have previously tried to accomplish a similar task, we are left with only naïve attempts and luck to prevent the loss of control. Unless there is a formally sanctioned mechanism to modify these procedures, either on a temporary or a permanent basis, the rigidity that typically

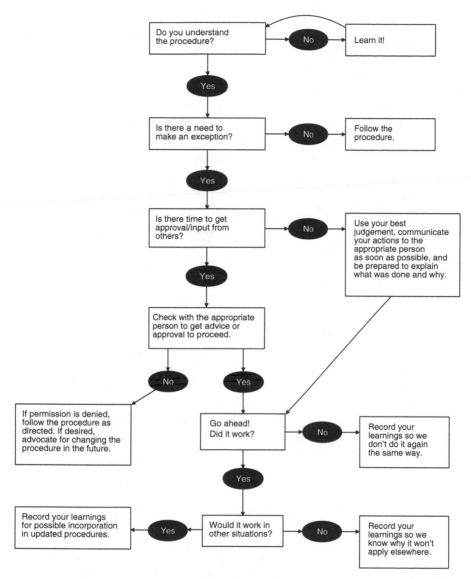

Figure 16.1 A framework for structured flexibility.

forms will not only encourage circumventive behavior, but will also leave problems and opportunities unresolved.

Sentar (fictitious name) had a sizable material management operation. In order to manage this important function, elaborate and detailed systems were put in place to ensure efficiency, consistency, and control. Individual procurement specialists were expected to abide by all established procedures or face serious sanctions for any deviations from the norm. While this system more or less guaranteed a predictable and therefore manageable operation, it was too cumbersome. For example, when vendors offered special, time-limited pricing options to Sentar, a procurement specialist often could not get the necessary approvals, from persons higher on the chain of command, to take advantage of the special pricing offer. Thus, the buying specialist had three choices: (1) stick with Sentar's procedures and end up paying more for the material; (2) break the rules, pay less, and risk being punished; or (3) spend more time than necessary (thus adding to company costs) circumventing the rules in ways that minimize the likelihood of getting caught.

Leaders from constrained organizations are usually afraid that their people will exercise bad judgment and do not allow the kind of fluidity that occurs with structured flexibility. What they can't grasp is that the worst that can happen is: current procedures will be periodically tested for relevance and either updated as necessary or confirmed "as is" after an experiment with an alternative to the standard. The best that can happen is: much more can be accomplished than the mere maintenance of a viable procedure. Structured flexibility means: (1) employees at all levels feel encouraged to act on their creative ideas and apply their closer-to-the-customer (or problem) perspective, while at the same time, (2) management can have confidence that the operation is still within their ability to influence. The system does not stay totally within predictable limits, but neither does it stray very far before management has an opportunity for corrective action. Structured flexibility is but one example of how to operationalize the pushing of a system into a contained slide at the very edge of the chaotic border.

Any element that contributes to strengthening the enterprise-wide envelope is a competitive advantage and, therefore, is usually expensive and difficult to achieve. If this were not the case, every rival would already be utilizing it. Both management and employees must make major investments in order for structured flexibility to become a part of day-to-day operations. Management must go to the trouble of adding an extra filtering mechanism to the hiring process—a screen that would reveal creative problem-solvers who are at ease expressing their opinions and ideas to management and, at the same time, can commit to supporting existing procedures unless and until they have been officially changed. Management must recognize and reward employees for their new ideas as well as be supportive of any person who takes the initiative to act when an exception is at hand and there is no time to follow the regular chain of command. Regardless of the ultimate determination of the actions, the fact that an employee pursued the initiative must be positively perceived. If not, structured flexibility is an empty phrase.

Ensuring Effective Implementation

We are at an important juncture in my description of the necessary conditions for an effective enterprise-wide envelope. Here, we cross over from those actions primarily designed to increase generic adaptation capability and focus on activities that are also intended to promote success with specific realignment initiatives. Setting up a strong sponsor network opens the way to building this bridge.

Everything described up to this point must be carried out by either the board or members of the senior executive team and cannot be delegated to others. But as we move into the sponsorship of specific initiatives, the activities to be outlined may or may not be done by the same leaders who set the nimble context for the organization. The criteria may fit the leader as well in that, with some strategic projects, the same individual, serves as both leader and sponsor. It would not be inappropriate, however, for a leader to feel his or her job had been adequately performed if the company's enterprise envelope included a network of managers and supervisors who could function as initiating and sustaining sponsors when the situation called for them to do so.

In this respect, the following framework for what constitutes a network of powerful sponsorship may or may not overlap with senior officers' leadership role. Regardless of who performs the sponsorship duties, without their accomplishment efforts at significant change are hopelessly doomed.

What Sponsors Must Accomplish

Sponsors are responsible for sanctioning the actions necessary to successfully implement major change initiatives. Specifically, they must:

- Understand the critical elements of providing effective sponsorship, and hold themselves accountable for performing this role well.
- Identify the network of other roles that must be played in order to successfully accomplish each change, including: additional sponsors, agents, advocates, and targets.
- Ensure that these roles are played effectively and that the following tasks are performed to completion in order to diagnose and address barriers to successful change:
  - —Making tough decisions about which changes to implement, keeping in mind the level of remaining adaptation capacity and the extent to which each change is a business imperative.
  - —Engaging each step in building a successful implementation plan.
  - —Executing the plan in a timely and effective fashion.

Characteristics of Effective Sponsorship

A key focus of our research over the years has been to distinguish winners from losers in the tactical management of change. Winners achieved the full human and technical value of their change decisions, on time and within budget. Losers either never accomplished their goals or did so only after investing a great deal more time or money than expected. Strong sponsorship proved to be, by far, the single most important difference between the two categories. We were able to identify very few people with sponsor duties, however, who fully understood this role. Most executives and managers described the sponsor as the maker or announcer of a decision. They displayed only a superficial understanding of the dynamics of change in general and the importance of the sponsorship role in particular. Consequently, their performance regarding change implementation was understandably low. We then took our learnings as to what made winners successful and developed a sponsor profile that serves as a guideline for strong sponsorship. For those with sponsor responsibilities, I offer the following characteristics for you to consider as critical to the success of change:

- Dissatisfaction with the present state—The level of dissatisfaction (pain) with the present state must be high enough to sustain sponsorship throughout the effort. An effective sponsor will be consistently aware that the organization cannot afford to fail at the change because the status quo is too costly. The initiative is considered a burning platform.

- Clear definition of the change—The effective sponsor will have as clear a picture as possible of the desired state. This vision ensures not only that the sponsor will lead in the proper direction, but that resources will not be wasted.

- Strong belief that change should occur—Organizations should avoid major change unless the sponsor believes that the remedy will eliminate the pain. Without a strong belief in its need and a commitment that it is the right solution, the sponsor will likely not be able to fully implement the change.

- The impact of the change—A change in one area often results in a significant impact on other areas. Effective sponsors understand the complex web of relationships that makes up their organization. They also understand how proposed changes will affect these areas in terms of both functionality and the human issues.

- Amount of resources necessary for change—Sponsors commonly underestimate the time, money, and people resources necessary to implement change. This mistake is the result of inaccurately assessing commitment, resistance, cultural impact, or change agent skills.

- Resource commitment—Effective sponsors must be willing and able to commit the necessary resources. They should make this commitment after realistically assessing the competing demands and anticipating future restrictions.

- Demonstration of public commitment—Sponsorship must cascade down an organization, but the target audience must have a sense that the change has been legitimized at the top. Initiating sponsors must, therefore, manifest their commitment publicly. Such displays of sponsorship will inform local targets that their immediate managers or supervisors are not acting without support from above.

- Strong private support—Skillful behind-the-scenes action communicates that the sponsor is not just paying lip service to the change project. Effective sponsors meet with key parties privately throughout the change process, to ensure continued support.

- Monitoring procedures—Procedures for monitoring are essential. They may take the form of periodic reviews of progress toward the change objectives. Monitoring procedures also help with early identification of any implementation problems that may exist, thereby allowing proper action to be taken.

- Consequence management—Effective sponsors must implement consequence management (i.e., the system of rewards and punishments used to sanction change). In most organizations, that which is measured and rewarded gets accomplished. Sponsors must therefore devise and maintain consequences that drive tactical objectives and strategic goals.

- Commitment to sacrifice—Major change often requires a personal and/or political price from those who play the sponsor's role. Effective sponsors understand that the costs for success are real, and they lead the way in paying them, thereby establishing that sacrifice will be required when the price of failure is prohibitive.

- Sustained support—Effective sponsors will do all of the above for as long as necessary to successfully implement the change. They will avoid short-term gains that are off the change path or will unnecessarily consume resources. They understand that no organization should undertake major change unless it cannot afford to fail at the effort.

The demands of being a successful sponsor dictate that no one can sponsor more than a few major change projects at a time. Poor sponsors often engage in far too many change initiatives, draining their time and energy to the point of being unable to adequately perform their duties.

Resolve

The real challenge in maintaining the course of change is the sponsors' resolve not only to initiate change but to persist in it. A major prerequisite for committing to change is the recognition that the cost of the status quo is significantly higher than the cost of change.

Initiating sponsors are those with the power to break from the status quo and sanction a significant change. They are generally higher in the hierarchy than those who must perform the duties of the sustaining sponsors. Sustaining sponsors are the people with enough proximity to local targets to maintain their focus and motivation on the change goals.

Although it may not seem plausible for a target to ignore a change directive from a senior officer of the company, it is a regular occurrence in most organizations. It usually happens like this: The initiating sponsor of a change may be the CEO, who makes a videotape announcing the firm's new focus on quality. The video is shown company-wide. Afterward, the local supervisor says, "Don't worry, it's just a bunch of hot air from the old man." The change is then poised on the edge of an abyss.

Any time there is a gap between strategic rhetoric and local consequences, targets will always be more responsive to the consequences. When the rhetoric the targets hear from senior management is not consistent with the positive and negative consequences that they see coming from their supervisors, an organizational *black hole* forms.

BLACK HOLES

There are spots in the corporate universe that seem to exert, on change projects, an effect that is similar to the effect of black holes on matter in space. Management's change rhetoric is pulled, as if by gravity, into bureaucratic layers and structures, wherein it forever vanishes without trace or effect. This phenomenon can yield, at all levels of management, withheld or distorted information. The information simply doesn't pass from one level of an organization to the next—or does so, but not in a form required for successful implementation. A network of strong sponsorship will prevent this problem.

Black holes form where there are local or sustaining sponsors who do not adequately support an announced change (see Figure 17.1). This occurs because of unintentional confusion, covert sabotage, or a lack of rewards and

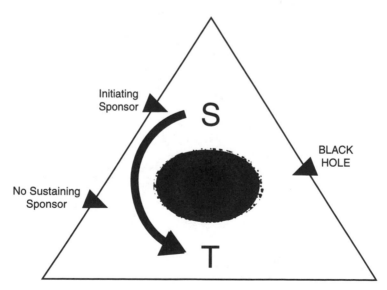

Figure 17.1   Typical ineffective sponsorship.

pressures directly connected to the change itself. Regardless of the reason, when sponsors fail to display the proper commitment to a change, the targets (T) below them will not fully support the transition.

Cascading Sponsorship

The remedy to the black-hole phenomenon is networked or cascading sponsorship, which begins with the initiating sponsor (S) and ends with the target associates (T). Change cannot succeed without a cascade of sustaining sponsorship that constantly reinforces the importance of a project as it moves through the organization (see Figure 17.2). With cascading sponsorship, initiating sponsors enlist the commitment of other key managers below them to support the change throughout the organization. These managers, in turn, do the same with those below them.

An effective network of cascading sponsors minimizes logistic, economic, or political gaps that exist between layers of the organization, and it produces the appropriate structure of rewards and punishments that promote achievement. Reducing the gulf between the rhetoric of change and

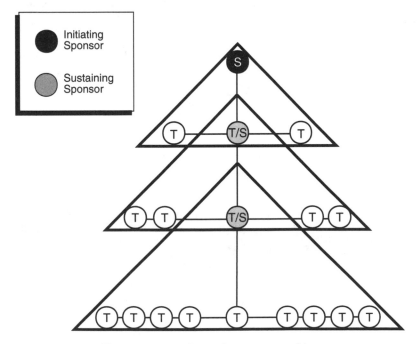

Figure 17.2 Cascading sponsorship.

the incentives and pressures that guide employee behavior dissolves black holes and thereby saves the unnecessary loss of adaptation capacity during project implementation. This is, in fact, the ultimate benefit of this book: the implementation of your change initiatives, on time and within budget.

Sponsors Reflect Leaders' Perspectives

The relationship between leaders and sponsors is important to the overall success of change endeavors. Leaders provide the context in which sponsors must operate. Whereas change leaders focus on the long-term implications of absorbing ongoing transitions, sponsors are centered on the short-term, tactical execution of specific initiatives.

In Chapter 10, we reviewed the six frames of reference most commonly displayed by senior officers playing key leadership roles during times of major change. Each tends to foster certain behaviors and actions by those functioning as sponsors. That is, sponsors often operate in ways that are consistent with their leaders' predisposition toward change (see Table 17.1).

Powerful Sponsorship

The primary description of effective sponsors is that they are scared and scarred. First, effective sponsors are scared, not necessarily that their change initiative will fail but that the cost if it should fail to be adequately implemented will be prohibitively expensive. They are scared of the implications rather than the probability of failure. Sponsors pursue business imperatives with the determination and compulsive tenacity that come from a burning-platform mentality. Also, effective sponsors benefit from the wisdom garnished from the scars left by decisions that were inadequately implemented because of a lack of applying Human Due Diligence to the human side of change. This scar tissue can be formed as a result of direct experience, vicarious learning, and/or mentoring by an experienced and trusted friend, colleague, or consultant.

If sponsors fail to fully comprehend the implications of the status quo or are unwilling or unable to properly execute their sponsor role, the change effort will fail. Without appropriate sponsorship—attention, energy, action, and other resources—the initiatives will falter. The only variables will be: to what extent does it fail; to what degree is the shortfall covered up by manipulated metrics and hyped rhetoric; and what, if any, learning surfaces that can be used to play the game more effectively on the next important project?

Table 17.1   Sponsor and Leader Perspectives

Leader's Frame of Reference	Sponsor Interpretation	Typical Sponsor Statement
Anti-change thinking	Be a goaltender.	"We don't pay you to think up ideas for change—you're paid to get your work done. If we ever change things around here, I'll give you a call. Until then, go back to work."
Rational change thinking	Use the "hammer" approach.	"Okay, listen up. Next week, we will be changing the way we do things around here. There will be new procedures, and some of you will be shifting your duties and responsibilities. The details, as well as my reasoning behind what we are doing, will be in my memo. It will be clear to you if you read everything carefully. Any questions? Good. Let's get back to work."
Panacea change thinking	It's a piece of cake.	"Sure, we've got some people upset with the changes we introduced, but hey, how hard can this be? Let's get Human Resources to order that videotape they were telling us about. Everybody should 'brown bag' lunch one day and we could all watch it. That would make the complainers feel like we're all in this together."
Bolt-on change thinking	Be careful when it is convenient to do so.	"I know how important this change management stuff is, yet I think you'll agree, it wouldn't be prudent to ask our people to slow down for any of that now. We'll be doing well to get the technical installation complete on time. We'll just have to wait until we have a little breathing room before we can afford to deal with the soft side of things. But, I promise you, we are going to do it. I'm not reluctant to use any of the techniques, I'm just trying to be practical about what we can realistically accomplish."

Table 17.1 (Continued)

Leader's Frame of Reference	Sponsor Interpretation	Typical Sponsor Statement
Integrated change thinking	Use a balanced approach.	"I have two messages for you, both of which are very important. First, this company's future, your job, and my job depend on hitting the new cost-reduction figures by year's end. We have absolutely no slack for tardiness or errors in hitting that mark.
		"The second message is that we are charged with not only implementing these changes and hitting the year-end numbers, but also sustaining that level of overhead for the foreseeable future. We may be able to use sheer force to hit the year-end deadline, but we can't maintain that kind of operation without our people behind us. So, I'm warning you now, when I ask for a status report, I want both the technical and the people issues addressed.
		"If you come back to me without your Human Due Diligence completed, you'd better have a note from your mother explaining why."
Continuous change thinking	Looking ahead.	"We can't afford to simply do a good job of applying a Human Due Diligence level of rigor to the human side of this project. Everyone here knows how important this initiative is to our long-term viability in the market, but we must not lose sight of the fact that even more changes are on their way—many we can't even see yet. We must not only successfully navigate this project through the cultural barriers that lie ahead, but do so in a way that further strengthens our company's overall capacity to respond in a nimble manner to future demands of change."

PART SIX

THE DESTINATION IS THE JOURNEY

Building a nimble organization is the most challenging task leaders face today.

Even scared and scarred leaders are cautious, as they should be, about taking that first step toward the rim of chaos. Of those who do venture forth, some will muster their resources to push ahead and eventually gain the skill and wisdom needed to succeed at the nimble game. Those who accomplish the agility they seek will learn that it is an arduous journey, fraught with trials, false starts, and defeats. Yet, at the same time, there is also the potential to gain an extremely high level of personal and professional satisfaction for yourself and your organization. The journey toward mastery of change is at once necessary, intimidating, and alluring. The thing to remember, though, is that setting out on the journey means never arriving, because change forever changes.

To ultimately prevail at the change game, we must understand the basics of how mastery is acquired and retained. It is the subject of Part Six.

Mastering the Leadership Role

The Journey

We have only begun to experience the change pressure that will continue to mount as the perpetual unrest era unfolds. Just as this level of change is a new challenge confronting business leaders, organizational Nimbleness as a remedy is equally untested. It appears, however, that by operating within the zone where a contained slide is feasible, organizations can enjoy the benefit of a faster and more effective adaptation capability than their competition.

Because Nimbleness is new and unfamiliar, our research in this area has uncovered only a few senior officers who displayed all the characteristics that promote a nimble environment. We have learned the most about nimble leadership by taking a composite approach, combining the best attributes from many different senior officers of nimble organizations. Some leaders were more skilled in some nimble aspects than others, and by focusing on them and what they were doing, we have been able to further our understanding of what senior executives must exhibit to expand their companies' capability for change.

I will refer to these leaders as masters of change, not because they have all the answers but because, relative to most executives, they have more of the right answers. Although these men and women from all over the world were involved in everything from mergers and downsizing to reengineering and introducing new technology, they all had one thing in common. Each in his or her own way had orchestrated a powerful agility in a company's day-to-day operations so that when important initiatives were announced, employees listened, understood the urgency, and accomplished their assigned tasks, usually on time and within budget. Sounds elementary, doesn't it? All these leaders did was build an environment where people could execute what they were supposed to around change when it was due. The sad truth is, this fundamental characteristic of leadership is no longer an assumed element of the corporate landscape.

In fact, accomplishing the full value of the changes business leaders have promised their boards, shareholders, and analysts has become the exception. This failure to deliver has not gone unnoticed by employees. Fewer and fewer people in the workforce believe that the various initiatives they are inundated with will ever really occur. Most workers in the corporate arena learned long ago not to confuse executive announcements with reality:

> When is someone up there going to grab the reins? Do they really expect us to get all lathered up every time they read the latest book from the "guru du jour"? This is the same crew who declared last year's panacea was our salvation, and the year before it was something on a little card I was supposed to keep in my wallet. The year before that, I think we all had to keep crystals on our desk and walk on hot coals—I can't remember.

To avoid this erosion of leadership's credibility, masters of change are very judicious about their transition pronouncements. They treat their strategic rhetoric as a currency that will be devalued if used in association with failed efforts. Their basic attitude is: "I wouldn't have announced the change unless it were essential to the business, and, therefore, we have no choice but to succeed at its stated objectives."

After years of studying exceptional and powerful architects of change, I continue to be intrigued not only with the lessons they have to pass on to us about organizational Nimbleness (which formed the contents of the previous chapters), but also with the manner in which they learn these lessons and gain their change-related wisdom.

On the Road

Based on what I have witnessed while working with senior officers over the past few years, there appear to be ten basic stops on the road to becoming a master builder of a nimble organization. Each of these junctures represents a critical crossroads in the process of learning how to translate strategic rhetoric into tangible actions. At each of these crucial points, if the traveler responds to the situation appropriately, learning occurs, and the next developmental phase of the journey is engaged. If any of the crossroads is not adequately addressed, the lessons necessary for mastery are blocked at that stage and further development is arrested.

IGNORANCE

The journey begins at ignorance.

When most new leaders or incumbents first take on a major initiative that represents more of a challenge than they have faced before, they enter the road to Nimbleness at a small community called *ignorance*. Ignorance, like everything else in the change game, is relative. This is not the ignorance that is associated with never managing change before. In fact, the executive[1] we will track on this road has an impressive record of implementing numerous change projects, some successful and some less so. The ignorance that places him at this point on the road is not so much tied to a general lack of change experience as it is due to his taking on a change project that's much more convoluted and demanding than any he has engaged before. He has promised more than he knows how to deliver—he just doesn't realize it yet. He not only doesn't know how to achieve a change of this scale, he doesn't know that he doesn't know. He assumes successful implementation is only minutes away and the trip will be uneventful, if not pleasant.

During this phase of the excursion, leaders are often doing such things as issuing memos, making speeches, and devoting portions of their executive meetings to explaining the remarkable results they expect from a particular initiative and the brief amount of time it will take to complete. If major change were this easy, it would mean we would seldom get in over our heads, and change-related wisdom would be nothing more than a trivial pursuit.

Critical corporate transformations are, of course, not that easy and the person who attempts to make change initiatives at the ignorance stage is bound to fail. Though painful, this failure is a necessary catalyst for the learning that must take place to proceed further down the road.

If somehow the initiative's goals are accomplished with simplistic memos and speeches, or its failure goes unheeded at this juncture, the likelihood that the executive will learn from the experience is minimal. For most people who are already successful, the really important lessons come from falling short of their goals, not from exceeding them.

But wait—can't we learn from success? Of course we can. In fact, success is particularly important early in the development of a new skill. That's why it is so important to be extremely encouraging to young children in their formative years or to adults when they first try something new. It is critical at these early stages of competency development to build the self-confidence that allows the student to see that proficiency is possible. For most people, facing too much failure too early in the learning process will drive out the motivation to continue the endeavor.

So, learning from success is important, but its primary value is achieved at the early and midterm phases of competency development. The more proficient people become in a skill, the more they draw from their failures to gain new ground. At the upper tiers of any profession, players of the game certainly relish the successes they achieve, but it is the missed opportunities and the poorly executed maneuvers that they focus on in order to strengthen their capability. If people at this level of the game improve, it is usually because they have paid close attention to what can be learned from their most recent failure.

The corporate culture that promotes this kind of learning can be perceived as either stimulating and inspiring or brutal and punishing. The match between the expectations people have about learning from mistakes and the need for such learning if one is to achieve the desired Nimbleness is key to a company's success. Misalignment between expectations and requirements for success can generate an environment where people feel unappreciated and overworked rather than valued and challenged. Someone who is not exceptional at his or her job, or is reluctant to push the limits of the personal skill base, and/or needs constant praise for yesterday's achievement is unsuited for an organization striving for or maintaining a nimble status.

Our executive traveler considers himself to be a world-class player in an organization seeking to be the nimble provider in its market. He not only has many years of experience in management, but in the course of his tenure as a senior executive he has successfully initiated several major change projects. Despite this background, he entered the journey at ignorance, not because he knows nothing about managing change, but because he is so unprepared to lead a company of this size, facing this much change. The scale and complexity of the game are unfamiliar to him, not the game itself.

Because our traveler considers himself already skillful at leading change, his most important lessons on this journey will come from his failures, not his successes. The ability to translate failure into learning will be essential.

For the executive, there are many hurdles to learning from failure. If he acknowledges failure but attributes it to someone or something else, there is no reason for him to take responsibility for corrective action. Also, if it is not expensive for him to fail, there is little motivation for him to seek less costly alternatives. Finally, if he can't or won't invest himself in identifying how to recover, the likelihood of future improved performance is low.

Managing failure at each of the crossroads on this journey is imperative for movement to occur from one phase to the next. We have found that progress will only take place if failure is acknowledged, responsibility is accepted, costs are perceived as significant, and the person is willing and able to pursue new, more effective ways to perform the task.

If, while at the ignorance stage, the traveler can convert his failure into learning, the key lesson to be acquired is that sophisticated change is not accomplished by simplistic announcements. Human beings have a complex network of defenses they can use to fight change. Remaining ignorant of these inhibitors and of what to do to manage the change process is a one-way passport to feeling victimized in a turbulent world. Only if a person correctly manages failure can he or she learn this lesson, and only if the correct lesson is learned can he or she advance to the next stage of the journey—toward mastery of the change game.

EDUCATION

When ignorance leads to recognizing and taking responsibility for the failure of an important change, and the cost of that failure provides the motivation to seek new answers, the traveler can choose to move on to the next stop, called *education*. Here, our executive can engage in any number of activities, from reading books and attending seminars to hiring private corporate tutors (consultants) or pursuing advanced degrees in the art of leading change. The objective here is to learn the dynamics of how people change or resist change in organizational settings, and what strategies can be employed, both before and while those dynamics are being executed. All this learning is in the service of increasing the likelihood of achieving the human and technical objectives of key initiatives on time and within budget.

The length of time the traveler chooses to stay in education can vary widely. It may range from the hours it takes to read a book on the subject, to three days in a public seminar, or to several years to pursue more formal training. Once the traveler is confident that he has accumulated all the knowledge necessary to successfully prepare for and execute major change, a new attempt will be engaged. Either the same initiative will be tried again (if it is a long-term effort) or the learnings will be applied to a different project. If he advances no further than education, however, the result will, once again, be failure.

Dealing with the human aspects of fundamental transformation within organizations involves much more than simply learning what should be done. Not yet realizing this, but armed with no more than the cognitive understanding of how change is accomplished, our traveler once again tries to engage change and faces defeat. As before, acknowledging and taking responsibility for this failure are critical if further learning is to take place. Not only is the desire to learn important, but the person must also possess the ability and willingness to learn the next and even more demanding set of lessons if progress on the journey is to continue.

INSIGHT

Failing twice now has gotten the attention of our executive traveler. Undaunted, however, he moves further down the road to the small town of *insight*. Here, the journey becomes more introspective. Our executive explores his previous change attempts and matches these experiences against what he learned while visiting education. What might explain his lack of success? If intelligence and ego are in their optimum ratio while this self-examination takes place, the executive can begin to separate theory from practical application and to identify nuances as well as the more obvious aspects of how the change process really works.

These insights can take many forms. For example:

> Now I can see what my instructor meant when she said people resist any major changes in their lives—even the positive ones. It wasn't that I didn't understand her when she first explained it during the managing change training program. In fact, I remember agreeing with her at the time. There is just something different about actually witnessing this phenomenon in real life. The very people who were originally promoting this change are now the primary roadblocks to its success. I now have a very different appreciation of what she was telling us in class.

Searching for these kinds of insights helps the executive identify the key strengths and weaknesses in his change-management performance. From these insights, he can now develop new strategies to compensate for his previous errors.

With a sense of pride at having covered so much ground, and with a belief that all the prerequisites for success have now been met, our traveler sets out for what he believes to be the last leg of the journey to successful implementation. Once again, however, the cost for mastery proves to be beyond what he expected. The next attempt to execute the same project (or a new effort) again falls short. It would be easy to succumb to denial or rationalization at this point. Only if our traveler can, again, admit failure and seek more learning will he be able to resume his journey toward the ultimate objective.

INTENT

Armed with fresh insight, the traveler starts again down the road of learning and eventually finds himself on the outskirts of a moderate-size city called *intent*. At this stage of the journey, the key lessons center around focusing one's resolve toward the change objective:

> It's time I get serious. I've got to crack the code on this—there is too much at stake to blow it. I know what to do, I learned that at "education," and then I determined what is really important about the approach I'm using when I was at "insight." If I just apply what I've learned, this project can come in on the mark.

Confidence buoyed, the executive traveler engages the same or yet another change effort, only to be thrown back by failure once again. Exhausted from the struggle and depressed by the lack of success, he now expresses doubts about whether succeeding at the change game is even possible:

> Is it just me and this particular project, or can anyone really change a large organization in a meaningful way? Maybe the gurus of change have simply charged such outrageous fees that no one will admit to the fact that their advice doesn't work. Maybe everyone knows but won't say that real change can't be orchestrated. Am I the last to know that it either happens or it doesn't, and change is really impervious to guidance?

Our traveler has dropped into the self-doubt and disillusionment that always come with informed pessimism. His sense of insecurity and betrayal will continue to mount until it either exceeds his tolerance for pessimism, resulting in a decision to abort the project, or a breakthrough occurs that energizes him to, once again, resume his journey on what now appears to be a dark, lonely, and dangerous road. Again, this kind of catharsis is dependent on the executive's ability to confront and manage failure and to draw the appropriate lessons from the experience.

COMMITMENT

Only as the executive pulls into the next metropolitan area does it become apparent that he has finally reached true *commitment*. Looking back, it seems embarrassingly sophomoric that he assumed "intending" to apply the change lessons he had previously learned could have produced anything more than it did—impotent hope, wishful thinking, and frustration. It is now clear that intending to apply a lesson learned reflects what one does with a good idea for change. Commitment to achieving something is the level of investment people make when they encounter not a good idea for change, but a business imperative—a change the executive and his company could not afford to fail achieving. It is the difference between merely wanting something and recognizing it as an absolute necessity.

The executive notices that, at this stage of the journey, the lessons about implementing change have grown harder to come by and are more cathartic. Correspondingly, their influence on him is also more powerful. It becomes clear to him that all the previous lessons learned would disappear like morning fog without this bond between desire and tangible results—the bond called commitment.

To solidify his new understanding of what commitment means, he establishes for himself the criteria by which he can recognize his own true resolve when it materializes. From now on, he decides, he will save the word commitment for when he:

- Invests the resources (time, energy, and money) to ensure the desired outcome.
- Consistently pursues his change goals, even when under stress and with the passage of time.
- Rejects ideas or action plans that offer short-term benefits but are inconsistent with the overall strategy for achieving the ultimate goal.
- Stands fast in the face of adversity and remains determined and persistent in his quest for the desired goal.
- Applies creativity, ingenuity, and resourcefulness to resolving problems or issues that would otherwise block his achievement of the goal.

"This was an important lesson," he thinks to himself, and he is proud of this milestone. True resolve will be the key source of the energy needed to propel him and his people, as well as the organization itself, through the transition process at the fastest and most effective pace possible—the optimum speed of change.

The learning needed to successfully manage major organizational change occurred many miles and numerous painful failures ago at education, and it was reinforced at insight. He now thinks the last puzzle piece must certainly be in place, so our executive continues his journey with renewed vigor toward the wisdom he seeks. There is a fresh spring in the traveler's step as he enjoys his newfound confidence. He anticipates that, a short distance down the road, he'll not only accomplish the initiative at hand but will also secure the coveted title of *change master*.

As he rounds what he believes to be the last turn in the road, he finds himself squarely facing a huge brick wall of implementation inhibitors. It catches him by such surprise that at first he is disoriented, as though he had just waked up in an unfamiliar hotel room in the middle of the night. He literally runs into the brick wall before he can stop. He is stunned by its mass. As far as he can see to the left and right, and as high as he can focus his eyes, there is nothing but solid resistance.

The details and implications of the sight before him are overwhelming. As the designated architect for the initiative he was charged with achieving, he recognizes he is doomed. The bricks in the wall are composed of dense resistance-creating materials: bureaucratic games, infighting, covert sabotage, and change rhetoric with no consequences. The wall is impermeable, and he knows it.

He turns and silently walks back a few hundred yards to a clump of bushes off the road. There, hidden from view, he slowly sits down, puts his head in his hands and weeps, overcome with despair and exhaustion.

His tears and remaining pride are finally drained, so he gets up and starts to walk in the direction from which he had originally come. After a few steps, however, a new realization overtakes him so powerfully that all he can do is groan and steady himself against a tree. He confronts a dreadful fact: Going back means the change he was committed to has failed. He became committed to this change only after realizing that its failure would incur a price that was prohibitively high. It's apparent that, despite the resistance he has encountered, going back to the old status quo isn't a viable alternative.

What is he to do? He can't go back; the price is too high. The overbearing image of the massive wall of resistance, however, continues to flash in his mind. He feels that trading places with someone faced with the mere dilemma of being between a rock and a hard place would be a welcome relief. He thinks, "I have no viable alternatives here; the change is insurmountable. But I can't afford to return to the way things were."

As he stands there, so stunned by his circumstances that he appears frozen in mid-stride, a scene from one of his favorite movies plays itself out in his mind. There they are, Humphrey Bogart and Katharine Hepburn on the *African Queen* deep in the jungle. Bogart's character (Charlie) has just pulled himself out of the water for a rest. They had become lost in the backwaters of the Congo and found themselves in water so shallow that Charlie had to manually pull the boat with a rope as he trudged through mud and the ever-denser foliage.

As he sits down on the deck of the boat to rest, he realizes he is covered with leeches. He goes into a panic and yells to Hepburn (Rosie) to help him get them off without leaving their heads in his body to fester.

Until this scene, Charlie has been portrayed as a powerful, tenacious, hard-driving personality. He has met each challenge presented to him by exhibiting the strength audiences expected from a 1950s portrayal of a man's man. Yet, when Charlie sees those leeches on his body, he crumbles and completely loses his composure. He is shivering like a scared child as he explains to Rosie that the one thing he can't deal with, never has been able to deal with, is leeches. It's his Achilles' heel.

Next is a close-up study of Bogart's face as Charlie absorbs the implications of his situation. If he does not reengage his worst nightmare, he and Rosie will die mired in the mud. No just-in-time, creative problem-solving technique can miraculously generate an easier, less gruesome alternative at the last minute. The film eventually ends on a happier note, but this scene is saturated with existential angst. Charlie must either go back into the water and face the leeches, which he feels he is emotionally unprepared to do, or he must confront the even more lethal option of staying in the boat and remaining stuck in the mud to die. Bogart's blank stare and measured movement as he slips back into the leech-infested water convincingly portray Charlie's plight: he is in a burning-platform type of situation.

In the few moments it takes for this scene to be played out in our traveler's mind, the answer to "What do I do now?" becomes painfully obvious to him. "For Charlie, it was leeches; for me, it's this wall of resistance. I don't know how I'm going to scale it, or find its weakness and break it down, but I do know confronting that wall is my last and best chance to avoid paying an even higher price if the change project fails."

With this mind-set, the executive evidences that he has learned another important lesson. Though it's perhaps hard to believe, even true commitment is not enough for successfully managing major organizational change. He doesn't know what comes next, but he knows he must find out, and the only way to do that is to continue his journey by confronting the wall of resistance that lies before him.

STRUCTURE

It suddenly occurs to our traveler that this stretch of the journey is particularly treacherous. Instead of moving down the road, which would reflect progress, he finds himself running from one end of this huge brick wall to the other, fighting all forms of resistance. The excuses he hears from the reluctant targets he encounters are endless: "Why can't we go back to the way things were?" "I don't think all this change is really necessary." "If we phase in the change, can my people be last?"

After many unsuccessful attempts to deal with the various forms of blockage, the executive's frustration mounts. At one point, he finds himself on a steep incline. The footing is loose, and confusion is everywhere. He stops to assess his predicament: "This isn't working—I'm not gaining any ground here. What else is there? I know what to do and I'm totally committed to doing it right. I no longer think turning back is an option, but what do I need to learn to go forward? There must be something that could help me." Finally it comes to him: "Tools! That's it—I need tools. I'm failing to manage this change because I'm relying on my knowledge and passion. What is missing are the mechanics."

Just at that moment, our traveler comes into a densely populated area positioned close to a section of the wall. The town's name is *structure*. As he enters the city limits, he says to himself:

> I shouldn't be guessing what the right questions are to surface my employees' resistance; I should be using well-documented diagnostic tools. I shouldn't be hoping I can remember to secure the proper mid-level management support before I engage a project; I should use a structured checklist like airplane pilots do to be sure they don't forget any preflight procedures. I shouldn't be hoping that people below me pay as much attention to the human issues as they do to the logistics and charts; I should require that our project management process have embedded within it the necessary steps to deal with such things as resistance and corporate culture.

Now, with knowledge, commitment, and structure in hand, the traveler moves in for what surely must be the final set of actions necessary for the initiative to succeed. Thinking that the requisite components have been secured and deployed, he begins to work on his acceptance speech for the ceremony at which he will receive his master of change accreditation.

At first, there were encouraging signs of progress, but now, to his surprise, the wall proves to be uncompromising and refuses to yield. Even with his new tools and techniques, the wall of resistance won't budge. He faces failure once again, and finds himself standing at a new crossroad. Like before, if this failure is not acknowledged—if he avoids responsibility for it, if he doesn't consider the consequences for the status quo to be prohibitively high, and/or if he can't or won't try to improve his performance—the necessary learning to enable him to move forward will not occur.

DISCIPLINE

Our executive traveler is now at his lowest emotional point of the journey: "If true commitment is applied to structured guidelines and tools, and still I'm not the leader of change I need to be, maybe the task is really beyond my reach." Just as he is about to feel sorry for himself and risk falling into the abyss of victimization, Bogart again flashes through his mind. Humbled by the actions of his cinema hero, he remembers the price he will pay if this change project fails.

He resumes the struggle. Because he must fight resistance battles on a lateral front along the face of the great wall, he makes little progress. Each time he maneuvers to penetrate the fortress, it recoils, absorbs his thrust, and dissipates his efforts into an infinite number of the bureaucratic bricks that make up its strength. As he regroups from each skirmish, he searches for that elusive factor that is missing from his arsenal:

> Knowledge, insight, intent, commitment, structure . . . what's left? If I apply these elements each time I attack the wall, how can it remain unscathed? How does it continue to parry and sidestep my advances? . . . That's it—I'm not utilizing all these components to my fullest extent each time I confront the resistance. Sometimes I'm focused on what I know I must do, but at other times I'm leading with my intuition and hunches. It must be this lack of consistency that is causing my downfall.

Just as these thoughts begin to clarify his strategy, he finds himself on the outskirts of a new, even larger city called *discipline*. Here, he will learn the value of compulsive tenacity—unrelenting resolve to persevere in the face of resistance. At this important juncture in the road to change mastery, he learns that doing what is necessary, doing it every time it is required, and doing it well each time it is called for is what discipline is all about.

The implications of his circumstances begin to dawn on him. Each time he implements a major change, he must employ all he has learned about the change process. Not when he can remember it, not when he has the time or the energy, not when he has the patience—he must pay his dues every time if he is to overcome the forces of resistance to major change.

The price for faltering in this discipline is nothing less than receiving a prohibitively expensive invoice for failing to execute the project. If at any time the pressure to sustain the discipline becomes too great, he can always opt to pay the bill he will have incurred for the failure. He can pay for being disciplined about applying what he knows he must do in order to succeed, or he can pay for the project to fail—but either way, he will pay.

He says to himself: "Knowledge, applied with true commitment, wrapped around structured guidelines and tools, and compulsively driven by the consistency that only comes from discipline—have I finally found the last piece to this puzzle?" Although he is hopeful that adding discipline to the previous learnings will increase his chances of success, he is cautious now as he prepares to reengage the wall. Too many times before, he thought he had deciphered the code for change wisdom and then was embarrassed by how little he really knew.

This time, he enters into battle with the wall believing he is better prepared than ever, but his past innocence is gone for good. He has suffered too many setbacks to ever again think he has all the answers. He applies all that he has learned and the confidence that can only come from his many expensive lessons; but he now also displays a spirit of inquiry only found in people who have decided to be lifelong pupils of their chosen craft. He is finally a true student of the change process.

When experience, confidence, and caution merge, the context for wisdom begins to form—and none too soon, for failure is, once again, staring into the eyes of our traveler. Though some important headway has been achieved by adding discipline to knowledge, commitment, and structure, a vulnerability remains that could jeopardize the change project's success. Again, the executive examines his actions to determine what remaining element stands between him and implementation success. This time, however, the answers do not come from within. Our traveler has exhausted all his resources for self-exploration and inspiration. He has to go beyond himself to search for the answer this time.

One day, after several fruitless attempts to solve this final conundrum, our executive expresses his frustration to one of the many managers he has asked to assist him on the project. After listening to her boss, this trusted ally asks whether he is open to her thoughts on the matter. She waits until he affirms his interest in her views and then says that, in her opinion, the answer to this final inhibitor is going to be particularly difficult for him because it is visible only to others. She says he will never be able to solve this particular problem alone because what is blocking him from further success is the limitations of his own perspective:

> Boss, if you could see yourself as others do, you would know that you aren't really doing half of what you think you are. You see yourself as knowledgeable, committed, and applying structured procedures in a disciplined manner. Most of us, however, see you as no longer dangerously naïve about how change occurs, but hardly knowledgeable about what to do every time; certainly interested in the change, but not fully committed to it; using some of the available tools and guidelines, but not nearly as many as you should; and disciplined, but only when it is convenient and it works easily into your schedule.

The executive is dumbfounded. He has no reason to suspect the manager's motives because he really trusts her, so he receives her statements as an honest, empowered expression of how she feels about his performance. He is perplexed, however: "How could she be so good at the rest of her job but so wrong about me?" There is no question in his mind that she has failed to grasp his new, but nonetheless real, passion and skill for leading change. He thinks to himself, "How could all this learning have gone so unnoticed?"

As they continue talking, the executive finds no solace in the fact that the manager feels he is clearly more prepared to lead the company through change than he was when stuck at the "ignorance" stage. Apparently, however, she and the other managers still think he is light-years away from demonstrating the kind of transition wisdom the company will need to survive, much less prosper, in the coming years.

"To be honest with you, it's not this change we are so worried about," she continues. "It's all the other changes coming our way that bother us. This company's future and our jobs are dependent on you leading us through the confusion. Boss, for all our sakes, I hope you figure out what to do, but you've got a long way to go."

It is becoming apparent to him that, because of his own blind spots, his view of his own behavior is markedly different from how she and the others see him. When he looks at himself, it is through a set of lenses that are biased by his need to live up to the self-image he aspires to. This kind of filtering system makes it impossible to perceive his actions without considerable distortion.

It occurs to him that this biased view of himself doesn't mean that how he sees himself is necessarily wrong, but it certainly helps to explain the difference in how others interpret his actions. This leads to a startling revelation: "I am probably not as good at applying all the change lessons I've learned as I thought, but even if I were, if my employees don't see these lessons reflected in my behavior, then, as far as they're concerned, I'm still inadequately prepared to lead them through a major transition."

ANTABUSE[2]

This last lesson was particularly difficult to learn. All during his professional career, this executive traveler had been reinforced to rely only on himself. He took pride in how self-contained he had become over the years. In part, he had made it to his current position of power within the organization by not looking for help from anyone else.

Being dependent on others for anything significant was clearly not his preference, yet he was now confronted with the fact that without honest—actually, brutally frank—feedback from those he led, he couldn't accomplish the task at hand. It was becoming clear that he was not a leader because of his title or the money he was paid. He was a leader only to the extent that others would follow his guidance.

This meant he was no more powerful than they perceived him to be. If his employees saw him as lacking the necessary education, insight, intent, commitment, structure, or discipline to guide the organization through turbulence, then, by definition, he was not the potent leader he had hoped he was. Regardless of his view about these tough, hard-earned lessons, if his people didn't see the appropriate behaviors in a way that was meaningful to them, for all intents and purposes they did not exist.

Back on the road, he was nearing the city limits of the biggest metropolis he had yet seen on this journey. As he contemplated the implications of this newest lesson, he noticed the sign on a large billboard near the road: "Welcome to Antabuse." His task here was obvious. He was to learn how to solicit input from others regarding how well his leadership behavior was being perceived as aligning with what was needed to achieve the stated change objectives. He knew the type of feedback he needed, but he was not sure he had the kind of relationship with his people that would lend itself to this level of candor.

In retrospect, he could now see that, for years, he had given people all kinds of subtle and sometimes even blatant signals that he was not very open to their opinions about his behavior. He had previously regarded the need for an executive to receive feedback from people who reported to him or her as a sign of weakness, and he therefore always tried to project an image of a strong leader who couldn't care less about how people interpreted his actions as long as they did as they were told.

Now that he really needed their honesty to become a better architect for this change project, he doubted their willingness to trust his request: "I can hear it now. 'Yea, right, boss—be honest with you about whether your actions match your words. The last three people who did that got their kneecaps shot off.'"

He wrestled with the problem for the next several days. By the end of that weekend, his wife had become aware of his preoccupation. He was obviously distracted; he had only gone through the motions of participating in Friday night's dinner out and movie, not to mention Saturday's picnic with the kids. Knowing the struggle he had endured getting to this point in his journey, she encouraged him to use her as a sounding board as he tried to understand the labyrinth he was in.

Past efforts at this kind of joint problem solving had proven invaluable to him. With previous problems he had faced, the combination of her personal support of him and her objectivity toward the emotional tug-of-war he had found himself in gave her just the right vantage point to help penetrate his blockage. At times like this, he was most grateful for the good fortune to be married to his best friend.

TOUGH LOVE

As she cooked the family's largest meal of the week, the "Sunday night feast," he sat at the kitchen counter and described his predicament. As usual, she listened well, and then asked a few thought-provoking questions. At that point, she said, "OK, I see," sounding much like the psychiatrist in the movie they had seen Friday night.

He waited, but she offered nothing more. He knew she was baiting him, so he didn't say a word. Finally, his curiosity got the best of him: "OK, OK, what do you mean—what divine inspiration has occurred to you?"

"Nothing . . . just the answer to your problem," she said playfully. "If you're interested, I could use some help cleaning out the utility room next weekend—can we cut a deal? A little sweat from you next week in exchange for some of my brilliance now?"

"You're on," he said. "What do you see?"

"Not so fast—I want more specificity from you. How about an agreement that I get two hours of your time to help me next Saturday to work on the utility room, if you don't get defensive about my interpretation of what's going on, but I get two additional hours on Sunday if you go into your typical denial/combative routine."

He looked at her with a smirk on his face.

"I'm serious, if you're going to make it harder than necessary to help you, I want to get paid extra for it."

"Is it really that hard to get me to see things?"

"Let me put it this way—the last time you asked for my opinion regarding one of your problems, I could have gotten you to repaint the whole house and replace the roof if I had negotiated properly ahead of time."

"OK, you got it. Two hours on Saturday for your opinion and two more on Sunday if I get argumentative and defensive. I assume I'm not obligated to agree with what you have to say—just to listen and not close down on your opinions too early."

"Yes, that's all I ask. I don't mind if you think about what I have to say and then discard it, but when you don't even let me finish a statement before you start explaining how I don't really understand what you're up against, it's apparent you're not open to any one else's opinion—at least not mine."

"OK, I get the message. Now, what do you see about this thing that I can't?"

"Problem: You're convinced that the next and hopefully last step in learning how to manage the changes at the office is to figure out how to get your employees to be really honest with you when they see you as not living up to your own rhetoric. You want them to tell you when you're giving mixed signals or not being disciplined enough about implementing an important new initiative. Am I close?"

"Did I marry you because of your irresistible charm, or was I secretly looking for my own personal consultant?"

"A simple 'yes' will do."

"Yes."

She paused at the refrigerator a moment to collect her thoughts. After putting up the milk, she went on: "If that's the problem, the answer is you're fighting the wrong side of the issue. Your staff is not the problem, you are. You don't really want what you say you want, and your people know it. Stop struggling with how to get them to believe you; they would if you were serious. If you could just . . . . "

He interrupts her: "Give me a break! I've poured my heart out to you over the past few months about how important this is to me. How can you stand there and say . . . . "

Prepared from the beginning for this, she said: "My recommendation is that if you get an early enough start Sunday morning, you could get my second two hours in before you had to miss your golf date with Al."

Realizing her not-so-subtle reminder of their agreement, he said, "OK, OK, I'm listening," with resignation in his voice.

"It's not that you don't want your people to be honest with you. You're probably ready to listen to what they have to say about you. I don't think, however, that you are ready for what it means to really let some of their impressions of you sink in. I'm not sure you're ready to actually change your behavior based on what they say."

"But I couldn't be any more sincere. I really do need their input about how they perceive me."

"You're not hearing me. I don't doubt that you're ready to listen to their honesty—that's not what I mean. I don't think you're ready to pay the price for what their honesty will mean for you. If they give you what you say you want, and you really listen and value their input, there is a strong likelihood you would have to change at least something about the way you operate. Despite what you say, I don't think you're ready for that."

He shot back: "You're not giving me enough credit."

"Wanna' bet?"

"Try me," he said.

"OK—What do you do if Scott comes into your office and tells you that if the implementation team you recently formed for this new project is really important to you, you would have to attend some of their status meetings instead of only reviewing their weekly reports as you do now."

"That's not realistic—pick something else."

"Why isn't it realistic? At the company party last month, I overheard Scott and some of the others talking about how they wish you could be more 'hands-on' with them during those meetings. They weren't complaining, they were just expressing a genuine need for your involvement."

"But they know I can't be at those meetings. It would be impossible."

"Impossible, meaning if someone put a gun to your head you couldn't get to at least a few of those meetings?"

"No, impossible meaning most of those meetings occur when I'm supposed to be with customers. Everyone knows we can't afford to lose a sale just for me to be in those meetings. Besides, I can keep up with their progress by staying on top of their reports."

"That's not the point. Of course you can stay abreast of their technical progress, but how do you convey your emotional investment and commitment to them if not in person?"

"This is ridiculous. It could cost thousands in lost sales if I went to those meetings. It's just not practical."

"Should I call Al to say you might be a little late for your tee time on Sunday?"

"But you're not playing fair. You're presenting an impossible situation. I can't afford to do what you are suggesting."

"Thank you. I rest my case."

"What?"

"I said at the beginning of this that you didn't want to pay for what you said you wanted."

"But the price you are suggesting is crazy."

"No it's not, it's just incredibly high. Besides, who said solving this problem of yours was going to be easy? If it were, you wouldn't have had to hire an expensive consultant like me."

"You can say that again. I think it's easier to deal with the ones we fly in from 'guru land' in their pinstripe suits than it is to be on the receiving end of your help."

"Poor baby."

"Seriously—I don't see how it's possible to do what you are saying. I couldn't afford what it would mean."

"Excuse me, I must have misunderstood. I thought I heard you say the other day that this was a change you had no choice about. It had to succeed. I thought I was talking to Bogie on the *African Queen* and it has time to pay one price you wish you could avoid in order not to have to pay another one that is even more expensive."

"Well, in this situation, there simply has to be another way to get Scott's team to see that I am serious about my commitment to the project," he said with as much bravado as he could muster. "They know how busy I am. They understand."

"Maybe there is another way to be convincing about the project's importance to you—that's not the point. The issue here is what would you do if there weren't another way and the answer was to either periodically attend their meeting or the project fails?"

After waiting a few minutes to let all she had said sink in, she followed with, "Do you really trust Scott?"

"What do you mean—you know I do?"

"What if Scott told you this was the only way to really get your message across to his team and without being totally sold on your resolve to see them through the project, he was convinced they would not take their task as seriously as they should. What would you do?"

"Foul—below the belt. I've already told you that's not a decision I could make."

She went on, "You know, I think you're right. Why didn't I think of that? I never considered indecision as an option. It's so simple now that I see your point. I'm sorry, Bogie, I guess what you want to hear is that everything is OK for you and Hepburn as long as you don't make a decision. If you'll carefully balance yourself on the side railing of the boat, we will declare that you are neither in nor out of the boat. That way, you don't have to face either the leeches or dying in the boat."

Exasperated at this point, he says, "Why are you being this way? I asked for your help thinking through my problem, not this unrealistic bantering back and forth."

"Ever heard of 'tough love,' my dear? The reason your expensive, pinstripe consultants at the office won't be this direct with you is they don't care enough about you to really be straight with you about your options. They can't make you this uncomfortable because you really don't want this kind of discussion and they know it. By the way, your employees are in on the same secret."

"Give me a break."

"You say you want your people to tell you what your behavior means to them, but I'm a good example of what happens when someone does—and I had it easy. They don't have the luxury of holding your Sunday morning golf game hostage as I do."

With a not-too-subtle dose of sarcasm he said, "I want you to know you have been a real help. I started off perplexed—now I'm depressed."

"Get over yourself. You're not depressed. You're feeling sorry for yourself because you can't have what you want without paying for it."

"You're not going to let up, are you?"

"I love you too much for that. Besides, if you don't figure out how to master change and lead this company through all these transitions, how are you going to get the bonus you need to buy me my new coat?"

"What new coat?"

"I'm better at this than I thought. My fees are going up."

"OK, just promise that the coat will be pinstripe to suit your character."

Knowing he needed some time to let the dust settle on their conversation, she suggested it was time to call the kids in for dinner. The boys were engaged in the usual playful antics that were part of their family ritual at mealtime, but she could tell our traveler was still distracted. After dinner, she sent the kids to do their homework and asked for his help with the dishes.

As she started loading the dishwasher, she said: "You know what really helped me a few weeks ago when it was my turn in the hot seat? I remembered your dad talking about his struggle with alcoholism and how, early in his treatment, he chose to take Antabuse. I was always impressed with his courage to take a stand like that."

With a pensive look, he said: "If you think it was impressive to hear him talk about it, you should have been there when it was happening. I was young, but I remember him telling me of his decision to do it. He didn't want me to be overly concerned if he should get sick when I was around."

She continued: "It makes all the sense in the world, but still—to set up a scenario where if you fail at your stated objectives you kick yourself in the rear end . . . . "

"Our family went through some very tough times before he went for help, but when he did, I regained a lot of respect for him. Deciding to take Antabuse meant he had to hold two seemingly contradictory notions about himself in his mind at the same time. On the one hand, by that time he was totally committed to stop drinking, yet he also accepted his humanity and figured he wasn't strong enough yet to be completely immune from back-sliding."

"That's tough. It sounds like one negates the other."

"What he taught me was that both can be true at the same time. He used to say that people in his AA group who selected only one of those views over the other never stayed sober long. His philosophy was that if you weren't ready to voluntarily take the Antabuse medication that would make you sick if you drank, you weren't ready to stop drinking."

"Your dad told me once that the effect of Antabuse was like getting a case of the flu about five minutes after taking one swallow of whiskey. He said it was terrible but the only way for him."

"Yea, setting up your own negative consequences for not achieving your goals is a pretty impressive act."

"Maybe that's what you have to do."

Thinking he could sidestep this newest thrust by interjecting some humor, he said, "What do you mean—I don't even drink."

"Oh, no you don't! You're not going to dodge this bullet. You know exactly what I mean. If you were as serious as you say you are about receiving feedback from your staff, you would believe it more yourself and therefore be more convincing with them when you tell them that you need them to be your Antabuse. You have to be so tenacious about learning how to provide the proper leadership for this change that you will ask them to tell you every time you don't come across as a committed sponsor. It may make you sick to hear it, but if you are really ready to listen, it would keep you sober."

They both fell silent for a few moments.

Her eyes suddenly lit up: "Bingo."

"What?"

"Wait, before I tell you, I want to cut a new deal."

"Don't they teach you gurus anything about professional ethics? We have a binding contract, remember? Two hours on Saturday for the utility room cleanup and that's it unless I argue. So, no new deal here at the last minute. As far as I'm concerned, I already have a claim on this bit of wizardry you're about to share with me. Plus, there's the new coat."

"OK, OK, but next time, it'll cost you double."

"You hired guns are shameless."

"Are you ready? Your staff doesn't want to be your Antabuse, and I know why."

"Why?"

"First, most of them came to work for you previously exposed to all kinds of bogus participative management training and rhetoric. None of them ever had a boss before that really meant it. In fact, all their lives they were taught just the opposite—by their parents, their coaches, their preachers, the government, and every place they have ever worked—people in authority have always told them what to do. This kind of long-term exposure promotes a sense of victimization. Now they work for a man who, by his own standards if not theirs, is exceptionally good at what he does. He not only prides himself on his self-sufficiency, but has previously devoted very little energy to asking employees for their views on his performance."

"I don't think I like where this is going."

She continued: "Think about it—your people started with a predisposition toward victimization, which was then further compounded by having a boss who is not known for being timid or indecisive, and who has always appeared uninterested in their views about his behavior. Gee, I wonder what's wrong with this picture?"

With a groan, he said: "Sounds like the perfect formula for intimidation, doesn't it?"

"Now add to this base of intimidation the fact that you are better at what you do than anyone at your office ever will be. They all have their talents, but they can't compete head-to-head with what you are good at. Not only do you and I know that, but, more importantly, so does your staff. Why would they think they could offer any feedback to you that you would listen to or would be meaningful to you?"

She waited a minute and then asked, "Have I lost you? Your eyes are kind of glazed over."

"Oh, I'm afraid I'm with you—that's the problem. I think your point is that they can't see any vulnerability in the areas of my competence, so they don't believe I really mean it when I say I need their Antabuse feedback to get better."

"Would you buy it if chess master Bobby Fisher walked up to you and said that only with your candid feedback could he improve his chess game?"

"Not a good example. My chess game has really improved lately, but I get your point. If my staff only sees me engaged in a game they know I'm already good at, they won't waste their breath giving me feedback, no matter what I say. I've got to convince them that it's not the three steps between them and me I'm working on, it's the ten steps between me and the edge of the game I need their help with. I've got to convince them that I really need their help if I am to recognize when I have new lessons to learn and when to cycle back and relearn old ones from previously covered territory."

"You can do it. I know you can."

Sensing he needed a break, she let the discussion die for a few minutes before saying: "My grandmother taught me that there is a good reason why people refer to life as a journey. I can hear her now, 'A trip is what you take when who you are at the end is no different from who you were at the start.' She used to say that, even on long trips, the most that changes is your age, so trips are measured in discrete units of time like hours, days, or years. Journeys, on the other hand, are measured in fuzzy, qualitative terms, not specific quantitative units. During journeys we don't become more of what we were or just pass time being what we already are—we go beyond who we were when the journey began."

They both became silent for a few moments, then she continued, "What I learned from her was that life's journeys are about substantive changes in our character. If these changes come fast, it's called trauma; if they come slower, we refer to it as growth. Regardless of the pace, a journey's purpose is to give us an opportunity, not a guarantee, for transformation."

"Not an insignificant little tidbit to learn from your grandmother."

"She was a very impressive woman. I wish you could have known her."

"All I got from my grandmother was that God would punish me if I didn't do my homework, and don't trust anyone who said TV wrestling was not legit. Maybe that's been my problem all along—I suffer from G.I.M.D. syndrome, and should not be held responsible for my shortcomings."

"OK, it's getting late. I'll go for it and ask the obvious question if you promise we can then go upstairs and start relaxing."

"Deal."

"So what is G.I.M.D. syndrome?"

"Grandparent-Induced Mental Deficiency Syndrome."

"I'm definitely charging you more next time."

MASTERY

Our executive traveler is back on the road again. We find him engaged once more in a fierce battle with the thick wall of resistance, but now significant strides are being made. The candid dialogue with his wife, uncovering why his staff was reluctant to be straight with him, has paid off. By securing the Antabuse feedback he needed from his staff, he was able to cycle back to re-learn the lessons he thought he had completed but in fact had left unfinished. The relationship building that was necessary with his staff in order to gain their confidence for the feedback he needed also had the effect of strengthening their mutual respect and sense of true interdependence. The net results were a unity within the team and a solidarity behind his leadership, neither of which he had ever enjoyed before.

The tide has now turned in his favor. Complacency and outright rebellion from his people have given way to genuine support. He would prefer it if all his people could honestly say that they believed the direction he was taking was fundamentally right for the company. He knows, however, that a few key staff members are still not in agreement with him. He recognizes that this is acceptable as long as they do everything in their power to achieve the goals he has set before them.

Most of those who could not support him decided on their own that this was not a work environment they could feel valued in, and they chose to seek opportunities elsewhere. He did find a couple of situations where it was necessary to force stronger support from people who were in important positions. After much dialogue, it came down to one of two choices: either they honestly got on board or they submitted their resignation.

When he took this definitive position, two groups converged to form the coalition of support he needed to finally create meaningful consequences to match with the rhetoric for change that now existed at all levels of the organization: (1) those who had always supported him in this change and (2) those who made a decision to back him now. There was a third group that proved important as well: those who left the organization, some voluntarily, and some not. Only when the resulting critical mass of support was generated did he have the political power to achieve the substance of his change objectives.

At last! Everything is not perfect, but there is no refuting that the change he has labored so long to achieve is beginning to be realized. Although the success of this particular initiative is important to the organization, the sense of accomplishment he feels is related to having met a much bigger challenge: he is now starting to understand what it is like to master the change process itself. To his surprise, however, the attainment of this long-sought-after goal does not bring the elation and joy he had anticipated. He does not have the sense of completion that he had expected. Instead of feeling he has finally finished a marathon that had begun at ignorance, he feels he has only begun his learning. He has covered a great deal of ground since his early days on the road to change mastery, but his most powerful learning is the one only now emerging.

It is becoming clear to him that along with the opportunities presented from his newfound proficiency comes the responsibility to avoid arrogance. Important lessons produce success only at the level of sophistication of the game where the lessons were learned. Success at one level leads either to complacency, which stifles further learnings, or to the humility that is necessary for advancement to the next level of the game. Winning at any one level is the motivation for either protecting the new status achieved or forging further into unfamiliar territory.

Winning the various games we play either produces a desire to be more conservative and protect what has been gained, or prompts us to risk what has been achieved in order to seek the next level of challenge. A third alternative is also available; do both:

1. Harvest the rewards from the latest victory while acknowledging the remaining limitations.
2. Search out new lessons that can only be found at the next level of the game.

Mastery comes from using one's knowledge and proficiency to not only profit from the game as it has been played, but to use the success that has been achieved as a foundation for pursuing the more advanced levels of the game's complexity.

At any point during the pursuit of proficiency, if it appears you have learned all the game has to offer, one of two options can be exercised: (1) You can either go comatose continuing to play a game that is no longer challenging (the price for this option is the forfeiture of passion); or (2) you can recognize the folly of thinking any game of real value can be completely mastered within a single lifetime. With this option comes the recognition that to pursue mastery means payments of your time, energy, and other assets for the rest of your life.

Mastery: The Map and Model

This book is about some of the more important lessons learned on the journey from ignorance to mastery of the game called organizational change. It is written for the newly assigned or recently challenged incumbent senior executive who is facing a level of change he or she has never before encountered, but who is also able and willing to learn. I assume that you fit this description. As was the case for the traveler who made the journey from ignorance to mastery, it is helpful to have a map. Figure 18.1 serves as both a map and a model.

The model is based on nearly two-and-a-half decades of observing senior officers throughout the world as they succeeded or failed at managing major transitions within organizations. It does not describe what they learned (covered in the earlier chapters). Instead, it is a model that describes how they moved—or failed to move—from one level of proficiency to the next in the change game.

The model describes 10 junctures representing key learning opportunities as a leader journeys from relative ignorance to mastery. Although these same learning opportunities would apply to any endeavor, the focus here is on gaining the wisdom to master the process of orchestrating large-scale change in major organizations.

The starting point of the journey to mastery depends on you.

The readiness to comprehend certain lessons fluctuates in relation to a person's previous edification and current placement along a continuum of experiences—it's a maturation process. The lessons progress through the 10 levels in a developmental manner, but the discovery process itself does not

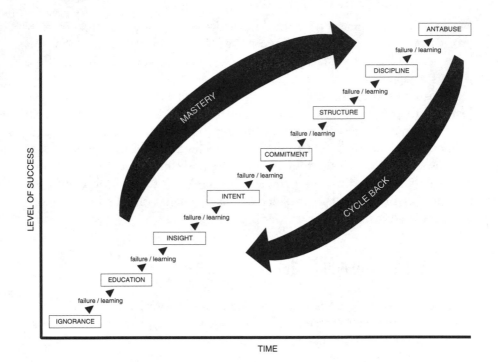

Figure 18.1   The journey to mastery.

unfold in the same way for each person. People will develop at their own pace and with varying degrees of learning intensity.

The 10 levels are separate, but they are also interdependent. An executive is likely to experience some degree of learning about the issues germane to a particular stage at any given time. Yet, each of the 10 learning junctures represents a period when certain concerns are more relevant and the lessons pertinent to those issues are more amenable to learning.

THE LEARNING WAVE

Instead of thinking about progressing from level to level in a one-at-a-time, linear manner, view advancement toward mastery as a wave moving through the critical levels or lessons to be learned. At any point in time, some degree of learning is probably taking place regarding each level along the journey; yet, during any one period, the search for answers is particularly intense regarding specific issues or concerns uniquely relevant to that level of development. As the lessons for each level are learned, the next level in the developmental sequence begins to take precedence. For example, only after education occurs is there much hope for insight and commitment. In the same manner, structure must be in place before discipline can be a priority.

HOW FAST CAN YOU LEARN?

Although no specific time frames are outlined in the description of the learning journey, the reader should know that the road from ignorance to mastery is measured at least in years. I have intentionally avoided any reference to the length of time needed to move from one level to the next so as not to establish a bias in the reader's mind about the time a person needs to learn his or her lessons. Take heart; the critical issue with regard to your time in achieving change mastery is not just your personal resolve to succeed, but also how you compare to your competitors. Minimally, you must stay ahead of them on this long journey, if only by a few steps, if you plan to be or remain the nimble provider in your chosen market.

Working in a learning-rich environment and understanding the various crossroads or junctures on the learning road will help you to manage yourself and your resources more effectively. Don't think, however, that the proper environment and access to the appropriate knowledge will allow you to skip steps or prematurely exit from one level to go to the next. It is important to become aware of and address the critical lessons to be learned at each level.

Movement from one level to the next will only occur when:

- There is enough success at each level to motivate continuance of the task without succumbing to complacency or arrogance. This, however, does not lead to the full accomplishment of the change objectives.
- The resulting failure is acknowledged.
- Responsibility for taking corrective action is accepted.
- The cost of the failure is significant.
- The person is willing and able to explore new ways to accomplish the change.

The complexity of the lessons, and your preparedness to learn, will dictate how long you will need before you move on.

It is admirable to seek ways to accelerate your learning, but keep in mind that increasing the pace of learning can be encouraged, but not dictated. You should seek learning-rich work environments and challenge yourself to acquire as much as possible, as fast as you can, at each level, but it will serve no purpose to become impatient and move from one level to the next before you are fully prepared to do so. If the lessons at any one level are not genuinely internalized, you will be back to learn them again. In this respect, failure to achieve your change goals represents the gateway to the remaining lessons required for success. If you manage your failures properly, you will always be led back to the lessons you have not finished.

Awareness of the 10 levels to master change won't help you move through your journey faster than you should, but it will help you to minimize the amount of time you waste being confused about what lessons you are to learn at any one level. The more resources that can be used for finding the right answers rather than searching for the proper questions, the quicker you will move through the journey.

The Journey: A Route Finder

LEVEL 1—IGNORANCE

"This is easy; send a memo."

The model depicts the entry level into the change game as *ignorance*. This is when senior officers don't know what they don't know about the implementation of major change. At this point, they typically think making a sound decision and announcing it confidently will achieve the desired result.

LEVEL 2—EDUCATION

"I got it—no problem."

If they are fortunate enough to learn from the inevitable failure that follows the initial effort, executives can move on to *education*. Here, they decide what the real problem is: they have not taken the time to learn from the experience of others. They may decide to read a book or hire a consultant, but the objective is the same: "I must absorb what others have learned so I can replicate their success with change."

LEVEL 3—INSIGHT

"Oh, *that's* what it means."

Armed with nothing more than information about how to proceed with change, even when this information is accurate, the executives will face yet another round of frustration. At this stage, there is learning about what should be done to orchestrate the implementation process. What is missing isn't the information about what to do, but the knowledge to successfully apply this information to achieve the desired objectives. If learning can be drawn from the failure at the education stage, the next level of work is at *insight*.

Here, senior officers are able to see the practical application value of the more important concepts and techniques they gained access to while at "education." From their firsthand experience, they can determine what portion of this information is truly relevant for their situation, and how to begin prioritizing the many implementation options and approaches they can now choose from. This level does bring a measure of success beyond education, but, without supporting mechanisms, the application of even brilliant insights will not achieve the hoped-for outcome.

LEVEL 4—INTENT

"I've really got to be careful this time."

For many people, it is difficult to learn that knowing what to do and even having keen insight about the realities of implementation are still not enough. Only if the failures at insight are translated into learnings can the next level of the journey be engaged: *intent*. It is here that executives significantly increase their motivations to accomplish the change they are focused on. Failure to achieve their change objectives is now generating far more serious cost implications. Seeking new answers, top officers come to the conclusion that they must marshal their resources and get serious about accomplishing their changes. Though seriously intending to change is a major step forward, it still falls short.

LEVEL 5—COMMITMENT

"This is serious. I can't afford to fail."

When good intentions to change do not produce the desired outcome and the resulting failure motivates executives to learn more about the implementation process, what they find at the next level is real *commitment*. Here, corporate leaders truly believe and declare to others that the cost for failing to achieve the change has become prohibitively expensive. Strong or even passionate commitment among senior officers, by itself, however, will not break the inertia of the status quo and turn an organization from its current course.

LEVEL 6—STRUCTURE

"Now I've got the process and tools I need. Let's go."

If the failure that comes from senior executives' relying on commitment alone can be translated into the proper learning, they can then move to the next stage, called *structure*. At this stage, they learn that unbridled commitment can consume many resources without producing much to show for it. A group of committed senior officers can put on an impressive display of rhetoric and passion, but their efforts will usually produce uneventful overall results unless they can channel their resolve into the use of such things as diagnostic tools, communication guidelines, and specific techniques for dealing with resistance.

LEVEL 7—DISCIPLINE

"I'll follow each step when it is required, and I'll do it well every time."

Even when tools and procedures are applied with commitment, the desired results won't be achieved if the structured guidelines are not followed rigorously. If the failure can be translated into useful lessons, executives can begin to value what is available at the next stage: *discipline*. Here, they learn that they must wrap their commitment around structure and then apply it consistently in a disciplined fashion.

LEVEL 8—ANTABUSE

"When, not if, I falter, I need direct, explicit, confrontive feedback and a reminder of the cost I'll pay if I don't succeed with this change."

The next sobering failure occurs when even commitment, structure, and discipline fail to gain the full measure of success from a change initiative. From this failure, there is an opportunity to learn one of the most difficult but most powerful lessons on the journey. It is here at *Antabuse* that executives can learn the importance of breaking free from the limitations of their own perspectives during change.

Just as recovering alcoholics sometimes use Antabuse as a negative reinforcement if they drink, senior officers serious about learning to manage change must set up a work environment where employees feel it is their responsibility to give management, including top executives, candid feedback about how they are viewed during the implementation of major change projects. The result of this feedback is that executives often come to realize they don't appear to others nearly as educated, committed, or disciplined as they thought they were.

While at Antabuse, executives often learn that employees are unimpressed with their change management skills, and for good reason—the task of orchestrating major transitions is often much more challenging than senior managers first anticipated or are prepared for. Some executives may feel this unflattering view of their change proficiency is unfounded. They believe they do possess the knowledge and talent needed to lead the change effort but circumstances have prevented employees from seeing those traits. The end result is, of course, the same whether the employees' lack of confidence in their leaders is well founded or not.

LEVEL 9—CYCLE BACK

"The only way to move forward is to go back to some earlier lessons and learn the nuances I missed."

When guiding change, you don't manage a singular reality, you manage multiple perceptions. Employee reality is defined by each employee's perceptions. If people don't perceive that they are being guided through change by competent leaders, then, as far as they are concerned, they aren't. Because this view represents their reality, they will behave as if the leadership is poor. Antabuse feedback is relevant regardless of how its accuracy is seen by the top managers who are receiving it, because it means, one way or another, the executive must return or *cycle back* for more learnings. Whether learning the substance of the lessons from an earlier stage or learning how to more effectively convey the lessons already learned, the executive is still a student of the process. Antabuse feedback usually sends executives back to an earlier level. For example, they may recycle to become more educated about the dynamics of change, to renew their commitment to the stated objectives of a particular initiative, or to become more proficient in the use of specific implementation tools and techniques.

LEVEL 10—MASTERY

"The confidence I have gained from my past success is proportional to the humility I feel because of how much there is left to learn."

Each return to an earlier stage starts the journey again from that point. Each level brings not only new learning but new frustrations and failures. An unending cycle is formed that represents the basic framework for life-long learning. *Mastery* of the game called organizational change begins when an executive's confidence from his or her past success is balanced by the humility that comes from knowing there will always be more levels of learning how to manage the transition process.

Applying the Model

The learning journey model is intended to help you gain as much as possible from the actions of nimble organizations described in this book. In this respect, the chapters you have read will be more useful if you can determine what level in the model best describes your current status relative to the issues and perceptions that were presented about navigating turbulent corporate waters. Throughout this book, I have described a number of lessons executives typically learn during their journey toward change mastery. As you review some of these, be aware of your placement on the model and the critical lessons to be learned at that level. You can locate your current level for any of these lessons by monitoring the reactions you had as you read earlier chapters. Table 18.1 offers some examples.

Table 18.1 Where Are You?

Reactions upon Reading What Masters Have to Teach You	Probable Stage of Your Journey	Your Current Learning Challenge
No way! How could that be true? I think Conner is making this up.	Ignorance	Realize you may not know what you don't know.
I had no idea! I never thought about it that way. Is he serious? Is that really what masters do?	Education	Learn the lessons being presented.
There is more to this than I thought. So, that's how I could use that approach. I didn't recognize that nuance before; that makes all the difference.	Insight	Uncover new implications of lessons already learned.
It's really not that hard. I just have to go out and do it. Why can't I get around to applying this stuff? If others can do this, so can I.	Intent	Stop denying the true cost of your failures.
I'm tired of paying for mistakes I know how to avoid. As soon as I finish this book, I'm going to apply this to my work. I can't afford not to use what I now know will work.	Commitment	Don't confuse passion with success.
So, that's the sequence you use. Great techniques—I'm using that one tomorrow. So, there is an actual procedure for generating commitment. I'll apply that at Monday's meeting.	Structure	Don't be seduced by the allure of technique alone.

Table 18.1   (Continued)

Reactions upon Reading What Masters Have to Teach You	Probable Stage of Your Journey	Your Current Learning Challenge
I'm ready to be relentless about what I just read. Do it right, do it every time. That's now my motto. No more skipping steps for me.	Discipline	Learn to value consistency during times of change.
I wonder what my staff would say if I were to ask for their honest feedback about what stage of the journey model I could perform better. I'm not looking forward to hearing the perceptions of my staff regarding my leadership of past changes, but I don't have a choice. Without their feedback, I'm in worse shape. In other situations, I learned some painful but important lessons from feedback. There is no reason why it wouldn't work around change as well.	Antabuse	Remember, views on your education, commitment, and/or discipline are in the eye of the beholder.
I know what stage I have to go back to for more work. It's so obvious now. Why didn't I recognize this aspect of that lesson before? I can see new levels of interpretation for what I thought I already understood.	Recycle	Learn that you're never through learning.
I'm proud of how much I know, but I also sometimes find myself unsure of my next move. I can now teach a "managing change" course to our new hires, but I would want to include in it my own past blunders and current challenges. How can I have come so far and still be so unprepared?	Mastery	Never let your confidence outweigh your humility.

Where from Here?

O DR, as a firm, has been conducting ongoing research regarding organizational change since 1974. In the past four years much of our research has been devoted to observing and analyzing actions that appeared to lead companies toward or away from operating in a nimble fashion. During the course of these investigations, I was in constant dialogue with senior officers as well as those who directly served them in some capacity. The focus of these discussions was what these leaders and advisers did and said to help or hinder their organizations' remaining agile and productive during periods of extreme instability. As part of these discussions, I would share with executives and their advisers what we were learning about nimble operations, and they would, in turn, relate their perceptions and experiences about trying to lead while their businesses were in constant transition. Although various opinions were expressed about some of the specifics, most of the top executives and key aides I talked with resonated with the majority of the descriptions and conclusions I have outlined in this book.

Despite this general concurrence with our findings, there were some important differences in their viewpoints. For example, a few of the executives and advisers with whom I talked could do no more than intellectually grasp what I meant by Nimbleness because they had never actually seen it firsthand. Others had a more practical understanding because they had been exposed to this kind of an organization somewhere in their career, but they didn't know how to intentionally create such an environment. Then there were those who had, somewhere, previously participated in a nimble work setting and were actively involved in trying to replicate that experience. Most of these leaders, however, were unable to discern the specific decisions and behaviors that had contributed to this outcome. They had nothing but their experience-based intuition and gut instinct to guide them.

It was this group, the unconsciously competent, who showed the strongest interest in our research of nimble organizations. They were leaders, key executives, and consultants who had one characteristic in common: they all had witnessed the competitive power of an organization more agile than most in its marketplace. They had had direct experience with and a value for Nimbleness, even though most of them had never used that term for what they were seeking. They were also the most frustrated, however, because they did not know how to replicate the magic. They could see what was missing from their companies' approach to change, but they lacked a set of tools and practical guidelines that could help them navigate the challenge.

A common reaction from those in the unconsciously competent category could be summed up with: "Experience has taught me that the pursuit of Nimbleness is a worthwhile, long-term quest for my company. I also know, however, that there are no fixed formulas about how to proceed that fit every organization. So, how do I get started? There must be some general framework for beginning the process." Well, the answer is: Yes, there is such a framework. The good news is that it is relatively simple to understand what must be learned and done to start moving your organization toward being a more nimble operation. The bad news is that it's not easy. Like most things in life, "simple to understand" does not translate into "easy to do."

So, where to from here?

The purpose of this final chapter is to provide one last checklist before the journey begins, and to give some guidance to leaders, and those who work closely with them, regarding how to keep moving forward.

Guidelines for Beginning the Path Forward

1. Focus on Nimbleness as a key to market success—Although it is critical to the organizational prosperity you seek, Nimbleness is not an end in itself. As you strive to achieve success in your chosen marketplace, you must continually identify and implement critical changes more quickly and efficiently than your competitors. Nimbleness is the "organizational fitness" that will enable you to do this. As outlined earlier, the process of identifying what changes an organization should make has several elements:

- Knowing what your business's key success factors are.
- Recognizing when they are being impacted by internal or external pressures.
- Identifying a need for adjustment in one or more success factors.
- Determining the specific nature of the required changes.
- Formalizing decisions to implement these changes.

The final step, *execution*, is undertaking the successful implementation of the changes in such a way that you not only achieve the desired results, but in doing so, you preserve as much human adaptation capacity as possible for future changes (see Chapter 1).

The primary reason for pursuing Nimbleness is: When you are able to move through this sequence of change identification (what) and implementation (how) more efficiently and effectively than your competitors, you will have achieved a decisive competitive advantage for your organization (see Chapter 3).

2. Focus on Human Due Diligence (HDD) as the means for achieving the desired Nimbleness—Once you have identified Nimbleness as a goal, your next task is to internalize the value of HDD. Fundamentally, this requires you to understand that human adaptation capacity is a finite resource that must be treated as carefully—and invested in as wisely—as financial resources are. This involves much more than paying cursory attention to the people issues in each project. It implies a range of responsibilities that spans the entire enterprise and is applied with structure and discipline (see Chapter 6).

3. Focus on raising capacity and reducing demand—To keep an organization functioning in a nimble fashion—on the edge of its limits for change—requires two simultaneously applied strategies: increasing adaptation capacity and reducing the unnecessary demands on an organization's existing adaptation resources. There are two considerations to note before increasing capacity:

- In settings where transition demands are already high and evidence suggests that more, not less, ambiguity and uncertainty is in the making, increasing the adaptation capacity beyond that needed to negotiate current levels of change is the only way to stay ahead of the demand curve.
- The decision to intentionally raise an organization's future shock threshold must be made far in advance of the rising tide of change. The optimum time to build a strong adaptation capacity is before high levels of dysfunction have been created.

There is always a certain draw on adaptation resources when an organization is facing the implementation of important initiatives. Above and beyond this inevitable drain, however, there are usually demands that unnecessarily pull down implementation capacity. Two primary contributors to this needless waste of resources are nonessential change initiatives and unskilled people in key roles:

- Nonessential change:
  —Success during perpetual unrest calls for sacrifices. What must be relinquished is the gluttonous appetite most leaders have for one of their favorite indulgences, innovation on demand. Reducing, slowing down, or giving up altogether other critically important change opportunities to safeguard an even higher priority is a costly act. Without this discipline to protect remaining adaptation resources, however, the typical appetite for innovation displayed by most corporate leaders quickly overruns any surplus that may exist.
- Unskilled people in key roles:
  —Leaders, sponsors, agents, targets, and advocates must be effective in performing their respective duties when engaging major change. If ineffective, people in these sensitive roles will not apply the proper mind-set, resolve, techniques, diagnostic tools, and planning to successfully execute their projects.
  —Poorly executed change not only jeopardizes the initiatives at hand, but also wastes precious implementation resources, thereby lowering the level of adaptation capacity available for future change efforts (see Chapter 8).

4. Focus on who does what—Ideally, HDD activities begin at the board of directors level. In their role as protectors of investors' interests, board members should recognize that their organization's readiness for change is a fundamental imperative for its long-term survival and success. This recognition is then manifested in two ways. First, the goals and priorities set by the board must reflect the importance of maximizing the organization's ability to identify and implement critical changes. Second, through selection and retention decisions, the board must ensure that the organization's leaders have the skills and desire to engage in activities that will increase the organization's Nimbleness (see Chapter 9).

HDD responsibilities continue with the senior leaders chosen by the board. They are responsible both for developing their own personal competencies and for undertaking activities that will enhance adaptation capacity throughout the organization. Specifically, each senior leader must be willing and able to:

- Set the corporate context by clearly articulating a guiding vision and mission that links individual employee efforts to enterprise-wide goals through strategy and culture.

- Within this context, commit to the change imperatives set by the board of directors or other governing body.

- Evaluate the level of change load facing the organization and adopt a mind-set, or style, toward change that will be effective in meeting this level of demand (see Chapter 10).

- Display and model personal resilience when faced with disruptive change (see Chapter 11).

- Recognize and manage the organization's vital operational paradigms (see Chapter 12).

- Master the change process through continued practices, and utilize failure as a catalyst for learning and growth (see Chapter 18).

- Shape an enterprise-wide change capability.

Among the specific actions leaders must be willing and able to undertake to create the necessary enterprise-wide preparedness for change are the following:

- Monitor the portfolio of initiatives being undertaken in the organization and the available capacity to assimilate new changes (see Chapter 7).

- Ensure that resilience is incorporated into the selection, development, and evaluation of individuals and teams (see Chapter 3).

- Set employee expectations at every level of the organization so that members are prepared to maintain high performance amid continually increasing levels of ambiguity and disruption (see Chapter 13).

- Ensure that people throughout the organization understand and apply a solid knowledge base regarding human responses to change (see Chapter 14).

- Delegate decisions appropriately, surround senior officers with empowered relationships, and insist that decision makers throughout the organization do the same (see Chapter 15).

- Ensure that there are structures to guide individual actions, and that they are balanced by enough flexibility to make sure they are continually refined and improved (see Chapter 16).

- Ensure that key people throughout the organization are prepared to plan and execute the proper implementation architecture necessary to succeed with critical initiatives.

The next set of activities that make up the HDD framework is more widely distributed throughout the organization. These activities pertain to the successful execution of major change projects, and thus are the responsibility of each individual who is charged with the sponsorship role in this process. In particular, the initiating sponsors of each major change have a critical role. They must:

- Make tough decisions about which changes to implement, keeping in mind the level of remaining adaptation capacity and the extent to which each initiative is a business imperative (see Chapters 7 and 17).
- Engage each step in building a successful implementation plan[1] (see Chapter 17).
- Execute the plan in a timely and effective fashion.[2]

The various roles and activities required for building a nimble organization are summarized in Figure 19.1.

Implications for Leaders

As the level of turbulence in the global, political, and economic environment increases, Nimbleness will become even more critical for future success. Furthermore, the long-term success of organizations will depend more and more on leaders' ability to minimize unnecessary change demands while undertaking every initiative that is needed to accomplish business imperatives. This means your organization cannot afford to implement any nonessential changes; you must become highly focused on identifying and engaging only critically important initiatives.

Creating an environment that is receptive to your efforts is a second challenge. If your board of directors has not yet adopted Nimbleness as a strategic goal and HDD as a mind-set, one critical task is to build strong advocacy for them to do so. In addition, you should work to build support among the community of financial analysts in your industry for a recognition of these two qualities as leading indicators of organizational health and competitiveness. In taking these steps, you will begin the process of aligning the metrics used to judge your performance with the activities you are undertaking to build a nimble organization, rather than leaving them at odds.

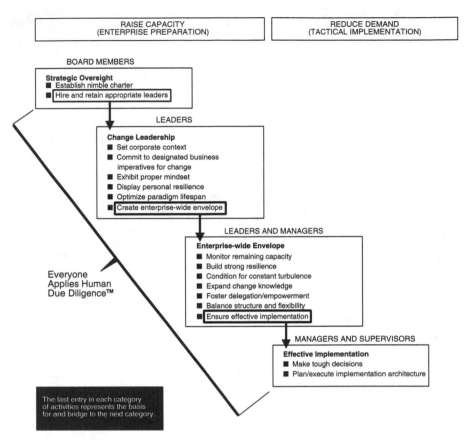

Figure 19.1   Who does what?

You must also be prepared to shape the direction of the senior leadership team within your organization. If you are the head of this team, you must ensure that each member is willing and able to undertake the personal and organizational activities that are outlined in this book. The ability to do this is not a "nice-to-have"; these competencies are vitally important. The force of change today requires an intense and disciplined focus on the human issues associated with maintaining alignment between key success factors and demands from the market. Leaders must consider creating an organization that addresses the human side of change to be a critical part of their job. The competencies mentioned in this book, therefore, need to be incorporated into the selection of senior leaders and into succession planning and development efforts.

LOC / MOC.

If you are a member of the senior team but not its leader, you must work to convince your CEO and/or COO to incorporate the issues, concepts, and actions discussed in earlier chapters into his or her thinking. Without the leader's support, you will not have the backing you need to undertake some of the critical activities that shape the organization's Nimbleness, such as establishing a clear, motivating, and achievable corporate context that is supported with realistic goals, objectives, and strategies; establishing and building a culture that values quick adaptation to the rapid changes in the marketplace; and intentionally hiring resilient people.

Wherever you are in the leadership hierarchy, you need to ensure that you have surrounded yourself with people whose ideas you value, and that you have set up means of allowing them to influence your decisions. You also need to ensure that they will give you honest feedback—that, in fact, negative consequences will occur if they fail to do so. Without this level of empowered candor, you will be unable to move through the stages of learning, and your skills at leading change will stagnate.

Once you and your fellow leaders understand the actions that HDD requires and the consequences for performing or failing to perform those actions, you should turn your attention to the organizational environment, evaluating each process and system for its support of quick, flexible, focused change. In particular, it will be critical to ensure that the metrics and reward systems are in place to support and reinforce nimble actions, and that individuals are given the training they need to acquire and practice relevant, change-related knowledge. People throughout the organization should (1) prioritize their change projects so that the weight of the current change load does not dramatically exceed the adaptation capacity of those affected, and (2) raise the organization's adaptation capacity through development activities and hiring/retention decisions.

For each critical initiative that is undertaken, you need to clearly articulate the alignment between the goals of the project and the achievement of critical business imperatives. You must ensure that the individuals who are responsible for implementing the initiative have the sponsorship authority to secure the commitment of those who must change, and that they will incorporate an HDD mind-set into their work *all the time,* not just when it's convenient or when they run into problems. Furthermore, you must ensure that the success of the all-important change projects is defined, tracked, and measured not only in terms of financial and technical objectives, but also in terms of human and opportunity costs so that the ROC_{hg} on the initiative is evaluated accurately.

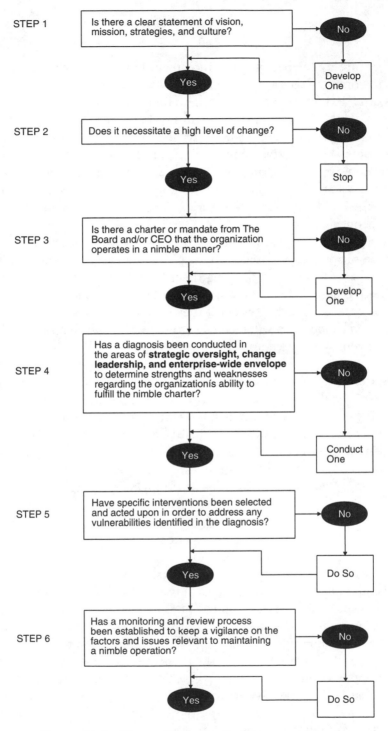

Figure 19.2   How to get started: Sequence of events.

300

Beginning the Journey

The guidelines and implications previously discussed represent the key elements in your role as leader of an organization trying to become more nimble in its response to change. With so many issues to consider, it would be easy to feel overwhelmed with the array of options. I offer a simplistic, but manageable, sequence for beginning your nimble journey (see Figure 19.2).

Implications for Those Who Serve Leaders

If you are not in a leadership position but are working in support of one or more leaders who are aspiring to build a nimble organization, you also face a particular set of challenges. Whether you aspire one day to lead or not, you are in a situation where you can learn a great deal and develop the skills that will serve you well both inside and outside of the organization.

Your first challenge is to ensure that you are operating in an empowered relationship—that your input to your leaders' decisions is valued and influential. Don't confuse this with a relationship in which your input is always (or even usually) adopted. Empowerment simply means that you are heard, and that your input carries weight. When you are in such a relationship, it is important for you to understand the priorities and goals that drive the leader's behavior; give straightforward, honest input as clearly as possible; and then demonstrate genuine loyalty to the decision that he or she makes (no carping behind the scenes!). In return, the leader owes you an explanation of the rationale behind his or her decision so that you can better understand it. If you are not in such a relationship, you have two viable choices: (1) work toward developing one by being explicit about what you would like the relationship to be, or (2) leave this work setting to find one in which you can become truly empowered. The third option—remaining in the situation and operating as a victim—will do nothing to further your own goals or help build a nimble organization.

Once you have established that you are in an empowered relationship, you need to recognize that you are dealing with human beings. Recognize that living in the midst of change brings with it a certain level of distress and dysfunction. Because your organization's leaders work under unremitting pressure, they will not always be perfect models of resilience. They may snap, they may retreat and communicate too little, they may forget what they know about attending to the human aspects of change. Your challenge will be to recognize their behavior for what it is, avoid perceiving it as a personal attack, and then give them feedback about the impact of their actions that is straightforward, as honest as possible, and framed in terms of the costs to achieve the outcomes they are striving for.

You need to be sensitive to several of the traps that people supporting leaders (even very good leaders) tend to fall into. The first of these is the tendency to pick up the slack when the leader is not doing his or her job. Even though you may believe it will help the organization and lead you to being perceived as a good scout, if you tend to rescue leaders in these situations, you may become part of the problem. If your boss or client is taking on more changes than he or she can appropriately address, or promising things he or she can't deliver, your role is to apply Antabuse feedback and be compassionately confrontive as you work toward getting the leader back on track. Without such feedback, the leader will most likely not see what he or she is doing and won't have a chance to learn.

The second trap is the tendency to take a leader's priorities at one point in time as an indicator of priorities in the future. Because of the shifting demands and pressures faced by senior leaders, they may move to the back burner something that had once been given a very high priority. If you see the commitment to a project flagging, it is your role to ask where that project stands on the priorities list and to operate accordingly. If the project is still a high priority, the leader needs feedback about the perceived support for it. If it does not have high priority, give feedback about the need to communicate a shift in priorities. Either way, you have an important task to accomplish.

The next trap to avoid also involves feedback. Leaders often underestimate the level of impact that changes will have on people throughout the organization, including you. When a leader hands you the twenty-seventh project in a week, you have a responsibility to push back and ask for clarification of priorities. If your response is always "Sure, boss, I'll get it done," he or she has no way of knowing what resources may be consumed by these requests, or the poor quality that may result. If, after stretching all the possibilities to accomplish the twenty-seventh project, a more appropriate response would be, "I can get this done when you want it, but you need to let me know which of these other projects I can delay in order to meet that deadline," you're asking him or her to set priorities and at the same time giving some good information about the human adaptation resources being used.

It may seem strange that most of your challenges are about standing your ground and giving honest feedback rather than overcommitting yourself, but that's what you must do. When leaders don't receive accurate information about resources, they can easily overdraw the change bank account. Please don't misunderstand. The task of building nimble organizations is not a comfortable one, and you have a lot of hard work ahead of you in supporting the leaders who aspire to this challenge. Most of the work, however, is in ensuring that leaders have good information, tactical support for the decisions they make, and clear, honest, and well-aligned feedback from people around them whom they trust and respect.

On the Nature of Things

And so your journey begins. But pause a moment for a final thought. Lucretius, a first-century-BC Roman poet, considered change in dark terms when he wrote his most celebrated work, *On the Nature of Things:* "Whenever a thing changes and quits its proper limits, this change is at once the death of that which was before."[3] Death? Yes, but out of the dust churned up by the traveler's footsteps comes another day and new life. We change with each footfall and commence dying only when the dust settles.

May your journey be filled with many dusty roads.

The Origins of the Investigation

There Is Much Left to Do

Though the content of this book is offered with a sense of pride, I feel compelled to remind the reader that our study at ODR of how people behave during change is far from complete. Because of the complexity of the human response to uncertainty, any claim of a comprehensive explanation for why people behave as they do is beyond anyone's reach at this time. We have only begun to uncover the array of forces at play when humans attempt to alter the thoughts, feelings, and actions of others in organizational settings.

Not only are there endless variables to account for, but applying the full weight of scientific rigor and artful imagination to these investigations has proven challenging, to say the least. We have found that one of the more common barriers to practical research is that many organizations are eager for information about how best to manage the human side of change, but few are tolerant of the kinds of detail and the procedures required for true scientific investigation. Many want the findings but don't want to participate in the process of serious inquiry. This limits the degree of exactitude that can be incorporated into the kind of investigations we would like to see when we are assisting companies to implement their change projects. Because of the complex character of change and the difficulty of conducting serious research in entrepreneurial and bureaucratic settings, the information in this book must be considered only a provisional report. With this disclaimer obligation now met, I also want to point out that the publication of this kind of report means that the study of humans facing change in organizational environments has moved well beyond the stage of alchemy, smoke and mirrors, and mysticism. It is no longer necessary for those who attempt major initiatives to rely only on trial and error, guesswork, and luck to achieve their goals. Without a doubt, the further our investigations takes us into the depth of the transition experience, the more will be revealed that can refine our understanding of the forces at play. For now, even partial glimpses into change dynamics provide opportunities to significantly increase the chances of success.

Where Did the Investigation Begin?

People usually feel helpless when they don't comprehend the things that are affecting their lives. One of the driving motivators behind our work at ODR is our belief that in order for organizational change to be successful, we must first understand its underlying dynamics. For me, the bias for gaining access to hidden forces that influence the outcome of change was established early. I first became intrigued with the process of change as a novice personal and family counselor in the late 1960s. I was often struck by the gap between the cognitive insights and emotional breakthroughs I witnessed among the people I counseled and by their inability to sustain the behavioral changes they desired once they tried to apply these realizations to their daily life. I recall my dismay when it first occurred to me how seldom the intellectual and emotional victories that occurred in the privacy of my office translated to prolonged, substantive alterations in my patients' behavior.

For example, let's say after months of working with a patient and helping him come to terms with a key issue in his life, the long-awaited cathartic moment arrived. He was finally able to converge his understanding of the problem that had plagued him for so long with his ability to identify what course of action he should take and his enthusiasm for resolving the situation with urgency and decisiveness. When these three forces intersected, the combination transformed his former victim mentality into a powerful resolve for action. I watched as he confidently walked out of my office to face the challenges in his life. He was armed with a heightened awareness of what he must do differently in order to succeed, as well as a passion for doing it.

The next time I saw him, however, I spent the entire session listening to him tell me all the reasons why "now was not the best time" for him to engage the strategies he had formulated. In a relatively short period of time, astuteness, eagerness, and optimism had been traded in for perplexity, reluctance, and pessimism.

After repeatedly witnessing this breach between intent and results, I concluded that my patients weren't failing—I was. I was sure that what appeared to me to be an impassable gorge between their display of understanding and motivation in my office and their inability to sustain prolonged behavioral change after leaving my office was probably no more than an easily crossed trench that my inexperience prevented me from seeing. Confident that the answer to bridging this gap was stored somewhere within the archives of psychotherapeutic technique, I sought guidance from my supervisor at the clinic where I worked. Fraught with emotion, I barged into his office without knocking and crammed all my frustrations into one long, uninterrupted monologue that lasted several minutes. After venting my dissatisfaction with my patients' results, I finished my outburst with: "What am I doing wrong?"

I'll never know whether the irritation in my supervisor's voice was attributable to my bursting into his office unannounced, or to the fact that he had been recently passed over for a promotion and was deeply resentful about being relegated to the lowly duty of answering incredibly stupid questions from young interns like myself. Nonetheless, after enduring my eruption, he looked at me with disdain and responded curtly. His answer was as poignant as it was short:

"First, don't ever come into my office again without knocking. Secondly, don't confuse what happens in your sessions with reality. We are magicians who marvel at our own tricks . . . if and when they work. Good day."

We all have defining moments in our professional careers; this was one of mine. The embarrassment I felt over my rude entrance into my supervisor's office faded quickly, as did the shock that an accomplished therapist would express such a jaded view of the profession I'd spent years studying and devoting myself to. What did not dissipate, but grew even stronger as time passed, was the realization that my supervisor, with decades of experience under his belt, was no less in the dark than I was about the inner workings of our profession. He didn't have much more of a clue than I had about how, why, or if people change as a result of our counseling interventions.

Though passed over for a promotion, this man was considered an excellent therapist who had many years of successful work to his credit. He had received numerous testimonials from former patients who attributed a large part of their recovery to his therapeutic skill. Here was an exemplary model of what I sought to accomplish professionally, yet he was revealing that he was ignorant of the formula for his own success, or, for that matter, the success of any other therapist in the field.

My initial reaction was what you might expect from a neophyte suffering his first of many confrontations with the sobering truth about his career choice. Surely the professional sights I had set for myself were loftier and more righteous than those of a master of deception performing sleight-of-hand tricks. Tell me there is more to my profession than the superficial powers of the Wizard of Oz. How could my supervisor be just as surprised as his audience when he was actually able to "pull a rabbit out of his hat?"

I'm not sure how long I indulged in this angst, but I do remember finally coming out of it to realize a pivotal point. My supervisor's curt statement hadn't disclaimed the value of the counseling he provided his patients; it just put it into proper perspective. This man was filled with self-esteem and took pride in his work. He knew that he was talented and that his therapy genuinely helped many people. What he was telling me was that he honestly didn't know why it sometimes worked and sometimes didn't. He was often just as amazed as his patients when their presenting symptoms would recede, if not disappear altogether, or when their problems would remain or grow even more pronounced. It wasn't that he didn't have a theoretical explanation for everything that happened in the sessions he conducted; he did. What he was trying to convey to me was that there was much more at play in these therapeutic sessions than he or anyone else really understood.

This incident induced in me a keen sense of sobriety about my career choice and a redirection of my interest. The seriousness came as a result of the implications the encounter signified for me. I learned that I had selected a profession that was guided as much by artful, intuitive maneuvers and serendipity as it was by validated conceptual foundations and well-tested prescriptive techniques. I came to realize that the counseling field was comprised of professionals who were, despite all their training, for the most part unconsciously competent. It occurred to me that the problem wasn't that psychotherapy was a useless hoax; it was that the profession as a whole lacked a deep knowledge of what led to its own triumphs. What I learned was that counseling was not always successful, but when it was, no one really knew why. Regardless of one's profession or level of accomplishment, without a full appreciation for what contributes to success, it is extremely difficult to gain ground on why failures occur and what can be done to avert them.

This brief encounter with my supervisor opened for me a completely new perspective on human behavior. It led me in a new direction that I was, at first, intensely curious about and finally became single-mindedly absorbed with: demystifying the process of how and why humans change. I became fascinated with the dynamics that unfold when people significantly change something in their life, and how they sustain that shift until it becomes fully incorporated into a new, embedded pattern of behavior. To this day, I remain engrossed with identifying the key features and properties that serve as the invisible code to successful transitions.

Early in my investigation of this phenomenon, somewhere around 1974, I realized there was ample evidence that some people knew more than others about how to implement change in their own lives and the lives of others. Among those who were skilled at this, there was a much smaller population who went beyond successful changes to mastering the art of piloting themselves and others through major transitions. At the time, there were not many guidelines for implementing the human side of change, so the question I started pursuing was: "What mysterious navigation system did these magicians use to maneuver themselves through change?"

Shifting Focus

So, although I began this quest as a means to better understand the successes that occurred in individual and family counseling, I gradually became more and more captivated by the dynamics that unfold when organizations successfully change. What I found in this arena were the same intuition-based success patterns I had seen in my own counseling industry. Leaders, managers, and consultants who were talented at managing organizational change were, for the most part, unconsciously competent in their accomplishments, just like the majority of therapists who were intuitively skilled in their craft. They did not know, and therefore could not articulate, how they worked their magic. I decided then that my life's work would be to investigate and identify the subliminal clues these people rely on to successfully implement change.

In attempting to unravel the mystery behind successful transitions, I was specifically interested in how important initiatives were executed, once a decision to proceed had been made. The questions that first triggered my interest in the dynamics of organizational change still comprise the focal point of my efforts today:

How can the secrets of those who are unconsciously competent at implementing organizational change be revealed and replicated by others?

What trace symptom, what hairline fracture in the process, what minute sign of pathology serves as the compass to guide these intuitively successful architects of corporate change?

To what degree can we bring structure and discipline to the process of orchestrating the emotional, social, and cultural implications inherent in altering the course of large institutions?

Some would suggest that these questions have been answered in recent years. They claim that, particularly in the past 10 years, much has been learned about how to introduce change, and most of the mystery around executing change has been solved. It is undoubtedly true that great strides have been made in implementing organizational change, yet we know nowhere near enough about how humans function in transition to guide an organization's destiny any more reliably than we did when we had nothing but our intuition to trust.

The challenge of learning enough to successfully pilot an institution through major transition is intimidating, but achievable. With an assignment of such scope, however, the only way to gain comfort in what has been learned thus far is to not look too closely at the magnitude of the mystery that remains. I believe those of us who profess some knowledge of the subject must admit that the complexities of human life are such that we are several generations of research and experimentation away from claiming full comprehension of the change phenomenon. For this reason, the content of this book gives no final answers, but aspires to a still evolving understanding of the human experience of change in organizational settings.

The Mechanics of the Adaptation Reflex

One thing that is assured in unfamiliar situations is that you will be surprised—and surprise is the primary symptom of loss of control. Without direct or indirect control, it is impossible to function effectively in what becomes an overwhelmingly confusing environment. If, during major change, loss of control is inevitable but control is essential to success, it becomes vital to have some means available for regaining balance each time it is disrupted. *The vehicle we humans use to recover our lost control is the process of adaptation. This is our retort to the surprises in life and it is called the adaptation reflex.*

Before I describe the adaptation reflex, let me remind you that modern cognitive research has resulted in great advances in our understanding of how we relate to the world and to changes in it.[1] This research is sometimes challenging to absorb and is, at the same time, a moving target. The model presented here is my attempt to distill and convey some of the basic research findings that appear to stand the test of time, in language that may be a little more user-friendly, at least for purposes of this book. I will also be adding some perspectives that resulted from the research conducted at ODR and that are unique to our view of adaptation.[2] Also, in the name of clarity, I present the model as binary when, of course, we know that the real process of learning and adapting to change is what some researchers call "fuzzy"—quite nonlinear and multifaceted. All in all, however, the adaptation reflex model should serve the purpose of helping us better understand loss of control and the reestablishment of dynamic balance.

The adaptation reflex is a four-step process. It involuntarily engages immediately following the first signs of lost equilibrium (see Figure B.1). Its aim is to enable us to make the necessary adjustments that will permit predictability and control to be reestablished.

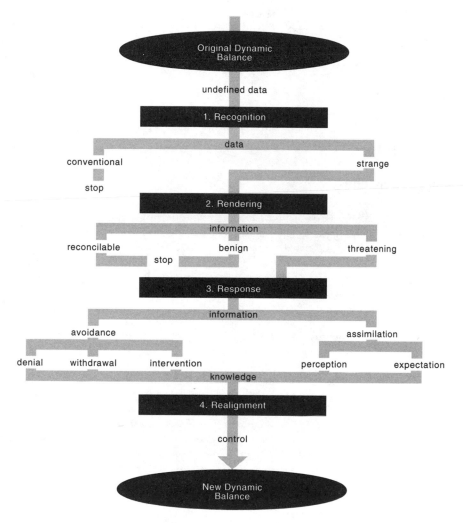

Figure B.1   The adaptation reflex.

The struggle for dynamic balance in our lives has endured as long as our species has walked in an upright position. We are genetically programmed to seek uniformity between our expectations and perceptions. This search for consistency is so strong because of our inborn proclivity for stable surroundings with minimal confusion and ambiguity. The innate drive to pursue and preserve predictability is so much a part of our essential nature that it does not require conscious volition. The engagement of the adaptation sequence to secure, protect, or regain balance is as natural and unconscious as the autonomic mechanisms that govern our bodies.

At each step of the adaptation reflex, we make decisions as to which of the options we face will result in the highest probability of success. Sometimes, we are cognizant of these evaluations and conclusions; at other times, they are as visceral and involuntary as jerking our hand away from unexpected contact with a flame. This is why the sequence is referred to as a *reflex action*. At each step, the election of one option over another occurs with or without willful intent. The four steps in the reflex are:

1. *Recognition* of the presence of unfamiliar data that could jeopardize previously established balance.
2. *Rendering* an interpretation or judgment as to the meaning of the new element.
3. *Response* to the situation by determining a strategy for restoring equilibrium.
4. *Realignment* of expectations and perceptions by applying the correct strategy.

Step 1: Recognition

Dynamic balance reflects the condition where few big surprises occur within the parameters of a particular situation. The consistency this creates forms a constellation of familiar prompts that signify what is understood to be true. Remember, success in all situations depends on the ability to translate data into information that can be applied as knowledge. When dynamic balance exists, the environment is filled with familiar signals that have been coded and indexed earlier so that, when they appear, they are quickly recognized and an appropriate response can be made. Because of the importance placed on equilibrium, when something that could possibly be unfamiliar data first appears, we immediately attempt to identify its nature. The first step of the adaptation reflex focuses on the recognition of data as conventional or strange.

Regardless of what type of situation is at hand, all human experiences are inundated with streams of data. *Conventional data* reflect stimuli that fit inside the limits of a previously established mind-set or understanding. These data are recognized as synonymous with or at least similar to existing information. As such, they are immediately accepted as new information that either reinforces what was already known to be true, or expands or contracts in acceptable ways what was already considered to be true. Dynamic balance can be maintained as long as conventional information is supported by most of the new data entering a situation.

Strange data reflect stimuli that are not recognized as being consistent with existing information chains. When the environment is filled with stimuli that are compatible with formally accepted information, what was anticipated to be true is reinforced by what appears to be happening. This allows expectations and perceptions to align; predictability is possible, and direct or indirect control becomes accessible. A very different reaction occurs when data are recognized as strange. Because strange data do not fit the existing framework of how things should look and work, they are seen as a potential threat to the prevailing order and balance. Their existence implies a gap between expectations and perceptions that could possibly disrupt the equilibrium in place.

Because dynamic balance always exists on a tentative basis, the sensitivity we demonstrate toward unfamiliar data is like that of people who are in a war-torn country and suddenly hear loud noises. No one waits to see whether a car is backfiring or the next rocket attack has begun. They just hit the ground. The purpose of this first step in the adaptation reflex is to quickly identify or recognize all new data that surface within a situation as either conventional or strange.

As shown in Figure B.1, into the original dynamic balance comes evidence of new unspecified stimuli that trigger the four-step reflex process. Undefined data enter the recognition step and what emerges are data labeled as either conventional or strange. Only data that are deemed strange (i.e., foreign to the established order) proceed to the next step. Here, during the second (rendering) phase, the data are converted into meaningful information.

Step 2: Rendering

Because of the potential threat they could represent, all data that are considered strange proceed to this next step of the adaptation reflex. Strange data are isolated, unattached expressions of nonconventional stimuli. They have no meaning other than possibly signaling danger. It is too early for the human brain to handle such data. When strange data first appear, there is no slot for them in any of the logic flows of the existing information clusters, much less any information patterns or chains. This is why strange data produce such an immediate discomfort for us.

The people and things we come in contact with must fit somewhere in our minds in order to protect the consistency we desire. All data must be classified as some form of information, or they cannot exist. Therefore, a determination must be *rendered* as to the implications of the strange new data that have surfaced. Strange data can fall into three categories:

1. *Benign* data represent a nonthreatening aberration that carries no significance.

2. *Reconcilable* data represent a new, but safe, interpretation of the data's implications. Even though these kinds of data add an innovative twist to existing information, the information created is considered nontoxic to the established order. That is, it is still congruent with, or at least not in opposition to, any of the other existing information patterns. The existing configuration of patterns of information remains relevant and viable to the situation.

3. *Threatening* data represent an intrusion into the internal consistency of the way the situation has been understood in the past. These kinds of data are potentially hazardous to the established dynamic balance. This means a new or dramatically altered variable has been introduced into the situation, and it could be powerful enough to make the existing frame of reference obsolete, if not totally useless.

BENIGN AND RECONCILABLE ARE PREFERRED

Most living systems try to maintain themselves at all cost. The struggle for self-preservation by the established order within your dynamic balance is no exception. One way this can be accomplished is by neatly cataloging or, if necessary, force-fitting any strange data that surface into either of the first two categories of Recognition (benign or reconcilable). When the third type of data (threatening) is recognized, the collapse of the current equilibrium is a real possibility.

If this collapse should occur, it means individuals or groups must operate without the benefit of predictability and control. This is so frightening for most people that, whenever possible, their existing internal logic will try desperately to reaffirm itself. This self-ratification is attempted by rendering the strange data as having either a benign or reconcilable relationship with the other existing forms of information. Even when all the evidence suggests the current configuration of understanding will no longer bring the success it once did, most of us will cling to our familiar frameworks until the last possible moment. This explains why it is so hard for our species to let go of familiar expectations.

Whether it's acknowledging the speed with which our bodies grow frail, or how quickly our children mature past our protective grasp, or the pace at which our organizational configurations fall into decay, it's difficult to accept how perishable life's brief periods of consistency really are. For most of us, it is with great reluctance and much anxiety that we try to come to terms with the passing of our personal existence on earth, much less the temporary nature of any one of its aspects. It's no wonder that we have such difficulty accepting the fleeting character of any stability in our expectations. We are often slow to accept—and, many times, outright rebellious—about admitting that the established formula for the balance in our lives is no longer relevant. This is why the illusion of change and the illusion of continuity are so prominent in our lives. In fact, usually by the time the third category (threat) is rendered, the symptoms of failure are overwhelmingly undeniable.

Given, then, how hard it is for people to acknowledge when their existing frame of reference no longer adequately explains what is happening around them, it should come as no surprise that few leaders are able to abandon their corporate strategies before they reach their point of failure. Most can't bring themselves to preclude the symptoms of strategy failure with preemptive action that would head off the inevitable decay that always occurs. The majority in leadership positions wait until their strategies and systems fail before they even consider alternative approaches.

It is an unusual leader, indeed, who will intentionally withdraw from a strategy that is still working in order to prevent complacency and arrogance from establishing a foothold. Those who do operate this way display a rare talent and conviction. What they do is seek out and sometimes even intentionally inject strange data, novel clusters, new chains, and creative patterns of information into their companies' existing framework before the old configuration of information defaults. These aren't leaders involved in change for its own sake. Like doctors who inoculate their patients against the flu by infecting them with a mild dose of a virus, these executives are trying to protect their organization and its employees from being unprepared for change. They are using preemptive actions to disrupt and ultimately strengthen their organizations' capacity to compete.

The timing of a leader's acknowledgment of data that are potentially threatening to the status quo seems to be a function of how tightly gauged his or her trigger-point is set for signaling danger. Most senior executives wait until customers, analysts, and/or shareholders have discovered problems before they act. A smaller number rely on early sightings of evidence, by people within the organization, that signal a breakdown in productivity or quality has occurred. It is an exceptional senior officer who preempts external or internal detection of problems by setting such a high standard of excellence within the organization that warnings are sounded at the first signs of data that could put the existing balance at risk.

Such leaders usually take action based on data that surface early—before actual breakdowns have occurred. They focus on leading indicators rather than trailing indicators, and they remain vigilant about the earliest signs that the current success is waning. They are prepared to take preemptive, corrective action even before any of the standard metrics can confirm a problem. This kind of leader views the appearance of threatening, scary data as an unwelcome but inevitable occurrence and actually treats it as an ally that must be embraced rather than shunned. A powerful and distinct competitive advantage is created because the majority of operations hold on to their outdated logic flows long after they should have released their clutch.

THE STRANGE DETERMINATION

If strange data are seen as possibly endangering the status quo, a further determination must be made as to the extent of the risk. This kind of risk assessment is based on four variables: (1) the degree of separation between expectations and perceptions; (2) whether the gap exists because of a problem or an opportunity; (3) whether the challenge is imminent or represents a threat that will take some time to develop; and (4) most importantly, the cost incurred if the gap is not closed.

The first three of these variables tell us that strange data can reflect a major or minor gap concerning a current or anticipated problem or opportunity that endangers the status quo. What clearly concerns us most, however, is a major breach involving a current problem.

The fourth risk variable is by far the most endangering to the status quo. This variable deals with the price a person will pay for failing to close a gap between expectations and perceptions. The more costly the breach, the more fearful people become about not being able to seal it again. As long as the hole is left open, predictability and control are lost and the likelihood for success diminishes. The degree of risk this represents is dependent on the cost incurred if failure should take place. When the price for maintaining the status quo reaches significant proportions, the break in the continuity of dynamic balance is causing drains on physical, emotional, and cognitive energy that are difficult to replace on a short-term basis. When these resources are depleted, the person or group can no longer continue the adaptation process and reverts back to the former ways of interpreting events and taking actions.

The purpose of this rendering is to determine whether the strange data identified in the Recognize step are: (1) different, (2) benign, but reconcilable with the previously established information chains, or (3) threatening to the status quo. In either of the first two cases, equilibrium is maintained and no further adaptation steps are necessary. However, should the unfamiliar data appear to be potentially threatening and the subsequent risk assessment confirm that the data are jeopardizing the integrity of the existing order, a recovery strategy must be formed and successfully deployed in order to reinstate the desired balance.

The outcome from these first two steps dictates the need for the remaining two steps of the process.

Step 3: Response

When dynamic balance is intact, we can rely on our expectations' being met. If this continuity is interrupted by strange data, it dilutes the predictability and control that are so important to success and our sense of well-being. This balance is highly prized. When strange data appear, a *response* mechanism is immediately evoked with the sole purpose of reestablishing the lost equilibrium.

Response generation consists of formulating a plan of action against the threat of loss of control. Once their purpose is severed, expectations and perceptions can be rejoined in many ways. The many scenarios that are possible, however, all fall into two basic strategies: One is externally focused (avoidance) and the other (assimilation) looks inward for answers to the lost balance. Three tactics are commonly used in the avoidance strategy, and two tactics are most often applied when assimilation is the strategy of choice.

AVOIDANCE STRATEGY

This approach calls for response plans that attempt to reestablish consistency between expectations and perceptions by focusing on dynamics taking place outside the person whose balance has been disrupted. Once avoidance becomes the strategy of choice, a second question is necessary to determine the proper tactic to deploy: "Will escaping the strange data be best accomplished by pretending it doesn't exist, sidestepping it, or doing something to fix the situation?" This question reflects the three primary tactics associated with the externally oriented avoidance strategy: denial, withdrawal, and intervention.

The first of these avoidance tactics—denying the existence of or the implications of a violation to the balanced order of things—is a common method for trying to maintain the viability of one's expectations. "I think all of you should stop worrying so much. Management has told us this merger will not in any way affect our jobs, and I think we should just believe them and go about our business as usual." Denial can be a useful strategy, but only if the threat is not a substantial one. If the change is significant, it's only a matter of time before the defense of disbelief is overtaken by the substance of the ensuing consequences.

The second main avoidance tactic is to simply flee the confusion of the unpredictable situation. Withdrawal can be a potent remedy for disorder, as long as the danger to continuity is geographically fixed, and physical distance from it increases the reliability of expectations. For example, Jerry, who is thirty-five and has been on his own for some time, goes home to visit his family for a holiday. The trip turns into a disaster because it provides the opportunity for his parents and siblings to recreate old behavior patterns that are no longer part of how Jerry sees himself. "Every time I come home, Harry starts needling me the way he did when we were kids, and, Mom, you jump in the middle to try and keep the peace." These kinds of emotional crises, though traumatic at the time, often resolve themselves when the sojourn is over. Once Jerry is back home in a setting and with people more attuned to the view he has of himself, the uneasiness and discomfort of the situation ease.

Regardless of the skill one has for denial or withdrawal tactics, trying to dodge the threat change represents does not always prove to be the prudent path. When a problem cannot be left behind in a physical space, or when the thoughts and feelings associated with the disruption are carried by the person wherever he or she goes, trying to keep a sensible distance from the burden can be difficult at best. For example, in most cases, running from the implications of an unexpected job termination or a surprise pregnancy is not a solution. In such situations, neither denial nor withdrawal will usually provide viable, long-term answers. Under these conditions, the third option may be more appropriate.

The third avoidance tactic, intervention, focuses on trying to fix what went wrong. Remember, we are able to experience direct control when we are able to intentionally influence the variables around us in such a way that we get what we want. When there is a significant breach between expectations and perceptions, we usually feel a problem has surfaced that needs fixing. The most common response to such a problem is to try to correct whatever went wrong—that is, to reach out or intervene into the objective reality around us and manipulate the buttons, knobs, and levers on life's dashboard so that the problem goes away (i.e., everything returns to the way it should have been).

Without question, this fixing of reality is the most popular way people try to deal with a disruptive situation. Yet, after looking at this tactic's track record, one has to wonder why. Attempts to directly control the challenges we face in our lives seem to run in the face of what common sense would dictate.

Much of the time, our efforts to directly control things around us just don't work. It would seem that this would set up an untenable contradiction between our reasoning capabilities (i.e., probability calculations) and our continued reliance on a tactic to fix reality that doesn't often generate what we want. To the contrary, however, most of us have actually learned how to dispose of this incongruity quite easily. Our species has never confused logic with what we are most comfortable doing. Whenever there is a choice between rational behavior and what would calm our fears and grant us serenity, we will consistently opt for emotional solace rather than cerebral integrity. Remembering the depth of the human desire for consistency and predictability helps explain our continued preference for familiar behavior patterns (even those that no longer work) rather than venture into the new territory that objective conclusions sometimes suggest. Tradition, established routines, and well-known procedures win most of their battles with logic and rational analysis.

To summarize the externally focused avoidance strategy, its basic intent is to circumvent the implications of a threatening change. This is done by denying, withdrawing from, or intervening to fix something outside the disrupted person.

ASSIMILATION STRATEGY

The second of the two main strategies in the response step is dedicated to absorbing the implications of change rather than trying to avoid them. This approach calls for a response that attempts to reestablish consistency between expectations and perceptions by focusing on dynamics inside the person whose balance has been disrupted. When denying, running from, or trying to modify tangible external reality doesn't seem likely to produce the desired results, people may choose to direct their attention to more of an internal focus. This second strategy for responding to information that jeopardizes the existing order of things is based on the assumption that it would be more productive to try to shift how the threat is viewed rather than attempt to avoid its presence. This inwardly focused, viewpoint-based approach employs two primary tactics: (1) reframing how something appears in order that it be perceived as more consistent with what was anticipated or (2) altering expectations to better match what appears to be reality. I refer to these tactics as *reframing perceptions* and *shifting expectations*.

The true human experience is never as binary as these two tactics, in their purest form, might suggest. Our perspective or frame of reference on something is comprised of both our expectations and our perceptions. They are intricately tied together, and modifications to either will have an impact on the other. Generally speaking, we expect to get more of what we already see, and we usually can only see that which we already expect. This is why it is so difficult to move away from a perspective once it's established. Even when we are able to relate to something or someone differently than we have in the past, we form new expectations that, to a great extent, are bounded by the limits of our original viewpoint.

For example, if we learn about a particularly unpleasant habit in someone we care about, we still tend to anticipate that he or she will behave in other, more positive ways.

This may be true despite new evidence to the contrary. In a similar fashion, we continue to expect the people we hate to fulfill our worst nightmares. When people do modify how they perceive a situation, it creates a set of expectations that is quite different from those that existed before.

Despite this meshing of expectations and perceptions, ordinarily the circumstances of a situation suggest one of these two tactics to be the better focal point to initiate a shift in someone's frame of reference. Regardless of which is selected as the primary tactic for assimilating a change, the result of any revision in one will result in some degree of alteration in both. With that said, let's explore each of these tactics separately.

REFRAMING PERCEPTIONS

When this option is selected, it centers on a person's frame of reference or orientation to a situation as the fulcrum for reestablishing continuity between expectations and perceptions. If someone believes he or she is in a situation where an unwanted external reality is both unavoidable and impervious to influence, that person may choose to *reframe* his or her bearing on the circumstances, and in doing so, develop an alternative disposition toward the situation. By doing this, the person is able to absorb or assimilate what has happened.

Our capacity to reframe our view of reality is an intriguing phenomenon. Although people are able to reframe themselves, the dynamics of this process may be easiest to see by looking at one person's efforts to reframe another. Communication between people always occurs on two planes: (1) the content level—the specific language used in the message a person is attempting to convey (e.g., a coded transmission); and (2) the context level—the frame of reference used by the sender regarding the intended meaning of the message. When the image of something or someone is reframed, its content stays the same, but the context in which it is presented is altered. For example, Mary says to her sister, "You don't have to spend the rest of your life dwelling on the negative aspects of our childhood. There were many wonderful qualities from our parents that you and I were exposed to that later served us well in our adult years." Or, John tells an associate at his office, "You have no control over the downsizing, but you can choose to focus your attention on the opportunities this challenge will uncover and not allow yourself to be unduly dragged down by all the fear and uncertainty you also feel."

There are endless components to a person's frame of reference that can be reframed. Some examples are:

- Definition—How the nature, properties, qualities, or scope of something is delineated.
- History—The explanation of past incidents that have led up to a current situation.
- Purpose—The description of what a person truly wants to achieve in a given situation.
- Requirements—What it really takes to succeed in a given situation.

Table B.1 shows how these components might be reframed.

SHIFTING EXPECTATIONS

If a foreign, external reality is irrevocable and no amount of reframing of the situation appears to offer any relief from the threat it imposes, another approach to assimilating a change is to redefine what is anticipated about the outcome from the experience. When this tactic is used, energy is concentrated not on the external reality or even the affected

Table B.1 Examples of Reframing

Framing Components	Original Situation Seen by Someone	Reframed Statement
Definition	"I'll never be able to work my way out of this problem."	"Maybe it's not a problem with a solution. Maybe it's a dilemma that must be endured."
History	"We have always demonstrated a capacity to grow, so why should we change now?"	"When I look back over the past several years of the Company's evolution, I don't see an organization with consistent, sustained growth. I see a few home runs that compensated for an otherwise poor performance record."
Purpose	"I can't wait until I get my hands on that guy."	"Given what has happened, how do you want to handle your next meeting with John? Do you want to vent your emotions or resolve the issue?"
Requirements	"I can't afford to confront her with this problem. She might get so angry that she would quit and then what would I do about her accounts?"	"To not discuss the situation with her could result in this problem never being resolved. That means you will continue to have the kind of low productivity you now have as a result of her operating as she does. What it really boils down to is how badly you want to address this problem. Are you willing and able to pay the price to achieve what you say you want?"

person's perception of its occurrence, but on the expectations developed about what will unfold as a result of what is happening or has happened.

Remember, the change-related stress being experienced by a person is due to an interruption in the continuity between what he or she anticipated and what is being perceived. All the other tactics for closing the gap are focused on aspects other than expectations. In the first strategy, the tactical options were denying a breach has occurred, trying to evade the point of its occurrence, or intervening to modify external reality to fit existing expectations. In this second strategy, we have already seen how the tactic of reconstructing perceptions may lead to the desired effect. This last tactic, however, is the only one that attempts to resolve the tension by dealing directly with expectations themselves rather than reality or perceptions.

When evidence suggests current expectations are unrealistic and should be recalibrated, there are many ways to proceed. One option is to lower the intended goal (e.g., "I don't think I'll ever make the kind of money here that I made when I worked at my last job"). Another approach is to redefine the criteria for success (e.g., "I should have never tried to get on the chairman's calendar during the same week that the board meets"). A third choice could be finding a way for the negatives to be less costly than originally anticipated (e.g., "This merger will create less political fallout than I thought").

A final example of how expectations can be shifted deals with a person who plans to move on with his or her life after a traumatic event. A person may say to himself or herself, "It's obvious this restructuring of the company is going to happen and it won't be pleasant—now where do I go from here? How can this inevitable negative be turned into an advantage for me?" There is no attempt to circumvent the reality of the situation or to emphasize the positives in what is going to be a terribly disruptive breakdown of what was predicted to happen. The person simply accepts the cards that were dealt, projects the implications of what will happen, and then focuses his or her energy on what to do next.

There are infinite numbers of ways that expectations can be expanded or contracted to create the missing continuity with perceptions. Any of these approaches can result in the construction of new expectations that are, hopefully, more in line with what actually seems to be unfolding. Rather than trying to close the disconnection between expectations and perceptions by manipulating the external reality (denial, withdrawal, intervention) or framing how it is perceived (perception), this last tactic is focused on preparing for the implications of what is about to happen. Though this may appear to be giving in or giving up, it, in fact, can be a very powerful and effective maneuver to accept short-term disappointment and pain in order that recovery and planning can begin for longer-term and more substantial success. Those who are unable to shift their expectations in the face of inevitable negative change deplete their resources by trying to avoid tactical defeat. In the process, they often lose sight of their more strategic campaign for success.

Whether reframing how an unfamiliar situation appears or developing new expectations to match what seems to be happening, the purpose of these last two tactics is to internalize or assimilate what has happened or will happen. Many people claim to have assimilated a change when, in fact, they have not. Many organizations allege that an important and costly initiative has been successfully embraced by its employees when, in reality, they have been taught how to mimic the symptoms of full acceptance. True assimilation of change is not an easy criterion to meet.

Listed in Table B.2 are indicators of whether someone has actually assimilated a major change or is holding on to a previous perspective long after it is feasible. For assimilation to occur, it is not necessary that all the positive indicators listed in the table be present; but as the number increases, so does the likelihood of successfully recalibrating expectations.

By the end of this Response step in the adaptation reflex, a basic strategy and specific tactic(s) have been determined to repair the breach between expectations and perceptions. If avoidance is the strategy of choice, the threatening information is to be denied, withdrawn from, or eschewed by fixing the situation. If the assimilation strategy is preferred, the disruptive information is addressed by somehow incorporating it into the person's frame of reference. This is accomplished by either reframing perceptions or redefining expectations so that the two are once again consistent with each other. To be successful, the broad strategy and particular tactic(s) engaged must be correct for the situation, and they must also be executed with sufficient skill and timing to elude the break in or reestablish the previous stable dynamic balance. The second part of this criterion is our segue into the last step in the reflex. The fourth step, realignment, is that point in the adaptation process where the response strategy and tactic(s) are actually engaged and the symmetry between expectations and perceptions is reunited.

Table B.2   Successful and Unsuccessful Assimilation

Unsuccessful Assimilation (Maintains old expectations, even though they no longer match current circumstances)	Successful Assimilation (Shifts from old expectations no longer relevant to expectations consistent with new circumstances)
Rejecting information that would threaten existing views	Being open to information that might lead to new perspectives
Continuing to apply previously established criteria for success even though they are no longer meaningful	Developing new criteria for success or new ways to achieve old success criteria
Continuing to pay attention to issues and ask questions that were relevant for previous circumstances but do not apply to current ones	Learning what to pay attention to and what questions to ask in the new environment in order to succeed
Applying previously established priorities and/or sequencing of activities to new circumstances, even though they do not generate success	Identifying new priorities and/or new sequencing of activities to match current demands
Continuing to apply outdated approaches to solving problems and/or exploiting opportunities	Identifying new ways to solve problems and/or take advantage of opportunities
Producing incomplete, superficial, and/or short-term application of desired behavior	Producing complete, comprehensive, and sustained application of desired behavior
Generating more resistance than necessary and/or less commitment than desired	Minimizing resistance, developing appropriate commitment
Feeling victimized by the lack of success in new circumstances	Feeling responsible for success in new circumstances, regardless of the challenge faced
Feeling resentful that previously successful behaviors are no longer rewarded	Feeling accountable to develop behavior that will address new circumstances
Displaying unnecessary levels of bitterness, blame, cynicism, and anger	Displaying high levels of accomplishments, self-validation, optimism, and pride
Requiring more time and money than necessary for implementation	Optimizing time and money needed for implementation
Requiring more time and money than necessary for maintaining desired behavior	Optimizing time and money needed to monitor and maintain desired behavior

Step 4: Realignment

The coveted dynamic balance we all seek was lost when the forces of change interrupted the stability of the old status quo. Once either external reality is modified or internal expectations and/or perceptions are recalibrated, a person once again can regain the feeling of being in control. The purpose of this last step of the reflex sequence is to reclaim predictability so a sense of direct and/or indirect control can be restored.

The realignment step does not really involve mending the equilibrium that was in place before the disruption of change. If minor repairs were all that were needed to regain balance, the intruding strange data would not have been seen as threatening in the first place. Moreover, without threatening data, the adaptation process would not have progressed past the Rendering step anyway. The old balance is not reclaimed or returned it to its pretraumatized state. *The previous dynamic balance is not revived; a new one is created.* The regeneration that takes place in this step entails overhauling, not patching up, the way external reality and internal expectations and perceptions relate to each other. When the variance between expectations and perceptions is severe, nothing short of a full rectification is sufficient for a new balance to surface.

With expectations reinstated, a renewed sense of control is once again possible. This means the response strategy created new realities, new expectations, and/or new perceptions, and the three domains are now functioning as integrated components with the other variables in the change situation.

Through repetitive application, these new elements (i.e., realities, expectations, or perceptions) acclimate themselves to each other, as well as to the other aspects of the situation, and eventually all are fused into a new established order. This new order means things once more make sense, and people feel like they are, again, in either direct or indirect control of their destiny. A new dynamic balance has been achieved.

SUMMARY OF THE ADAPTATION REFLEX

The adaptation reflex involves moving from one state of dynamic balance to another. When the desired uniformity between expectations and perceptions is first achieved, control and the opportunity for success in a given situation are secured. This balance is always tentative, though, because of the unstable nature of the surrounding environment. Due to the constant bombardment of new stimuli, stability eventually wavers. Each time the provisional symmetry collides with strange data, the adaptation reflex is engaged. The reflex process may stay enrolled throughout all four of its steps, or it may terminate if results from the reconnaissance effort (either of the first two steps) indicate no further action is needed.

The first facet of the adaptation sequence occurs when unspecified stimuli enter a person's preexisting dynamic balance and trigger the reflex action. Undefined stimuli are processed in the Recognition step and with the exit from this step comes a determination as to its nature. It can be recognized as either conventional (i.e., within the limits of the existing balance) or strange (i.e., perceived to be different than expected). If the data are viewed as strange, the Rendering step is automatically engaged. In this second step, the unfamiliar data are transformed into useful information when meaning is attributed to them. As this conversion takes place, a key judgment is made. The data are classified as unlike anything else in the existing information chains but reconcilable enough to be incorporated easily into one or more chains without much effort; distinct from any existing chain but benign to the overall existing balance; or dissimilar from other chains and posing a potential threat to the current order. Data go into the Rendering step and out comes meaningful information.

If the judgment rendered is that the strange data jeopardize the preexisting balance, the process moves on to the Response step. Here, the available information is used to craft a reply to the lost control. Like other aspects of the adaptation reflex, composing a plan to respond to the breach in continuity can be done in a highly intuitive fashion or approached with conscious intent and forethought. When approached unconsciously, the results often look more like a sketch or outline than a detailed design. When deliberate, calculated purpose is involved, the outcome is likely to resemble a precisely organized blueprint for the proposed course of action. Whether done spontaneously or intentionally, the outcome of the Response step is to formulate a plan of action to rebut the lost control.

At the fourth step, Realignment, the information created in the two prior steps is applied to create application knowledge. The successful execution of the strategy devised in the Response step reestablishes the vital connection between expectations and perceptions. The new bridge between what was anticipated and what appears to be happening is accomplished.

This final step is where fresh realities, expectations, and/or predictions are matched with each other to form a new order. With this new order comes the feeling of, once again, being in control. When direct or indirect control is achieved, the situation may or may not be as desired, but it is again understandable and therefore more likely to be managed. Success in what was an unfamiliar situation is now at least possible.

Key Lessons

I'm sure you are asking yourself, "All this may be interesting, but what do I do with it? How does understanding the mechanics of the adaptation process help me be a better leader for my organization as it faces major turmoil?" Well, for one thing, it's difficult to manage something you don't understand. CEOs who are uneducated about the basics of operating a computer are at a disadvantage when it comes to making strategy decisions about the use of information systems in their organizations. If they lack a working knowledge of the subject, they are at the mercy of their expert advisers. They lack the ability to include in the decision-making process their own sense of what to do.

The same is true when considering the strategic value of being the nimble competitor in a market. Without a working knowledge of how change unfolds in an organization—in this case, specifically how the adaptation process operates—leaders are at a distinct disadvantage. In addition to the value of understanding the basic mechanics, three key lessons associated with the adaptation reflex are important for leaders to know:

1. The *time* it takes for people to adapt to change varies by person and circumstance.
2. Physical, emotional, and intellectual *resources* are required to accommodate change.
3. The outcomes from adapting to change produce a variable *harvest*.

TIME VARIATION

The time frame for moving through the entire adaptation process may be, for some people, no longer than the wink of an eye; others, however, may ponder some of the decisions interminably. Sometimes, the process is never completed and the breach between expectations and perceptions is left unresolved. When this happens, if a person stays in this kind of situation for extended periods, it can lead to chronic, long-term dysfunction and failure may result.

Typically, the faster the steps are engaged, the less conscious we are that an adjustment to change has even been made. We are painfully aware of the adaptation process when it appears to move forward at a snail's pace—for example, following a divorce; adjusting to children's leaving home for college, job, or marriage; or the loss of a dear friend. The process of accommodating change can become all but invisible, however, when its pace dramatically accelerates.

When Michael Jordan begins one of his famous leaps into the air to slam a basketball into the net, he does so after (1) making an instantaneous assessment of the competitive variables he is contending with and (2) determining what he believes will happen if he attempts the shot. Let's assume that, given his skill level and years of experience, the confidence he has in predicting the outcome of this particular move is high as he begins his leap. This means he starts the play in a state of dynamic balance—that is, he believes there is a likelihood that the basket he is about to attempt will, in fact, be completed.

As is the case in all fast-paced environments, between the moment when Jordan's feet leave the floor and the officially recorded time of the anticipated goal, the variables shift. Two players move out of their projected positions and suddenly are in his path, making his expected flight plan impossible. In what seems to be an instantaneous reaction, he alters his course of movement. In less than a second, he completes all four steps of the reflex, adjusts himself to the unanticipated shift in position, and completes an unbelievable pass to one of his teammates, who then makes the score. Few people in the sports arena who witness these split-second adjustments would think of Jordan's actions as a demonstration of the adaptation process in action. More common references would be to think of this as just an example of his great "moves" and his natural "instinct" for the game. Beneath the more obvious interpretation of his phenomenal talent, however, lies another explanation for his agility: the speed of his adaptation reflex.

The time required to complete the four-part adaptation reflex appears to be greatly influenced by how well acquainted a person is with the kind of conditions in which the change is occurring. People have the capacity to move through the process at lightning speed if they are familiar with the circumstances. Returning to the basketball court, let's say this exact situation had never occurred for Jordan before, where all the variables (e.g., players, his mental/physical condition, everyone's placement in the court, time left in the game, and crowd enthusiasm) were precisely the same. Even though a particular situation may be new, his years of playing professional basketball have made him extremely accustomed to at least similar circumstances. The precise placement and status of all the variables may be different, but the variables themselves are not. His familiarity with them allows him to make the necessary modifications in a fraction of a second.

The adjustment process slows considerably when people contend with less familiar situations. Jordan is an incredible all-around athlete, but he may not be able to bring his phenomenal speed of reflex to games other than basketball. This was the case when he left the Chicago Bulls for a brief period and tried his hand at professional baseball. The same man who is the very definition of greatness on the court became a third-string, average-at-best player who couldn't compete well in the professional ranks of baseball.

His move from one sport to another represented more than a shift from hardwood courts to grass ballfields and from a large to a small round ball. The more important inhibitor to his success was his lack of experience with the kinds of circumstances that commonly occur in baseball. He went from recognizing frequently repeated conditions and executing habitual movements to engaging in actions and reactions he was a relative stranger to, and he could not react to them with his normal grace and speed. The master became a raw recruit. As a green, unseasoned, awkward baseball novice he could not perform competitively, much less dazzle the crowd as he had while playing basketball.

When we are familiar with the kinds of unanticipated things that can happen to us, we tend to react much faster than when we are faced with totally novel situations. The agonizingly slow pace at which our companies sometimes adapt to disruption occurs, in part, because people are not only surprised by a specific unforeseen event, but are also unaccustomed to the general circumstances in which that surprise occurs.

Required Resources

Regardless of which strategy and tactics are used, it is a resource-consuming activity to recalibrate either external reality or internal expectations and/or perceptions. This kind of recalibration draws on three types of assimilation resources: cognitive, affective, and behavioral. Each is necessary for realignment to occur. The deployment of the chosen strategy and tactics has to be logically thought through, any strong feelings associated with the situation have to be addressed, and new skills may be required and may have to be developed. It follows then that intellectual, emotional, and physical energy is required to carry out any response to disrupted equilibrium. Every time a maneuver within the adaptation process is executed to help close the expectation/perception gap in a particular circumstance, these three forms of energy must be applied successfully. Actually closing the gap may require many such maneuvers, but each one is fashioned by creatively investing the proper resources.

The adaptation reflex is so embedded into our day-to-day functioning that the process is engaged hundreds of times each day without our awareness or our conscious intent to do so. Because of this, the full extent of the resources used to drive the adaptation process are often overlooked. To set the proper context for examining resource consumption during change, let's review, once again, the steps that generate the energy invoice incurred when adapting to change:

- The majority of the intrusions that disturb our sense of order and balance do not warrant the engagement of the entire adaptation sequence. When conditions are perceived to be relatively calm, new data are recognized as being mostly conventional in nature, and if they appear to be strange at all, they are usually either benign or reconcilable with other already-established information. An environment low in turbulence means most of the stimuli that surface fit well with our preexisting understanding of how things are. These are situations where the adjustments necessary to accommodate the inevitable surprises we encounter are modest and without much consequence.

- Change of any magnitude happens when the dynamic balance we try to achieve and maintain is thwarted by unfamiliar circumstances. Minor change takes place when the gap between expectations and what is perceived is slight to moderate. These occurrences usually don't make it past the Rendering phase because they are not seen as very threatening.

- Major change takes place when there is a powerful interruption between expectations and perceptions. When this happens, the entire adaptation sequence must be engaged to restore order. Once established, the coveted dynamic balance is disturbed by unspecified stimuli that are recognized as strange data. If a judgment is rendered that the data represent information threatening to the existing order, a response is formulated to guide the necessary actions, resulting in either altering external reality and/or internal perceptions/expectations. Once this response strategy is successfully deployed, expectations and perceptions are once again aligned.

The energy required to go through this entire adaptation sequence in order to address a major change is significantly greater than that required for minor adjustments. Accommodating dramatic change is more of a resource-draining activity than accommodating small, secondary adjustments. Each of the four steps in the adaptation reflex requires physical, emotional, and intellectual energy to accomplish. The precise mix of resources needed to successfully adapt to a change varies, based on such things as personal characteristics of the individuals involved, the severity of the disruption, and which step of the sequence is being engaged. A summary of each follows:

- Personal characteristics—Someone who is more resilient[3] to disruptions in his or her life will require fewer resources to accommodate change than someone with, for example, a low tolerance for ambiguity and/or an inability to identify opportunities within challenging situations.

- Level of disruption—Though all major change requires the physical, emotional, and intellectual means to narrow the gap between expectations and perceptions, the energy necessary when the rupture is traumatic is greater than when it is less forceful. As the size of the breach expands, so does the amount of resources needed to reinstate it.

- Phase engaged—Most of the time, the first two steps of the adaptation reflex draw on more cognitive than emotional resources to accomplish. Stronger emotional feelings are typically associated with the adjustment processes in the last two steps (reclaiming activities). Powerful feelings often surface once new data are deemed a threat, and a response must be generated and deployed. The physical demands are, of course, increased anytime a person processes both cerebral and heartfelt information. In the Realignment step, a gap has been closed, and the need for these three resources is usually lessened. This is where control is once again available. Normally, this part of the process is much less demanding than the others. Finally, the call for all three of these resources is at its lowest as long as the new dynamic balance can be maintained.

ADAPTATION HARVEST

Major change occurs when there is a significant fragmentation in the continuity between expectation and what is perceived to be occurring in matters of importance. Adapting to this kind of change takes place when objective reality is altered, perceptions are modified to align with established expectations, or expectations are adjusted to fit more closely with existing perceptions. By recalibrating reality, expectations, and/or perceptions, direct or indirect control can be rescued, and success in what was an unfamiliar environment is possible.

As previously stated, the consignment of the physical, emotional, and intellectual energy needed for this kind of recalibration can be considerable, but the yield from the investment can also be very beneficial. When all four steps of the adaptation reflex are engaged, one of three outcomes can occur: recovery, gain, or growth. Each of these three options reflects a form of accommodating change, but the perceived cost/benefit ratios and associated comfort with each kind of experience vary greatly:

- Recovery—This kind of outcome is the weakest of the three harvest possibilities. In cases where recovery is the outcome, the intellectual, emotional, and physical investment necessary for recalibration was viewed by the person involved to be inordinately high when compared to the value he or she received from the ordeal. The individual would gladly retract the change if possible, because, from his or her standpoint, little payoff occurred in relation to the cost of the adaptation process. This person accepts the change as irreversible, but sees only a slim chance of succeeding well enough in the new environment to compensate for the difficulties experienced during the migration. For this reason, people in these kinds of situations often carry with them a great deal of bitterness, and they tend to blame others for what caused the change or what happened during the transition.

- Gain—The person who achieves this outcome also believes the change he or she experienced was too expensive for the results received; however, with this kind of harvest, there is more of a return for the transition investment made than is true with recovery-type harvest. The physical, emotional, and intellectual energy it took to recalibrate was costly, but, from the person's standpoint, the success that resulted created a value that made the effort at least worthwhile. Although the individual reports a positive yield was secured from the experience, the trouble and hardship he or she withstood left such an impression that if there were now a choice to reenter the same change situation, it would be declined.

  People in these circumstances consider themselves fortunate to have profited from the discomfort and aggravation that were suffered, but overall they wish the experience had never happened and they would still prefer for things to have stayed the way they were before the change. Because of this, even though people in these situations have achieved more because of the change than they otherwise would have, they often hold on to a great deal of cynicism, anger, and resentment long after the transition is complete.

- Growth—This kind of assimilation outcome reflects an individual who pays no less of a price for his or her change outcome than individuals who have recovered or gained from theirs, but this person believes the investment was more than worth the trouble and pain that were experienced. The cost/benefit ratio is viewed in an extremely positive light, and he or she would never wish to return to the preexisting state before the change. Even though a very high price was paid for the rewards received, this person believes whatever was required to accomplish the transition was worth the investment. The physical, emotional, and intellectual invoice may have been much greater than this person ever thought possible before entering the transition process; but if offered the chance to do it all again, he or she would. Even knowing beforehand what the full price would be, he or she would not hesitate to pursue this change again.

  People who grow from change typically carry little, if any, negative baggage from their difficult and costly ordeal. If injustices were done to them along the way, they forgive and/or move on with the rest of their lives. If they made mistakes, they don't indulge in much guilt or self-incrimination, because they believe they were making the best decision they could at the time. People who grow from their trials and tribulations tend to be more grateful than resentful about the price they paid to achieve what they ultimately accomplish. They often report that everything they have experienced in their life, both good and bad, was necessary for them to be prepared to achieve and embrace the rewards they eventually enjoyed.

The difference in yields from the recovery, gain, and growth outcomes has very little to do with the cost of each type of transition, because the invoices are basically the same. The distinction lies in the ultimate benefits received by the people involved. Much like a mother who can't recall the almost unbearable pain she experienced during her child's birth, the price tag for the things we are truly committed to usually becomes insignificant once the bill is paid and gratification is secured.

The People Side of Realignment Initiatives

et's move forward to Human Due Diligence (HDD) by going backward to briefly examine the origins of the old change management framework that proved so useful during the Contiguous era. I start by drawing a distinction between the objectives of *project management* and that of *people management*. HDD represents only half of the ingredients organizations need to implement important initiatives. Project management is its counterpart, and without the value it brings, HDD would never deliver the kind of execution architecture so essential for today's unending modifications and conversions.

Once you select a strategic initiative, successful implementation requires two types of planning and action. As a senior officer, you may not personally engage in these activities, but it is part of your role to assure that they take place. The first of these activities is devoted to issues associated with logistics. Here, typical questions are: What will be the sequence of events and key milestones? What technology requirements will be incurred? What financial resources are needed, and how will the funding be secured? Is training necessary, who will attend, and when? Issues like these are customarily addressed in an organization's project management process.

The second type of planning and activities centers more on the ways in which people feel, think, and behave as they respond to the changes they are being asked to accept. Typical questions are: When, why, and to what extent will people resist initiatives they are being asked to accept? To what degree are people prepared to work effectively in unfamiliar teams as they respond to new demands? How important is it that people feel involved in the making of various decisions as implementation unfolds, and how will their participation be managed? The focus here is on the people management process.

These two processes are vital to implementation success. Project management is necessary to deal with tangibles like budgets and schedules, while people management is important in addressing the more emotional factors such as people feeling threatened, secure, victimized, or empowered. With acknowledgment to the always present exceptions, it has been my observation that most poor execution, that occurs all too frequently, is due not to weak project management but to inept or nonexistent people management.

Regardless of the nature of an initiative, people will always struggle if it requires them to significantly alter their expectations or perceptions about such things as job requirements, policies, procedures, with whom they work, or how they will be evaluated and compensated. Humans don't like unpredictable work environments; introducing major changes, even ones people say they want, typically generates a level of ambiguity and uncertainty. Unless this inevitable reluctance to change can be planned for and appropriately addressed, impeccable solutions will fall prey to the powerful forces people invoke to protect the predictability of their status quo.

Generally, leaders have either been unaware of or did not place much value on the interdependent relationship that exists between the project and people management processes. Most leaders have long been familiar with the benefits of project management and how it contributes to getting things done. In fact, many leaders see project management as all that is needed for successful execution of their change efforts. Some know people management concepts and techniques are available, but do not see them as value-added and, therefore, often avoid using them. Other top officers are aware of and value both processes, but see the two as separable, independent variables affecting the outcome of implementation efforts. For example, because of time premiums or budget constraints, leaders often will attempt to proceed with a change endeavor, addressing only the issues raised by project management. Though not as frequent, there also have been plenty of cases where leaders invested in the concerns of those people affected by a project to the exclusion of providing the kind of tangible project management necessary.

Although each of these processes often has been dealt with as a stand-alone approach to executing decisions involving change, the two actually represent distinct but highly interrelated components of a single phenomenon called *implementation*. With today's turmoil to contend with, the operational/utilitarian (project management) and cognitive/affective sides (people management) of executing major changes must be addressed if the desired alterations in an organization's key success factors are to take place.

Both processes are equally important to implementation success, yet the paths of their separate development have only recently converged. The project-management mechanisms were the first to develop. The project side of managing the introduction of innovations has a long history. Certainly the logistical concerns of the ancient Egyptian engineers in moving from the use of techniques for building the early step pyramids to that of building the Great Pyramid at Giza took precedence over any concerns they may have had for their slaves' expectations.

By the 1950s, the more tangible aspects of executing change were well established, and project management had gained respect as a key component to accomplishing important initiatives on time and within budget. Starting in the 1950s, traces of the people-management component were beginning to form, and by the 1960s, it was starting to enjoy some legitimization among corporate officers. The two features continued to evolve, however, in parallel. First, they developed as related, but autonomous parts, and then finally they became more and more closely reciprocal in nature. By the early 1990s, the two distinct processes had reached a point of asymptote (i.e., very close together, but never fully touching). They had become intertwined, yet were still treated as two units that could be segregated, and often were. Because of their true interrelationship, however, many leaders saw the need for their project-management attempts to closely coordinate with their change-management efforts.

As we entered the 1990s, the struggle to keep the two elements separate gave way to a more unified approach that started to reflect genuine synthesis. This new, still forming perpetual unrest paradigm represents a true merging of the two formerly independent aspects and serves as the basis for the next generation of approaches and techniques being developed to orchestrate the human side of transition. Within this new framework, people-management components remain distinguishable but can no longer be disentangled from the project management elements. When the two were separate, they could be deployed individually. With the emergence of a need for a nimble work environment and the use of HDD to achieve it, the formally divided components can be fused into a single process where each can be addressed and focused on, but no longer can either one be completely isolated from the other.

The unification of these two processes required a parity between the two that was not possible until the people management component matured enough to reflect a similar level of sophistication to that of its project-management counterpart. Given that project management has been in existence much longer, it has only been in recent years that the people management perspective has had enough of this seasoning to be on par with project management.

From the 1950s to the 1990s, the human side of change evolved through a rich legacy that culminated in what became known as *change management*. By the 1990s, an area of specialization called change management had surfaced that dealt exclusively with how people could be better prepared for and managed during the implementation of major initiatives. As a field of professional guidance, it had been influenced by its human resources (HR) and organizational development (OD) ancestry, but it evolved with much more of a bias for prescriptions, procedures, and methodologies.

An important distinction was that HR and OD professionals often were seen as being more identified with the trauma experienced by employees rather than the pressures experienced by leaders during change. Warranted or not, as a result of this image, many executives thought the HR and OD functions interpreted their role to be that of ministering to the victims of change, not supporting the architects who had implementation responsibilities. To senior officers scarred from their battles with change, they felt they had little in common with these esoteric specialists who appeared to avoid being too closely aligned with the hard realities of leadership during tough times. It seemed to these veterans of many change battles that HR and OD professionals did not want to risk being connected to the fallout from some of the more unpopular change decisions (e.g., the emotional trauma of downsizing, painful restructuring, or threatening new technology). To many in the senior management ranks, "the marshmallows from the soft side of the tracks" were fair-weather friends, at best.

For the most part, change management practitioners aligned themselves differently from decision makers. Although they usually defined their role as being a resource to anyone at any level of the organization, they typically formed their alliances no lower than the mid-tiers of management, and occasionally with senior officers. Most felt they were there to help build whatever implementation plans were needed, even for the most unpleasant of change initiatives. For this reason, they were usually better received by leadership. They also were generally held in higher regard than their HR and OD counterparts, because senior management perceived them as more focused on what they, as top executives, considered to be the real issues. These issues concerned such ideas as how to:

- Stay centered on market success and avoid getting overly focused on any one change project as the ultimate goal.
- Demystify the change process, so that it is understandable and manageable.
- De-emphasize emotionalism without avoiding the legitimate concerns people have about adjusting to new demands.
- Identify the critical risk factors to track during implementation and how to generate metrics to measure them.
- Formulate practical methods line managers can use to deal with employee resistance and generate tangible results that actually help complete projects.

With these kinds of objectives constituting its charter, change management gained a high degree of acceptance among many in mid-level management and some senior-level executives. It became recognized as something executives actually wanted associated with their major change efforts instead of the political placating that often occurred with various HR and OD efforts.

The lack of structure that had characterized many OD practitioners did not go unnoticed by the specialists of this later period. Early in the change management time frame, many practitioners worked hard to build methodologies for implementing major initiatives. These approaches varied in detail and scope according to the view held by the developer. The one thing that most had in common, however, was their purpose: to provide an integrated framework to orchestrate the change process. As these methodologies were unveiled, they provided practitioners with the intellectual road maps that had been missing in the OD period. In doing so, the competence of these professionals deepened and their confidence soared with regard to the value they could provide to the organizations they served.

As more and more implementation methodologies were developed and released, it became easier for many of the concepts and techniques that had been independently developed over the years to be rationalized and interconnected. Once these cognitive guides became available, change-management practitioners started using more standardized terms, procedures, principles, and diagnostic instruments to which leaders were easily able to relate. This consolidation of terminology and diagnostic guidelines made it significantly easier for everyone to communicate with each other and in so doing, they were able to more productively address the impediments to successful change.

Though change management has served us well, the onset of the perpetual unrest period has created a need for an alternative, HDD, that brings a fresh perspective to orchestrating major organizational transitions. In fact, HDD represents a fundamental break from the change-management framework. This latest developmental phase for the change profession is no mere extension of the previous period. The change-management approach offered a view of executions geared to mid-level management and their employees with only occasional influence granted at the upper tiers of the executive ranks. The new HDD framework is calibrated to operate from a more strategic frame of mind. It is designed to address human issues at all levels of the hierarchy, but its primary purpose is to serve the concerns and challenges of those in executive-level positions. Far from ignoring or excluding the change-related struggles of middle- and lower-tier management—and those

Table C.1   Change Management versus Human Due Diligence

Change Management	Human Due Diligence
Focus is on the process used	Focus is on the results achieved
Change projects are viewed as terminal objectives valued for their own sake	Changes are seen as a means to a more important end: market success
Center of activity is mid- to lower-level management and employees	Center of activity involves senior-level leadership
Applied to separate change projects that may or may not have overlapping impact	Applied to specific projects as well as to preparing the overall organization for ongoing transition
Generates a cursory, truncated review of people issues affecting project success	Generates an extensive, comprehensive analysis of the implications impacting change success
Applied as a discretionary, piece-meal reaction to people problems that have already surfaced during implementation	Applied as a mandatory, comprehensive, preventive action intended to maximize commitment to change goals
Focuses on damage control after resistance has been created	Focuses on preventing unnecessary resistance and managing that which is inevitable
Designed for leaders who think of managing the human side of change as an expense	Designed for leaders who think of managing the human side of change as an investment
Mostly concerned with helping people feel better as they endure transition trauma	Mostly concerned with managing current adaptation capacity and maintaining adequate resources for future initiatives
Language calibrated to the Human Resources community includes beginnings, endings, letting go, and comfort zone	Language calibrated to senior officer's perspective includes due diligence, human capital, ROC_{hg}, structure, and discipline
Applied primarily to tactical, nice-to-have projects	Applied primarily to strategic, business imperative initiatives
Used when it's easy, not too expensive, and doesn't take too much time	Used despite the effort, cost, and time involved
Used mostly to fix existing operating paradigms	Used mostly to break from old and shift to new operating paradigms

(continued)

Table C.1   (Continued)

Change Management	Human Due Diligence
Success criteria include helping people express their concerns and ventilate their frustrations, reducing pain and discomfort of people in transition, receiving additional requests to help with other projects	Success criteria include expanded market share, increased net earnings, enhanced shareholder value
Use advocated by practitioners	Use demanded by leaders
Practitioners primarily rely on their instinct for guidelines	Practitioners primarily rely on structure, principles, objective information, and discipline supported by instinct and intuition
Practitioners often believe they lack support from leaders, and therefore feel insecure about themselves and ambivalent about the concepts and tools they use	Practitioners enjoy full support from leaders, and therefore feel more sure of themselves and confident in the methodologies they use
Practitioners are facilitative in style, less confrontational and more political with leaders than is helpful	Practitioners are direct and prescriptive, appropriately confrontational, and display little political behavior with leaders they serve
Practitioners are grateful when occasionally allowed to apply their knowledge and skill	Practitioners expect to be treated as valuable assets and to function in a way that reflects their considerable expertise

who report to them, HDD addresses these issues directly, but within a context that also respects the pressures and opportunities faced by senior leadership.

The boundaries between change management and HDD are depicted in Table C.1. These characteristics represent the bridging from one change era to the next in the evolutionary development of the capacity we humans have to direct our own destinies. With the rise of HDD comes the beginning of a new framework for the leadership and orchestration of human variables associated with organizational transformation.

NOTES

PREFACE

1. ODR (Organizational Development Resources) is a research-based consulting firm headquartered in Atlanta, GA. ODR works exclusively in the area of helping organizations prepare for and implement major change initiatives.

2. Whenever there is a reference in the coming chapters to something I have researched, witnessed, heard, concluded, or speculated about, I am conveying more than my own personal perspective. Throughout this book, my comments will reflect the combined views of the staff at ODR as well as our many clients who have joined us in exploring the convoluted layers within the process of human change. Human Due Diligence is a trademark of ODR.

CHAPTER 1 EXECUTION, EXECUTION, EXECUTION

1. "How IBM Became a Growth Company Again," *Business Week*, December 9, 1996.

2. Joseph B. White, "Next Big Thing Re-Engineering Gurus Fake Steps to Remodel Their Stalling Vehicles." *The Wall Street Journal*, November 26, 1996, p. A1.

3. "Movement" refers to the difference in the status of the organization before implementation of the initiative, compared to its status after implementation.

CHAPTER 2 CONFRONTING THE CHALLENGE OF CHANGE

1. These terms are addressed in more detail in Chapter 4.

2. Unconscious competence is based on unexamined, instinctive behaviors that nonetheless produce correct outcomes. Conscious competence stems from explicit knowledge and deliberate acts that are intended to yield a desired outcome.

CHAPTER 3 THE CONSTANT QUEST

1. Resilience is described in more detail in Chapters 11 and 13.

Part Four Nimble Leadership Capabilities

1. Rhoda Thomas Tripp, "International Thesaurus of Quotes," *The New York Times Magazine,* May 12, 1968.

Chapter 11 Leadership's Personal Resilience

1. Resilience and exercise—Margaret A. Colgate, *A Secondary Analysis Assessing the Personal Resilience Questionnaire and Exploring the Relationship between Resilience and Exercise.* University of Maryland, Doctor of Philosophy dissertation, 1995.

2. Resilience and leadership—*Organizational Level and Resilience: An MOC Databyte,* 1995, ODR, Inc.

3. ODR utilizes the *Personal Resilience®* Questionnaire to measure the characteristics that are linked to individual resilience. This tool is available for individuals interested in investigating their own resilience, and for organizations wishing to assess and improve the overall resilience of their employees.

Chapter 12 Optimizing Paradigm Life Spans

1. "Paradigm" is a relatively recent entry into the lexicon of organizational leadership. Due in large part to the books (e.g., *Paradigms: The Business of Discovering the Future*) and videos (e.g., *The Business of Paradigms*) by Joel Barker, the term has gained wide currency. The term's popular origin dates back to Thomas Kuhn's use of it to describe the spread of innovation (or its absence) in the scientific community (*The Nature of Scientific Revolutions,* 1962).

2. Figure 12.1—Reprinted by permission of The Progress & Freedom Foundation, copyright © 1994.

3. Building phase—The period when a paradigm is conceived and realized. If, as an organization forms, it is able to survive—if not prosper—it can be said to be progressing, to some degree, toward achieving its purpose. This progress is the result of learning to successfully align unconscious assumptions, stated beliefs, measurable behaviors, effective systems, and meaningful methods.

4. Fixes—The actions directed at the systems, methods, or behaviors of an existing paradigm that are effective in correcting relatively short-term deviations from performance goals. Some fixes are directed at strategic issues, like marketing of products or use of technology; others are more tactical in nature, like reorganizing a department or conducting a training program to develop better teamwork. Regardless of the scope of the effort, all fixes share a common goal of protecting the general framework of "how things are done around here."

5. Harvest phase—The period when an organization reaps the benefits of the operational configuration assumptions, beliefs, behaviors, methods, and systems) developed during the building phase.

6. Assumptions—The unconscious and, therefore, mostly unquestioned views regarding what is important and how people and things operate. Beliefs—The conscious and often stated expectations that employees have of themselves, others, and their work. Beliefs result from an integration of values and expectations that provides a framework for shaping what people hold to be true or false, relevant or irrelevant, and good or bad about their environment. Whether in oral or written form, belief statements can entail both intended and unintended messages regarding what people plan or think they should do. Behaviors—The observable actions that are based on expectations and ideally aimed at carrying out an organization's purpose. Systems—The interaction of assumptions, beliefs, and behaviors that aim to achieve the organization's purpose. Organizational systems are the mechanisms that power the guidance and functioning of an enterprise. Methods—Artifacts developed to help people function within a system (e.g., rules, policies, tools, forms).

7. This occurs when an organization's response to a crisis results in the preservation of obsolete assumptions and beliefs. Here, the leader has either mistaken "strange data" as conventional in nature, and rendered those data benign; or he or she has otherwise denied the data altogether. The dynamic balance lost during the crisis accelerates the system out of control. Corrective measures primarily directed toward methods, systems, and behavior (fixes) are continued even though they have become ineffective. Renewal—The period when a new paradigm is built to replace the old one. This occurs when an organization's response to a crisis results in the reshaping of its fundamental assumptions and beliefs to significantly enhance its productivity and quality. Renewal takes place when fix-type corrective measures are acknowledged as no longer effective in resolving critical business challenges.

CHAPTER 18 MASTERING THE LEADERSHIP ROLE

1. The masculine singular is used throughout this story only for ease of expression. All references to a male leader are to be interpreted *as a leader of either gender*.

2. Antabuse® is a registered trademark of Wyeth-Ayerst Labs.

CHAPTER 19 WHERE FROM HERE?

1. Implementation—The critical issues, patterns of behavior, general guidelines, and particular approaches related to building and executing implementation

architecture for a specific initiative are covered in my previous book, *Managing at the Speed of Change*.

2. Execution—Other aspects of the sponsor's role can be found in *Managing at the Speed of Change*.

3. Translated by H. A. J. Munro.

APPENDIX B THE MECHANICS OF THE ADAPTATION REFLEX

1. Research—Marshall, Sandra P. *Schemas in Problem Solving*. Cambridge, United Kingdom: Cambridge University Press, 1995.

2. Perspectives—Brewer, W. F., & Pani, J. R. The structure of human memory. In G. H. Bower (Ed.), *The psychology of learning and motivation: Advances in research and theory* (Vol. 17). New York: Academic Press, 1983.

3. Characteristics that make up the resilient personality are fully discussed in Chapter 11.

BIBLIOGRAPHY

Ackoff, Russell L. *Redesigning the Future*. New York: John Wiley & Sons, 1974.

Ames, Joan Evelyn. *Mastery: Interviews with 30 Remarkable People*. Portland: Rudra Press, 1997.

Andrew, A. M. *Self-Organizing Systems*. New York: Gordon and Breach, 1989.

Argyris, Chris. *Knowledge for Action*. San Francisco: Jossey-Bass, 1993.

Argyris, Chris. *Strategy, Change and Defensive Routines*. Marshfield, Massachusetts, Pitman, 1985.

Argyris, Chris, and D. Schon. *Organizational Learning*. Reading, Massachusetts: Addison-Wesley, 1978.

Aspinwall, Lisa G., and Shelley E. Taylor. A *Stitch in Time: Self-Regulation and Proactive Coping*. American Psychological Associations, 1997.

Bahlmann, Tineke. "The Learning Organization in a Turbulent Environment." *Human Systems Management*, 1990.

Barker, Joel Arthur. *Paradigms: The Business of Discovering the Future*. New York: HarperCollins, 1992.

Batten, Joe D. *Tough-Minded Management*. New York: Amacom, 1963, 1969, 1978.

Beckhard, R., and R. Harris. *Organizational Transitions*. Reading, Massachusetts: Addison-Wesley, 1977.

Beer, Michael. "Why Change Programs Don't Produce Change." *Harvard Business Review* (1990).

Beer, Michael, R. A. Eisenstat, and B. Spector. *The Critical Path to Corporate Renewal*. Boston: Harvard Business School Press, 1990.

Bennis, Warren. *On Becoming a Leader*. Reading, Massachusetts: Addison-Wesley, 1989.

Bennis, Warren G., Kenneth D. Benne, Robert Chin, and Kenneth E. Corey. *The Planning of Change*. New York: Holt, Rinehart & Winston, 1976.

Bennis, Warren, and Patricia Ward Biederman. *Organizing Genius: The Secrets of Creative Collaboration*. Reading, Massachusetts: Addison-Wesley, 1997.

Bergquist, William. *The Postmodern Organization: Mastering the Art of Irreversible Change*. San Francisco: Jossey-Bass, 1993.

Bernstein, Peter L. *Against the Gods: The Remarkable Story of Risk.* New York: John Wiley & Sons, 1996.

Bolman, Lee G., and Terrence E. Deal. *Leading with Soul: An Uncommon Journey of Spirit.* San Francisco: Jossey-Bass, 1995.

Bridges, William. *Transitions: Making Sense of Life's Changes.* Reading, Massachusetts: Addison-Wesley, 1980.

Capra, Fritjof. *The Turning Point: Science, Society, and the Rising Culture.* New York: Bantam Books, 1982.

Chaleff, Ira. *The Courageous Follower: Standing Up to and for Our Leaders.* San Francisco: Berrett-Koehler, 1995.

Ching, I. *The Classic of Changes.* New York: Columbia University Press, 1994.

Cohen, Jack, and Ian Stewart. *The Collapse of Chaos: Discovering Simplicity in a Complex World.* New York: Penguin Books, 1994.

Conner, Daryl R. *Managing at the Speed of Change.* New York: Villard Books, 1992.

Davis, S. M. *Future Perfect.* Reading, Massachusetts: Addison-Wesley, 1987.

Davis, Stan, and Bill Davidson. *2020 Vision: Transform Your Business Today to Succeed in Tomorrow's Economy.* New York: Simon & Schuster, 1991.

Davis, Stanley M. *Future Perfect.* Reading, Massachusetts: Addison-Wesley, 1987.

De Bono, Edward. *Lateral Thinking for Management.* American Management Association, 1971.

DeGeus, Arie. *The Living Company: Habits for Survival in a Turbulent Business Environment.* Boston: Harvard Business School Press, 1997.

DePree, Max. *Leadership Is an Art.* New York: Dell Publishing, 1989.

Drucker, Peter F. *Managing for the Future.* New York: Penguin Books, 1992.

Drucker, Peter F. *Managing in a Time of Great Change.* New York: Truman Talley Books, 1995.

Edvinsson, Leif, and Michael S. Malone. *Intellectual Capital: Realizing Your Company's True Value by Finding Its Hidden Brainpower.* New York: Harper Business, 1997.

Ellis, Christian M., and Elizabeth J. Hawk. "A Recipe for Success: Redesigning Reward in Organizations with Mature Teams." *Target,* 1994.

Etzioni, A. *A Responsive Society.* San Francisco: Jossey-Bass, 1991.

Farson, Richard. *Management of the Absurd: Paradoxes in Leadership.* New York: Simon & Schuster, 1996.

Galbraith, Jay R., and Edward E. Lawler & Associates. *Organizing for the Future: The New Logic for Managing Complex Organizations.* San Francisco: Jossey-Bass, 1993.

Gardner, Howard. *Frames of Mind: The Theory of Multiple Intelligences.* New York: Basic Books, 1983.

Garvin, D. A. *Building a Learning Organization*. Boston: Harvard Business School Press, 1987.

Gleick, James. *Chaos: Making a New Science*. New York: Viking Penguin, 1987.

Goldman, Steven, Roger Nagal, and Kenneth Proiss. *Agile Competitors and Virtual Organizations*. New York: Van Nostrand Reinhold, 1994.

Goldstein, Jeffrey. "A Far-from-Equilibrium Systems Approach to Resistance to Change." *Organization Dynamics*, 1988.

Gross, N., J. Giacquinta, and M. Berstein. *Implementing Organizational Innovations*. New York: Basic Books, 1971.

Hamel, Gary, and C. K. Prahalad. *Competing for the Future*. Boston: Harvard Business School Press, 1994.

Hammer, M., and J. Champy. *Reengineering the Corporation*. New York: Harper-Collins, 1993.

Handy, Charles. *Age of Unreason*. New York: McGraw-Hill, 1992.

Handy, Charles. *The Age of Paradox*. Boston: Harvard Business School Press, 1994.

Harmon, Frederick G. *Playing for Keeps: How the World's Most Aggressive and Admired Companies Use Core Values to Manage, Energize, and Organize Their People and Promote, Advance, and Achieve Their Corporate Missions*. New York: John Wiley & Sons, 1996.

Hesselbein, Frances, Marshall Goldsmith, and Richard Beckhard. *The Drucker Foundation: The Organization of the Future*. San Francisco: Jossey-Bass, 1997.

Hesselbein, Frances, Marshall Goldsmith, and Richard Beckhard (Eds.). *The Leader of the Future*. New York: The Peter F. Drucker Foundation for Nonprofit Management, 1996.

Hesselbein, Frances, Marshall Goldsmith, and Richard Beckhard (Eds.). *The Organization of the Future*. New York: The Peter F. Drucker Foundation for Nonprofit Management, 1997.

Hickman, Craig R. *Mind of a Manager, Soul of a Leader*. New York: John Wiley & Sons, 1990.

Homa, Bahrami. "The Emerging Flexible Organization," *California Management Review*, Summer 1992.

Hurst, David K. *Crisis and Renewal: Meeting the Challenge of Organizational Change*. Boston: Harvard Business School Press, 1995.

Jacobs, Roberts W. *Real-Time Strategic Change: How to Involve an Entire Organization in Fast and Far-Reaching Change*. San Francisco: Berrett-Koehler, 1994.

Jantsch, Erich. *The Self-Organizing Universe: Scientific and Human Implications of the Emerging Paradigm of Evolution*. New York: Pergamon Press, 1989.

Jaworski, Joseph. *Synchronicity: The Inner Path of Leadership*. San Francisco: Berrett-Koehler, 1996.

Kuhn, Thomas S. *The Structure of Scientific Revolutions.* Chicago: University of Chicago Press, 1962.

LaMarsh, Jeanenne. *Changing the Way We Change: Gaining Control of Major Operational Change.* Reading, Massachusetts: Addison-Wesley, 1995.

Land, George, and Beth Jarman. *Breakpoint and Beyond.* New York: Harper Business, 1992.

Lewin, Roger. *Complexity Life on the Edge of Chaos.* New York: Macmillan, 1992.

Macdonald, John. *Calling a Halt to Mindless Change.* American Management Association International, 1998.

McFarland, Lynne Joy, Larry E. Senn, and John R. Childress. *21st Century Leadership: Dialogues with 100 Top Leaders.* New York: The Leadership Press, 1994.

McWhinney, Will. *Paths of Change: Strategic Choices for Organizations and Society.* Newbury Park, California: Sage Publications, 1992.

Mohrman, Allan M. Jr., Susan Mohrman, Gerald E. Ledford, Thomas G. Cummings, and Edward E.Lawler III & Associates. *Large-Scale Organizational Change.* San Francisco: Jossey-Bass, 1989.

Nadler, David. *Champions of Change.* San Francisco: Jossey-Bass, 1998.

Nadler, David, Robert B. Shaw, and Walton A. Elise & Associates. *Discontinuous Change: Leading Organizational Transformation.* San Francisco: Jossey-Bass, 1995.

Nonaka, Ikujiro, and Hirotska Takeuchi. *The Knowledge-Creating Company: How Japanese Companies Create the Dynamics of Innovation.* New York: Oxford University Press, 1995.

Nystrom, Paul C., and William H. Starbuck. *To Avoid Organizational Crises, Unlearn.* American Management Associations, 1984.

Olesen, Erik. *12 Steps to Mastering the Winds of Change: Peak Performers Reveal How to Stay on Top in Times of Turmoil.* New York: MacMillian, 1993.

O'Toole, James. *Leading Change: The Argument For Values-Based Leadership.* San Francisco: Jossey-Bass, 1995.

Peck, M. S. *The Road Less Traveled.* New York: Simon & Schuster, 1978.

Quinn, Robert E. *Deep Change: Discovering the Leader within.* San Francisco: Jossey-Bass, 1996.

Schwarz, Norbert, Michaela Wanke, and Herbert Bless. *Subjective Assessments and Evaluations of Change: Some Lessons from Social Cognition Research.* New York: John Wiley & Sons, 1994.

Seligman, Martin. *Learned Optimism.* New York: Simon and Schuster, 1990.

Senge, Peter M. *The Fifth Discipline.* New York: Doubleday, 1990.

Sheldon, Alan. *Organizational Paradigms: A Theory of Organizational Change.* New York: Amacom, 1980.

Siu, R. G. H. *The Master Manager.* New York: John Wiley & Sons, 1980.

Siu, R. G. H. *The Craft of Power*. New York: John Wiley & Sons, 1979.

Smith, Douglas K. *Taking Charge of Change: 10 Principles for Managing People and Performance*. Reading, Massachusetts: Addison-Wesley, 1996.

Stacey, Ralph D. *Managing the Unknowable*. San Francisco: Jossey-Bass, 1992.

Stamps, David. "The Self-Organizing System." *Training*, 1997.

Steele, Fritz. *Consulting for Organizational Change*. Amherst: University of Massachusetts Press, 1975.

Taylor, James, and Watts Wacker. *The 500 Year Delta: What Happens after What Comes Next*. New York: Harper Business, 1997.

Terry, Robert W. *Authentic Leadership: Courage in Action*. San Francisco: Jossey-Bass, 1993.

Tichy, Noel M. *Managing Strategic Change: Political and Cultural Dynamics*. New York: John Wiley & Sons, 1983.

Tichy, Noel M., and Mary Anne Devanna. *The Transformational Leader*. New York: John Wiley & Sons, 1986.

Toffler, Alvin. *The Adaptive Corporation*. New York: McGraw-Hill, 1985.

Treacy, Michael, and Fred Wiersema. *The Discipline of Market Leaders: Choose Your Customers, Narrow Your Focus, Dominate Your Market*. Reading, Massachusetts: Addison-Wesley, 1995.

Watzlawick, Paul, John H. Weakland, and Richard Fisch. *Change: Principle of Problem Formation and Problem Resolution*. New York: W. W. Norton, 1974.

Wheatley, Margaret J. *Leadership and the New Science: Learning about Organization from an Orderly Universe*. San Francisco: Berrett-Koehler, 1992.

Wheelis, Allen. *How People Change*. New York: Harper & Row, 1973.

Woodward, Harry. *Navigating through Change*. Burridge, Illinois: Irwin Professional Publishing, 1994.

Yates, F. E. *Self-Organizing Systems*. New York: Plenum, 1987.

Zimbardo, P., E. Ebbesen, and C. Maslach. *Influencing Attitudes and Changing Behavior*. Reading, Massachusetts: Addison-Wesley, 1977.

ABOUT ODR

ODR is an Atlanta-based consulting and training firm helping organizations apply Human Due Diligence to increase their Nimbleness. For our next book, we are seeking stories and examples about individuals and organizations that have successfully applied one or more of the principles described in *Leading at the Edge of Chaos*. If you have a story to share, or would like to contact us for additional information about our work, we would be delighted to hear from you.

Linda Hoopes
Leader, LOC Team
ODR, Inc.
2900 Chamblee-Tucker Road, Building 16
Atlanta, Georgia 30341
800-242-6438

E-mail: leadingchange@odr.odnet.com
Web site: www.odrinc.com

INDEX